Microsoft

Office 97
Internet Developer's
Guide

Microsoft Office 97 Internet Developer's Guide
Copyright © 1997 by Kevin Marlowe and Jeff Rowe

Library of Congress Catalog Card Number: 97-60915

First Edition 9 8 7 6 5 4 3 2 1

Printed in the United States of America

Ventana Communications Group
P.O. Box 13964
Research Triangle Park, NC 27709-3964
919.544.9404
FAX 919.544.9472
http://www.vmedia.com   SEP - 1997

Ventana Communications Group is a division of International Thomson Publishing.

Limits of Liability & Disclaimer of Warranty
The authors and publisher of this book have used their best efforts in preparing the book and the programs contained in it. These efforts include the development, research, and testing of the theories and programs to determine their effectiveness. The authors and publisher make no warranty of any kind, expressed or implied, with regard to these programs or the documentation contained in this book.

The authors and publisher shall not be liable in the event of incidental or consequential damages in connection with, or arising out of, the furnishing, performance or use of the programs, associated instructions and/or claims of productivity gains.

Trademarks
Trademarked names appear throughout this book and on the accompanying compact disk, if applicable. Rather than list the names and entities that own the trademarks or insert a trademark symbol with each mention of the trademarked name, the publisher states that it is using the names only for editorial purposes and to the benefit of the trademark owner with no intention of infringing upon that trademark.

President
Michael E. Moran

Vice President of Content Development
Karen A. Bluestein

Director of Acquisitions and Development
Robert Kern

Managing Editor
Lois J. Principe

Production Manager
John Cotterman

Art Director
Marcia Webb

Technology Operations Manager
Kerry L. B. Foster

Brand Manager
Jamie Jaeger Fiocco

Creative Services Manager
Diane Lennox

Acquisitions Editor
Neweleen A. Trebnik

Project Editor
Paul Cory

Development Editor
Diane Haugen

Copy Editor
Paulette Kilheffer

CD-ROM Specialist
Adam F. Newton

Technical Reviewer
Russ Mullen

Desktop Publisher
Kristin Miller

Proofreader
Tom Collins

Indexer
Lynn Brown

Interior Designer
Patrick Berry

Cover Illustrator
Lisa Gill

About the Authors

Kevin Marlowe is a systems analyst with Computer Sciences Corporation at NASA's Langley Research Center in Hampton, VA, where he develops databases and user interfaces for Windows and the Web for the management of scientific data. He has an M.S. in Computer Science, and 10 years of experience in information systems management and application development.

Jeff Rowe is the president of Beowulf Enterprises, a computer consulting company run from a beach chair on the island of Oahu in Hawaii. He is a leading authority on connecting databases to the World Wide Web and the author of *Building Internet Database Servers with CGI* (New Riders). He has done work for NASA and Southwestern Bell, among others. When he isn't playing and calling it work, Jeff follows his Air Force wife, Major Amy, from base to base, changing e-mail addresses like most people change socks. (You have changed your socks today, haven't you?) Jeff can be reached for now at beowulf@lava.net. Catch him quick before he moves again.

Acknowledgments

Thanks to Jeff Rowe, who got me into this mess, and whose easy humor and skeptical attitude have made the last couple of years of cubicle-dwelling a lot more bearable; to Laura Belt, for finding the diamond projects in the rough; to Diane Haugen, both Muse and Oracle; and to my family—Jill, Daniel, and Shannon—for letting me do this and still remembering my name after it's all done.

—*Kevin Marlowe*

Thanks to my agent, Laura Belt, for bringing me the opportunity to write this book. Thanks to my co-author, Kevin Marlowe, for being so easy to work with, both on the job and on this book. Thanks to Diane Haugen for being such an excellent wordsmith. Thanks to Greg Kochaniak of Hyperionics for letting us use his HyperCam software to capture the videos for the book's CD-ROM. And finally, a big thanks to my wife Amy, and my son B.J., for letting me do fun things like write about toys, um, I mean software.

—*Jeff Rowe*

Dedication

To Jill, my wife and friend, who still makes the sun rise, the stars shine, and time and tide ebb and flow after all these years.

—*K.M.*

To my mother, Sue Rowe. Without you I wouldn't be who I am today. And in loving memory of my father, Paul Rowe. I think Dad would be proud.

—*J.R.*

Contents

Introduction

Your phone rings only once—it's an internal call. Before 9:00 a.m. on a Monday morning, that can only mean trouble. You pick it up. It's your project manager, well, really your boss's boss, the kind of person who happens to like to dole out his special projects personally. That means that whatever he wants, it's going to be in addition to the things that are already sitting on your desk this morning.

"You interested in a little high visibility, creative work?" he asks. Sure sign of trouble.

"Um, sure—what do you have in mind?" you say, not really sure you want to hear the answer. You can hardly say no.

"I've been thinking we need one of those Web things, you know what I mean, don't you?"

"A Web site? OK . . . what do you want on it?" (Pepperoni, you're thinking.) The stream-of-consciousness advertising-brochure babble that begins to flow into your earpiece tells you that he doesn't really know, but he'll know when he sees it. He sounds like the teacher on the old Peanuts TV specials—blah, blah blah-blah.

"OK," you say, getting into the idea, looking for the catch—after all, Web design looks like fun. All of those cool graphics and hyperlinks and the glamour of the Web might be yours if this works out, and if not . . . so you ask the obvious question. "What's my budget?"

A short silence on the other end of the line and then the dreaded response:

"Why do you need a budget for something as simple as this?"

Zip. Nada. Work with what you have. And he does mean you, not you and a staff. Use the machines in the office. Buy a book if you have to. There's only one thing that can make this worse, you think, and then he tells you that he'd like to see a prototype a week from today. Five work days to put up a Web site, with no tools and no staff.

Lucky for you—you just happen to have the *Microsoft Office 97 Internet Developer's Guide* sitting on your desk—your force multiplier on the battlefield of low-cost Web site development. With a little creativity and patience, you're going to find out how to use Microsoft's Office 97 (Professional Edition) to turn spreadsheets into Web tables, documents into Web pages, paper presentations into online tutorials. With a little guidance from a couple of old hands, you'll be embedding database tables in your pages and creating links to your customer billing data with a minimum of frustration.

Office 97 isn't the perfect Web development environment, and we can't pretend that it is. However, it does basic Web pages very well, does some advanced features pretty well, and doesn't impede you from doing the hard stuff manually if you want to. If you're familiar with the primary applications in Office (Word, Excel, PowerPoint, and Access), you have the foundation for what you need to get started. We'll assume that you don't have a lot of time, so here's a summary of what you'll find inside this book:

- a little history to help you gauge the temperature of the water you're about to jump into;

- some thoughts on where the industry is going so you know where the far end of the pool is;

- details on how to get Internet service and set up a Web server, so people can see how well you swim;

- step-by-step Web swimming lessons for each and every application in Office 97 Pro;

- a fully functional sample Web site based on the examples throughout the book, so you can get a sense of what the crowd at poolside may be hoping to see.

(Enough of the swimming analogy.)

If you're a newbie, rest easy—we'll tell you what you need to know to build a functional, adequate Web site using the tools you have in a short time. If you already know the basics, but want to know more about the Internet-enabling of Office, we'll tell you all there is to know about the Internet and Web features of Office 97.

And if you're a Web guru, you can show this book to your fellow gurus as proof that Microsoft hasn't perfected the mousetrap yet, so long as you admit that these tools provide an easy way to build a functional site fast.

After some background information, each chapter will focus on a specific Office application, including a discussion of how to integrate it with the other Office components. We'll build a few Web pages with each tool to show you the high points, and we'll tell you where to find the details. We'll even show you where the riptides lurk. (Sorry, couldn't resist.)

We have put several kinds of information in sidebars:

Our Take

We don't always agree on the best way to do some things, and we've worked together and separately long enough to know that there's more to the creative process than step-by-step instructions can provide. Each Our Take column discusses a particular issue of relevance to the Internet, the Web, or computing in general. We (Kevin and Jeff, the authors), both lend some insight to the topic currently being discussed. Jeff is a UNIX guru and proud of it: he enhances perfectly good programming languages for fun, dreams in bytecodes, and looks forward to seeing Diablo ported to SunOS. Kevin likes working on PCs because he can break them and fix them again faster than you can say "call a system administrator." He dreams in SVGA and organizes his childrens' toys into program groups. Each brings unique perspectives to application development and Web design.

FYI: Good to Know Stuff

These provide additional detail about how a particular feature works, an alternate method of performing a certain task, or related topics that you might wish to refer to if the core discussion isn't detailed enough for your taste. Tips provide nice-to-know information that may be interesting, but isn't critical.

CAUTION

Wisdom borne of dozens of re-installations, crashes, and just plain bugs is inscribed for you in Caution notes. Before trying the technique being described, check out any Cautions in that section.

What Is...

If you already know what a *user interface* is, you might not need to read these. But if you don't, they're here for you. We've tried to keep the definitions on the pages where the words appear so you don't have to page back through the book to refresh your memory about a term.

So keep a sense of humor, remember that patience is a virtue, and dive in. The water's fine.

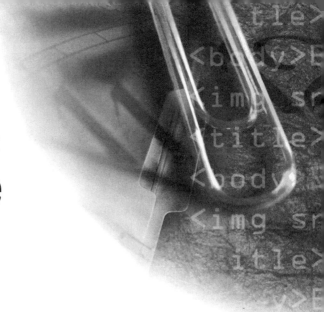

chapter 1

Life on the Internet

Many people are frequent users of Microsoft Office 95 and are making the jump to Office 97 because of the integration and Internet-enabled features of Office 97. If you are familiar with MS Office but don't know much about the Internet, this chapter is for you.

Once we have explored the useful features of the Internet, we will explore the World Wide Web in Chapter 2. The Web is built on top of the Internet and gives it a pretty face, but the Internet is still doing most of the work.

The new features of Office 97 let you do some powerful things, but you are required to know a good bit about the new environment you are working in. The Internet can be a potent tool for you if you know what you are doing. This chapter will bring you up to speed and give you the basic knowledge you need to use your new tools.

The Internet & the Web: Two Different Things

If you already know how the Internet works, you may still pick up a pointer or two that fills in a blank spot in your knowledge or explains something that puzzles you.

If you think you know enough to jump right into using Office 97 and its new capabilities, feel free to skip on to Chapter 5, "Microsoft Word 97." You can always come back to this chapter if you need to.

If you are continuing into this chapter, take a deep breath and read on. There will be a lot of terminology thrown at you, but the terms are not as important as the ideas behind them. The Internet is a highly technical artifact, but you don't need to know everything about how it works in order to use it.

Do you need to know everything about how an internal combustion engine works in order to be a good driver? No, but it helps if you know what the steering wheel and brakes do, and how to check engine fluid levels. This chapter will lift the hood on the Internet and point out some useful features, but many people who make a living using the Internet are kind of hazy on the hardcore details and they do just fine.

The Internet and the Web are different creatures. This chapter will acquaint you with the Internet, and Chapter 2 will acquaint you with the Web. These chapters will help you to understand both, explain why they are so different, and tell you what each can and cannot do. Some features of Office 97 use the Internet (and can also be applied to an intranet) while other features are focused at creating documents for the Web.

Understanding the difference can help you decide how to create and target your documents. You should also understand a little about the vast new world you are about to experience. There are pluses and minuses to joining the Internet community and using it for yourself.

In its simplest form, the Internet is a worldwide collection of machines that communicate via high-speed telephone lines. Some parts of the Internet carry huge amounts of data, while others carry only a little.

Machines are connected to the Internet all over the world. The Internet community is a true global village. You can use the Internet to communicate with people you would never know about otherwise. In addition to the social aspects of a global communication medium, there are many things the Internet allows you to do with documents and presentations that can enhance your business or organization. Just like the U.S. Postal Service, the Internet is a service that makes your life easier and takes care of a lot of the details that you have no need to know, but are necessary for smooth operations.

The Internet: Your Personal Postal Service

The numbers and diversity of the people who use the Internet on a daily or infrequent basis are huge. Some people work on computers that are hooked directly to the Internet 24 hours a day. Others never use the Internet except from their home PC for a few minutes a week to check their e-mail.

There are literally millions of machines connected to the Internet, from single-user PCs, to multi-user UNIX boxes, to routers, bridges, hubs, and even printers. How does information go from one machine to another without getting lost?

What Is. . .

Intranet: a computer network usually used within a company. An intranet works in exactly the same way as the full-fledged Internet, but it's safer because it has no connection to the outside world. If your network is isolated from the Internet, no outside force (such as a hacker) can get to the computers on your network by using the Internet.

UNIX boxes: this is a term used by those who work closely with big computers that run the Unix operating system. There are so many different types of Unix computers that instead of trying to identify one, it's easier just to refer to one generically as a "Unix box."

routers: all of the information that travels around the Internet has to come from somewhere and go somewhere else. A router is like a network traffic cop, directing information in the right direction to reach its destination.

bridges: a bridge is a simplified type of router. It acts as a "bridge" between two networks by passing all traffic through without inspecting it for its final destination. Bridges are often used to strengthen signals over long distances.

hubs: a hub distributes network traffic from one source to several destinations. The destinations may be individual machines, or entire networks. Hubs often include the ability to act as routers.

When you do something such as sending e-mail to a user on another machine somewhere on the Internet, you send the e-mail to an address such as user@machine.domain.extension. Each part of that address has a specific meaning:

- **User:** name of the account on the target computer the e-mail is going to. A machine may have one or many users, depending on its processing capabilities.

- **Machine:** name of the destination computer. Machine names may be silly, such as *Hackmeister*, or descriptive, such as *sun_sparc_20*. Each machine has a unique name within the domain it belongs to.

- **Domain:** name that identifies the company or organization that owns the computer. Domain names such as *microsoft.com* or *beowulf.com* can identify a large collection of machines or a single machine.

- **Extension:** identifies what kind of organization owns the computer. Government computers have a .GOV extension, colleges and universities have an .EDU extension, and commercial organizations have a .COM extension. Other extensions are .MIL, .ORG, and .NET. New extensions such as .WEB, .STORE, and others are in the works to further identify different types of Internet machines.

This may look to you like enough information to find a machine, but a computer needs more. A computer doesn't even use the name of the destination computer to send it information. The human-readable name must be converted into a form that is usable by computers, as explained in the next section.

What Is This Funny Internet Address Anyway?

The first thing a computer does with data intended for another computer is to resolve the name into an *IP address*. IP stands for "Internet Protocol" and is a standard way of assigning a unique address to a computer. Every machine on the Internet must have a unique IP address.

Even so, how do computers locate the IP address of another machine on the Internet? Computers come and go all the time and it would be impossible for every computer to keep a list of all other computers and keep it updated.

What Is. . .

IP: stands for Internet Protocol, and defines the common language that Internet computers use to talk to one another.

InterNIC: the regulatory body that controls the dispersal of computer names to make sure a computer name is not used by more than one machine.

IP addresses are controlled by an organization called **InterNIC**. InterNIC handles domain name and IP address registration. It is vitally important that no two machines on the Internet have the same name or IP address so information can get to the correct computer. InterNIC takes care of this vital function.

Our Take: InterNIC

Kevin: If you have a connection to the Internet, you can browse the list of the thousands of domain name registrations at InterNIC. In Windows, start your Internet connection. Then click on the Start|Run. Type **telnet rs.internic.net**. When the prompt appears, type **whois microsoft**. You'll see Microsoft Corp.'s registration information, as well as some others. You can type **whois <somebody>** as many times as you like. Type **logout** when you're done.

Jeff: What I find amazing are the really stupid names some people have registered. Try typing in something silly and chances are someone owns it. This can be a hilarious party game. Of course, one reason the silly names are registered is because the first, second, third, and fourth choices were already taken.

This means at least one organization on the Internet has a list of all the computers attached to the Internet, right? Not so. An organization can reserve a block of IP addresses and a single domain name, then name their machines as they want to and assign IP addresses to their machines as they want to. Some IP addresses might not be used for a long time, as the company purchased enough IP addresses to allow for adding more computers to their network at a later date.

Identifying IP Addresses

There are two ways for your computer to find the IP address of a remote machine. The simplest method, used by most Unix machines, is to keep a list of machine names and their IP address in a special file on your computer called the *hosts* file. You can add machines you know about, or that users on your system send a lot of e-mail to.

The other way is to use a *Domain Name Server* (DNS). There are machines on the Internet that attempt to keep track of every machine on the Internet. Once a computer is connected to the Internet, it is generally registered with a DNS. Different DNS machines can share and pass around new versions of the computer list.

Your local machine must know the IP address of a DNS machine in order to use the DNS service on the remote machine, and this is usually done by adding one or more DNS machines to your local hosts file.

When resolving a machine name, your local machine will look in its hosts file for the computer name you want to communicate with. If the name is not on the local machine, each DNS listed in the hosts file is contacted to see if it can resolve the given name into an IP address. Figure 1-1 gives you some idea of how a DNS works.

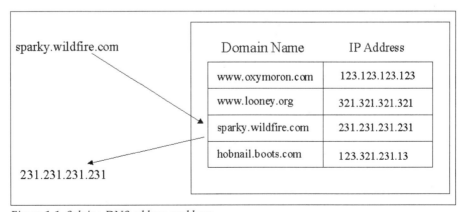

Figure 1-1: Solving DNS address problems.

Your computer sends a machine name to the DNS server for resolution. The DNS server looks up the machine name in a table and tries to find the associated IP address. If the IP address is located, it is passed to your machine and the outgoing e-mail is addressed with the IP address accordingly. If the name can't be found, you will get an error about an "unknown host" or the destination machine "has no DNS entry" and your e-mail will not be delivered.

If this happens, and you already know the IP address of the destination computer, you can substitute the IP address for the machine name. No name resolution is needed, and your e-mail message can be sent out immediately.

Most people find it easier to remember fred@sparky.wildfire.org than to remember an IP address that is just a string of unrelated numbers. Like anything else, however, you must pay a price for convenience. Looking up IP addresses takes time, and can fail at any time. Using the IP address directly makes things harder on your memory but easier for your computer to send information to a remote machine.

FYI: Loopback Address

When you connect your machine to the Internet, it either uses its own, unique IP address, or it is automatically assigned one by your Internet service provider. While it can be tricky figuring out your IP address (if you want to know) when it's dynamically assigned, you can always count on the special IP address **127.0.0.1.** This address, called the *loopback address*, always refers to your own machine. So if you send mail to 127.0.0.1, you'll get it back! This is a good technique to use when setting up a computer to see if the network is working correctly.

Learning How the Data Flows

If the destination machine is down the street or across town, the e-mail message will probably never travel across the main Internet, but if the message must go a long distance, it will probably be routed onto one of the major sections of the Internet, called *backbones*, that have the *bandwidth* necessary to carry huge amounts of Internet traffic.

What is...

backbone: A major piece of the Internet designed to carry enormous amounts of network traffic.

bit: A single piece of computer information. At the lowest level, a computer only recognizes two signals: on or off. A bit is the representation of this signal as a 1 or a 0.

baud rate: This is a measure of the rate at which bits flow across a communication line.

byte: 8 bits. It takes 8 bits of computer storage to represent a single character. Those 8 bits are called a byte.

Communications: Pass the Bandwidth, Please

Bandwidth is a measure of the amount of data a communication line can carry in a specified time. For instance, if you have a 33.6 modem, that means your modem is capable of broadcasting or receiving 33,600 *bits* per second. The number of bits per second is called the *baud rate*. So, your modem is capable of 33,600 baud.

A bit is a single 1 or 0, and it takes 8 bits to identify a single character. The 8 bits making up a single character are called a *byte*, so your 33.6 modem can transmit 4200 bytes, or characters, every second.

This may seem like a lot, but if you have a 33.6 modem, you know how rare it is to connect at the full 33.6 transmission rate. Depending on the quality of your local phone lines and switches, you may not be able to connect at any more than 24,000 or even 19,200 baud. Figure 1-2 shows how larger bandwidth allows you to get more work done. A business with a faster connection to the Internet can use it to do far more than the average user at home can do over their modem.

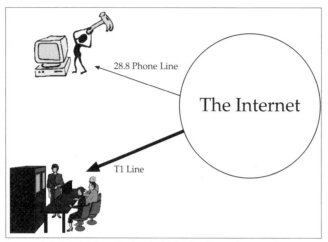

Figure 1-2: The higher the bandwidth, the faster the data flow.

What Is...

noise: communications lines carry signals. If something interferes with that signal, it introduces errors and the signal must be retransmitted until it is received correctly. The errors in a communication line are collectively called *line noise*.

efective throughput: no matter what the advertised transmission rate of a communications line or piece of equipment might be, that is only under ideal conditions. When you subtract the degradation of line noise from the maximum possible line quality, what is left is the *real* transmission rate which is called the *effective throughput*.

Thunderstorms or ground water collecting around underground power lines can affect the speed of your phone line by introducing *noise*, or random electrical pulses, into the phone lines. If you have a noisy line, your modem must continuously retransmit information so it arrives at its destination in the correct format. Line noise can seriously degrade the *effective throughput* of your phone line, which is the actual amount of data that gets through once errors are corrected.

If you have tried to download a large file over a slow or noisy phone line, you know how quickly a 33.6 modem starts to seem like a bottleneck.

If you consider that ordinary phone lines were never intended to carry the amount of data your modem pumps out, and that the only way today's high-speed modems achieve ever-increasing baud rates is by using new methods of data compression, you begin to understand how important bandwidth can be to users of the Internet.

ISPs: The Internet Federal Express

If the Internet was limited to using conventional phone lines, it would never have evolved into what it is today. In addition to normal phone lines, telephone companies also have communication lines of much higher bandwidth.

If you think of data flowing around the Internet in the same way water flows through a pipe, then the bandwidth of the communication line corresponds to the size of the pipe. Water flows faster through a larger pipe. Once a lot of water gets to its destination, the water can be fed into smaller and smaller pipes until it eventually ends up at your kitchen sink. This is how data flows across an Internet backbone.

Not only can a bigger pipe carry more data at once, but the data flows faster as well. More water can be pushed through a bigger pipe at a higher rate of speed because more water passes a fixed point in the pipe at any given time. The Internet backbone works in much the same way, as shown in Figure 1-3.

What Is...

ISP: an Internet Service Provider. They effectively rent you a piece of their Internet connection for your own use. They support the computers and communications equipment and you pay them for the service.

T1: a communications line that can transmit large amounts of information very quickly. Not many individuals need one of these.

T3: a very large communications line that can transmit truly phenomenal amounts of information in an astonishingly tiny amount of time. Not many governments need one of these.

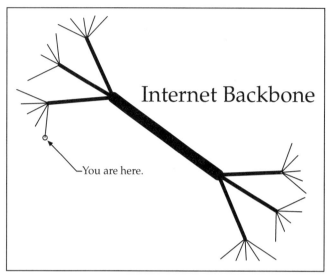

Figure 1-3: Data flow on an Internet backbone.

The original Internet was created by the National Science Foundation (NSF) with taxpayer money. The Internet backbone was begun in the United States as a way to hook high-speed computers together. During this era of budget cuts, the NSF decided they simply could not finance the Internet any longer. Private enterprise in the person of big telephone companies stepped in and funded it, passing the cost on to customers. ISPs and local telephone companies attached smaller lines to the backbones and tied the whole thing together. Phone companies around the world joined in to make the Internet an international artifact.

A common high-bandwidth line is called a *T1* and can carry 1.5 million data bits per second, which is roughly equal to 50 regular telephone lines. Many *Internet Service Providers* (ISPs) have a T1 connection to the Internet to carry all of their customer's data. Some big ISPs have multiple T1s or T3s. A T3 is equal to about 30 T1 lines. Even larger pipelines are available.

A piece of data leaves the transmitting computer and flows out into a larger pipe where it mixes with other data. More and more data is packed together as the pipe size increases. If your data travels a short distance, it may never be routed across a backbone segment. If your data has to travel across the country, or to another country, it will travel across a backbone.

Once your data gets close to its destination, it will be routed off the backbone into a local, smaller pipe. Your data will flow through smaller and smaller pipes until it reaches the destination computer. This process is repeated for every piece of your data until it is all collected together as it was at its origin. Individual pieces may travel different paths and arrive out of order, but once all the pieces arrive, they all get put back together as they should be.

Packets: Data Packaging & Delivery

The individual pieces of data travelling the Internet only move in one direction at a time because electrons can only move through a piece of wire in a single direction. Groups of electrons in a wire form an electric pulse that carries a voltage. The voltage is either low or high to signify a 0 or 1 bit. Groups of these pulses are packed together in a *packet,* which is a standard-sized piece of information transmitted over the Internet.

What is....

packet: A standardized piece of information which travels over a network. Any machine receiving a packet can read the information to make sure the packet gets to its destination.

hop: A hop is the transmission of a packet from one machine to the next. Data moves in a series of hops until it arrives at its target machine.

dynamic routing: If a piece of the Internet goes down, computers send information via another route so packets can still get where they're going. If the broken piece comes back up, they can go back to using it. This is called dynamic routing.

Even though data is broken up into packets, if the data had to travel from origin to destination without stopping or allowing other data transmission to occur, it would be like every freight train in the country traveling on the same track. No matter how small the trains are made, the entire track would be dedicated to a single train from the time it left the station to the time it arrived at its destination. Obviously, this would not allow much freight to be transported.

Railroads often employ sidings, which are short sections of track designed to let one train pull onto the siding and let another train go by. The Internet uses the same sort of design, but the sidings are the individual machines hooked up to the Internet. Each small *hop* traverses a little piece of the total network.

Packets travel across the Internet in a series of short hops from machine to machine. While a packet is on the wire from one machine to the other, that section of the Internet is in use, but with the multitude of machines attached to the Internet, packets can travel a variety of paths to reach the same destination.

Once a packet reaches the next machine in its path, the machine holds the packet until it decides which machine it should be sent to next. When the line is clear, the packet is sent onward. If the first machine chosen is busy, a second machine will be selected and the packet sent to it. In this way, packets can travel virtually infinite paths and still arrive at the same destination.

The ability to send packets to different machines depending on machine load is called *dynamic routing* and is the cornerstone of making the Internet work as efficiently as possible. It is possible for great chunks of the network called the Internet to be destroyed, and data can still find its way across what network is left. The bandwidth will be greatly decreased, and some data may have to be transmitted many times to reach its destination, but the Internet will continue to function.

Our Take: No Dead Ends on the Information Superhighway

Kevin: The Internet pioneer John Gilmore has said that "The Internet interprets censorship as damage, and routes around it." What this means is that any part of the Internet that denies passage to a particular piece or type of data probably cannot prevent it from reaching its destination, because the structure of the Internet ensures that it will just be routed around the problem segment. Similarly, it would take a lot of physical damage to disable the Internet, because every machine on the network is potentially a gateway for data to pass through en route to other machines.

Jeff: This is true. The Internet is configured to supposedly withstand a nuclear war and continue to function, certainly more slowly, but still function. I certainly hope we never find out, but it's comforting to know my e-mail will still get through to its destination when my home town is melted into radioactive slag.

Data Flow: Finding Detours

When a machine sends out a packet to another machine, it waits for a confirmation signal from the destination machine to be sure the packet arrived safely. If not, it resends the packet until it arrives safely.

If the signal takes too long to come back, the sending machine assumes the receiving machine is either too busy or down, so it sends the packet again. This process continues until the packet gets to its destination. Figure 1-4 demonstrates dynamic routing to bypass a broken communication link.

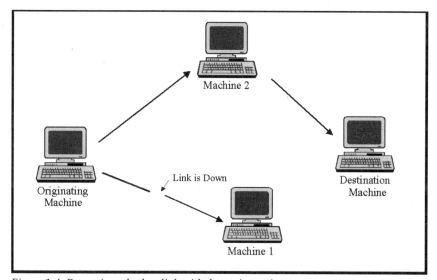

Figure 1-4: Bypassing a broken link with dynamic routing.

The originating machine tries to send a packet to the destination machine via Machine 1, but the Internet link between them is down. The originating machine looks in its routing table to find the name of another machine that might have a link to the destination machine and sends the packet to Machine 2. Machine 2 can see the destination machine just fine, so the packet arrives safely.

It is possible to send a packet to a machine that simply cannot find a route to the destination machine. In this case, the destination machine never sends back a confirming signal, so the sending machine tries again. If a packet cannot be sent to the next hop, the originating machine will generate an error message that the destination machine is down or nonexistent.

What Is...

packet: A standardized piece of information which travels over a network. Any machine receiving a packet can read the information to make sure the packet gets to its destination.

packet storm: If too many packets are being sent across a network due to network errors or users generating too much network traffic, this can result in a large amount of data flooding a network at one time, possibly overwhelming the network. The network will slow down for a time as it tries to handle the load.

POP: Point-of-Presence. A major hub of one of the major telephone companies. A POP is usually placed where there is a large amount of network traffic, such as in a large city, so they can be assured of enough bandwidth to handle the load.

router: All of the information that travels around the Internet has to come from somewhere and go somewhere else. A router is like a network traffic cop, directing information in the right direction to reach its destination.

routing table: Just about every computer on the Internet has a database of computers and IP addresses. Computers consult this "routing table" so they know where to send packets.

As traffic on the Internet increases, these error messages pop up more and more often. Recently, the Internet has become a victim of its own popularity. As more data is transmitted across the Internet, more sections are busy at any given time, and packets simply cannot be sent anywhere.

This causes even more congestion as the packets are resent in an effort to find a path to the destination. Many networks connected to the Internet are protecting themselves from these *packet storms* because their private networks can be overcome by externally transmitted packets. Networks can be protected in a variety of ways, at the expense of slowing down the Internet.

Routers: Traffic Directors

Major intersections on the Internet which are required to handle the most traffic are generally in the hands of the big telephone companies, such as AT&T, MCI, Sprint, and others. These intersections are called a *POP* which stands for Point-of-Presence, and are the main arteries where pieces of the Internet backbone begin and end.

The major intersections handle phenomenal amounts of data during peak periods. One of the functions of a POP is to take data from the backbone and feed it into the smaller pipes connected to the Internet, or to take data coming from the smaller feeds and stuff it onto the Internet. All of this is done by a specialized piece of hardware called a *router*. A router is not intended to slow down network traffic, but it can happen.

As its name implies, a router does one thing: it receives a packet of data, sends a confirmation signal to the transmitting machine, checks to make sure the packet has arrived intact, reads the destination address, decides which pipe the packet goes into, and routes it appropriately. If the packet cannot be delivered, the router sends it to another router in the hopes the next router knows the destination machine. A router does nothing but send and receive network packets.

At first glance, routing might seem to be a simple thing. But consider: a single packet can travel the length of the country in a few milliseconds across an Internet backbone. Packets from millions of machines all hopping across the Internet at the same time come crowding into a single machine: the router.

A router may be required to handle several *thousand* packets a second. Could you read the address on a letter, look at a wall with holes in it labeled for the 50 states, and poke the letter into the correct hole, over and over, many times a second?

A lot of money has been poured into developing faster and more efficient *algorithms* for routing network traffic. An algorithm is a repeatable series of steps for completing a task. Developing really sophisticated algorithms requires the use of advanced mathematics and people whose brains are too big for their own good. Even so, routers across the country are beginning to bog down under the amount of traffic travelling the Internet.

When a router becomes completely overwhelmed, it begins to lose some of the packets it has received because they are arriving faster than it can send the old packets out. The originating machine never receives a confirmation signal so it must resend the packet.

When data packets arrive at the destination machine, they are reassembled in order. If a piece is missing, the data may be corrupted. If the receiving machine is smart enough, it can send out a request for the missing piece, but this increases network traffic too. If the data is corrupted, yet another request for the entire data set must be issued and the process begins all over again, increasing network traffic once more.

As illustrated in Figure 1-5, the number of packets lost on the Internet is growing due to the high levels of network traffic. Lost packets are bad enough in themselves, but resending packets that are not received, and repeating downloads to replace corrupted data further increase Internet traffic. A large increase in network traffic can overwhelm an Internet site.

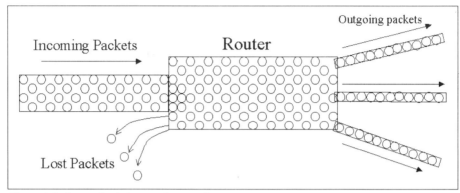

Figure 1-5: An overloaded router loses packets.

Hackers: Protecting Yourself From the Internet

It is possible for a hacker to deliberately send so many packets to a computer that no one can use the machine because it becomes overwhelmed trying to handle the network traffic. This kind of attack is called a *denial of service* attack because it denies legitimate users access to their system.

What Is...

hacker: The term "hacker" used to be a term of honor, used to designate a computer person who showed exceptional ability. Thanks to the media misunderstanding the term (and much of everything else they report on), the term has acquired a negative connotation.

ping: A computer program used to see if another computer is alive and receiving packets.

denial of service: If I send so many packets to your machine that other users can't get access to your system, I'm causing your computer to deny them service.

firewall: This is usually a computer running special software that an external network is connected to. The firewall acts as a security guard for your network, making sure unauthorized network packets do not get access to your network.

ports: A computer uses a port to send and receive data. The more powerful the computer, the more ports it has available. Each port has a number so you can attach a program to a port and outside computers can attach to just the right port and gain access to the program.

One such attack is the *Ping of Death*. A *ping* is a simple packet sent from one machine to another to see if the remote machine is up and minimally functional. The receiving machine responds to the ping with a message that says essentially "Yes, I'm alive and I can see your packets." If a flood of ping packets is directed at a machine, it can be overwhelmed just trying to answer them all.

Hackers can be devious in their attacks on an Internet site. In many cases they use obscure knowledge of the way the Internet works or a subtle flaw in a particular operating system. Often, the compromised site never knows it has been invaded, or at least not until the invaded machine is used to launch an attack on another machine. When the attack is traced back to the offending machine, no one on the machine has any idea what is going on and the hacker quietly disappears and uses another machine to continue the attacks.

FYI: HTTP Packets Now Boarding at Port 80

Computers across the Internet behave in a standard manner. If they didn't the Internet simply would not work. Each computer has a variety of channels, called *ports*, that it can communicate through. The e-mail server listens to the same port on all machines, the ftp server has a standard port, and many other services all have a port that is the recognized standard for them to use.

There is nothing to prevent a machine from being completely reconfigured to use different ports, but if that is done, the machine cannot communicate with other machines in the Internet.

For these and many other reasons, diligent system administrators will attempt to protect their local networks from outside attacks by limiting access with a *firewall*. In an automobile, a firewall is a substantial plate of metal that separates the engine compartment from the passenger compartment. If a serious accident occurs, the firewall protects the passengers from the heat and fire than can possibly erupt in the engine compartment.

The firewall is not a solid piece of metal, however. A few things must come through the firewall in order to control the vehicle, such as the accelerator and brake cables, the engine gauge units, electrical wiring, and so on. Small holes are poked in the firewall to pass the necessary elements into the passenger compartment, but anything that has no business on the inside of the vehicle is excluded.

A computer firewall works the same way. The firewall software is configured to accept only certain packets, based on what the packet is intended to do. Figure 1-6 demonstrates the pickiness of a good firewall program.

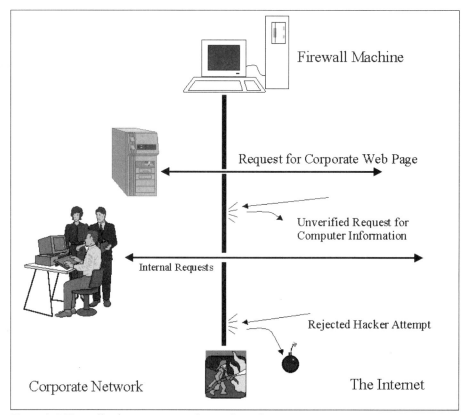

Figure 1-6: Firewall software accepts only certain packets.

When a packet arrives at a firewall, the firewall examines it to see where it is coming from and where it is going. If the originating machine is not on the list of trusted machines, the packet is rejected and never gains access to your network. If the packet is trusted, and is headed for the right place, such as the e-mail server on the standard port, it is accepted. If the packet is headed for a protected port, it is rejected. A firewall can work in both directions, disallowing users inside the firewall from using the Internet in a proscribed manner as well.

While too much paranoia is unhealthy, leaving your system completely open and unmonitored is an invitation for violation. The power and usefulness of the Internet is not without price. With a little foresight and work, a computer system can be reasonably protected and still provide a full range of functionality. The Internet offers too many features not to use them.

Using Your Personal Post Office

Now that you have all of this information about the Internet, what good does it do you? Well, for one thing it helps you understand just how wonderful the Internet really is, and the enormous resources required to keep it running.

In addition, you may now understand a little more about how your computer interacts with the Internet, so the next time you have a slow connection or another computer on the Internet can't be located, you will be able to tell the problem lies with the Internet machines, not your own.

Having a global communications network is a really neat thing, but other than sending lots of e-mail messages, what can you do with it? There are a lot of standard programs associated with the Internet that you use once you learn a little about them.

Office 97 lets you use some of these common Internet features from within the Office 97 applications. One application may get more use from a particular feature than another, and the Internet-enabling of the Office 97 applications may differ in degree, but all of the Office 97 applications have expanded their usefulness and scope by being made more fully aware of the Internet.

Note: You may have never seen the programs mentioned and illustrated in the sections below. In fact, compared to other e-mail, newsreader, and other Internet programs (and Office 97) you may be familiar with, they will probably seem simple, spartan, and unfriendly. However, despite all the flash and glamour of their graphical user interfaces, the Internet programs (with the exception of Web browsers) you might be familiar with don't do anything more or better than these programs. Which is why we chose them to illustrate this chapter—to show just how basic Internet tools really are.

E-Mail: Let's Do Lunch

Yes, everyone who has an Internet account uses e-mail. The first thing most of us did when we logged on for the first time was to send ourselves e-mail, or send the person sitting next to us e-mail. It is amazing that a piece of text can be flung off into the void with a weird address such as sally@bigduck.quack.com and have it arrive safely three seconds later.

Once the novelty wears off, the useful applications of e-mail still remain. For one thing, e-mail is easy to use. There are no pens and paper, no envelopes, no stamps, and no licking of glue. Just pop open your e-mail program, pick an address from your address book, type a few characters, and send the message. Figure 1-7 shows the menu screen of the common Unix e-mail program, PINE.

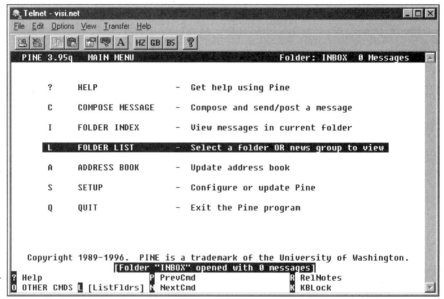

Figure 1-7: PINE is a common e-mail program.

As you can see, PINE is not an exciting program. It has no buttons to push with a mouse, and in fact you can't use a mouse with it at all. You must type all commands using the keyboard using arcane commands you must memorize because the online help is minimal at best. It works, however, and can send e-mail to anyone in the world.

This single feature alone would bring every mother on the planet onto the Internet if they realized how much more they would hear from their children if everyone had an e-mail account. Kids would be more inclined to write home if it was this easy.

Perhaps politicians should jump on the bandwagon of "an Internet account in every pot" considering e-mail can bring families together, promote good writing skills, and foster World Peace. The Internet can be used for great things indeed.

In addition to serving humanity, e-mail is also being used increasingly by technical support people to help customers. Instead of waiting on hold for hours only to talk to an idiot who knows less than you do, you can send e-mail to a tech support account. The technicians on the other end can take a while to give you back an answer, but chances are it is correct because they had time to find the right answer instead of just telling you the first thing they could think of.

As many technical support people can tell you, one of the dangers of e-mail is getting too much of it. Communication is a good thing, but like anything else it must be used in moderation. It is easy to be overwhelmed by the volume of e-mail you receive.

Conscientious people who feel obligated to answer every e-mail message they receive soon find themselves spending all their time answering e-mail. Because e-mail is so easy and cheap to use, people send more of it. This can cause you problems until you learn to deal with it more efficiently.

Remember: some e-mail does not deserve an answer. If you ignore an e-mail message, it doesn't make you a bad person. It's okay, really. E-mail should be answered at *your* convenience, or it does not serve a constructive purpose. Especially if the e-mail is asking you to buy something or it's from someone you don't know who is asking for a favor or calling you an idiot.

Now that you've received your sermon for the day, let's move on to some of the other useful features of the Internet that can give you all kinds of excuses for wasting time, entertaining yourself, avoiding work, looking busy, or even actually accomplishing a task.

Telnet: Window on the World

If you have an account on more than one computer connected to the Internet, you can use all of them at the same time. Skeptical? It's true! All it takes is a Telnet client on your end and a machine that accepts Telnet connections on the other, and many of the machines on the Internet are set up to use Telnet as a matter of course.

Telnet is a bare-bones method of connecting to a remote machine and using its resources, and is depicted in Figure 1-8. Any command that can be issued from a command line is available in a Telnet session. In today's era of point-and-click user interfaces, Telnet is not very glamorous, but it is the workhorse of many a system administrator and programmer.

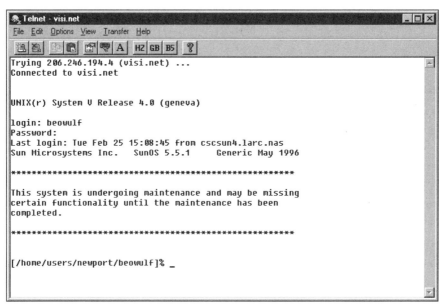

```
Trying 206.246.194.4 (visi.net) ...
Connected to visi.net


UNIX(r) System V Release 4.0 (geneva)

login: beowulf
Password:
Last login: Tue Feb 25 15:08:45 from cscsun4.larc.nas
Sun Microsystems Inc.    SunOS 5.5.1      Generic May 1996

**********************************************************

This system is undergoing maintenance and may be missing
certain functionality until the maintenance has been
completed.

**********************************************************


[/home/users/newport/beowulf]% _
```

Figure 1-8: A Telnet window.

If anything, the Telnet program is even more boring than the PINE program. A Telnet window can communicate with any computer in the world, but it may bore you to sleep before you get there.

Once you have a Telnet window open to a remote machine, you can run programs, monitor system activity, administer a database, edit files, and many other things. If you have a window manager that is compatible with the remote machine you can even run programs that require a graphical front end.

The program uses the CPU of the remote machine and sends its output to your machine across the network. Your window manager captures mouse clicks and typed input and sends them to the program running on the remote machine. In this way, you can do things from home that used to require physical access to the remote machine.

So many lucky people are making use of this procedure that it has been given a name: *telecommuting*. Simply dial up over a phone line and modem to connect to a remote machine, log in with your username and password, and you can do most anything from home that you can do sitting at a desk in a stuffy office.

What Is...

CPU: Central Processing Unit. The main computer chip that runs all of the programs on a computer.

telecommuting: One day I will sit at my computer at home and do my work on a machine many miles away, *and I will get paid for it.* This is telecommuting.

FTP: File Transfer Protocol. Used to transfer files from one machine on the Internet to another.

Telnet: A program that establishes a connection to another machine and lets you issue commands to execute programs on the remote machine.

FTP: Reach Out & Download Something

Ever find yourself at your work computer and realize you left a file on your home computer that you really need? If your machine at home is connected to the Internet, you can easily transfer the file to your work computer. Once you do so, you should really seek professional help, because only massively nerdy people have a home computer with a permanent Internet connection.

Our Take: Nerd Defined

Kevin: Jeff has the next best thing: a separate phone line for his home computers. His *three* home computers, one for each of the three people in his family. He's well-qualified to know what's nerdy and what's not.

Jeff: Ah, so you agree I know massively nerdy? And I have *four* computers, not three. I need a backup in case one goes down. Deathmatch anyone?

Files are transferred across the Internet using a program called FTP, which conveniently stands for *file transfer protocol*. FTP is another of those bare-bones, unglamorous, workhorse programs that many people cannot do without. Figure 1-9 shows you just how boring FTP can be.

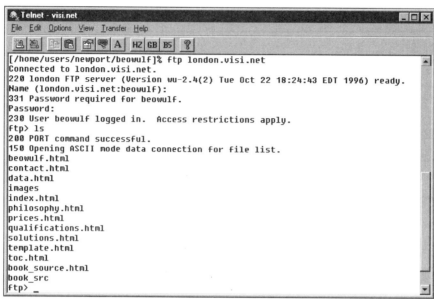

Figure 1-9: An FTP window.

Once again, this is a good example of an Internet application that does a good job, does only what it is supposed to, and requires the user to know what they are doing in order to use it. Nothing is automated, and the user keeps track of what is going on because the FTP program only does what you tell it to.

Using FTP is simple: connect to a remote machine using the FTP program, enter your username and password, find the files you want, request them, and copies of the files are transferred to your machine.

Really large files may take a long time to transfer, but FTP is reliable and no other process has replaced it. The FTP process has been prettied up by putting fancy front ends on top of the FTP process, but the purpose remains the same.

In fact, FTP is so boring these few paragraphs describe it as well as necessary. Even so, the Internet would be a large ocean of isolated machines if it were not possible to transfer information between them.

An Internet feature with far more flash and glamour is *Usenet Newsgroups,* which many people consider the heart of the Internet and the best thing about the Internet community.

MUDs: Games People Play

Lest ye think the Internet is nothing but a dry and boring place where egg-heads and losers who have no lives spend their Saturday nights, there is another side to the Internet as well. Not everything on the Net is work oriented.

What Is...

Chat room: One of the most useless, most maligned, and most popular features of the Internet. People who might not speak a word to anyone around them will log onto a chat room and use the computer keyboard to talk to anyone who will listen.

MUD: Multi-User Dungeon. The real reason the Internet exists, MUDs are much more fun than chat rooms and give you rewards for killing things. It doesn't get any better than this.

Usenet: A collection of newsgroups that are published to computers all over the world. Readers can post new messages or respond to other messages. If you post something stupid, you better be wearing flame-proof underwear.

TIN: The Internet Newsreader. One of a large number of useful, arcane programs used to read Usenet newsgroups.

As an example of the fun content of the Internet, consider the *MUD*, or Multi-User Dungeon. There are many variations on the features and attractions of a MUD, but the underlying theme is the same: kill things, meet people, drink alcohol, and generally run amok. No, a MUD is not a redneck bar, but a computer program that thousands of people play every day.

A MUD uses the Telnet protocol to allow users from all over the World to connect to the MUD at the same time. As each player logs in, they use a username and password just like a normal computer account, but from there the similarity ends.

As a player logs in, he or she assumes the character of their username. Some first-timers use their real names, but once they see characters with names like Zeus, Beowulf, Deathstalker, Fang, and Phish wander by, they soon realize they are no longer in Kansas, Toto. A representative screen of what you might see in a MUD is shown in Figure 1-10.

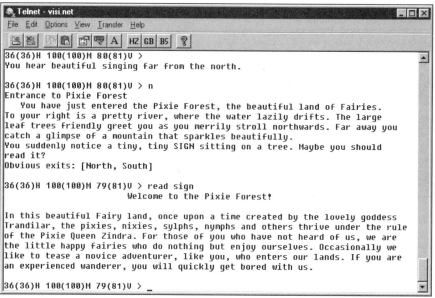

Figure 1-10: A MUD adventure.

As you can see, a MUD is a text-only adventure game. The room you are currently in is described by the words on your screen and your imagination fleshes out the rest. Everything else on the Internet is done with text, why not the games too? We don't need no stinkin' graphics!

A MUD character starts out as a weenie character of level 1, with little or no armor, weapons, potions, or magic. The general idea is to find yourself a weapon and some armor (the general store across the street looks promising) and go find something to kill. As you kill monsters, you gain experience points. As you gain experience, you advance in levels and grow more powerful so you can kill bigger monsters and get more experience points, and so on.

Some players, however, never advance very far because they are on the MUD just to talk to their friends. People from Australia wander into the local bar to chat with people from the United Kingdom, Canada, and Brazil. The MUD culture is the origin of the chat rooms now found all over the Internet.

With a wide variety of MUDs to choose from, players tend to pick the MUD that is best suited to their own characteristics. A MUD should be fun, but there is much more to the decision than that. The same description can be applied to another Internet feature called *Usenet News*.

Usenet: The Internet News Desk

One of the single most useful and biggest time-wasting features of the Internet is a Usenet news feed. Do you want to find out how to write something really complicated in an obscure programming language? Have you ever wondered who *really* shot JFK? Do you need a recipe for goat's-head soup with just a touch of mint?

A newsgroup is an amorphous beast that is targeted at a particular audience. There are over 50,000 individual newsgroups that can see 1,000 messages a day, or 5 messages a year depending on the popularity of the subject served by the newsgroup.

In general, Internet users are not a shy lot. Usenet is a forum for many knowledgeable (and not-so-knowledgeable) experts to answer questions for the edification of the people who read the newsgroups.

Once you discover the vast amounts of information available from users of the Internet, you may never be seen again. Remember, we warned you. The TIN newsreader is shown in Figure 1-11.

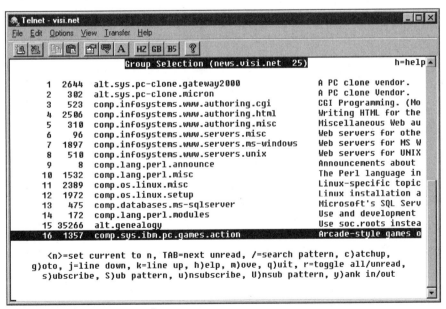

Figure 1-11: The TIN newsreader.

What Is...

Usenet: A collection of newsgroups that are published to computers all over the world. Readers can post a new message or respond to other messages. If you post something stupid, you better be wearing flame-proof underwear.

TIN: The Internet Newsreader. One of a large number of useful, arcane programs used to read Usenet newsgroups.

post: Send a message to a newsgroup.

moderated: A human being reads each posting to a single moderated newsgroup before it is posted to determine its acceptability.

unmoderated: No one reads posts before they are posted. Welcome to chaos.

flame war: Ouch, that hurt! If you say something dumb in a newsgroup, millions of people will read it and some of the less socially acceptable will "flame" you with posts that melt your eyeballs. If you respond in kind, hundreds of strangers will happily join in by posting their own flames. Pretty soon, the newsgroup will melt into slag and warriors will gather in bar rooms around the world to toast their cleverness.

A message that appears in a newsgroup is called a *post*, and sending a message to a newsgroup is called *posting a message*. There are many software programs designed to help you search for and select newsgroups, organize the postings, and send and reply to postings.

FYI: Posting a Message

The UNIX program rn, used to read and write messages to newsgroups, gives the following warning before it lets you post a message to a global newsgroup: "This message will be posted to machines all over the World, costing hundreds if not thousands of dollars. Are you sure you want to do this?"

A *moderated* newsgroup has a person or group who is responsible for the content of the newsgroup. Postings are read by the moderator and judged for appropriate content. Different moderators and different newsgroups have different standards for appropriateness. A newsgroup for heart transplant recipients would hardly be the place for a posting asking for help killing garden weeds.

A newsgroup that accepts any post by anyone is an *unmoderated* newsgroup and posts can be about any subject, regardless of the topic of the newsgroup. Newsgroup posters are great believers in the right of free speech and exercise it to the breaking point.

Any unmoderated newsgroup is a study of anarchy in action. If someone asks a really stupid question that shows the poster obviously did no research to find the answer on their own, the poster will be the deserving recipient of a *flame* posting, which can insult them, their family, and their family pet. Lack of IQ and personal grooming habits are often mentioned as well.

If the original poster takes offense and flames back at the flamer, newsgroup readers are more than happy to choose up sides and jump into a *flame war*. No one is as nasty as someone who can sit at their computer and say anything they want with no chance of physical reprisal by the recipient. Knowledge of the subject at hand is of no consequence in a flame war. The point is to emotionally scar your victim as deeply as possible. Unmoderated newsgroups are not for the softhearted or slow of wit.

Some mentally challenged individuals consider it fun to actually start a flame war by posting messages that are so stupid they deliberately provoke readers to flame them. These posts are called *trolls* because they are trolling for fools to respond to them.

To avoid being flamed, the vast majority of newsgroup readers don't post a single message, but simply *lurk* and read messages posted by others. These *lurkers* may never post a message, or they may respond to a post via a personal e-mail message to the author of a post.

What Is...

spam: Not only an unappetizing meat (by?)product, spam is also a name applied to unwanted junk postings or e-mail sent to large numbers of people, usually for the purpose of getting money.

FAQ: Frequently Asked Questions. Many newsgroups see the same questions asked over and over again, so some kind soul will collect them and put them in an easily reachable spot in the hopes that newbies will read the FAQ instead of asking the same question Joe Blow asked yesterday. Sometimes it works and sometimes it doesn't.

Online Ms. Manners

People who are new to the Internet and Usenet are called *newbies*. First-timers are looked down upon by frequent posters because the newbies are ignorant of the unwritten rules of newsgroup posting called *Netiquette*. Netiquette is a code of behavior expected of you to make using the Internet more productive for everyone.

Many newsgroups see the same questions asked over and over by newbies. These are called *Frequently Asked Questions* and referred to as *FAQs* (pronounced fax). Frequent readers of a newsgroup may collect these FAQs together into the newsgroup FAQ which new readers are supposed to peruse before asking questions on the newsgroup.

A common question posted to newsgroups is "where do I find the FAQ for this newsgroup?" but that question is in the FAQ so the poster should have read the FAQ before posting. Here comes another flame war.

Spam

The recipient of the most vicious flames are *spam* postings. Spam postings are messages posted to a large number of newsgroups at the same time, whether they apply to the newsgroup topics or not. Spams are usually advertisements or "get rich quick" pyramid schemes. If you spam Usenet, you better don your flame-proof underwear because your e-mail box will fill up fast with flaming e-mail.

Why is it called spam? The origin of the term is the subject of some debate, but if you really want to know, perhaps you should hunt up the appropriate newsgroup and ask that question yourself. Best of luck.

Fast Answers

In spite of all this negative commentary, newsgroups can be the best, fastest source of information in the world. Literally millions of people read Usenet news, so any question you post can receive an answer in just a few minutes. Internet users are among the most knowledgeable people anywhere on any subject.

All you need to do to receive a quick, courteous reply is to first search for the answer yourself, then find an appropriate newsgroup, read the FAQ (if you can find it), and then post your question with enough information about the problem to show you at least tried to find an answer. If you follow this formula, many people will be more than willing to help you. It is these generous people who hold the promise of the future of the Internet.

The Future of Your Personal Post Office

Many people have predicted many things for the future of the Internet. Some predict the Internet's total collapse from overuse and lack of bandwidth. The recent growing pains of the Internet have fueled these doomsayers, but while small sections may have collapsed for a short time, the Internet as a whole has proven to be remarkably resilient.

Others predict unlimited bandwidth "real soon now" and the eventual hookup of every household in the world. To these people, the Internet is the Borg of Star Trek fame, and resistance is futile. Unlimited bandwidth is unrealistic, and must be paid for. Those who expect the Internet to remain free while expecting infinite bandwidth are doomed to disappointment.

The Internet is in a critical time of transition. More people use the Internet than ever before, and are straining resources. Plans are being developed to deal with the problem, but they will take time and money.

Our Take : Where Is the Internet Going in the Next Year?

Jeff: The next phase will probably take place more on corporate intranets (what a stupid word! Why not "innernets"?) than the real Web. The innernet is where most real Web programming will take place because there is a market for it, and it will pay better. You can standardize on one platform and Web browser on an innernet and write programs that work with your choices.

Kevin: Disk and memory will only get cheaper (although not quickly), meaning that software (like Web browsers, servers, suites) will become fatter and less efficient as it becomes less cost-effective to make code compact and adequately debugged. AOL will either raise rates or give up the unlimited hours plan, and the Web will be a better place for it. Jeff says he was in a store that had a whole aisle of PCs dialed-up and connected to AOL from 8 AM to 9 PM. No wonder the lines are always busy.

Modernize Equipment: Build Me a Bigger Pipe

The biggest Internet bottleneck is outdated transmission lines and telephone switching equipment. Some equipment still in use today was installed in the 1930s and simply cannot keep up with the demand for ever-greater bandwidth.

High-traffic sections of the Internet have been or are being upgraded to fiber optic transmission lines which increase bandwidth many-fold. Fiber optic technology allows many packets to be transmitted through a communication line at the same time, and in both directions at once.

Another solution to the bandwidth problem is *private Internets*. Large corporations who need guaranteed bandwidth are contracting with major ISPs to support high-speed communication lines that are available only to corporate users. Data is routed away from the overloaded Internet and onto the private Internet. This costs a pretty penny, but if a company needs the bandwidth and they can afford it, it is the best solution. This also reduces the load on the Internet just a little bit.

Cost: Internet Postage Stamps

Another hotly contested issue is the rate paid by Internet users. The telephone system was designed to handle short telephone calls that lasted a few minutes. Internet users can stay logged on for hours at a time. There are some who argue that those who use the lines the most should pay the most.

Until just a few years ago, the Internet was funded by the National Science Foundation (NSF). During these days of cutbacks and budget crunches, NSF underwriting of the Internet is a thing of the past. The cost is now borne mostly by long distance telephone companies, and private industry takes a dim view of not making a profit.

The Internet will probably be upgraded considerably, but it won't be cheap. The cost will be transferred to those who use the Internet and those who use it most will probably have to pay more. The Internet will be the better for it, but a nostalgic Internet community will not give in without a fight.

Addressing: More Confusion

One of the most pressing issues about the Internet is the availability of new IP addresses for all of the new computers connecting to the Internet. The present scheme should support over four billion computers, but many addresses are reserved for special use, and some companies have reserved huge chunks of IP addresses for their computers to use.

Back before the Internet was the buzzword of the year, large companies such as IBM, Southwestern Bell, AT&T, and others licensed a major portion of the available IP addresses for their own use.

IP addresses are in the form xxx.xxx.xxx.xxx, where 'xxx' can be any number from 000 to 256. In reality, usable addresses are constricted more than that. In addition, companies can receive a Class C or even a Class B license.

A Class C license awards a fixed set of IP addresses to a particular company. A Class C license for the 123.456 prefix, for example, grants the use of any IP address of the form 123.456.xxx.xxx to the licensee.

A quick bit of multiplication shows a Class C license grants the use of 256 * 256 or 65,536 possible IP addresses to the license holder. That is a lot of computers! That's also a lot of IP addresses that may never be used and are unavailable to assign to other machines.

A Class B license is even more generous. It grants the use of IP addresses of the form 123.xxx.xxx.xxx which is 256 * 256 * 256 or 16,777,216 computers. If these were handed out freely, only 256 companies could possibly have machines on the Internet.

New IP addressing schemes have been proposed and are slowly being approved, but the implementation of any new scheme would be a long and arduous project. Every machine on the Internet would have to be upgraded to recognize the new format which will not happen overnight, or without cost.

Moving On

What has caused this new and overwhelming interest in the Internet? The Internet itself is not particularly user-friendly, and while the basic tools that make the Internet usable are perfectly serviceable, as you have seen, they aren't easy to master. It took a totally new innovation to make the Internet the hottest topic in technology today. It took the birth of the *World Wide Web*, which is covered in Chapter 2.

chapter 2

The Birth of the World Wide Web

The Internet is a great tool, but it's hard to use. The Internet was built on mostly UNIX computers, and UNIX is as friendly as a grumpy badger unless you know how to deal with it. Not many people sit down at a UNIX workstation and feed a badger very often.

For most of its lifetime, the Internet has been the province of college students and professors, researchers, and scientific programmers who used the Internet to communicate with one another, download obscure academic papers, and flame each other in newsgroups.

Our Take: The Next Year on the Web

Jeff: The Web will spend the next six months just stabilizing where it is now. It has grown too far, too fast, and the underlying Internet is showing the strain. Bandwidth problems, usage payments for Internet service, online credit card transactions, and some stable programming platform for Web browsers will have to be taken care of before the next phase of Internet growth.

Kevin: Here's what's going to happen in the next year: IPng or some variant thereof will be adopted as a standard, if not in practice. HTML 3.2 will be generally accepted and every browser and editing environment worth anything will support it, but everybody will continue to add their own "extensions." We'll see pay-for-use private Internets become popular, providing no-delay information highways for those who can afford them.

Then along came Tim Berners-Lee who came up with a great idea: Why not give the Internet a *GUI*, or graphical user interface? (GUI is pronounced "gooey", by the way.) What's a GUI? If you use Microsoft Windows, you use a GUI. A GUI makes using a computer easier by putting computer commands in drop-down menus, letting you use a mouse to select things, and letting you *see* what you are doing.

What is...

graphical user interface (GUI): Uses graphics to display what is being done on a computer, like pull-down menus full of commands or buttons to push with a mouse.

server: A computer that serves software to users or a software program that provides a service to users, such as a Web server or database server.

browser: A software program that lets you interact with the features of the Internet using a GUI.

When using a GUI, you are isolated from the complexity of the underlying operating system. You don't have to know how files are stored on the hard drive or the commands needed to move files around. You just click on a filename in a window and drag the file picture to another part of the window. The GUI executes the command to move the file for you. From this simple idea, the World Wide Web was born.

The Web made the Internet usable for regular people, not just computer geeks. By giving the user a visual representation of what is going on, a Web browser gives those of us who rarely use a computer a way to use the powerful features of the Internet in a simple way.

If your boss just told you to create the company Web site, and you don't even know what the Web is, tomorrow when the boss asks you how things are going, you can cough up everything you learned from this chapter and watch his eyes get big. You'll be on the fast track to management for sure. You have our sympathies.

Our Take: The Best Thing About the Web

Jeff: There are so many great things about the Web, it's hard to pick just one, but since I thought up this stupid topic, I have to answer it. I like using the Web as a research tool. I don't mean just for finding white papers on physics projects, but also for things like finding cheats for computer games, finding information for school reports, or finding prices for computer hardware.

So many people have put so much information on the Web, bless their hearts, that you can find just about anything, good or bad, on a Web page somewhere. Sure there's smut, and there is trash, but the good stuff is in the overwhelming majority.

Kevin: I'm constantly entertained by the growth of the Web, both in size and in content. The pace at which things are moving is so fast that no one person can expect to keep up with all of it; reading the trade magazines these days almost leaves you breathless. "Hey!" you think, "I just figured out what ActiveX is; now they want to change it again?" It can overwhelm if you let it.

But the craziness of it all, like driving too fast on a winding road through a forest, is exhilarating. The best thing about the Web for me is that there's always something new out there, something to grab hold of and learn. No excuse for boredom in this business. And if what's already out there is so interesting, who can say that what's next won't be better?

It Takes Two to Tango

The World Wide Web (WWW, or just "Web") operates on the GUI principle, but it lets you access files on other machines around the Internet, not just on your own. You don't have to know the commands needed to tell your computer to go out and get a copy of the file and bring it back for you to look at. The Web does this with two pieces of software: a *Web server* and a *Web browser*.

Our Take: The Worst Thing About the Web

Jeff: The hype. The Web is just another tool for people to use, but the media and software companies looking to cash in on it have promoted the Web into some huge thing that can't help but disappoint those who believe the hype.

The Web is at its best when presenting information to you in an interesting format. Online stores, corporate Web sites, Web search engines, all of them give you information. If you listen to the hype, I'll be able to walk my dog, make dinner, and pilot a moon buggy, all from the Web. Hey, I don't even have a dog. The moon buggy part is cool though.

My second worst thing about the Web is Java. In two years, Java will be a usable language that will hopefully replace the bloated inefficiency of C++. For now, it's a kid's toy that can do some really neat things very, very slowly.

Kevin: Traffic. When you promise a silk purse from a sow's ear, a lot of pigs are going to be purchased. It's nice to promise all-you-can-surf to everybody, but the fact is that the infrastructure just isn't there to support 100 million full-time users of the Net.

The silver lining to this is that the traffic will eventually result in road construction, but it's not going to be cheap and the new highway that's agreed upon isn't necessarily going to be the best road that could be built. In the meantime, we're going to have a lot of people who could really benefit from the use of the Web who are going to be frustrated by the cost and the delays, and they'll probably give up. That's a shame.

The Flashy Web Browser

The Web browser gets all the good press. Why? Because you can *see* it. Web browsers are glamorous. Web browsers show you pictures and have lots of neat buttons to push. You can change font types and sizes, turn Java and JavaScript on and off, change browser colors, switch languages to Chinese, and so on. A cool Web browser is shown in Figure 2-1.

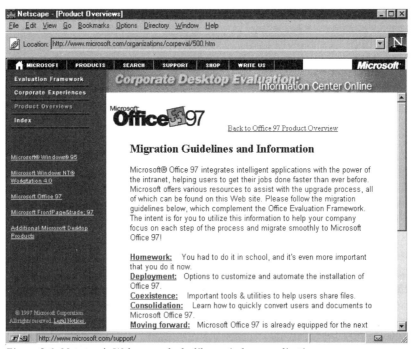

Figure 2-1: Netscape's Web screen looks like a windows application.

Even if you've never used a Web browser before, you can just keep pushing buttons until something happens. If you figure out what two buttons do, you're on your way around the Internet. While using a Telnet window or FTP program, there is no way you'll "accidentally" discover how they work.

Browsers are cool, and they are interactive. We all want the coolest browser with the newest features so we can draw stuff interactively on an Internet white board while we chat with someone using our Internet phone.

Web browsers support neat scripting languages like JavaScript and VBScript, which let you embed scripts in your HTML code—and the user's browser runs them like real programs. You can move the user around your Web site automatically, pop up message boxes, scroll messages across the bottom of the Web browser, and just generally annoy the heck out of anyone who visits your Web site. This is considered to be very cool.

Our Take: What's Next for Web Browsers?

Kevin: Let's see. Lynx was a text-only browser, circa 1993. Mosaic added images in '94, then data streams showed up in Netscape 2.0 in '95. Internet telephony was '96. So we get a new browser feature about every year. I think we'll probably see browser/desktop integration in late '97, with the next installments in the Windows and Navigator sagas. Soon, maybe in '98 or '99, I'm looking forward to voice recognition. "Computer! Find Blue Screen of Death and NT, and ignore README files!" Cool.

Jeff: Next will be a completely new application that says it's a Web browser and isn't. Honestly, when is enough enough? I can't even find a Web browser that does the minimal things I want it to do without having to put up with the code bloat caused by collaboration software, Java support, e-mail, news, and back-rubbing software.

Stop already! Microsoft has begun the same process with Web browsers that they have pushed over the limit with office suite software. They keep adding more features and telling people they can't live without them. Bleh! I don't need three-fourths of the features in Word 97, but can I get a slimmed-down version of Word that only takes up 5 megs instead of 30? Of course not.

Ahem. I happen to believe the Web is a great idea that is being mercilessly forced to do a lot of things it doesn't do well, nor should it be expected to do them at all. Maybe that makes me a curmudgeon, but so be it.

If the Web does something well, use it. If not, use something else. As for the question of what comes next, what's left? We now have radio and TV broadcasts over the Web, fishcams, satellite weather maps, pictures of naked women, bulletin boards, database interfaces, Web search programs, and who knows what else?

The Invisible Web Server

Then there is the Web server. You can't see it, you aren't even sure it's really there until you get one of those annoying *Server cannot be contacted* messages. The only time you think about the Web server is when you can't connect to it. If it works, you don't think about it. If it doesn't, you yell at it. The only press Web servers get is bad press.

What Is. . .

JavaScript: A programming language invented by Netscape for use in their Web browsers.

VBScript: A programming language invented by Microsoft for use in their Web browsers. Netscape had one, and Microsoft wasn't about to use it because that would have implied Microsoft thought Netscape had a good idea.

HTML code: The language of the Web. HTML is not a programming language because you can't write programs in it, but it's a markup language that is intended to format text for viewing.

Java: The savior of civilization, if you listen to Sun. No big deal, if you listen to Microsoft. The truth is somewhere in the middle. Java is a new programming language invented to run TV cable boxes. Someone decided it would be neat to use on the Web, and some of the greatest hype in history was born.

There is no cool graphical front end for a Web server (except when you use the Web browser to do Web server administration, but the browser is the cool part), so the Web server is pretty much invisible. It just runs "out there," sending the stuff you request back to your browser.

Web servers are not glamorous. They require you to configure stuff, know about port numbers, and worry about server security. If you want to do something cool with a Web server, you have to actually write real programs and make them work with the server, using some pretty strange programming techniques. Web browsers are easy. Web servers are hard.

Speaking the Language of the Web

Okay, you say, I have a Web browser and I know there are millions of Web servers out there on the Internet, so how do I make the two talk to one another? Initiating a connection between a Web browser and server requires a magical incantation called a *Uniform Resource Locator* (URL).

Understanding the Uniform Resource Locator

The Uniform what, you say? When you start up a Web browser for the first time, even if you've never used the Web before, your browser will display a default Web page. The page will be different depending on who makes your browser software, but the page displayed will be the *home page* of the browser maker.

What Is. . .

Uniform Resource Locator (URL): A magical incantation used in a Web browser to find a site on the Web. The URL tells the Web browser what machine to look for and what Web page to look for.

home page: A person or organization's main Web page.

hyperlinks: Text or an image that lets you click on it and go to another Web page.

A home page is like the front door to a house. Anyone can have a home page if they have an Internet account that allows it. Your home page is an introduction to you, your company, and your Web site. Browser makers generally include on their home page a table of contents of their Web site, a way to search their Web site for information, and a list of *hyperlinks* to other Web pages.

A hyperlink is an image or a string of text that includes a URL to another Web page. If you click on the hyperlink, your browser sends a request for a Web page to the Web server specified in the URL. The Web server finds the page and sends its contents back to your browser. Your browser hums for a little while and then displays the new Web page.

If you look in the little box at the top of the browser, you will see a really ugly-looking string of characters. This string is the URL of the Web page you are currently looking at in your browser. Each part of the URL contains a piece of the information required to find a Web page somewhere on the Internet. When all of the pieces are put together, the URL becomes a unique name for a specific Web page.

A URL is composed of four main parts:

1. The protocol

2. The machine name

3. The port number

4. The path information

What Is. . .

protocol: A standardized language computers use to communicate.

port: A computer uses a port to send and receive data. The more powerful the computer, the more ports it has available. Each port has a number so you can attach a program to a port, and outside computers can attach to just the right port and gain access to that program.

path: Where to find a file on a computer's hard drive.

parameter: A value given to a program to tell it what to do. Based on the value of the parameter, the program can do different things.

DNS: Domain Name Server. A computer program that accepts human-readable computer names and returns the computer-readable IP address.

IP: stands for Internet Protocol and defines the common language that Internet computers use to talk to one another.

Let's take a closer look at a few URLs to see what all the parts mean. The Microsoft home page can be reached by using the simple URL:

```
http://www.microsoft.com
```

The first part of the URL, *http://*, tells the Web browser which protocol to use when initiating a connection. Protocols are discussed more fully later in this chapter, but for now you should know Web servers and browser communication using the HTTP protocol. Now the Web browser knows it will be contacting a Web server.

The next part of the URL, *www.microsoft.com*, is the machine name. This specifies the complete machine name of the computer that hosts the target Web server. Once the Web browser software resolves the machine name using a DNS, it will have the IP address of the target machine.

You'll notice, however, that the Microsoft home page URL does not contain the other two pieces of information required in a URL. This is because the port number and the path are optional parameters.

If no port number is specified in the URL, the Web browser uses the *default* port number. A default is a standard value used whenever no other value is specified. The default port number for a Web server is port 80. Web servers can be attached to any available port on a computer, but to find a Web server on a nonstandard port, you must know the port number. Other programs such as FTP, Telnet, and e-mail have standard port numbers too. Putting standard programs on known port numbers makes the Internet work much more smoothly.

The final part of the URL, the path information, is also optional. If no path information is specified, the default is assumed. In this case, there is no standard default for the path information. The default is set as part of the Web server configuration. Each Web server can have a different default page, and your Web browser has no idea what that could be. Therefore, your Web browser requests a default page, and the Web server returns whatever page it has as a default.

A more complicated URL might look like so:

```
http://cscsun1.larc.nasa.gov/~beowulf/db/web_access.html
```

Once again, the protocol used is http://, but the machine name is cscsun1.larc.nasa.gov, and the default port will be used. The *~beowulf/* portion of the path information indicates this Web page is under the directory of the user account "beowulf." The target file is *web_access.html* in the *db/* subdirectory.

Understanding File Extensions

The .HTML extension on the target filename designates the type of file being returned by the Web server. In this case, the document is written in the HyperText Markup Language (HTML), which will be covered in the next section. HTML is the native language of the WWW.

What Is. . .

file extension: The part of a filename that comes after the '.'. The extension often identifies the type of file format used to store information within the file. By identifying the extension, you know how to process the file.

.HTML: The file extension used for HyperText Markup Language documents. Some machines use .htm instead because they can't handle more than three letters in a file extension.

.GZ: The file extension used for files compressed with the 'gzip' program. Some other file extensions for other types of compression are '.zip', '.arj', and '.lzh'. The file extension identifies the type of compression used.

.GIF: Identifies images stored in the Graphics Interchange Format.

.JPEG: Images stored in the Joint Photographic Experts Group format.

helper application: If a Web browser can't process a file type itself, if a helper application is defined for a particular file extension, the browser can start up the helper application and it can process the file.

tags: Tags are HTML identifiers that tell a Web browser how to display information.

Other possible extensions are .TXT for plain text documents and .GZ for a compressed file that will be downloaded to your machine instead of displayed in the Web browser.

A Web browser comes to you preconfigured to recognize a large number of file extensions. Some extensions are simply displayed by the browser. Other extensions signal the browser to find a *helper application*: another application on your system that is able to process and display that file type. The Web browser hands off the file to the helper application as soon as it finishes downloading it.

If the Web browser encounters a file extension it doesn't recognize, it gives you the option of saving the file on your computer for later processing. You can also add new file extensions to the list your browser understands if you need to, by using the browser's configuration options, shown in Figure 2-2.

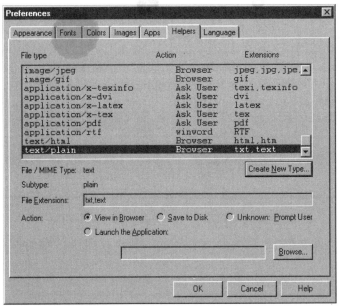

Figure 2-2: The Helpers tab of a browser preference dialog.

As you can see in Figure 2-2, a Web browser contains the code to process some file types, such as HTML, text, GIF, or JPEG, internally. The type of file is listed in the first column, with the associated file extensions in the last column. The middle column identifies what program will be used to handle files of that type. If the middle column says Browser, the Web browser itself contains the programs to process files of that type.

Other file types require external helpers, such as RTF, which will open Microsoft Word to display documents with the .RTF extensions. Other file types are unknown and default to asking the user what to do, as indicated by Ask User.

While a Web browser can handle an astonishing number of file types, most of the documents written for the Web are written in HTML, as mentioned before.

HTML: The Language of the Web

HTML is a collection of commands, called *tags*, that tell the Web browser how to format and display the contents of a Web page. Tags generally come in pairs, and they are placed before and after the text they affect.

There are many good books on the shelves at your local bookstore, such as *HTML Publishing on the Internet, Second Edition* from Ventana, that cover HTML and many of its extensions. Teaching you how to write raw HTML is beyond the scope of this book.

HTML is not a complicated language, but it is fairly extensive. New additions are regularly being added to the language to increase the functionality of HTML as Web designers continue to push the limits of the language outward.

There is a standards group charged with identifying and standardizing the changes made to HTML. Unfortunately, they do not move as quickly as the rest of the Web and browser makers, anxious to have the best product, add their own proprietary HTML tags that are only recognized by their own browser.

In many cases, other browser makers will adopt the new tags into their own browsers, but in some cases the new tags have the same name but do not behave the same in different browsers. A Web page that looks fine in one browser will look terrible in another because of the conflicting interpretation of how HTML tags should be handled.

In the browser wars, users who want to create pages available to anyone on the Web are faced with a few options:

1. Try to write HTML that can be understood by any browser and keep a copy of every known browser so they can check the format.

2. Pick a browser and write code specifically for that browser.

3. Ignore the HTML extensions added by browser makers and use only HTML tags that are part of the approved HTML standard.

Option 1 is harder to do than it sounds. If a person who develops on a UNIX computer wants to support all browsers, he must also have access to Windows and Macintosh machines to check the format under those operating systems as well. Some browsers are not available under all operating systems.

Option 2 is an acceptable choice if you are developing a private intranet and you can dictate the browser that will be used to view your company Web pages. You can't prevent users from bringing in their own favorite Web browsers, but if they can't read Web pages correctly, you are not obligated to change the pages.

Option 3 might sound the same as option 1, but it isn't. There are many useful HTML extensions recognized by most browsers that are not part of the HTML standard. Some extensions, such as HTML tables, were adopted by browser makers long before they were approved as part of standard HTML. Also, not all browsers recognize every HTML tag that is part of the standard. The standard keeps changing, but old browsers that don't know the new changes are still being used.

Accepting option 3 as your standard assures your Web pages can be viewed by anyone on the Web regardless of the browser they use; but it also means your Web programs will be harder to write, and you might not be able to do everything you want with your Web pages. The new HTML extensions make it easier to do some things and make some things possible for the first time. If you cannot use the new extensions, it might be harder to do what you want with the limited HTML you have available.

In the browser wars, the users are the ones who lose, as the browser makers try to force you to choose their product. This is generally excused as being part of our capitalist economy, with competition creating new and better products.

Maybe so, but it hasn't worked for long-distance telephone companies and it doesn't work for Web browsers. The World Wide Web was founded on the premise that any user on any computer using any Web browser can have equal access to information. To foster this notion, the Web is built on standard *protocols* that were already in use on the Internet.

Protocols: Keeping the Playing Field Even

The word "protocol" has been used several times in the course of this part of the book. Every aspect of the Internet and the Web operates on a standard set of protocols that allow all kinds of software on all kinds of hardware to interact and accomplish a task in a consistent manner.

A protocol is simply a method of communication agreed upon between the two parties that are communicating. If one party speaks one language and the other party speaks another language, the two cannot exchange information. The Internet is built on several different protocols that are used to accomplish different purposes.

The Internet uses the Internet Protocol (IP), File Transfer Protocol (FTP), and Telnet protocol among others. The Web has its own protocol, the HyperText Transfer Protocol (HTTP), for transferring HTML documents from a Web server to a Web browser. The Web protocol is layered on top of the standard Internet protocol, which simply means HTTP uses the Internet to transport information between the server and browser.

Web browsers and servers spend a large portion of their time sending HTML documents across the Internet, and because all Web servers and all Web browsers understand HTTP, any Web browser can communicate with any Web server. Users don't need to know how it works. All they need to know is that it does.

From the Web developer's perspective, the programs you write can be vastly different. Web programs can be written in different computer languages, get data from files or a variety of databases, or produce output as HTML, text, or graphics. The user might never know or even care how a Web page is created, but behind the scenes is where the fun is.

Web programming has become more sophisticated and more complicated in the short lifespan of the Web. Programs written to run on the Web server and produce output for the user's browser can make use of many new programming methods, some of which will be explored in the next section.

Programming for the Web

Once the world was a simple place. If you wanted to write a program for the World Wide Web, you used the Common Gateway Interface (CGI) provided by the HTML standard. Whether you used Perl, C, the Bourne Shell, the DOS batch language, or some other language, your Web programs had to work within the confines of the CGI standard.

That simple world exists no more. Today there are many more methods of Web programming available, and each has its own set of characteristics, strengths and weaknesses, zealots and detractors. Needless to say, the Web is a lot more fun, and confusing, than it was a short time ago.

The Web is where some of the newest technology is being developed, and as usual the "bleeding edge" attracts some of the brightest minds in the world to write new software that makes the previous versions look old and hackneyed.

Our Take: How We Use the Web

Jeff: I'm a UNIX programmer by choice, and proud of it. I write Perl programs that use mod_perl and the Apache Web server to bypass CGI and access a database from a Web front end. I couldn't do any of that under MS Windows. I run Windows at home for games, but I run Linux for any programming. The tools are better, and cheaper, and more fun to use.

I also use the Web whenever I want to find the answer to a question, read the daily news, find a good price on a new hard drive, or help my son do research reports for school. I live and work on the Web on a daily basis. It's a good thing, in my opinion. I blew it off at first, but it has won me over.

➡

Kevin: I find that my bookmark lists tend to grow to about a hundred pages as I mark things and then shrink to less than 30 as I cull the ones I really don't need. I'm a news junkie, and there's nothing better than up-to-the minute news and stocks, and I'm really enjoying the growth of the consumer products discount sites online. I practically live in the Microsoft Knowledge Base and knew Alta Vista when she was a baby. Looking for information? I can find it. Should have been a reference librarian.

The thing that I *don't* use the Web for but wish I could is detailed technical support. I'm really steamed by the corporate attitude that says "if we put a troubleshooting guide on the Web, we don't need to provide phone support." Believe me, before I'll call somebody, I've already exhausted all of the online resources and I'm in dire straits. I hate having to hunt for phone numbers. Try to find the tech support phone numbers on Microsoft's pages. They're there, but the only link to them is hidden in a paragraph somewhere.

The pace of development on the Web is phenomenal and cannot be completely attributed to the fact that programmers are bespectacled nerds who have no life and have nothing better to do than write super-software.

Mega-corporations such as Sun, Microsoft, and Oracle are copying the short design cycles made infamous by NCSA and Netscape, devoting millions of dollars to develop software they give away for free. The Web is like nothing ever seen before. New ideas, tools, and programming methods are popping up at a dizzying rate.

This section is intended to give you an introduction to some ways to communicate between an external program and a Web server or Web browser.

By exploring the use of these new programming methods, you can decide if your Web applications would perform better or gain added functionality by using a programming method other than CGI. On the other hand, your CGI programs might work just fine, and using another programming method would just complicate your code for no good reason.

Office 97 gives you the option of using no programming at all, incorporating VBScript or JavaScript into your Web pages, adding programs written to use CGI, or using "hooks" built into the Microsoft Web servers that give your Web site extra functionality.

The next few sections talk about three of the most popular methods of Web programming: CGI, Web server application programming interfaces (API), and Java. You can incorporate programs using programming tools outside of Office 97, or you can use the more limited native methods included in Office 97.

Using a Common Gateway Interface (CGI)

CGI is the old standby. CGI has some very real limitations that can increase the load on your system, and it is very limited in how it can transfer data from a Web server to an external program.

What Is. . .

VMS: An operating system run by old, antiquated mainframe computers that will stop being used any day now um, any day now. . .

Perl: A programming language that has taken the Web by storm because it incorporates many of the good features of some popular existing languages and throws out many of the bad, plus it adds some new ones of its own.

UNIX: A powerful, robust, unfriendly, hard-to-use operating system that gave birth to the Web.

Windows NT: a moderately powerful, limited, friendly, easy-to-use operating system that is trying to take over the Web.

Understanding CGI Processes

A Web server implements CGI differently depending on the operating system the server runs under. A method used under UNIX would probably not work under Windows or MacOS, and vice-versa. In spite of this, there are some things that must happen in order for CGI to work under a specific platform.

Our Take: Using Perl for CGI Programming

Kevin: If you absolutely must write CGI code that will run on UNIX machines, Macintoshes, and PCs, consider learning Perl. Variants of Perl are available for free for just about every UNIX variant, the Mac OS, and for Windows NT, and the differences between the versions are minor.

Jeff: While the programming differences might *seem* minor, some major changes had to be made under the hood of the Perl for Windows executable. The people who ported Perl to Windows are to be commended. The people who ported Perl to VMS should be considered very strange.

When a request comes in for a Web server to run a CGI program, the Web server creates a computer process to execute the CGI program. In the UNIX world, this is called forking a child process. The child process inherits a copy of the parent's current environment, which is the set of conditions the Web server is currently operating under.

If the Web server environment changes after the child inherits it, the environment of the child does not reflect the changes. Once the child is created, the parent cannot affect the child's environment.

The environment can contain several parameters. One is the unique ID of the parent-and-child process the operating system uses to identify the processes. Another is information about the parent process, such as the configuration parameters the Web server is operating under. This can include the root directory of the Web server, where the log files are located, and so on. Thus the child process can produce error messages that show up in the Web server logs or access files in the Web server file space.

What Is...

Parameters: Values given to a program to tell it what to do. Based on the values of the parameters, the program can do different things.

child process: A computer process spawned by another process in order to run a program while the original process accepts new requests for processing.

ID: Each process running on a computer must be uniquely identified so the operating system can allocate resources and keep track of what a process is allowed and not allowed to do. Each process is given a number, or ID, that identifies it to the operating system.

log files: As a program runs, it can generate a report of what it is doing. Errors are reported, program requests by users are reported, and so on, and all of these reports must go somewhere. A Web server writes all reports to a set of files, which make up a fairly complete log of what the server is doing.

root directory: A file system is constructed something like an upside-down tree, with the root being the topmost directory. By defining a root directory for your Web server, you prevent Web users from accessing anything outside of the specified directories.

Sockets: A socket is basically another term for port.

One of the most important things the Web server does before creating the CGI process is to set the values of several environment variables that are needed by the CGI process. If you have written many CGI programs at all, you know the important ones, such as REQUEST_METHOD, QUERY_STRING, CONTENT_LENGTH, and others. These environment variables are used to pass important information to the CGI process.

Different platforms manage this parent-child communication in different ways. Under UNIX, the two communicate directly via sockets using standard input and output, as shown in Figure 2-3.

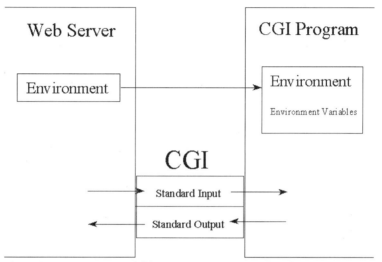

Figure 2-3: UNIX parent-child communication occurs directly between sockets.

When a Web server starts up a CGI program, the server gives the CGI program a set of variables to tell the CGI program what is going on. A communications pipe is set up between the Web server and the CGI program so the server can send information entered by the user to the CGI program, and so any results produced by the CGI program can be passed from the program to the server and eventually back to the user's Web browser.

Under Windows 3.1, sockets do not work in the same way, so the Web server might create a file that contains the environment variables, and the first thing the new CGI process does is read the file. Other platforms might have their own method of inter-process communications, but this should be largely transparent to the Web user. The Web server takes care of how all of this is done. The user just pushes a button and gets results. None of the behind-the-scenes activity is shown to the user.

Once the child process is created, the CGI program is loaded into memory and processes the information passed to it by the Web server; executes; produces output, which it passes back to the Web server; and terminates. The output is passed to the user's Web browser by the Web server, and the connection to the Web browser is closed.

This is all done as a single monolithic event. The CGI program cannot halt in the middle of execution to ask the user a question to determine what it does next. If the program needs user input to continue, it must output an HTML form and terminate. The user enters information and submits it to the Web server, which invokes yet another instance of the CGI program for it to process the new information.

CGI Advantages	CGI Limitations
Use any programming language to write CGI programs.	Can be resource hogs.
No proprietary programming interface.	Can be written in inefficient languages.
Most Web servers support CGI.	No communication between CGI processes.
	Each CGI request requires a new process.

One of the biggest pluses to using CGI is the freedom to use any programming language for your Web programs. Whether it's C, Perl, Tcl, Ada, or any other language, as long as the language can read data from standard input and write to standard output, it can be used to write CGI programs. There is no proprietary programming interface.

Another big plus is the universality of the CGI standard within any Web server. No matter what platform your programs run on, the Web server supports CGI. Unfortunately, the differences between operating systems force differences in the way CGI programs must be written, but between Web servers that run on the same platform, CGI works pretty much the same way. This makes your Web programs portable within the constraints of a particular operating system. This reduces programming time when upgrading or switching Web servers.

However, CGI programs are expensive in a programming sense. Programs that use CGI can use up a lot of operating system resources. Not even considering the resources required by the CGI program itself, the process created by the Web server to run the program is very inefficient.

Each time a CGI program is accessed, a separate process is needed. If you have a busy Web site, that can lead to a lot of redundant CGI processes running on your machine, which increases the system load and reduces the system resources available to the Web server or the operating system itself.

If each CGI program is written in Perl, some operating systems will load a copy of Perl into memory for each CGI process. This can bring a Web server to a grinding halt in a very short time if your computer doesn't have enough memory or a powerful enough CPU to handle the load.

Another limitation is that CGI processes cannot communicate with each other without some very convoluted programming, and it would be rather pointless for processes that exist for such a short time to try and interact with one another.

It would be nice if the Web server would facilitate communications between CGI processes so you could write one process to handle one function and another to do something else, and the two could be synchronized by the Web server, but this cannot be done with simple CGI.

It would be even nicer if the Web server could start up a CGI program and then keep it alive after using it, so the next CGI request would use the copy already created and save the expense of creating another CGI process. Neither of these methods are supported by the CGI standard.

These limitations are balanced by the universality of CGI availability. If you want to do something as easily as possible and you only want to learn a single method of Web programming, you need look no further than CGI. If you need more functionality, however, you should look at other methods.

Using the Server Application Programming Interface (API)

Some Web servers provide you with an application programming interface that allows your programs to interact directly with the Web server itself. When you write server API programs, you have access to the internal code of the Web server. How many times as you have written CGI programs did you want to be able to add just one more function to your Web server? With the server API, you can do that and more.

Many Web servers offer their own API. Netscape, Microsoft, O'Reilly, and Apache, among others, all give you a set of functions that let you interact directly with their Web server. Each API might work a little differently, but they all do much the same thing.

Understanding APIs

Where CGI programs are external programs that exist independently of the Web server, programs written using a server API are loaded into the same piece of memory, called the *memory address space*, of the Web server. This gives API programs access to any functions the Web server software makes available to programmers, as indicated in Figure 2-4.

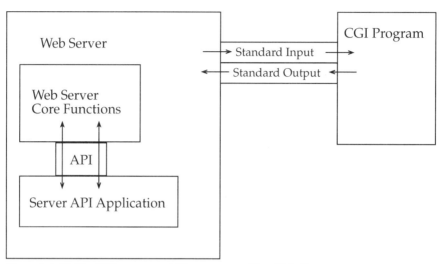

Figure 2-4: Unlike CGI programs, API programs reside within the server.

Commercial Web servers' APIs give you a selection of functions that can control how the Web server behaves or can make use of internal functions such as URL encoding and decoding, sending and receiving messages to and from Web clients, and allocating and deallocating memory resources. This can greatly increase the flexibility of your Web programs.

What Is...

compiled: A programming language is a convenience for humans. Computers only understand 1s and 0s. Once a program is written in a programming language, it must be converted into machine language for the computer to execute. Not only that, but different types of machines require different machine languages. A compiler is a program that takes programs written by programmers and turns them into machine language. The machine language program, often called *executable code*, is the version that is run by a computer.

scripting language: Scripting languages allow programs to be compiled "on the fly" instead of all at once. With a programming language such as C, you write the program and then compile it into an executable. If you need to make changes, you have to recompile the whole thing. This can be a time-consuming process. Scripted programs, such as Perl programs, can be easily changed because they are compiled each time they are run. Compiled programs are a bit faster because they are compiled once and can be run directly. Scripted programs are a bit slower because they must be compiled before they are run, but they are easier to modify quickly.

> **dynamic link library:** If a program needs a function that is present somewhere on a computer, there are two ways the function can be made available to the program. One is the compiler locates all necessary functions and puts them into the executable code when the program is compiled. The other way is the compiler locates the functions, but only puts the location into the compiled program, and the program only loads the functions it needs. Functions that are loaded on demand, or dynamically, are contained in computer code libraries. If a library is intended to be loaded dynamically, it is a dynamic link library (DLL).
>
> **run time:** The moment at which a program is run.

Your API programs must be compiled (unlike Perl or other scripting languages) and, if written for a Microsoft Web server, must be in the form of a dynamic link library (DLL). A DLL can contain code that is a program in its own right, but a DLL uses the code as an extension that can be loaded by the Web server program.

A DLL written to use a server API can be one of two types: pre-loaded or on-demand loaded. A pre-loaded DLL is loaded into memory by the Web server as the server program starts up. An on-demand DLL is loaded into memory the first time it is needed by the Web server and remains in memory for subsequent requests.

By executing inside the same memory address space as the Web server, a DLL function can interact with the server during execution. Where a CGI program is isolated from the server process and must execute completely before returning results to the server, a DLL function can continuously pass information back and forth with the server as it executes.

Deciding When to Use the API

There are many benefits to using a server API, some of which are detailed in the following sections.

API Benefits	API Limitations
Programs can be loaded at run time, making them seem faster.	Requires more complex programming.
Better program performance.	Hard to migrate CGI to API.
A single process can handle multiple program requests.	Requires compiler to create linkable code.
	You only get access to functions provided by the API.
	Badly behaved code can crash your server.
	Proprietary API interfaces.

One of the benefits of using an API is the ability to create functions that replace or enhance existing Web server functions. For instance, you can create your own error-handling routines. You can replace the cryptic error messages emitted by a server with custom functions that do different things, depending on what the error is.

As an example, whenever a request comes into your server for a filename that can't be found, instead of returning a File Not Found error immediately, you can write a routine that tries other filenames in case the user made a typo. If they enter 'BigFile.htm', you can search for BigFile.html, bigfile.htm, BIGFILE.htm, and any other combination of upper and lowercase letters, extensions, and directories.

This can ease the frustration of users, plus keep users from leaving your Web site in exasperation. After searching for any file that might closely fit what the user typed, if no file is found it would be nice to return the filename entered by the user and a polite message indicating they might need to check spelling, capitalization, or the extension for errors.

Another benefit is the ability of the Web server to load a DLL if a function contained by the DLL is needed. If none of the functions in a DLL are needed, the module is never loaded, preserving system resources.

Also, because the DLL code is executed directly by the Web server process, there is no overhead required to create a separate process for program execution. This can greatly increase the performance of your code.

Another advantage is the reuse of loaded DLL modules. As more requests are handled by the Web server that require your DLL code, the DLL is already in memory and immediately available to the server process. This eliminates the startup and shutdown overhead of creating new processes under CGI.

If multiple requests for a DLL function are received at the same time, the Web server can take two approaches to satisfying the requests. If your DLL code is single-threaded, which means it can only process one request at a time, the Web server can invoke another instance of the DLL and continue to do so until all requests are satisfied. The pool of DLL resources continue to exist to process requests if needed.

If your DLL code is multi-threaded, which means multiple processes can use the same instance of the code at the same time, the Web server simply calls the same DLL function as needed. Both of these methods use operating resources efficiently (though multi-threading does more so), which enables your Web server to handle more traffic.

FYI: Multi-threading

Some Web servers such as Microsoft's Internet Information Server (IIS) require you to write your DLL code as a multi-threaded application. This increases the efficiency of your code, but can greatly increase the complexity of it. Multi-threaded programming is not for the inexperienced or the faint of heart.

The multi-threading issue can also make it hard to migrate CGI programs to use a server API. Compiling a multi-threaded DLL involves issues that simply never arise when writing CGI programs, whatever language you use. The new complexity can force you to rewrite existing programs from scratch, instead of just adapting them to use a new interface.

What Is...

memory leak: When a program runs, it uses computer memory. The program asks the operating system for a piece of memory, and the operating system finds an unused portion and reserves it for the program. If the program keeps asking for memory without reusing what it already had or giving it back to the operating system, these memory leaks can cause a badly behaved program to use up all computer memory and crash the system.

DLL: Dynamic link library. A library of computer functions that can be loaded into a program as they are needed by the program.

deallocate memory: Give memory back to the operating system when a program is finished with it.

In addition, using a server API requires you to have a compiler that can create a multi-threaded DLL. You might have to move to a commercial compiler if you don't have one or you use a free compiler available on the Internet. Changing compilers can be bothersome if it involves moving to an unfamiliar or proprietary development environment.

While server APIs greatly increase your access to Web server functionality, you still only get access to functions that are provided by the API. If you want the server to do something not provided by the API, you can't do it.

FYI: Researching APIs

If you have a specific objective in mind that requires access to certain Web server functionality, it would certainly be a good idea to explore what functions are exposed by the various Web server APIs before choosing a server for your Web site. This assures you of getting the functionality you need before committing to a server. Not all Web servers give you access to the same internal Web functions.

One of the biggest drawbacks to using a Web server API is that badly behaved code can crash your Web server, and memory leaks can do the same. Because the DLL code inhabits the same memory as the Web server, if your code does something to corrupt memory or if it fails to free resources needed by the Web server, the entire Web server can collapse, either immediately, or after resources run out over time.

Some Web servers have methods available to minimize the effects of badly behaved code in an effort to prevent loaded modules from causing server crashes, but there is nothing that can be done about memory leaks that accumulate over time and eventually cause the server to crash due to lack of resources.

CAUTION

If you write DLL modules for use with a Web server, you must aggressively contain memory leaks. As a program is used repeatedly, any minor failure to deallocate memory grows into a major problem over time.

Another thing to consider is the proprietary nature of server APIs. There is no API standard, nor is there any standards body that is waiting to approve one. A proprietary interface locks you into using a particular Web server, unless you want to repeat the investment of time and resources required to learn to use a different one.

The Web has become a battleground for companies trying to gain market share in the Web server war. At this point there is no clear winner, and the competing API standards make choosing an API a gamble. If it is too much of a gamble for you to be comfortable, maybe another alternative to CGI is what you need. Read on for another option.

Using Java

Java is completely different from any of the other methods mentioned in this section, because Java programs run on the user's machine, not your Web server machine.

Using Java as your Web programming language can reduce the load on your server and reduce the possibility of insecure server-side programs that open your machine to hackers. Your programs can still take advantage of the platform independence of the Web by running on any operating system that can support Java.

Our Take: Do Applications Written in Java Have a Future?

Jeff: Certainly. Not a big future until Java gets better, but a future nonetheless. Java has a lot of excellent features. It is like C++ Lite, without all the underlying junk. Java has taken the good features of C and C++ and put them into an object-oriented language designed to be object oriented from the ground up, and not grafted onto an existing language like C++ was to C.

Now the growing pains start. It took C++ several years of development to devolve to where it is now. Compilers had to get better and faster, and the language had to grow. The same thing will happen to Java. Hopefully, it will get fast enough to be usable on the Web. Right now, it's hopelessly slow.

And, if you think about it, the Web is a silly place to use a language as full of promise as Java. Java should be used to create full-blown stand-alone applications that can run on any machine that has a virtual Java engine. Restricting Java to run inside a buggy Web browser hurts both Java and the Web browser.

Kevin: A short-term future, certainly. Java at this point is no better than any other high-level programming language in its infancy. Until it's stable and reliable, why write mission-critical code in it? Microsoft's End-User License Agreement for Windows NT sums it up: "Java technology is not fault tolerant and is not designed for use in hazardous environments requiring fail-safe performance, such as the operation of nuclear facilities, air traffic control, and direct life support machines." And these guys are selling the code!

As Java matures, it might become a reliable, useful language, like C++, or it might become an overhyped albatross, like Ada. Time will tell.

Understanding How Java Works

Java is a language in its own right, such as C or Perl. You can create stand-alone Java applications or Java applets that run in Java-enabled Web browsers. Either way will work on the Web, but the applet version is the one with the most obvious Web connection because it is executed directly by the browser.

What Is...

object-oriented (OO) language: This one is tough to describe to non-programmers and to some programmers. Basically, an OO language lets (forces?) you to write programs as if they are a cabinet. If you want users to reach into the cabinet and pull something out or move it around, you must program a cabinet door in just the right place. This keeps users from pulling the wrong thing out of your cabinet.

compiler: A programming language is a convenience for humans. Computers only understand 1s and 0s. Once a program is written in a programming language, it must be converted into machine language for the computer to execute. Not only that, but different types of machines require different machine languages. A compiler is a program that takes programs written by programmers and turns them into machine language. The machine language program, often called "executable code," is the version that is run by a computer.

high-level programming language: Some languages require the programmer to do more than others. A high-level language tries to make things easier for the programmer by making the commands easier to understand and use. They don't work very well yet.

SQL: Structured Query Language. SQL is the language used to interact with a database.

JDBC: Java Database Connector. A standardized method of communicating with a database using the Java programming language.

Where other Web programming methods are used in conjunction with a programming language or are constructed to allow you to use a programming language with them, Java is a programming language itself. The tool and the method for using it are one and the same.

Java programs are machine independent when run by a Web browser. Java applets are compiled into *bytecode*, which is then executed by the browser. The browser contains a *virtual engine* that is specific to the platform on which the browser runs. The browser provides a generic environment for the Java bytecode to execute. A simple overview of Java is shown in Figure 2-5.

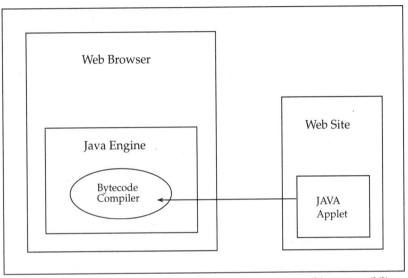

Figure 2-5: Java programs run by the user's browser overcome machine compatibility problems.

When a CGI program is invoked, the Web server machine is responsible for running the program, producing results, and sending them back to the Web server, which passes them on to the user's Web browser.

When a Java program is run, the user's Web browser executes the code, and the only resources expended by the Web server machine are those needed to transfer the Java code across the Internet to the Web browser. Once that is done, the Web server and host machine are out of the processing loop. The Java program handles any networking or external programming connections that are necessary.

Java has many built-in methods that allow your Web browser to interact with external programs such as a database. Your Web browser can act as a client-side database front end. Java code can construct SQL statements based on user input, connect to a local or remote database server, and retrieve the results, all without connecting to a Web server.

Access to a database via Java is so promising that a new specification for a Java Database Connector (JDBC) is under development and has been implemented by several companies for their Web/database products.

Deciding When to Use Java

JDBC is an API implemented in Java specifically for connecting to databases. Many major database vendors have endorsed the standard and are working on their own JDBC applications.

JDBC works much the same way as the Open Database Connector (ODBC). In fact, it is possible to use a JDBC-ODBC bridge so JDBC methods can be translated into ODBC function calls. This provides compatibility with many existing ODBC drivers.

JDBC does not implement the full ODBC API, however. Some things such as scrolling cursors (the ability to move forward and backward through a result set retrieved from a database) are not available in JDBC.

Web/database gateway products that use JDBC are already beginning to be introduced, even before the JDBC specifications are finalized. Because of this, the new products might implement proprietary JDBC interfaces that add functionality but are not interchangeable. You should be aware that products implementing the JDBC API might not adhere to the complete specifications.

The Importance of Standards

If I, as an American, want to communicate with a French person, one of us has to speak the other's language, or we must both know a third language. If I speak English only, and the other person speaks only French, we can both talk all we want and never understand each other.

In fact, the French government has a law that French citizens may speak only French to conduct business of any kind. This can cause a lot of inconvenience and frustration on both sides of an international business meeting, but it's good business for French interpreters. It's not always so good for French or American businesses.

The Internet is a shining example of a truly international medium that benefits those who use it. The Germans and the Japanese have their own newsgroups, just like any other country connected to the Internet. Worldwide newsgroups tend to be dominated by English, but posters who don't speak English very well might prompt a flurry of Spanish or French postings to explain a point. There are enough people on the Internet to translate for most any user.

The Internet works because the machines connected to the Internet adhere to common standards. There are various committees and groups who informally govern what gets changed and what doesn't, but no one government or corporation controls the Internet, despite some attempts to do so.

Change and improvement are inevitable, but the Internet will maintain its value only if those changes are agreed upon by a wide audience of users.

Our Take: Can Anyone Make Money on the Web?

Kevin: I'm sure somebody is, but there are a lot more people trying to make a living out there who aren't. Isn't it a little sad that the Web is becoming like newspapers and magazines, depending on advertising revenues to pay its content providers?

Bill Gates has suggested that the real money will be made when the day comes that "micropayments," payments of less than a dollar, are cost effective to charge and collect on the Web. I'd pay a few cents for access to a good, up-to-the-minute newspage, like the Wall Street Journal's site; what if my browser could authorize a merchant to charge me the cost of a newspaper when I first access their page in the morning? I think Gates is right. There's a mint to be made, a few cents at a time.

Jeff: Sure, those who make the Web software for other people to use when creating their Web sites are making a few bucks. Few companies actually using the Web to make money are getting rich.

The Web is all over the newspapers and the trade magazines, but in spite of the hype, the Web is not in enough homes in America to generate the revenue that TV and radio do. I choose what I look at, and I have millions of Web pages to choose from. I can ignore advertisements and pick the pages I want to read. The Web forces marketing people to admit they have no clue how to read a market.

In a couple of years, early adopters of the Web will find out how to use the Web to their best advantage. Their experience will shake out a lot of the bugs in Web information delivery, and the new version of the Web will attract more users. A couple of years, considering the speed of the Web? Yep, considering the Web has gone from full speed to a dead stop because the Web is overloaded in the past year, why not?

Moving On

The Internet and the Web are not the same thing, but one lives on top of the other. The two together are a tool, an opportunity, and something to do on a lazy Sunday afternoon besides sleep. Life on the Internet is never the same, is always interesting, and changes by the minute.

Now that you can live and work on the Internet and surf the Web like a native, it's time to understand Microsoft's place in the larger scheme of things and where Office 97 fits into that place. The next chapter, "Microsoft & the Web," will clue you in.

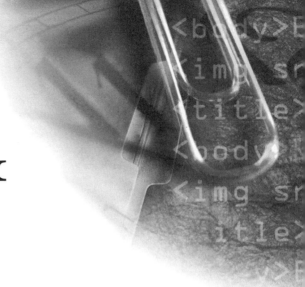

chapter 3

Microsoft & the Web

W hen you decide to use one company's products to produce and manage a Web site, there are many factors to consider before you actually begin using the products. The software applications themselves are only a portion of what must be considered when committing yourself to use them.

Your boss (the one who told you to create the company Web site in Chapter 1) has been surfing the Microsoft Web site (or having someone do it for him) and has read about this cool new product from Microsoft called Office 97. He wants you to investigate using Office 97 to create the Web site. In fact, he wants you to look into using an all-Microsoft solution. Where are you going to find objective information on Microsoft?

The purpose of this chapter is to acquaint you with some topics that deal with Microsoft, the Internet, and Microsoft competitors. Once you are fully informed about the issues that surround Microsoft, Office 97, the Internet, and the Web, you can make marketing and development decisions with more confidence.

You might have heard a lot of talk about how Microsoft is trying to take over the Internet. Most of this talk comes from Sun and Oracle, who also want to own the Internet. Is Microsoft so evil and everyone else so nice?

Our Take: What Place Does Microsoft Have on the Web?

Jeff: I don't like Microsoft's business practices, but they have as much right as anyone to take advantage of the Web. More power to them. Just stay away from my Linux box.

The Internet is big enough for any number of people and companies. If Microsoft learns how to play well with others, they will be welcomed. If not, they won't. But they will still play on the same playground, regardless.

Kevin: Like it or not, it's tough to compete with a company that has a year of revenues in the bank in cash and has a well-respected and competent product line. Let me go out on a limb here: If it weren't for Microsoft, computer geeks and college students today would inhabit the Web, and that's about it. Windows brought GUIs to the masses in the same way that Mosaic for the X Windows System made the Web worth surfing. I don't know what the next innovation will be, but I hope to be writing about it while it's still new and interesting.

Deciding on Open vs. Proprietary Software

The argument goes something like this: The Internet is based on open standards, which are decided upon by committees whose purpose is to open up communications standards for everyone to use equally well. The machines connected to the Internet use these open standards to communicate so all machines can understand what other machines are saying.

Microsoft, on the other hand, wants to Rule the World(TM) by forcing everyone to use the proprietary Microsoft versions of these open standards, which just coincidentally only run on Microsoft operating systems.

Is this true? Like most things, the answer is yes and no. Yes, the Internet is based on open standards and yes, Microsoft wants to Rule the World. No, Microsoft is not the only company that pursues this goal and no, they are not the only company that wants to force you to use their products.

So then, why the big stink over Microsoft's entry into the Internet and Web market? The Internet is a big place, and more competition just gives users more choices so things are better for everyone, right?

Not necessarily.

Using Products From Several Vendors

If a system is open, it does not necessarily mean you get a copy of the source code. Products such as the Linux operating system and the Perl language compiler pretty much define the highest level of openness, but other products can be open and still remain proprietary. Confused?

What Is...

operating system: Software that runs on a computer and translates commands entered by the user into instructions a computer can understand. Linux, Solaris, MS-DOS, and OS/2 are operating systems.

compiler: Takes a computer program written by a user and turns it into instructions understood by a computer. How is that different than an operating system? The operating system is a program, and a compiler turned it into computer instructions. The operating system automates the process of converting user instructions into machine instructions.

protocol: A method of communication agreed upon between the two parties that are communicating. If one party speaks one language and the other party speaks another language, the two cannot exchange information. A protocol is a formally described method of communication.

Network driver: A piece of computer hardware must have a piece of software that communicates between the hardware and the operating system. This is called a driver. A network driver is software that goes in between a network card and the operating system.

TCP/IP: Transmission Control Protocol/Internet Protocol, which explains why it is abbreviated to TCP/IP. TCP/IP is the communications protocol used by every machine on the Internet to send data back and forth.

Teletext: A simple, text-only form of communications used in the good old days, not unlike teletype.

The term "open" refers to how well a product conforms to a set standard in the way it behaves. There are many standards documents floating around the Internet that define how a program should accept input, produce output, and conduct itself while it runs. If a program wants to say it conforms to one of those standards, it must conform to ALL of the tenets of the standard, not just a selected few.

An excellent example is the TCP/IP protocol. If a machine uses a version of TCP/IP that is different from the standard, its messages cannot be understood by other machines, and will be effectively ignored. Because TCP/IP is an established standard, no one can force all TCP/IP users to change their version of the protocol, try as they might.

However, just because a TCP/IP network driver must be able to communicate with other machines in a defined manner does not mean the network driver must be written the same way as all others. In fact, companies who manufacture networking hardware generally write their own network drivers for their hardware, because software written for another piece of hardware either won't work with theirs or won't perform well enough. The TCP/IP standard itself is "open," but the network hardware can remain proprietary and still use the open protocol.

The networking hardware becomes "open" if the hardware vendor publishes the specifications for the hardware so other people can write their own versions of TCP/IP drivers and users can choose which driver to use. Drivers written by a company that specializes in network drivers will probably outperform drivers written by someone who has less understanding of networking.

Open systems allow the user to pick and choose the pieces that comprise their entire system. This allows users to custom tailor their system to meet their own needs. This is diametrically opposed to proprietary systems.

Using Products From a Single Vendor

If the networking hardware company does not release specifications for their hardware, that forces users to use only software written by the hardware company. That's proprietary. If the networking company has some really great features in their products that people really want, standardizing on a single network card is not such a bad thing. Or is it?

Let's say the networking company creates a new network router that transfers data twice as fast as any other on the market. That's neat, and a lot of people want it. What's the catch? It only works when used with their network cards. If you don't use their network card, you can't use the new hardware. If you decide to use the new hardware, you must replace your existing network cards with theirs. If the company's future products all require the use of some other piece of their hardware, this is known as a "closed" system.

What is...

router: Accepts data traveling across a network, consults an internal map of the network, and sends the data where it is supposed to go.

open system: A system produced by one company that allows others to write their own programs to interact with the system.

closed system: A system produced by one company that forces others to buy products from the company in order to use their system.

What's so bad about it? Well, what if you don't want to pay for replacing your current network cards to get the neat features of the other piece of hardware? What if, once you buy all the hardware you thought you needed, you discover the new proprietary software conflicts with other software you use. Your solution is to replace your current software or do without the really neat features in the hardware you bought, or buy still more hardware that uses different software.

If you are the type of person or company that picks a single vendor for all of your products, a closed system will not concern you. If you pick and choose each piece to get the best value for your money, or to get just the features you need, you require an open system. Now that we've defined the terms, let's see how all of this applies to Microsoft. (And many other companies, don't forget.)

The Microsoft Approach: Proprietary All the Way

Microsoft got its start writing Basic language compilers for various hardware platforms. Bill Gates and friends pulled many an over-nighter to get code working and shipped out on time. Then one day, IBM was looking for an operating system for their new computer, called a Personal Computer, and Microsoft just happened to acquire the rights to an operating system called DOS, which stands for Disk Operating System. They promptly renamed it MS-DOS, for obvious reasons.

Developing Brand Name Recognition

MS-DOS showed up on thousands of new IBM clones and made the fledgling Microsoft quite a bit of money. Naturally, other companies wanted a piece of this good thing, but Microsoft and IBM stuck together and MS-DOS became the standard operating system for the PC architecture.

What Is...

MS-DOS: The most common PC operating system.

PC: Personal Computer. Popularized by IBM.

IBM DOS: IBM's own version of a PC operating system.

DR DOS: Digital Research's version of the PC operating system.

graphical interface: Uses graphics (buttons, menus, scrollbars) to make interacting with a computer easier.

command line prompt: The only way to interact with a computer before the graphical interface arrived.

operating system: What a computer runs that lets it do things.

Windows: Microsoft's graphical interface to MS-DOS.

There were other PC operating systems that emulated or even surpassed MS-DOS, such as PC-DOS, DR DOS, or even IBM DOS, but MS-DOS had entrenched itself in the mind of PC users as the "real" DOS. This "brand-name" recognition was merely the first in a landslide of campaigns by advertisers trying to capture mind share for a product. In spite of Microsoft's dominance of the DOS market, there was enough competition from other operating systems to give users a choice.

Each new version of MS-DOS generally included all of the good stuff the competing versions of DOS included in their last version, plus a few more features such as disk compression and memory managers copied from standalone products. In this way, users could keep using MS-DOS and feel they weren't being left behind by new products. The new features of MS-DOS were generally not the best on the market, but they were good enough for most computer users.

In addition to MS-DOS, Microsoft was working on another nifty little product called Windows that gave the user a graphical interface that used a mouse to point and click instead of a boring command-line prompt that required users to remember operating system commands.

Packaging MS-DOS With Windows

Windows had a lot of really neat features that a lot of people wanted. What was the catch? Microsoft wanted you to run Windows on top of MS-DOS. At first, Windows wouldn't run on other versions of DOS. The other vendors quickly fixed the problems, but Microsoft kept producing new versions of Windows and advertising MS Windows and MS-DOS as a package deal, so users started to think they had to use the two together.

Then Microsoft executed the maneuver that started them on the road to becoming the software giant they are today. They convinced major computer sellers to bundle MS Windows and MS-DOS with every computer they sold. Microsoft charged the computer dealers a much lower price per copy than the software sold for in stores. Computer dealers liked the idea because it added perceived value to their wares, and consumers liked it because they got the software cheap.

Before other DOS competitors could react, Microsoft had most major manufacturers locked into exclusive contracts. Microsoft was on its way to becoming a major software company.

However, an operating system and a pretty interface were not enough to keep users from discarding Windows, replacing MS-DOS with something else, and running the DOS programs they were comfortable with. Users needed a reason to use this neat new interface.

Throwing in MS Word as Well

Microsoft wrote a lot of Windows-based software, but their first big hit was MS Word 2.0 for Windows. It had lots of really neat features that a lot of people wanted. What was the catch? Word required MS Windows in order to run. Regardless of the version of DOS you had, Word would not work if you weren't running Windows.

What Is...

MS Word: Microsoft's word processing software.

applications: Computer programs.

Microsoft Office: Microsoft's suite of programs including a word processor, a spreadsheet, presentation software, a database (in the professional version), and whatever other application they choose for the current version of Office. In three versions of Office, the fifth application has changed three times. In Office 97, it's Outlook.

computer platform: The combination of computer hardware and operating system.

suite: Multiple applications packaged together and hyped as everything you ever needed.

Other vendors saw how much better the Word 2.0 looked and acted under Windows, and Windows took care of a lot of the icky details for them, such as video and printer drivers. At that time, any program running under DOS had to provide its own video and printer drivers, and they were a never-ending source of headaches for the user. Windows was inviting because it promised to end all that.

Microsoft continued to produce software for Windows, creating versions of popular software designed to replace competitor's versions that only ran under DOS and were ugly compared to the Windows versions.

As the next logical step, Microsoft went back to the computer dealers who were shipping Windows with every machine and offered them the same sweet deal on the Windows applications that they had offered on Windows itself. Not only that, but they put several programs together into a suite called *Microsoft Office* to make the deal even sweeter. Dealers snapped up copies of Microsoft Office and shipped them out the door. Before long, software vendors moved their products to Windows or created new products that never existed under DOS. The applications produced for the Windows operating system finally convinced users to keep Windows on their computers.

Microsoft's Accomplishments

Microsoft practically gave their software away in order to capture the market and the minds of computer users. Is this anti-competitive business practice, or shrewd business? Software prices have dropped dramatically to keep up with Microsoft pricing. How can this be bad?

Our Take: Microsoft Envy

Jeff: In my humble opinion, a lot of the invective directed at Microsoft is based on simple jealousy. Microsoft is successful, other companies want to be just as successful, and Microsoft is the natural enemy. Add to that Microsoft's brute-force approach to throwing yet another software application at a problem, and the two sides fan the flames. Microsoft didn't get where it is today by being stupid, mean, or illegal. Many people would have you believe otherwise, but Microsoft has been investigated by the Justice Department a few times and come up clean.

Kevin: So far.

Let's take a step back and look at what Microsoft accomplished. Microsoft did two things for PCs that no one had done for any computer platform ever before.

Leveling the Playing Field

First, no matter who made the hardware, the software had to be compatible with DOS and Windows. Even those who are fanatical UNIX users frequently bemoan the incompatibilities that exist between various versions of UNIX. Anyone who makes UNIX hardware makes their own version of UNIX. A program created to run on one version often requires a lot of work to run under another version. Not so on the Windows-based PC platform.

What Is...

UNIX: a powerful, robust, unfriendly, hard-to-use operating system that gave birth to the Web.

architecture: The physical construction of the guts inside your computer.

standard operating system: A common operating system that doesn't change from computer to computer, even if the computers are manufactured by different companies.

PC clone: When IBM introduced the PC, other companies created their own copies of the PC called "clones." Eventually the clones became more popular than IBM's version because they were cheaper.

Why is a single standard platform a good thing? Because vendors who write software only have to write for a single operating system. Companies who write UNIX software are fairly rare. Why? Because they have to write five different versions of their software for five different versions of UNIX. Companies who write software for Windows write one version, support one version, and have only one set of programmers to pay. It's much more efficient to write software for the Windows platform than to write for the fragmented UNIX market.

Microsoft created and marketed MS-DOS and MS Windows into a level playing field for the IBM PC architecture. Software companies looking to be as profitable as possible no longer had to guess which operating system would sell the most software for them. However, while a standard operating system is a good thing, it isn't enough.

Creating a New Market for Software

The second good thing Microsoft did was to attach their product to the IBM PC architecture. Many people believe that Apple's products were superior to the PC at the time, but when PC clone makers began to make cheaper machines, the PC market exploded and took Microsoft DOS and Windows with it. After all, what better way to prove the new clones were compatible with IBM computers than to have the same operating system as IBM? MS-DOS became the basic operating system on every machine. Windows was the pretty interface that made it easy to use.

Putting Microsoft Windows into millions of homes and offices offered those writing Windows software a vast new market that had never existed before. Many companies hitched their wagons to Microsoft's star and rode into profitability. Or, at least some of them did.

Companies that produced software that competed directly with Microsoft applications could not match Microsoft's deep pockets and marketing strategy, and some companies began to fade, leaving MS to control the market. However, Microsoft's success depends largely on the fact you must run Windows in order to run Windows applications.

There are many DOS emulators that allow you to run Windows under various flavors of UNIX, but while they replace DOS, they cannot replace Windows. Windows applications are closely tied to the internal workings of the Windows environment and cannot exist on their own. Microsoft had established their proprietary, closed operating system as the standard for PCs.

Microsoft Caught Napping by the Web

The Web caught Microsoft completely by surprise. It caught a lot of other people and companies by surprise as well, but none as big as Microsoft. On its surface, the Web just looks like a bunch of diverse Web pages that you look at using a browser.

Look at the Web from Microsoft's point of view, however. The Web is comprised of any type of computer you can imagine, and there are more of them than there are of PCs. The user side of the Web doesn't require any specific software other than a Web browser, which will run on any computer platform.

The Web Threatens Proprietary Software

Hold on! *A Web browser is a graphical interface to a world-wide operating system that runs on any computer.* If the Web turns out to be The Next Big Thing, no one will need Microsoft products any more! Programs written using free tools such as C, Perl, Java, and the Apache Web server will own the Web and users will discard Windows and pick their own operating system.

What Is. ..

graphical interface: Often called a "GUI," which is pronounced "gooey" and stands for Graphical User Interface, a GUI is just a way of using graphics to make a computer easier to use. If you use Microsoft Windows, you use a GUI. The combination of a mouse used with windows and icons to select commands and activate programs gives the user a computer interface that doesn't require them to know much about the underlying operating system, unless they want to.

OLE: Object Linking & Embedding. Another attempt by Microsoft to reinvent the wheel; OLE is a standard way of making programs that run under Windows share data. For example, OLE allows an Excel spreadsheet to be embedded in a Word document. If a user double-clicks on the spreadsheet, the Excel application is started to edit it. This is different from having Word edit the spreadsheet directly.

Java: An overhyped programming language that might actually turn out to be useful in a year or two. Java is different from most programming languages in that it's intended that code written in Java can be reused on any machine.

VBScript: Microsoft's version of a Web browser scripting language, offered as an alternative to Netscape's popular JavaScript scripting language.

ActiveX: A renamed version of OLE tailored to the Web and the new version of Office.

Windows NT: Microsoft's workstation-class version of Windows, intended for use in business environments where the demands the user places on the operating system are more extensive than those imposed by a typical home user.

To Microsoft, the Netscape Web browser looked like a slavering wolf poised to break their near-monopoly of the PC operating system and eat their software empire. In short, they got scared. In true Microsoft fashion, Microsoft reinvented itself as an Internet company.

To prove it, Microsoft produced their own Web browser in no time flat. Hi, I'm Internet Explorer—use me, I'm free. Now use my proprietary extensions and you must use Windows as well. Hey, use ActiveX and the Microsoft version of Java and you have a really cool Web development environment! Only Internet Explorer can read them, and that excludes anyone on a UNIX or Macintosh platform, but that's insignificant.

The Ill-Fated Microsoft Network

Scarcely five years ago, Microsoft was preparing to launch The Microsoft Network (MSN); MSN promised to be a CompuServe with the added benefit of a slick, MS-engineered interface. The Internet was an enormous network connecting primarily academic and U.S. Government sites, and its use was incidental to the way people worked. You could easily complete a day's tasks without once noticing that the network was down. Sophisticated users used Gopher and Veronica to search for what little information was made available by kind souls who saw the potential of the medium. And a simple Teletext terminal was sufficient to take advantage of most of the power the Net afforded. But in the unheralded city of Urbana-Champaign, Illinois, a group of students was working on developing a graphical front end to the chaos that was the Internet. We all know the story of Mr. Andreesen and the other wunderkinds who brought color and style to the information-sharing subset of Internet called the World Wide Web (WWW). But Mr. Gates and company maintained that Microsoft's future was in office-enabling applications, not the worldwide dissemination of your secretary's spreadsheets.

But you can't fault Gates's error. Nobody could have foreseen the explosive growth of the Web and the impact that information sharing via the Web would have on the American society of the late 1990s. *Time* named The Computer the "Man of the Year" in 1982, but Otto Friedrich's cover story in that issue makes no specific mention of the Internet (although the value of global networks is discussed, presciently recognizing their value and potential problems). Even in mid-1995, it wasn't clear exactly how Microsoft was going to approach the "Web phenomenon," even after it had missed several years of burgeoning opportunities. Creating an "Internet" division at Microsoft would be akin to creating an "Electricity" division at a manufacturing company, Gates said; the network is the medium, not the product. He was right, of course, but the importance of Internet-enabling applications is akin to electricity-enabling a factory, and Microsoft was still creating very nice oxcarts while the world was getting wired for power.

Microsoft Stuck in the Proprietary Rut

Microsoft has the resources to be a major player in any software market, and that includes the Web. Unfortunately, Microsoft has approached the Web as it has any other market. The Internet has existed for decades without Microsoft and hopes to continue that way. Microsoft is just protecting its own interests. Something has to give.

Microsoft has made itself no friends by trying to co-opt Java, by creating its own version of JavaScript called VBScript, and by renaming OLE as ActiveX and trying to make it an Internet programming language that only works with its own browser.

On the other hand, people applauded Netscape for doing much the same thing. There is no accounting for the media perception of some people and events. Everyone roots for the underdog and likes to see Goliath vanquished. Microsoft is not a team player, but they are only doing what Netscape had been doing for the preceding months.

The Web is not a quiet place, but things will settle down. Microsoft will own the Web, or they will not, but you and I will find a way to use the Web any way we please with no one telling us how to do it. The Internet, and now the Web, are two steps away from becoming living, breathing entities. Not even Microsoft can stop that.

In fact, Microsoft might turn out to be the hero of the Web event. Windows NT has made massive inroads over low-end UNIX systems to position itself as a viable corporate operating system. UNIX vendors have finally awakened from their smug slumber and are slashing hardware prices to stave off the Microsoft invasion. How bad can that be? Stay tuned to find out.

Coming Up to Speed With Office 97

Microsoft has committed itself to making money off of the Internet and adding functionality to all of their products that allow users to take advantage of the new medium. Each product will be explored in depth later in the book, but for now, let's take a look at the underlying philosophy that drove Microsoft to *Internet-enable* Office 97.

What Is...

Internet-enabled: Software that can use the Internet to do things, like send and receive mail and share data.

user interface: A way to convert the requirements of a person using software to commands a computer can understand. The DOS command line is a user interface. The channel changer on your TV is, too.

toolkit: A set of software tools that makes programming a computer easier.

suite: Multiple applications packaged together and hyped as everything you ever needed.

LAN: Local area network. A computer network that is (usually) comprised of machines located in close physical proximity.

Internet Assistant: Microsoft's add-on to an application that makes the application Internet-enabled.

NetBEUI: Microsoft's networking protocol for sharing Windows computer resources.

WfW: Windows for Workgroups. Windows 3.1, updated to version 3.11, and with networking features added. Windows 3.11 is not the same as Windows for Workgroups, which is sometimes erroneously called Windows 3.11.

Schedule+: The predecessor to Outlook.

network: A collection of computers connected together so they can communicate.

While Microsoft might try to have you believe that the newest release of its flagship application line is the greatest thing since sliced bread, well, it's not. There is certainly no great advance in the underlying theme of each component application; Word is still a good WYSIWYG word processor, Excel still uses columns and rows. What you already know about using PowerPoint and Access, for the most part, still works. And for most people, the modest improvements in the user interface and programming tools will not make worthwhile the expense of a new toolkit and, quite possibly, a bigger disk drive to hold it.

But Office 97's real strength is exactly where Mr. Gates and company intended it to be—in its smooth incorporation of features to support the development of content for the Internet. Microsoft's recent corporate about-face has been marked by almost frenetic attempts to "get with the Web," and Microsoft excels in corporate reinvention like no other large modern corporation.

The Hard Copy Days (Office 4.0)

When Office 4.0 was released in 1994, the most probable final destination of most Office "documents" was paper. In those ancient times, the amalgamated "suite" was a new idea, and most people still purchased their software application by application. Office 5.0 (1995) was still Internet-unaware, although small bows to the emerging corporate LAN began to appear: for example, the concept of revision marks in Word allowed co-workers to make independent revisions to a basic document without destroying its original structure. This would have been wholly unnecessary if people had not begun to share work via interoffice networks.

Office 95 (1996) assumed the existence of some kind of network, but not necessarily the Internet. The essentially ignored Schedule+ application first shipped as an unannounced component of Windows for Workgroups (WfW) in 1994. It disappeared with the release of Windows 95, but showed up again in Office 95 as a means to assist in the coordination of an entire office's schedules. Using Microsoft's proprietary NetBEUI network protocol (first appearing in WfW), Schedule+ could query every machine on the local network and compile a conglomerate office schedule—perfect for those impossible-to-plan office meetings. But the component applications of Office 95 still did not recognize the Internet (or the Web) as a native environment. Microsoft's slick-but-kludgy Internet Assistants, released as afterthoughts, attempted to take these applications' products and convert them from "intended-for-paper" to "intended-for-the-Web" and, like many last-minute hybrids, they didn't work very well. They certainly weren't good enough for professional content development, and a host of tools were born to fill the niche market for Web authoring aids. Microsoft was still hedging its bets on the direction that the new push towards a true global Internet would take.

The Office Network Days (Office 95)

After Office 95 gained a sizable market share and Microsoft had finally come to recognize the impact that this technology would have on its business, Microsoft began releasing the Internet Assistants. These freely available add-on software components enabled existing Office applications to write (and sometimes read) the language of the Internet, HyperText Markup Language (HTML).

Once you had installed Office and had gotten accustomed to it, you could connect to the Internet (natch) and download these modules from Microsoft's Web site (now running and garnering millions of visits a day). Typically, the Assistant you chose would add an entry to your Save menu: Save as HTML. Generally, these produced acceptable-looking, simple HTML documents that could then be placed on a Web server (like the then-new Internet Information Server, available for Windows NT Server version 3.51).

Unfortunately, *simple* was the key for documents created this way. The HTML created by the Internet Assistants was static; that is, they did not permit full-featured hypertext authoring tools, including those necessary for precise text placement, most form design, and programming. Many popular features of the HTML language were not supported in the early Internet Assistants, and even the later ones created imperfect and difficult-to-maintain HTML code. For example, a typical error that the early Assistants made was to try to replicate the font size of the starting document in HTML. This imposition of the HTML font tag was typically repeated for every work or sentence in the generated document, even if it was only required once at the beginning. The end result looked the same to the viewer, but a human editing the code was confronted with a screen full of <FONT> commands (tags). If Microsoft was going to play in the Web game, it was going to have to build its core applications with network enabling as a design goal, not an afterthought.

The Information Beehive Days (Office 97)

Enter Office 97. Microsoft apparently still intends that users should work on their desktops and use the network as a tool, rather than an environment. There is no talk here of a central server that runs the code (can you say "mainframe?"), or of automatic software updates, much less of Java and network computing. Office 97 is like an information beehive. The queen bee, whose name is Microsoft Outlook, sits in the hive and waits for the drones (Word, Excel, PowerPoint, Access) to go out and bring back information. Whether that information is on the local machine (in the form of a local document), on the local network (in a shared folder), or on the Internet (as a Web page) makes little difference. Queen Outlook keeps track of everything the workers bring back and how it relates to every other piece of information in the hive. In Office 97, it is not even difficult to imagine a document in any of the Office applications that references a document somewhere else on any attached network, and the origin of information is almost irrelevant.

Nowhere is this more evident than in the Outlook Journal, which shows all of the interactivity among the various Office applications. Taking a glance at the records that it automatically keeps (Figure 3-1) leaves no doubt that Queen Outlook is keeping pretty careful tabs on what's happening in the hive.

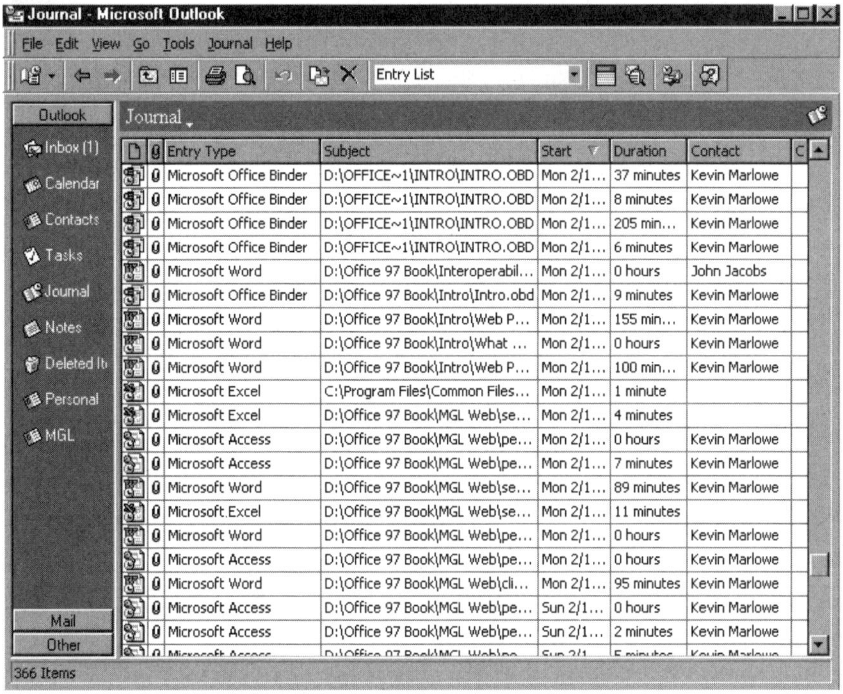

Figure 3-1: The Outlook Journal tracks Office application activity.

As competently as Office 97 keeps track of the information it collects, it's not as good as getting information out. If your office consists of a homogeneous group of PCs, all running a version of Windows developed since 1994 (practically the Dark Ages, in Web time), and you are happy running Microsoft applications, you can safely assume that information sharing is not going to be a problem in your office.

What Is...

NFS: Network File System. A method used by UNIX computers to share file systems across a network. This is not sharing files, mind you, but actually sharing the hard drives themselves.

UNIX: A powerful, robust, unfriendly, hard-to-use operating system that's commonly used in high-end computing applications, especially in science and academia.

PostScript: A language for constructing documents that will be sent to a printer. The printer must understand PostScript for this to work.

However, once the whole-office-on-Office 97 paradigm is broken, things get harder. Got some perfectly useful PCs, maybe running Office 95? Sorry; Word 97 doesn't save natively in Word 7.0 format (it can be selected for each individual document, one at a time, or you can download a patch to Word 7.0 that will let it read Word 97 files). Macs? Real trouble—everybody's going to have to agree on a common file format, and then a file server will have to be set up, using third-party software and hardware (an NFS-mounted UNIX machine is a good choice). Heavy-duty users running any flavor of UNIX are out of luck entirely; Office documents will need to be saved as text (or printed to a file in Postscript) to be useful to them.

Our Take: The Importance of Standards

Jeff: Can't we all just get along? Sorry, but I get really tired of the problems involved with sending files back and forth between operating systems. Even during the writing of this book, trying to find a common file format between the editor's Mac and our Windows machines cost us a couple of days. I never even tried reading the files under UNIX. It was not an efficient use of my time to figure it out twice. This is not just a Microsoft problem, but a problem endemic to the amorphous nature of the Internet.

Kevin: Even standards aren't always standards. Take, for example, the new RTF format in Word 97. You used to be able to depend on RTF as a common denominator, but not anymore. There's a fortune to be made on a Web server that translates incoming and outgoing documents into a format the people on the other end can be guaranteed of understanding.

Other Web Players Nip at Microsoft's Heels

But wait, you say—what about the Web? Well, that's still not Microsoft's home turf. Mr. Gates has run power lines to his log cabin, but he's still not convinced of the value of light bulbs.

Netscape's Open Software

Netscape's single-handed effort to create a fully functional Web browser for nearly every operating system in common use represents more than a phenomenal effort on the part of Netscape's staff. More importantly, it heralds the birth of an information-gathering application that works everywhere, using the same data. As a boon to the heterogeneous operating environment, this development is unparalleled. The development of a universal translator for the Babel of competing operating systems might be noted as a landmark achievement in the recent history of computing, but for one thing: It threatens those who have vested interests in maintaining the language barrier.

Since Netscape's corporate emphasis has been on information gathering (browsers and servers), one can only assume that Netscape's "enhancements" to the HTML standards have been in the interests of making the Web a more useful place. With the exception of the universally hated <blink> tag (the code that makes text blink endlessly in your browser screen), one would have a tough time arguing that Netscape's modifications to the standard are anything but beneficial. Almost everybody's browser supports Netscape's tags.

Microsoft, on the other hand, has taken a slightly different tack. "Our browser is better," they claim, "because it supports features that you can incorporate using our proprietary tools, and those features are better than Netscape's because almost anybody can write them." This is a thinly veiled effort to maintain the language barrier. Programmers incorporating Microsoft's "ActiveX" modules doom their code to partial functionality on any browser but Microsoft's. Even Microsoft's implementation of its own tools is weak; look in Word 97. And that's how the Web fits into Microsoft's strategy: Use Microsoft's authoring tools (Visual Basic, Visual J++, etc.) and productivity tools (Office 97) and operating systems (Windows) and everything will be just fine. Such a monopoly can be a good thing in certain environments—corporate intranets, for example. But it's not a useful starting place for such a pervasive and potentially border-shattering tool as the World Wide Web.

However, Office 97 is not the only game in town. There are other, often forgotten software companies that make similar products. How good are they, when compared to Office 97? How much of the market can they expect to conquer and hold? Let's take a look.

What Is...

Visual J++: Microsoft's Java programming environment. Careful, there's proprietary code in that there Java.

ActiveX: OLE in disguise.

Visual Basic: Microsoft's programming environment for their Basic programming language.

intranets: Also known as a LAN, these are computer networks not connected to the Internet.

Our Take: HTML Extensions

Jeff: I'm ambivalent about HTML extensions. The Internet Committee charged with standardizing HTML can't keep up with the demand for new HTML features. Microsoft and Netscape are just giving customers what they want. However, the Web was *founded* on the concept of a universal interface to read Web documents. HTML extensions hurt the very thing they are attempting to improve.

Kevin: Not to be a curmudgeon here (because Jeff is absolutely right), but some of the best features in HTML today were originally extensions, like tables and background images. The standards bodies move pretty slowly (relative to most Web development), and it's useful to see which features are being used in practice before they become standards.

Lotus Notes the Web

The danger one courts when trying to be all things to all people is that you might end up as nothing to all people. Even if your product is technically superior to everything else on the market, the sheer luck of being in the right place at the right time may or may not come to you, and you'd better have a fallback plan.

What Is...

VisiCalc: An old spreadsheet program.

Lotus 1-2-3: VisiCalc's successor.

CP/M: An operating system that is the predecessor to DOS.

spreadsheet: A way of organizing information into columns and rows for easier analysis.

suite: Multiple applications packaged together and hyped as everything you ever needed.

Notes: Lotus Notes. A popular computer program for sharing information among a group of people.

hub: A hub distributes network traffic from one source to several destinations. The destinations can be individual machines or entire networks. Hubs often include the ability to act as routers.

Internet hooks: Functionality added to Microsoft Exchange so Exchange can use the Internet and, therefore, so can its users.

OS/2: An advanced operating system produced by IBM (with some help by Microsoft, long ago) that has rabid fans but doesn't get the publicity that Windows does.

Take spreadsheets, for example. Who would have guessed that the brainchild of a tiny company called Lotus Development could displace the product that practically defined the spreadsheet, VisiCalc? Lotus's 1-2-3 looked almost identical to VisiCalc, but it ran on a new, niche operating system—something called MS-DOS. VisiCalc's user base was entrenched in CP/M, and you'd have to look hard to find someone working today who remembers CP/M. For Lotus, all of the planets aligned and they were ready.

Now, fifteen years later, Lotus has become a division of the mighty IBM, and has begged, borrowed, and stolen to create an office suite of its own to compete with Office (made by a formerly tiny company whose flagship products, Word and Excel, ran on a new, niche operating system). Lotus's suite is now Internet-enabled in much the same way that Office is, but its market share is tiny. The relative merits of Lotus SmartSuite notwithstanding, the real player in the office automation ring is Notes.

With Notes, a workgroup uses client applications on their local machines to produce content, and then it's posted to a Notes server. The Notes server stores the documents uploaded and makes them available to Notes clients, wherever they are. When used in conjunction with a Lotus Domino server, a Notes installation is more or less Web-enabled, permitting the information residing on the server to be accessed via the Net. Sound familiar?

By including Outlook's Internet capabilities in Office 97 and adding Internet capabilities to the Exchange Server program, Microsoft is saying to Lotus, "Hey, guys, we can play in that game, too." The biggest difference is that Microsoft's products only run under Windows. Domino also runs on several variants of UNIX and OS/2, as well as NT. And Lotus provides an easy upgrade path for offices already using its clients.

Our Take: Is It possible to Create a Web Site Using Only One Suite?

Kevin: I don't think so; not yet. If I had my choice of any tools to build a site, depending on the mission of the site and the environment it was to run on, I might choose the following:

- a management utility like Microsoft FrontPage or Netscape LiveWire Pro;

- an authoring tool like Netscape's Communicator HTML editor in conjunction with a good text-editing tool like Programmer's File Editor (or vi, if on UNIX)

- graphics editors like Corel Draw and Paint, or Paint Shop Pro if I wasn't doing any original art;

- maybe a GIF animator and a whole bunch of clip art to pull ideas from.

It won't be long before someone puts together a package that can handle the whole site (I have high hopes for Corel's new Web editing suite, and I'd like to get my hands on a copy), but by then, I expect that good sites will require features that won't be in the package.

Jeff: Sure it is. My suite of products looks like this: the vi editor to write HTML, xview for image manipulation, and Perl for Web programs. I toss in a few other software goodies like the Apache Web server, mod_perl, DBI/DBD, and Mini SQL, and I have a Web development suite that will outperform any other on any platform.

What Is...

LiveWire Pro: Netscape's product for writing Web applications that communicate with a database.

FrontPage: Microsoft's Web site creation and management software.

Paint Shop Pro: A shareware graphics program.

GIF: Graphics Interchange Format. A popular image format.

Apache Web server: A free Web server produced by the Apache group, hard-working, dedicated guys who want users to have a free, high-quality Web server. I get all misty eyed just thinking about it.

SQL: Structured Query Language. The programming language used to communicate with a database.

DBI/DBD: A Perl programming interface for writing programs that communicate with a database.

MiniSQL: A shareware database server.

Vi editor: A common editor found on every UNIX computer.

XView: A shareware graphics program for UNIX.

Perl: A programming language that has its own religion.

Netscape Communicator: Netscape's Web browser.

Corel Draw: A vector-based graphics creation and manipulation program.

Corel Paint: Like Corel Draw, but specifically for working with bitmaps.

vector drawing tool: A drawing program that works in lines and shapes (a la Picasso) rather than dots (a la Matisse).

Considering the installed base of Notes servers, Microsoft sees both a business and a technical opportunity here. If one assumes that almost 10 times more people use Microsoft's office tools suite than Lotus's, there seems to be a huge number of people who can benefit from a groupware solution—a market which Lotus has recently dominated. And if some of the Notes installations can be prodded to switch on the basis of Microsoft's better integration with the desktop, or licenses provided at no additional cost with new machines, then it's the more the merrier.

Corel Draws Notice

As if the playing field isn't crowded enough, from the Great White North comes Corel Corporation, whose vector drawing tool, CorelDraw!, was so good that they decided to take over the world. Purchasing the venerable WordPerfect word processor from Novell in a fire sale, Corel has thrown together a suite with essentially the same features as Lotus's and Microsoft's. Furthermore, they've got the fiercely loyal user base that WordPerfect brings with it, as well as the dedicated fans of their drawing products.

Corel's got one more advantage worth noting, and it's their pricing structure. For $900, an office can install one copy of Corel Office on a central server machine and *any number of directly connected PCs can use the tools at no additional cost*. Considering that Microsoft Office 97 Professional retails for about $250, it doesn't take a lot of users to make the Corel suite more cost effective. Add the fact that Corel's suite includes Corel's phenomenally capable drawing tools, and there is a lot of bang for the buck coming out of Ottawa.

And then there's Java. The young but well-supported programming language for the Web is gaining visibility outside of developer circles because of its inclusion in office tools suites. Lotus plans to include support for small, integrated applications written in Java ("applets") in the next release of its suite. By the end of 1997, Corel plans to release Corel Office for Java, a distributed software suite that keeps most of its code on a server machine and runs thin (meaning relatively small and fast) clients on local CPUs. This is *real* Internet enabling.

What Is...

Java: An overhyped programming language that might turn out to be useful in a year or two.

applets: Programs written in Java that are intended to be run in a Web browser.

CPU: Central Processing Unit. The main chip in a computer.

distributed software: Software that runs on more than one computer at a time.

server: A computer program that provides a service to users running a particular piece of software.

Office Suite Components

Application	Microsoft Office Professional 97	Corel Office Professional 97	Lotus SmartSuite 97
Presentation	PowerPoint	Presentations	Freelance
Database	Access	Paradox	Approach
Personal Information Manager (PIM)	Outlook	InfoCentral	Organizer
Drawing	WordArt	CorelDraw	
Web Browser	Internet Explorer	Netscape Navigator	
Other		Time Line (project management), CorelFlow (flowcharting)	ScreenCam (multimedia)

Note: Only significant applications are included in listings. All of these suites include various small "value-added" applications included at no additional charge.

Table 2-1 : Office suites, side by side.

Do We Have a Winnah?

There is evidence that Microsoft might be losing some of its historical dominance in the office tools market. If one considers products shipped with PCs ("original equipment manufacturer" copies, or "OEMs"), Microsoft's market share seems pretty steady. At about 75 percent of all installed office suites, things seem locked up.

However, Corel's pricing structure is sure to make a difference, especially among home users, and IBM is incorporating Lotus's suites in new IBM PCs—a move that is sure to help Lotus's share. At retail outlets, Lotus's sales are abysmal, but Corel seemed to be selling more of its suites than Microsoft until recently. Every new release of a line causes a spike in sales, and Microsoft is currently enjoying the Office 97 spike.

It's not clear where this is all going to end up. Anybody betting on Lotus in 1980 or on Microsoft in 1990 would be very wealthy today, and that's the nature of this market. One missed opportunity can spell the end of an empire.

The old adage used to go, "Nobody ever got fired by buying IBM" in the days when IBM was the recognized leader in technology and standards, but that banner seems to have passed to Microsoft.

Going With Microsoft

Office 97's HTML authoring features have come a long way since the Internet Assistants of Office 95. Save As HTML is immediately accessible from the main menubar of every Office application except Outlook. Typing something that looks like an Internet Uniform Resource Locator (URL) in any Office application creates an active link to the document it describes. But no Office application can yet produce HTML code that is as maintainable or effective as the code of any dedicated HTML authoring tool currently available. The drag-and-drop functionality of Windows that we have grown to appreciate doesn't extend to the Web, and in fact can produce misleading results. It's just not right—not yet.

Office 97 is an excellent suite of applications for doing everyday office management tasks—crunching accounting data, writing letters, scheduling appointments, making presentations. It's even a little more, since Access has become a formidable PC database with all of the features anyone would wish for in a $199 database engine. But, despite the marketing claims on the back of the CD box, it's not Internet friendly. It can, however, be used as a tool to put content on the Internet, especially with a little help from some inexpensive third-party tools and a knowledgeable author. This book seeks to help you, the reader, make effective use of the applications that Mr. Gates has given us to produce top-notch Web sites. It *can* be done.

Office 97 seems like a safe bet for today, and if your goal is to get your data on the Web from Office 97, a little effort will get you there. But Corel certainly bears watching, and Lotus has a 500-pound bear backing it in the corporate persona of IBM.

Moving On

Microsoft is not the "Evil Empire" that Luke Skywalker will destroy in his Tie-fighter (written in Java). Microsoft is just in business to make money. One of the products they have produced to ride the wave of Internet popularity is Office 97. It isn't perfect, but nothing is yet. Don't count Microsoft out. It usually takes them three tries to get it right.

Now that you understand the issues behind investing in Microsoft applications and you have decided to use Office 97, you need to set your Windows environment up correctly to use it. Chapter 4, "Web Publishing With Windows," will help you set up your computer to use Office 97, complete with a Web server and e-mail server.

chapter 4

Web Publishing With Windows

Nothing is ever as simple as it seems. When you were assigned this job, you knew that it was going to fall on your shoulders to write Web pages. But how are you going to get the pages you write onto the Web? Print them out and mail them to "Webmaster, Washington DC"? Start up a Web browser on your PC and hold a disk up to the screen? You need to make some arrangements with people who maintain full-time connections to the Web. You need to decide the name under which your company will do business online. And you need to figure out how your pages, the primary product of your efforts, will end up online.

What You Need to Publish on the Web

In general, unless you contract the entire job out to a third party (which is an option worth considering, especially if you aren't going to add staff to manage this effort eventually), there's only one way to do this. The decisions you'll have to make are in the details—who will own and maintain which pieces of the hardware and software that get you on the Net.

The global Internet consists of thousands of computers of all types that speak a language called TCP/IP, which stands for Transmission Control Protocol/Internet Protocol. By virtue of being connected through any number of types of wires and all understanding TCP/IP, these computers are eligible to have "IP addresses," which are guaranteed to be unique worldwide. IP addresses are assigned, upon request, by a standards body called the InterNIC.

With an IP address, the connection of the appropriate wiring, and the installation of the software necessary to understand TCP/IP, any computer can be a member of the Internet.

Most computers also have descriptive names, which are much easier to remember. If you're setting up your site to be available to anybody anywhere, you almost certainly want to arrange with InterNIC for one of these names, called a "domain name"; if you don't care that the address of your server is hard to remember, you might not. Use of domain names is not required, but it's customary.

In our case, one particular computer needs to be connected to the Internet—your Web Server. Furthermore, the server machine needs to speak the special language of the Web, which is called HyperText Transfer Protocol (HTTP). The details of HTTP and TCP/IP aren't important. What you need to know is that your machine must speak both of those languages, and you have to contract with a company called an Internet Service Provider (ISP) to connect it to the Internet.

What Is...

TCP/IP: Transport Control Protocol / Internet Protocol—the language used by computers to communicate on the Internet.

IP address: The unique number that identifies a specific computer on the Internet.

HTTP: Hypertext Transfer Protocol—The primary language used, in conjunction with TCP/IP, by computers to communicate on the World Wide Web.

ISP: Internet Service Provider—A company that provides connectivity services for individuals or other companies wishing to attach computers to the Internet.

domain name: A common name identifying a group of computers attached to the Internet.

InterNIC: The organization that maintains the master registry of domain names.

protocol: A communications language used by computers.

Teaching a PC a language (or protocol) is a lot easier than teaching a person, but it's best left to an experienced network engineer. Depending on the method you're using to connect with your Internet Service Provider (described in more detail below), he'll probably install some hardware, install the TCP/IP protocol from your Windows (either 95 or NT Server) CD, and set some configuration options. One of those options will be the IP address and name of your server, described above.

There's one more thing to do—teach your server how to speak HTTP. Your network installation person might be able to do this for you, but you can do it yourself with this book. Later in this chapter, we'll go through all of the options and steps you need to know to install two popular Web server software packages—Personal Web Server on Windows 95 and Internet Information Server on Windows NT Server—on your server PC. There's a lot to do, so you'd better get started. First problem: how are you going to connect to the Net?

Choosing Your Internet Service

If you are creating a site for personal use or for a small business, an account with an Internet Service Provider (ISP) might be appropriate for you. To connect your PC to the Internet, you need to become a part of a network that is already connected. You do this with a connection to an ISP, usually via your telephone line and a modem in your PC. Most ISPs maintain full-time, high-speed connections to even larger hubs, which in turn connect to larger sites, and so on. The collection of all of these hubs, and everybody they connect, comprise the global Internet.

> **Our Take**
>
> **Jeff:** Don't expect much performance from a phone line and a modem. If you get more than about 12 hits a day on your Web pages, you'll need an upgrade.
>
> **Kevin:** Consider this—a typical 33.6 kbps modem actually transfers no more than about 4 kbps of data via FTP or HTTP. So if you're up 24 hours a day, the most data you'll transfer is less than 350MB. That's a lot of data, but it's darned little for a Web site.

Online service providers, such as America Online (AOL), CompuServe, and The Microsoft Network (MSN), might hold interest for you if your Web hosting needs are minimal. These services provide a small amount of space for posting your Web pages, plus access to the Web and their internal pages, which typically include special stories and features intended for entertainment (AOL) or business (CompuServe). You have no control over the capabilities of their Web servers, and your site is competing with thousands of others for access to their communications lines. For personal sites, this is probably not a problem. Costs range from $10 to $30 per month for unlimited access. Typical complaints with these services include inability to get through to the host computer and slow network response during peak traffic periods (usually evenings and weekends).

What Is...

FTP: File Transfer Protocol. The most common language Internet-connected computers use to transfer data files (blocks of data destined for storage on a disk, not for immediate viewing). FTP, like HTTP, requires TCP/IP to work.

bit: The smallest piece of information used by a digital computer. Bits can have two values: on or off (or true or false, or 1 or 0, etc.). One bit doesn't generally tell you a whole lot.

kbps: Thousands (K) of bits per second (bps). Usually refers to the speed at which data is sent over a wire.

byte: Eight bits. A byte is typically (but not always, depending on the computer system) required to express one character.

MB: Millions (M) of bytes (B), pronounced as "megabyte." Typically used to express amounts of data, usually for files or disks.

Microsoft Network (MSN): Microsoft's own little part of the World Wide Web, to which they'll allow you to have access for a fee. This kind of commercial outcropping on the Internet is typically referred to as "value-added service," even when the value of it isn't immediately obvious.

Factors to Consider When Selecting an Internet Service Provider

"Retail" ISPs range in size from enormous (AT&T, Sprint) to mom-and-pop operations run from somebody's basement. This option is the most common choice for small businesses and individuals who do not require the added content made available by an Online Service Provider. The size of the company providing the service is not one of the critical factors to consider in choosing your service, any more than it is when choosing a long distance phone carrier. When choosing an ISP for retail service, you should consider price, services, support, and availability.

Price

For a single connection from a home or small business, typical prices run from $10 to $25 per month for unlimited use. Note that "unlimited" does not mean "full-time"; you are expected to release the line when you are not actively using it. Pricing generally drops for longer-term commitments.

Services

Most ISPs provide "PPP" accounts; these allow your PC to connect directly to the Internet via their servers, but not to have any direct access to their servers' internal resources. For most people, this is fine, but programmers and UNIX gurus might prefer "shell" accounts, which provide both PPP and access to the server's programs and internal resources.

Support

Is technical support readily available and at convenient hours? Murphy's Law dictates that your hard drive will develop a problem requiring you to reconfigure your Internet connection late at night before an important demonstration, and long tech support hours make this infinitely easier.

Availability

How many local phone numbers does your ISP provide for you to call? (Several large ISPs provide 800 service.) How many phone lines does each modem handle (the fewer the better; less than 10 is ideal)? How often are all lines full?

If your Web site is (or is going to be) extensive and you expect a lot of traffic, you might wish to consider more capable, pricey options such as the virtual domain, machine hosting, or local hosting.

Virtual Domain

You pick a domain name (usually of the form "megacorp.com") and enter into an agreement with an ISP that they will register and maintain your name, as well as handle any traffic destined for that site. Your ISP's computers host your site, but it appears to the outside world as if the computers belong to your company. Registering a name costs $50 per year (with the first two years payable when you register), and hosting services typically run from $150 to $300 per month, depending on the traffic your site generates. Your local ISP can give you more information on their virtual domain services.

There are scores of companies who will do you the favor of registering your name with InterNIC, for a fee. Generally, they're not doing you a favor, since the registration process is quite simple and can be completed online for no additional charge (see http://rs.internic.net/cgi-bin/itts for registration information and a tool to search the database of already registered names). However, when you register, you must supply the IP address of an already running machine (called a "domain name server") that will route traffic intended for your PC to it. Generally, this is a machine at your ISP's office, but you need to tell your ISP that you're doing this before you do it. Otherwise, they won't add your machine's newly registered IP address and domain name to their databases, and nobody will be able to connect to it. Your ISP (which might offer to take care of all of the registration paperwork for you) will almost certainly be happy to oblige for a few dollars.

Machine Hosting

You purchase a computer capable of acting as a server and you install your server software and Web pages, and your local ISP keeps the machine in their offices, connected to their high-speed communications lines. You are responsible for registering and maintaining your domain name, and you depend on the ISP for nothing more than power and communications. This service is typically inexpensive, but is not offered by all ISPs.

Local Hosting

You purchase a computer capable of acting as a server, install your server software and Web pages, buy several pieces of equipment to manage communications services (called "routers" and "CSU/DSUs"), and arrange for high-speed communications lines with your local phone company or communications provider. The phone lines might not be expensive, depending on the speeds you require and the capabilities of your local phone company. A T1 line that handles 1.5 megabits of data per second (more than 50 times the speed of a typical PC modem) can cost as little as $300 per month in some places. The equipment can be expensive to purchase and support, however. On the other hand, your storage capacity is essentially unlimited.

What Is. . .

T1 line: A digital phone line, as opposed to the analog phone lines most of us use in our homes. A digital T1 can generally carry up to 50 times the data a standard 28.8 kbps analog modem can pump out.

domain name: A name that all of the computers in a given, arbitrary group, answer to. Like surnames among humans, domain names are augmented with other names that identify specific machines. For example, megacorp.com is a domain name that probably doesn't belong to any one machine; batman.megacorp.com is probably one machine somewhere in Megacorp's network.

router: A device that receives streams of network traffic and segregates it so only data intended for machines attached to its other end passes through.

CSU/DSU: A device that converts digital telephone signals to data computers can understand. Used in conjunction with high-speed communications lines, like T1s.

Comparing Relative Capacity to Cost

The relationship between relative capacity (site disk storage, access speed, software choice) and cost (for equipment, communications, and services) in setting up a Web site can be roughly sketched as in Figure 4-1. It's pretty clear that, after a certain dollar value is reached, some pretty incredible increases in site capacity are possible for only a little more money.

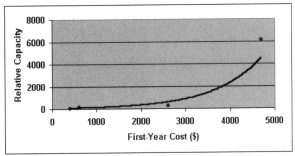

Figure 4-1: After the initial investment, costs stabilize.

The First-Year Cost values above are very rough estimates based on current market prices for the hardware used for each solution listed in the previous discussion. The Relative Capacity values are calculated using the following formula, presented here for the first time:

`Data connection speed (Kbps) x Disk storage (GB) = Relative Capacity`

For example, in the graph above, the following figures were used to calculate the cost and capacity of the "machine hosting" model:

Cost:	
Pentium-200 CPU, 2GB disk, no video	$2,000
ISP domain serving fees	$200
ISP connection fees	$200
Local modem for administration	$200
Total	*$2,600*

Capacity:
1540 kbps (standard ISP T1 line) x 2GB hard disk = *3080*

There's no particular significance to the calculation above taken by itself. It's only there to show you how to come up with a more or less objective estimation of how much Web service a given ISP contract offers you so you can make intelligent comparisons while price shopping. Comparing ISP service packages can be like comparing PCs on a shelf at a retailer: one has a faster modem, but one has a bigger hard disk. Which is better? You have to decide; this formula might help.

Your criteria for evaluating capacity might be very different from the ones used above. For example, you might wish to consider the cost of technical support, or mean system time between failures. In any case, as long as you are consistent, your graph should assist in your evaluation of possible solutions.

The interesting thing about the graph in Figure 4-1 is that there comes a point where the trend line starts to rise exponentially. There is a point in your spending where you will purchase your own equipment rather than using the ISP's servers. It might be that you want more control, or you want to move the machines into your own office, or the ISP might not have the hardware you need. In any case, once you buy your own server hardware, your other costs pale in comparison. You might not need so much capacity that you ever reach that point, but if you do, it's nice to know that the worst is over.

The quandary for you, the content developer, is how much money you want to invest in publishing on the Web. For individuals, an online service provider or retail ISP will allow you to publish a few pages about yourself and your hobbies or to keep in touch with friends. For most small businesses, either retail hosting or virtual domains are appropriate choices because they provide adequate capacity and service at a reasonable price. For larger companies, machine hosting or a locally administered site might be more appropriate because they permit detailed configuration and control and capacity limited only by your budget.

Whether you choose one of the more-or-less-free servers from Microsoft or you choose to run a server designed and supported by a third party, you can be assured that you will get reliable, efficient HTTP service for your customers. While the simplest servers provide no more than that, additional services available from Web server software range from a simple file-transfer server to secure transaction management and detailed statistics. Your choice of a server depends to a great extent on which of these services you require and how much you have to spend.

Using Windows 95 for Web Development

If you have a choice as to which platform to run your Web server on (i.e., you own your Web server, whether it's physically located at your ISP's site or your office), you can choose the operating system on which to run your server as well. For most people who have the flexibility to choose an operating system for their server PC, Windows NT Server is the obvious choice. It's designed to support multiple users (hundreds of them, if you like), it includes features to support the remote management of client machines and remote users, and it's well supported by the manufacturer, by other users, and by a legion of certified technical support people.

What Is. ..

ISDN: Integrated Services Digital Network. The cheapest digital phone line you can buy. Data transfer rates over ISDN range from 64 Kbps to 512 Kbps (depending on configuration), as compared to today's typical modems at around 30 Kbps. ISDN service requires some specialized equipment up front, and you pay by the second rather than paying a flat rate.

LAN: Local area network. Any number of machines, usually in close geographic proximity, connected by some kind of data communications system.

intranet: A LAN that supports the TCP/IP protocol, thus mimicking a small chunk of the global Internet.

PPP: Point-to-Point Protocol. A common way to connect computers to the Internet using a modem and a standard phone line.

URL: Uniform Resource Locator. The unique "address" of a page of the World Wide Web.

Front Page: Microsoft's low-end World Wide Web authoring tool.

configuration: The set of options that make up the current state of a computer or piece of software.

FTP: File Transfer Protocol. The standard method of transferring files across the Internet.

Our Take: Internet Use & Response Time in the Future

Kevin: I believe that something's got to give on the bandwidth issue. Either people will get tired of waiting for response and they'll get off the Net (easing traffic) or infrastructure will be built to support the demand, for a price. Actually, you can do that today: if you can afford a T3 for your company, I'd like to surf on your network. But the price of communications hardware will decrease over time as data rates increase.

Somebody with access to the numbers can figure it out, but I'm willing to bet that the cost of consumer-grade data communications stays about the same in real dollars over time as the capacity of the medium increases. What I'm trying to say is that for whatever you're paying now, you'll be able to afford better and better response time as the years go by.

Jeff: Again, I must take a contrary attitude here. I do not believe the number of people using the Web will continue to climb indefinitely. The number of Web users will drop in the next year or two simply because of the limited uses of the Web and the technological barriers to overcome before the Internet can live up to its hype.

The biggest problem is the antiquated telephone equipment that home telephone customers are forced to use. Bad wiring, slow switches, and lousy connections drop phone line performance and decrease efficiency. I worked for Southwestern Bell for a while, and I still can't make a phone call today without being amazed my call goes through. There is so much old equipment out there held together with spit and prayer, it's no wonder the Internet is bogging down.

That said, the next problem to overcome will be the amount of money paid for a reliable Internet connection. If I could get a high-speed connection such as ISDN for about two to three times the cost of my analog phone line and no per-minute access fees, I would snap it up. As it is, the phone companies are too greedy to get my business. Reliable, high-speed computer data lines that run into the home are what is needed. Data should be routed across a data network, not a voice network.

For a few, however, Windows 95 will be the operating system their Web server runs. If you're working on a machine that is attached to a large network and you want to run your local PC as a Web server, you might well be running Windows 95. If your office has a small LAN and you're setting up an intranet and don't want to incur the expense of installing NT Server, you might choose to have a Web server run in the background on a PC already running Windows 95. Whatever your reasons, Windows 95 is a viable Web server, if somewhat limited in capacity.

You should note that your ISP, if you are connecting to their network via PPP, might not permit you to run a Web server on your local PC. Maintaining a Web site adds significantly to the traffic level on a local network, and the dynamic nature of PPP addressing makes assignment of a URL to a PPP-connected machine a headache. There are also legal implications to your controlling the content that is freely and publicly available from a machine in their domain.

If your ISP does allow you to run a site from your local machine, they will probably assign a permanent IP address and require you to register a hostname with them. This arrangement is essentially the same as a virtual domain (see "Setting Up Your Internet Service," above), and you will probably be asked to establish a business account with the ISP.

Microsoft bundles server software with its FrontPage authoring environment called Personal Web Server. It's also available via the Microsoft home page. Personal Web Server is a perfectly capable Web server that runs on your Windows 95 PC and allows browsers to retrieve pages stored on your local disk. It's not suitable for sites that will experience dozens of concurrent hits or sites that require detailed statistics. But for a small installation, it might be sufficient, and you can't beat the price. As an added bonus, it allows your Windows 95 PC to act as an FTP server and permit anonymous access (if you desire) to files on your local hard drive.

FYI: Run the Latest Versions of Software

Make sure you're running the latest versions of Microsoft's Web products for best results. Standards change and bugs are fixed frequently. As of this writing, the following versions are current:

Windows 95 requires Service Pack 1, available at http://www.microsoft.com/windows95/info/service-packs.htm.

Microsoft Exchange Server version 4 or newer is required for workgroup sharing using Microsoft Outlook, but is not required for Web publishing.

Installing & Configuring Personal Web Server

Once you've downloaded the Personal Web Server distribution file, double-click on the filename in Windows Explorer to install it. This action only installs the server; there is still a lot of configuration to be done.

You will need to restart your PC to allow the changes to your Windows system files to take effect. When your PC restarts, you will notice two changes immediately: There might be a button entitled Personal Web Server on your taskbar and a new icon in your taskbar tray (Figure 4-2), and there is now an icon titled Personal Web Server in your Control Panel. You can set up and administer the Personal Web Server by double-clicking on any of these.

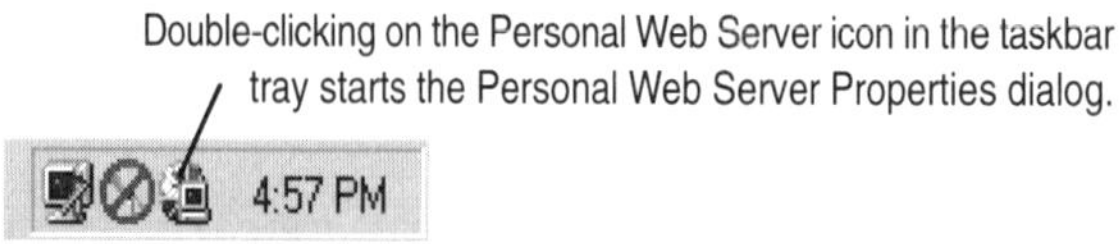

Double-clicking on the Personal Web Server icon in the taskbar
tray starts the Personal Web Server Properties dialog.

Figure 4-2: Personal Web Server in the Taskbar.

Our Take

Jeff: Installing a Web server is not a simple thing. Can't it be made easier? Well, installing a Web server under Windows is about as simple as it gets. Microsoft has made installing an operating system as simple as possible, and the Windows built-in installation program tries to make installing all software as simple as possible. Ask anyone who has tried to install OS/2 or any flavor of UNIX how easy it is. Windows has a long way to go before it is idiot proof, but installing anything under Windows is much more pleasant than the alternative.

The Personal Web Server Properties dialog includes four tabs, each of which might be selected to display the associated property sheet: General, Startup, Administration, and Services. You should review all four to become familiar with their functions, but you're unlikely to use all of them at any one time. When you need them, however, you'll be glad that you know they are there.

The General dialog (Figure 4-3) contains two critical pieces of information: the URL of your Web pages and the directory on your hard drive in which they should be saved. The value shown for your URL is drawn from your Network settings and includes the name of your machine and its domain. In the event that you are using Personal Web Server from a machine connected to the Internet via a PPP account, it is highly unlikely that this entry will be correct. You should note the name of the "Default Home Page" and its location to make it easier to change later. Personal Web Server, by default, installs itself in C:\Webshare; local Web pages are saved in the subdirectory called wwwroot.

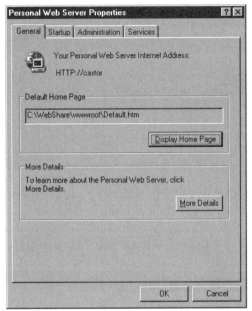

Figure 4-3: The General tab of the Personal Web Server Properties dialog.

FYI: Task Switching

You can't use the Windows task-switching keys to switch between a foreground application (like a Web browser) and the Personal Web Server Properties sheet. To return to the Property sheet, minimize all other applications so they don't hide the Property sheet.

The button marked Display Home Page in the General dialog starts up your default Web browser and loads the designated page. The More Details button verifies your network connection and displays server statistics.

FYI: Connection Failing

Pressing Display Home Page connects to your PC using the HTTP protocol, just as if you had called up your home page from a machine located elsewhere on the Internet. If pressing this button returns an error message or if nothing happens, either your network connection is not set up correctly or your machine name is not recognized by the network.

FYI: Documentation for Personal Web Server

The default home page Personal Web Server creates for you is pretty simple and is intended to be replaced (it automatically lists your hobbies as "movies" and "reading," for example). It contains one very useful link, however—to the online documentation for Personal Web Server. Click on the words "Personal Web Server" at the bottom of the page to load the server documentation main menu.

Selecting the Startup tab brings up options for starting and stopping the Web server (Figure 4-4). The Start and Stop buttons at the top notify the Web server that it is to begin or stop answering requests from the Internet to return its Web pages. The two check boxes below determine whether or not the Server starts when the PC is booted and whether the Web server configuration dialog is available from the Windows taskbar while it is running.

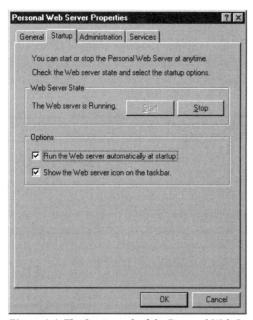

Figure 4-4: The Startup tab of the Personal Web Server Properties dialog.

The Services dialog (Figure 4-5) lists the two Internet services that Personal Web Server provides—File Transfer Protocol (FTP) and HyperText Transfer Protocol (HTTP)—and allows the starting or stopping of either. You might want to disable FTP if you don't want remote users to access files on your PC, or you might want to disable HTTP if you are only using Personal Web Server to configure your PC to serve files to the Internet or your office intranet.

Pressing the Stop button on the Startup dialog stops both the FTP and HTTP services.

Permitting FTP access to your PC doesn't make it an open book for the world to read. Access is only allowed to certain directories, specified in the FTP configuration options below.

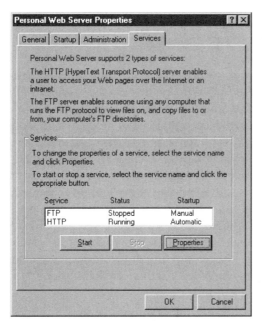

Figure 4-5: The Services tab of the Personal Web Server Properties dialog .

To start or stop each individual protocol, click once on its name and then select Start or Stop as appropriate. To make it automatically start whenever Personal Web Server is started, press the button marked Properties at the bottom of the window after selecting the protocol you wish to configure (Figure 4-6).

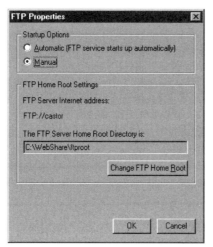

Figure 4-6: FTP Properties dialog of the Services tab.

Your choices in either case are to make the protocol automatically available when Personal Web Server is started or to make it start only when desired (manual). The FTP Server can be reconfigured to move its home directory to any location on your PC; this and many more configuration options (described below) become available when you press Change FTP Home Root. The HTTP protocol (Figure 4-7) permits the same startup and home directory choices, plus an option to change the default home page. This is the page that people connecting to your PC will see if they do not explicitly choose any other page (e.g., if they connect by typing http://www.megacorp.com without specifying any specific page in the Megacorp Web). Both configuration options permit the administrator to change the default; pressing either Change Home Root or Change Home Page makes available a myriad of other options. For most users, the default options are appropriate.

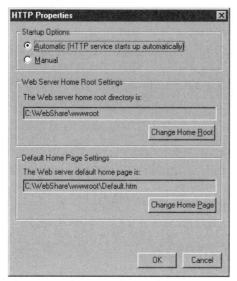

Figure 4-7: The HTTP dialog of the Services tab.

Selecting Administrative Options

The Administration tab doesn't directly permit any changes to configuration. Selecting the Administration button on this property sheet, or choosing any of the additional configuration options from the Personal Web Server HTTP and FTP Property sheets, starts the default Web browser to manage more advanced configuration options. These settings should not normally be changed unless there is good reason to do so, but inspecting them is informative.

Detailed configuration is performed via HTML forms viewed in your browser. This conceivably makes it possible to administer your server remotely, from a machine located elsewhere on your company's LAN.

If your Internet connection is not active, your browser will report an error attempting to connect to your PC's Web server. Even if you don't intend to make outside administration possible, you must have an actively running Internet connection to perform detailed configuration.

It's not possible for anybody on the Internet to administer your Personal Web Server. Only a user account on the local Microsoft network, with specific permission set ahead of time, can perform administration.

Selecting Administration from the Administration tab in the Personal Web Server Properties dialog starts the Internet Services Administrator, a central point for all detailed configuration of your Web server.

The default administrative options will probably work fine for you. If you're curious as to each individual option and what it does, you can either try it or check Appendix C for detailed instructions on every single configuration option. There's nothing in Appendix C that's necessary for the basic operation of your server, so we'll move on.

Other Windows 95 Server Options

If you don't want to use Personal Web Server, perhaps because you require better logging capabilities or remote administration, you have several other choices. Other options range from free to not very expensive, and some are more capable than others. Some possible choices:

- **Alibaba** (http://alibaba.austria.eu.net/DOCS/index.htm)
- **Website** (http://website.ora.com)
- **FastTrack** (http://home.netscape.com)

A performance analysis of all of these products would be impossible in this space, but all are very capable, handling up to 1,000,000 requests/day over a standard T1 (1.54 mbps/sec) line, running on a Pentium PC. A quick comparison of features follows (Table 4-1):

	Personal Web Server	Alibaba	Fast Track	WebSite
Manufacturer	Microsoft	Computer Software Manufaktur	Netscape	O'Reilly
List Price (US $)	$0	$99	$299	$129
Secure Sockets Layer (SSL) security		✔	✔	✔
Multihoming				✔
ImageMap support		✔	✔	✔
Cookie support		✔	✔	✔
HTML Editor included			✔	
One-step publishing	✔		✔	

Table 4-1: Windows 95 Web server features compared.

What Is. . .

Secure Sockets Layer (SSL) security: A generally accepted security standard for Web servers that makes the transfer of information between Web client and server somewhat more secure. It's typically used for financial transactions over the Web.

multihoming: The ability of the Web server to answer to more than one name, say, www.megagcorp.com and ftp.megacorp.com.

image map support: Some Web pages include images that are actually hyperlinks to external documents. If the image has different behavior depending on the point in the image that's clicked, it's called an image map. One method of image mapping requires support from the Web server.

cookie support: Some Web sites "remember" when you were there last and what you did when you came. They do this by placing an entry in a file on your local computer and checking to see if the entry is there the next time you come to their page. That entry is called a cookie, and checking the status of cookies requires server support.

HTML Editor: Some kind of authoring environment for Web pages, like Microsoft Word.

one-step publishing: A more-or-less automated way of sending pages you've authored to the server, like Microsoft's Publish to the Web Wizard.

Server selection is largely a matter of preference, and you stand to gain by trying as many as you have time for (all provide free trial copies) and making your decision based on subjective factors, such as ease of use and performance on your own network. For a list of other Windows 95 Web servers to consider, see the Yahoo! Directory listing at http://www.yahoo.com/Computers_and_Internet/Software/Internet/World_wide_Web/Servers/Microsoft_Windows_Windows_95/.

Using Windows NT for Web Development

So, you've settled on Windows NT as your server platform. Microsoft's latest release, version 4.0, combines the familiar Windows 95 interface with a robust, capable network server operating system. A Web server running on Windows NT, configured properly and with adequate hardware to run it, can handle almost any level of Web activity.

FYI: Use the Latest Software Versions

Make sure you're running the latest versions of Microsoft's Web products for best results. Standards change and bugs are fixed frequently. As of this writing, the following versions are current:

Windows NT Server is at version 4.0 with two Service Packs (available at http://www.microsoft.com/msdownload/default.asp).

Internet Information Server is at version 3.0 (note that the version shipping with Windows NT Server 4.0 is version 2.0 and should be updated; update files are at the above URL).

Microsoft Exchange Server version 5.0 is required for workgroup sharing using Microsoft Outlook, but is not required for Web publishing.

Choosing Between NT Workstation or NT Server

Unfortunately, the world of commerce intersects the world of science when one begins discussing the differences between Windows NT Server version 4.0 and Windows NT Workstation version 4.0. In a nutshell, they are the same piece of software, with the titles changed on the windows to make them look slightly different.

One setting in the Windows system registry determines whether the operating system allocates its resources as a server or as a workstation, and a software catch is installed in the product to prevent users from changing the setting. If a copy of NT Workstation ($199) has that registry setting directly modified, it suddenly starts calling itself NT Server ($499), and it acts like NT Server, too. For the definitive analysis of this characteristically profit-minded issue, see O'Reilly's analysis of the situation at http://www.ora.com/oracom/win/index.html, which makes for fascinating technical reading.

Having noted the nonexistent differences between the software, we need to explain that Microsoft prevents the use of NT Workstation as a Web server through legalese. The standard license that comes with NT Workstation states that "you may permit a maximum of ten (10) computers to connect to the Workstation Computer to access and use services of the software product."

There is no longer any physical restriction that would prevent you from running a Web server on NT Workstation. But to do so would be a violation of your license with Microsoft. *Caveat emptor.*

The bottom line is that you can't legally use NT Workstation as a Web server, although it would work fine, especially if it were tuned properly by an experienced NT administrator.

Using Peer Web Services for NT Workstation

If you've already read the section above on configuring Personal Web Services, you have a pretty good idea how to configure Peer Web Services and Internet Information Server (IIS). That's because they are essentially the same product, and Peer Web Services and IIS are identical except for the titles on the windows. For a brief discussion of this behavior, see Andrew Schulman's analysis at ftp://ftp.ora.com/pub/examples/windows/win95.update/ntwk4.html.

CAUTION

> *Don't try to install Personal Web Server on a PC running Windows NT. You will corrupt the system registry beyond repair and have to reinstall Windows NT to correct the problem. The Web servers for Windows NT are installed slightly differently than the Web server for Windows 95, as discussed below.*

The Web server included with Windows NT Workstation is called Peer Web Services. Note the inclusion of the word Peer in the title; this is generally taken to imply that this Web server is for use on an intranet or other local office environment where you and your "peers" will be sharing data. Microsoft's license, as discussed above, effectively prohibits you from using NT Workstation as a World Wide Web server on the global Internet.

What Is...

applet: In the context here, an applet is a program that makes up part of the Windows Control Panel. It's also often used to refer to a certain type of program written in the Java programming language, but that's not discussed here.

peer: A member of the same group. In "Peer Web Services," Microsoft is implying that the NT Workstation version of their Web server is only robust enough to handle small numbers of clients.

There are a couple of added bonuses to using Peer Web Services. As in Windows NT 3.51, the so-called "simple Internet services" (FTP, Gopher, etc.) are built into the operating system—you just have to know where to find them. Unlike NT 3.51, they're not system services, available from the Services applet in Control Panel. In NT 4.0, they're Networking services, installed from the Network applet. Same church, different pew.

Installing & Configuring the Workstation

When you install NT Workstation, the setup utility for Peer Web Services is automatically installed and is waiting for you to activate it. To begin the installation, do the following:

1. Go to the Control Panel: click on Start | Settings | Control Panel.

2. Double-click on the Network applet to start network configuration.

3. Click on the Services tab.

4. If Peer Web Services is not already installed as a service, click on the Add button and select Microsoft Peer Web Services, and OK.

5. You will probably be prompted to insert your installation CD-ROM. Follow the prompts and click OK when the copyright notice for Peer Web Services appears.

    You should now be seeing the Peer Web Services Setup dialog (Figure 4-8), and a plethora of options are available to you.

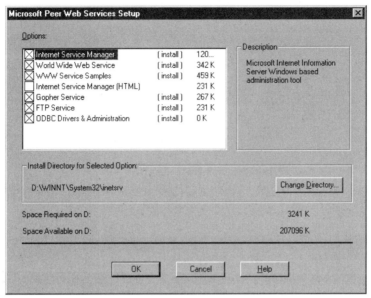

Figure 4-8: Peer Web Services Setup dialog.

6. You should now check the boxes adjacent to the names of the services you wish installed. Your options are as follows:

- **Internet Service Manager:** This is the application that you will use to configure the Web server (and other services). Install it.

- **World Wide Web Service:** The HTTP server. If you don't want to use this machine as a Web server, you don't need this, but why are you reading this chapter?

- **WWW Service Samples:** Some sample pages that use Microsoft's proprietary HTML extensions, including database connections and ActiveX components. Worth installing if you have any interest in these products, but realize that they highlight features that will only work on Microsoft's Internet Explorer Web browser.

- **Internet Service Manager (HTML):** The Web server configuration screens, intended to be used through a browser. You've seen this before, in the configuration discussion for Personal Web Server, above. You should install this.

- **Gopher Service:** This is not a dating club for large rodents. Gopher is a nearly obsolete Internet information service that allows remote users access to specially indexed information residing on an Internet server. The Web has largely replaced it. You probably don't need to install this.

- **FTP Service:** Permits remote users to send to and retrieve files from your server without viewing them. Of the many original UNIX utilities designed for the Internet, this one is still alive and well and is indispensable. Install this.

- **ODBC Drivers and Administration:** If you will be writing Web pages that will access a PC database (like Access), install these drivers. Otherwise, you don't need them.

What Is...

IIS: Internet Information Server, the Web server that is bundled with Windows NT Server.

ODBC: Open Database Connectivity, a standard for using online databases. See Chapter 7 for more information.

The default installation directory for all of these applications is \WINNT\system32\inetsrv. Unless you have a reason to change this, don't.

When you've selected the options you require, press OK. If you're asked if it's OK to create a directory, select Yes.

You will be prompted for the root directory for the HTTP (World Wide Web), FTP, and Gopher services (whether or not you're installing all or none of these). The defaults are \InetPub\wwwroot, \InetPub\ftproot, and InetPub\gophroot. This is where you will put files for remote users to see. Unless you allow it, they will not be able to access any other part of your system. If these choices are satisfactory, select OK and create them if prompted.

Peer Web Services will install from your CD-ROM drive.

CAUTION

If your network adapter or modem is not configured properly (or is not installed), the installation process will probably hang your system as the software installs and tries to communicate with the network.

Once installed, Peer Web Services will appear as a network service under the Services tab of the Network applet in Control Panel.

To configure options for Personal Web Server, you don't use the Control Panel at all. You'll notice a new addition to your Start menu after you restart your PC: under Programs, Microsoft Peer Web Services (Common) has been added. There are four programs available from this menu (Figure 4-9). They are:

- **Internet Service Manager.** The application you'll use to configure Peer Web Services.

- **Key Manager.** An application for configuring and managing encrypted (Secure Sockets Layer, or SSL) communications between remote clients and your Web server.

  Use of the Key Manager application is absolutely necessary if you require a secure, encrypted site. For example, if you are developing a site that permits the transmission of credit card numbers or other personal or proprietary information, you might want to enable SSL and use the Key Manager to configure your security environment. This security feature is in addition to the standard authentication security provided by Peer Web Services; Key Manager and SSL are strictly needed only if you require encryption of the data stream. For most Web sites, this will not be necessary. If you think your site might require SSL-level security, read the discussion in Chapter 5 of the Peer Web Services documentation, entitled "Securing Your Site Against Intruders." A description of how to use Key Manager is beyond the scope of this book.

- **Peer Web Services Setup**. The same setup program that you just ran, in case you want to add or remove components later. Since you've already seen the Setup program, we need not discuss it again.

- **Product Documentation**. The documentation is, well, documentation. Actually, the documentation, in HTML, is extensive and comprises as good a reference as you'll find for the individual functions of the Web server.

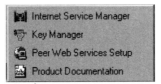

Figure 4-9: Peer Web Services menubar.

What Is...

SSL: Secure Sockets Layer, the operating system support for encrypted communications between your Web server and clients.

key manager: A utility to control the encryption options for your server.

The critical application you need to understand is the Internet Service Manager. As in the Personal Web Server, there are dozens of configurable options in a Web server, and this is where you set them all. Additionally, Internet Service Manager can be used to configure any Windows NT machines on your local network that are configured as Web, FTP, and/or Gopher servers (assuming that you have Administrator rights on each machine). This can be a real boon to a network administrator.

Selecting Administrative Options With Internet Service Manager

The Internet Service Manager (Figure 4-10) provides a central control point for all detailed configuration of all of the Peer Web Services. From this point, you can configure, start, and stop all FTP, WWW, and Gopher services on all of the machines on your local network. With a glance, you can evaluate the state of your network's remote services and see problems immediately. To start the Internet Service Manager, select Start I Programs I Peer Web Services I Internet Service Manager.

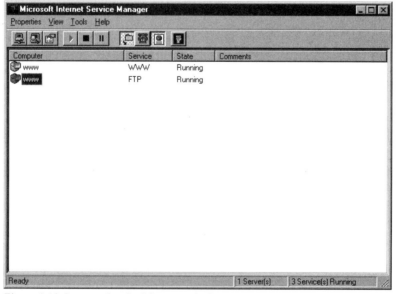

Figure 4-10: Internet Service Manager window.

You must have Administrator access rights on remote machines to change their configuration settings.

The Internet Service Manager toolbar reproduces all of the functions of the menubar above it. There are four groupings of controls on the toolbar, as shown in Figure 4-11.

- The first group facilitates searching the network for servers and editing their properties; this group includes the Server Selector button, the Search for Servers button, and the Server Properties button.

- The second group starts, stops, and pauses the currently selected service.

- The third selects which services are displayed in the current window; the buttons correspond to the FTP, Gopher, and WWW services.

- The final button starts the Key Manager.

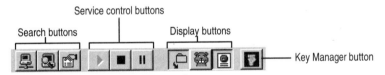

Figure 4-11: The Internet Service Manager toolbar.

As was the case with Personal Web Server under Windows 95, you might never need to use any of these configuration options. Just knowing how to get to them to explore them is a feat in itself. In the event that you do wish to explore them, we've included a detailed description of each option and what it does in Appendix D.

Using Internet Information Server for NT Server

The Internet Information Server (IIS) is exactly the same product as Peer Web Services. There is no difference between the dialogs in Peer Web Services and in Internet Information Server, except in the names at the tops of the windows. To install IIS in Windows NT Server, follow the directions above for Peer Web Services, except that you should select Internet Information Server from the Add dialog in Network Services under Control Panel, as in Figure 4-12.

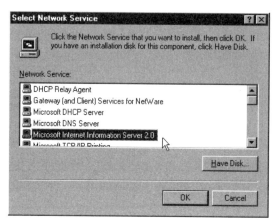

Figure 4-12: The Select Network Service dialog for Internet Information Server.

The version of Internet Information Server that ships with Windows NT Server version 4.0 is IIS 2.0. The upgrade to version 3.0, which adds such features as Active Server Pages (permits better integration of Microsoft Office with IIS and includes a service pack for Windows NT), Microsoft NetShow Server (video streaming and conferencing), the Microsoft FrontPage Server Extensions (site management), and the Microsoft Index Server, is available for download at http://www.microsoft.com. All of the above features will work with Personal Web Server on Windows 95 and are also available for download separately and at no charge.

Other Servers for Windows NT

You can view an extensive list of Web servers for Windows NT at Yahoo!; see http://www.yahoo.com/Computers_and_Internet/Software/Internet/ World_Wide_Web/Servers/Windows_NT/. Unlike the Windows 95 market, however, IIS is a much more prominent player in the Windows NT market, as is evidenced by the relative paucity of its competitors. Some of the more prominent options include:

- **EMWAC** (http://emwac.ed.ac.uk/)
- **Netscape SuiteSpot** (http://home.netscape.com/comprod/ server_central/product/suite_spot/index.html)

Whether you're using your own server or not, you'll need to have a way to get the pages you create onto a server in order for them to be read. The Web Publishing Wizard provides a good way to do this. Since you haven't created any pages yet (that's in the following chapters), it's likely that you'll want to bookmark this section and come back to it later, when you have something to upload. On the other hand, if you want to follow along and you've got a particular Web server in mind you want to try this with, it will work with any files you choose—say, the contents of your \temp directory. Just remember to remove whatever you upload later if you were just practicing.

Using the Web Publishing Wizard to Upload Files

In most Office applications, Microsoft has performed enough user testing to know what kinds of things users find difficult to do. So they've tried to make it easier with online helpers called wizards.

Wizards are programs within programs that automate parts of processes that typically require some detailed knowledge or require many steps. For example, the process of sending your Web pages to your Web server, whatever it is, requires a little knowledge about the server. You might not have that knowledge, or you might not remember; this isn't much of a problem, because Microsoft is going to do most of the work for you with its Web Publishing Wizard. A wizard is no substitute for a knowledgeable technician, by the way, but it's usually a good start.

Making Sure Your ISP Supports Microsoft's Wizard

For the ultimate in Web publishing ease, Microsoft has made arrangements with several large ISPs to permit its products to communicate directly with their servers and automate the process of moving files from the developer's PC to the ISP's server. This service, while convenient if you frequently change your pages, might not be the least expensive way to run your Web site. You might be able to find a local ISP that either has or will support the Microsoft server extensions. Otherwise, Microsoft's Web Publishing Wizard information page (http://www.microsoft.com/windows/software/webpost/default.htm) lists several large ISPs (including AOL and CompuServe) that participate. The Web Publishing Wizard is included on the Office 97 CD in the directory \Valupack\Webpost.

Using the Web Publishing Wizard is not difficult once you have authored your pages and ensured that your ISP will support the Wizard. To use the Wizard, you will need to know at least two pieces of information:

- **Where are the Web pages you want to post?** Note that the Wizard assumes that you will be publishing either a single file or a whole hierarchy of files, stored locally under a central directory.

- **Where will your ISP store your pages?** The Uniform Resource Locator (URL) of your personal Web page area is what you'll need; contact your ISP if you don't know it.

Entering the Appropriate Information About Your ISP

Let's get started. The Web Publishing Wizard is started by selecting Start | Programs | Accessories | Internet Tools | Web Publishing Wizard. Hope your mouse finger isn't too tired after all that. You'll see a friendly startup dialog (press Next to continue), and then you'll be asked where the files that you wish to upload are (Figure 4-13). Hit the Browse button and select the directory the files are in. Then click on the Next button.

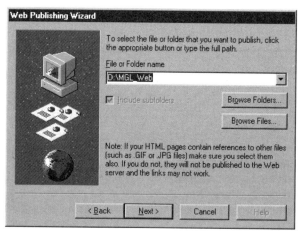

Figure 4-13: Web Publishing Wizard opening dialog.

CAUTION

If your pages are located in subdirectories of one top-level folder, be sure to check the Include Subfolders button on the file selection dialog. Otherwise, only the top-level directory's pages will get published. Note that this might be what you intend, if the subdirectories all contain temporary files or historical copies of your pages.

The wizard presents you with some default choices for ISPs. If none of the suggested ISPs are correct (as will be the case if you use a local mom-and-pop ISP or if you host your own site), you will need to enter the appropriate information for your ISP.

Since this is pretty likely the first time you have run the Wizard, let's go through it. Click on the New button to set up a new ISP. Figure 4-14 is what you should see; already the tough decisions begin.

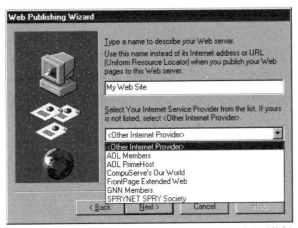

Figure 4-14: Selecting your ISP for setup with Web Publishing Wizard.

Pick a name, any name, for your server. This name will be seen by nobody but you, and only when you're running the Web Publishing Wizard. If you're maintaining pages in several different directories (say, for different users or business units) of a given Web server, you could use different names in this dialog to distinguish them.

You can save yourself some work if you can choose one of the ISPs listed in the pulldown list at the bottom of this dialog. If you can't (which is likely, since you're setting up your own server in this scenario), select Other Internet Provider. More questions. Click on the Next button to continue.

The next dialog, in Figure 4-15, asks for the URL of the pages you're going to post. Your ISP should have told you this if you're using a commercial provider; if you're running your own site, you needed to know this to install it. Enter it here and press Next to continue.

CAUTION

> *This is where you could enter the specific URL of individual users or divisions in your company if you desire. Just make sure you set up these "virtual directories" in your Web server software, as detailed in the previous sections, before you try to use the Web Publishing Wizard this way.*

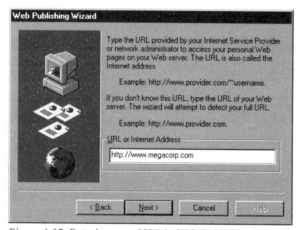

Figure 4-15: Entering your URL in Web Publishing Wizard.

Now it's time for some networking lingo. Figure 4-16 shows the Connection Type dialog. Is your ISP connected to the same local area network to which you are? If so, you can choose the first option, Local Area Network (Intranet); if not, you'll need to use Dial-Up Networking. Ideally, you've already set up the Dial-Up Networking entry for your ISP; if not, you can click on the New Dial-Up Connection button to set one up. That's a topic for another book.

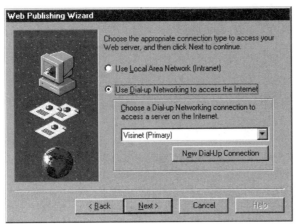

Figure 4-16: Selecting your type of connection with Web Publishing Wizard.

After you've selected an ISP (and after Windows restarts, if necessary, and you've restarted the Wizard), the wizard will use your existing Dial-Up Networking connection to connect to your ISP. Once connected, it will attempt to ascertain whether the remote server supports the Web Publishing extensions the wizard prefers.

If the remote server does not support the Web Publishing extensions, you'll see a heart-wrenching message like the one in Figure 4-17.

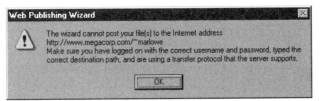

Figure 4-17: Error message for ISPs which don't support Web Publishing Wizard.

The Front Page Server Extensions, modifications to Web server software from various manufacturers that make the servers accept various FrontPage innovations, are freely available from Microsoft's Web site, and your ISP can install them if they like at no cost (except for their time). If they (or you) are running a Microsoft Web server, the extensions are installed automatically.

More questions follow, and we'll answer them all. The first is shown in Figure 4-18.

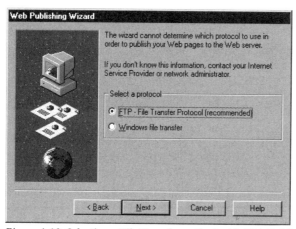

Figure 4-18: Selecting a File Transfer method with Web Publishing Wizard.

Do you want to use the Internet File Transfer Protocol (FTP) or Windows Networking to transfer your files? The answer to this question should almost always be FTP, as every Web server will support it. If your server is located on your local network, you can choose Windows File Transfer if you know the path to where the files will be stored (not the URL). The path can be local (C:\InetPub\MGLWeb), mapped (Q:\InetPub\MGLWeb), or a network path (//BABY-HUEY/ImetPub/MGLWeb). Pressing the Next button spawns the dialog in Figure 4-19:

Figure 4-19: Entering your server password with Web Publishing Wizard.

Enter your username and password here; these will be sent to the remote host (either by FTP or through Windows, if required). Your password will be displayed as a line of asterisks in case someone is looking over your shoulder.

A word to the wise: If you type your password wrong here, you will spend many painful hours trying to figure out what went wrong. Be careful of the Caps Lock key and get it right the first time. Then press Next; if you're using the FTP connection method, you'll see the dialog in Figure 4-20. If not, you're probably done and can skip to the head of the class.

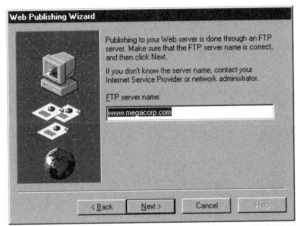

Figure 4-20: Entering the name of your FTP server in Web Publishing Wizard.

Enter the name of the machine you'll transfer the files to or through. Your ISP might use the same name as the Web server machine, or it might use something else. If you're not sure, call your system administrator or ISP to find out what the FTP server is called. Press Next to continue. The dialog in Figure 4-21 appears.

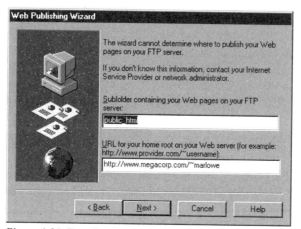

Figure 4-21: Entering the Server Directory Name for your Web page files in Web Publishing Wizard.

Because of the nature of FTP, you need to tell the Web Publishing Wizard exactly where to put the files on your Web server machine. Enter the directory name it should write to (not the URL) and the URL of the top level of the site, as shown in the example in the dialog.

In the best of circumstances, you just sent your pages (if any) to your ISP. If the Wizard maintains that it cannot connect to your ISP, check the following:

■ Is the machine you specified for FTP access correct? You can verify this using Windows's built-in FTP client:

1. Click on Start | Run.

2. Type **ftp** and press Enter.

3. In the box that appears, type **open** *hostname*, where *hostname* is the name of your ISP's FTP server.

4. When prompted, enter your username and password.

5. If the server lets you log on, you know you have the correct information. If not, call your ISP and ask for FTP instructions and be sure to ask these questions:

■ Are your username and password correct?

■ Is the Web subdirectory on your account correct? Most ISPs use "public_html," but some do not.

- Is your account using all of its allotted file space? Even if there's nothing in your Web server directories, files elsewhere can count against a disk quota, if you have one. This is especially common if your ISP is using a UNIX-based Web server.

Moving On

Whether you're running your Web site on Windows 95 or Windows NT, your remote clients can expect excellent performance while you reap the rewards of a relatively inexpensive architecture.

O'Reilly's analysis (http://www.ora.com) claims that any competent Web server product, running on any 32-bit version of Windows (Windows 95, Windows NT Workstation, or Windows NT Server) can easily saturate a standard T1 data communications line. This implies that, for most sites, any shortfalls in the quality of service will be due more to telephone communications than to the capabilities of your server hardware or software. The quality of your Web site hinges primarily on an issue more critical than the server, however; to paraphrase Bill Clinton, "it's the content, stupid."

Now you know all about the Internet and the Web, you have your Web development configured and running, and you're finally ready to begin putting content on the Web and sharing files over the Internet using Office 97. The next chapter gets you started with Web publishing using Word.

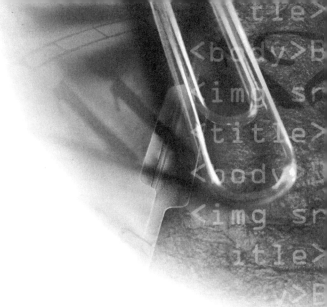

chapter 5

Microsoft Word 97

It's time to get to work. You know what you have to do, but where do you start? Will it just happen, or is there some planning involved? What tools will you use? Who invented liquid soap, and why? Maybe it would be easier to just pop up a Web browser and go check the latest news headlines, maybe the weather. How's your Microsoft stock doing today? A quick trip to the rec.humor.funny newsgroup to catch up on the latest jokes before someone sends them to you in e-mail.

Wait a minute. You've got a PC and a copy of Office 97, or you wouldn't be reading this book. You have a task at hand, and plenty of room for creativity (maybe too much). Try this. Start Word, then click on File | New | Web Pages Tab | Web Page Wizard. In less than five minutes you can create a functional starting point (a home page) for the Megacorp Web site. There's a lot more to creating a good Web site than this, but consider this illustration an example of just how easy it can be to get something on the page.

In fact, you can get quite a bit on the page using nothing but Word 97. Since most Web pages are, at heart, just text files written in such a way that a browser understands how to make them look good, any text editor can theoretically create gorgeous Web pages. In fact, the best Web pages are still written in simple text editors by people with an impossibly complete understanding of the language of the Web. Now, you probably don't want to develop that kind of oneness with your PC; you want to get a Web site up. Word can help you do that quickly and easily if your needs are basic, and passably if your needs are more involved. If you are setting up a site from scratch using Office 97, you should definitely start in Word.

Word 97 includes more features than any one person could ever hope to use in a single document, or even in a whole book. It creates the simplest of documents with deceiving ease and manages multi-document tomes as if you write those all of the time. Turn a database into mailing labels? No problem. Send a fax to everybody who sent you a Christmas card last year? Can do. After working with Word for awhile, you might begin to wonder what it *can't* do.

Despite the temptation, we'll avoid saying that it can't do HTML. You're going to love the built-in graphical bullets and lines, for example. On the other hand, you're not going to like tables that run off the right edge of your screen, or OLE objects that don't update after linking them. But we'll tell you how to deal with that and the other things you'll find as you explore the Land of Gates.

In this chapter, we'll start with a picture of a page we want to develop, and we'll explore how Word can be used to accomplish that goal. Beginning with relatively simple pages and moving on to some pretty complicated designs, you can either use the examples given as training tools or follow the same process with your own page designs.

About Web Page Design

Just as you can't expect to jump into a pool for the first time and know how to swim, you can't expect to jump into a Web publishing system and create great Web pages. If you try, you will die of frustration before you get very far.

One could spend an entire career learning how to create effective graphical design elements on Web pages, languishing in the minutia of the effectiveness of round bullets vs. square ones and the appropriate use of white space. You don't have time for that, but you should make time to organize your thoughts and borrow the best features from pages you like.

If you're interested in the discipline of page design for the Web and in software in general, you might consider any number of books on these topics. Two of our favorites are *About Face: The Essentials of User Interface Design*, by Alan Cooper (IDG, 1995), and *deconstructing web graphics* (New Riders, 1996), by Linda Weinman. You can see previews of both books (or order them) at their publishers' home sites, (http://www.idg.com including a nice list of handy tips) and http://www.lynda.com/bookstore/ respectively. Another Web page design guide is *Looking Good Online* (Ventana, 1996). There are also several good sites on the Web that discuss page design (use your favorite search engine and search for "Web page design").

Content Is Key

Before you can start creating your Web pages, you need to decide what will be on them. It's OK to get started, build a few mostly blank pages, and then fill them in later, but the best sites are carefully planned and maintained from the start. You don't have to get too fancy with your plans—after all, you'll probably have ideas as you start writing—but if you don't have a goal, you won't know it when you get there.

Reinventing the wheel can be avoided in Web design by doing a little surfing. Find the pages of organizations (or individuals) with similar needs and see what they have done. Make notes of their best ideas and make notes of the things that just don't work. Roam around, following links from page to page, jotting ideas as you go. Make screen prints (use the print button on your browser) of both good and bad pages, and note on the printouts what you liked and didn't like. Do the pages you like flow well? Can you find information you're looking for? Are they so full of gadgets and gizmos that they take forever to load? Is their use of fonts and graphics consistent? Does it make you want to come back? You can save yourself a lot of agony by taking advantage of the learning pains of others.

Our Take: Page Titles

Kevin: There's another good reason for printing out samples of sites you like. Most browsers will print the URL of the page you print at the top (Netscape) or bottom (Internet Explorer) of each page of the printout. When it comes time to reproduce a technique or feature that you especially liked, you'll be able to use this printout to find the page again and view its underlying source code to see how it was built. In most browsers, hitting the "Print" button at the top of the browser window will print this way.

Alternately, you could add the page to your bookmarks; but this can become unwieldy quickly, and you have no way of remembering why you bookmarked that page.

Jeff: This is a good reason to have a descriptive title on each of your Web pages. Anyone bookmarking one of your pages will be able to tell what the page is two weeks later when they look at the bookmark for the first time.

What You See Ain't What You Save

When you work in Word, the keys that you press on the keyboard are represented as characters on the screen in front of you. For every key you press, no more than one character appears on the screen (unless you hold a key down, and that's another story). When you use the built-in tools that Word provides for adding special effects to your page, you don't usually see any more characters on the screen. Making a line **bold**, for example, requires a couple of key presses, but there is no net increase in the number of characters on the screen.

Our Take: Is There an HTML Editor That Handles HTML as Well as Word Handles Text?

Jeff: Not yet, though they are getting closer very fast. Consider: Word processing software has been around for quite a while, and the first versions were pretty bad. Anyone remember LotusWorks or WordStar? Word processors have the luxury of being able to define their own document format for storing information, so they can do neat things to make the text look just right. They have vastly improved the editing features over the years as well.

HTML editors, on the other hand, must all use the same output format (namely HTML) and try to make the text in the editor look just like it will look in a Web browser. Considering no two Web browsers will display a Web page in the same way, the concept of a WYSIWYG HTML editor is not as easy as everyone assumes it should be.

Kevin: The biggest factors holding back the development of a really good HTML editor are the built-in limitations of HTML. You just can't do some things in HTML that you can do on a printed page, and those of us who expect our word processors to turn our thoughts into beautifully formatted text are invariably disappointed when things don't look as we expect them to. I'm not sure that we'll ever see an HTML editor that we can all agree is as good as a high-end WYSIWYG word processor if our standard is the appearance of the output. I, for one, would be happy to see an editor that could support all of the standard HTML tags correctly and consistently in a WYSIWYG mode. I haven't seen one yet.

Internally, however, there's a lot going on. Word is putting your keystrokes on the screen (Figure 5-1), but it's also storing a record of everything you type, deletions and all, internally. That's how it can undo your errors. As long as your PC's memory holds out, Word can save an almost unimaginable number of keypresses and reverse them, if requested. So the representation of your document in Word's memory is not at all the same as the representation you see on your screen.

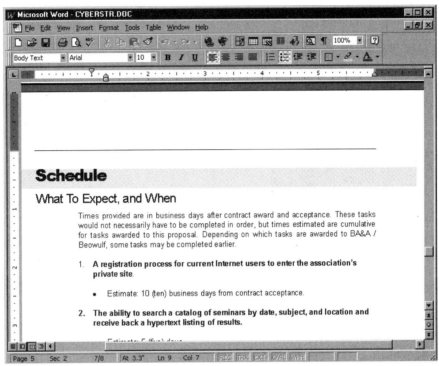

Figure 5-1: A sample Word document.

Similarly, when you save your document to a disk, you have a choice of several different "formats" in which to save it. By default, Word 97 uses a format all its own—one that virtually no other word processing program can read or write, for now. This format is completely dependent on a machine to read it; it makes no sense if you look at it directly (Figure 5-2). This way, Word can save all of your formatting, bullets, and so on in a manner that is convenient to Word for reading later.

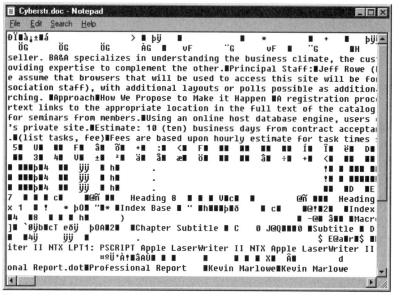

Figure 5-2: The same document's representation on disk.

There are several other formats available to you in Word 97. Various types of plain text are available as options, but saving your document as text invariably loses some of the formatting you applied to it while creating the document: margins, emphasis, bullets, and such niceties will all disappear. This is because, using simple text characters, there's no way to make certain characters bold and no way to define margins. You can save your work in Word 6.0/95 format, which is the "language" an earlier version of Word used, but some of the new features of Word 97 might be lost, and Word warns you of this if you try. For maximum portability among other brands of word processors, you can use the almost-standard Rich Text Format (RTF), which most word processors can read. RTF looks almost like what you typed into your document, with a few formatting "tags" added (Figure 5-3). This way, Word preserves all of the formatting of your document while saving it in a generic format. This is possible only because RTF (in this incarnation) is capable of representing all of the formatting you might apply in Word in its native tongue.

FYI: Rich Text Format

Word 97's RTF isn't the same, standard RTF that other word processors expect. "Enhancements" made in this latest version of Word make its RTF unreadable by most other programs, until they're updated to handle this new format.

Also, when you save a document in Word 6.0/95 format, you're really saving it in RTF, but with a .doc extension. Go figure.

Microsoft has promised fixes to these problems, and they should be available on Microsoft's Web site by the time you read this.

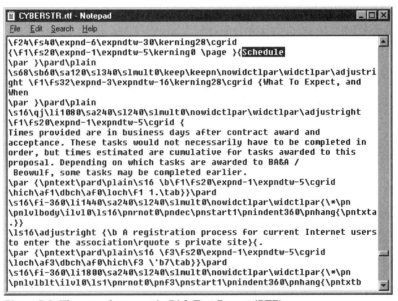

Figure 5-3: The same document in Rich Text Format (RTF).

HTML Mode in Word

The language of the World Wide Web is called *HyperText Markup Language*, or HTML. HTML, like RTF, can be read by mere humans trained to understand it; this makes it relatively easy to write and read (Figure 5-4). On the other hand, this simplicity also means that HTML can't do all of the fancy formatting that a word processor can produce. HTML provides no easy way to precisely place an image on a page; it doesn't understand simple tabs, and there's no way to force a page break.

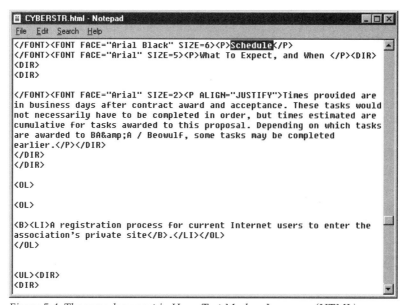

Figure 5-4: The same document in HyperText Markup Language (HTML).

Our Take: HTML Tags

Kevin: You'll notice that HTML isn't all that different from regular text; some words or phrases are surrounded by "tags," which are enclosed in triangle brackets, thus: <B>Bold!</B>. The first tag starts a particular format (in this case bold text), and the second one (identical to the first except for the addition of a slash) ends the format. With few exceptions, all HTML formatting is done this way.

You can see that someone who knows the tags could probably write HTML without the help of a special editor. In fact, most experienced HTML authors do just that, using a Web browser to help tweak their code into just the right shape.

Jeff: Yes, I do. No HTML editor works just right for me yet.

These shortcomings are partly by design and partly because the language and its medium are young. In Word 97, you can write a whole document and then try to save it in HTML format; like the "plain text" above, Word warns you that "some of the formatting might be lost." In fact, most of your formatting will probably be lost, especially in a document of significant length or complexity. The limitations of HTML are so great that Microsoft has provided for you a whole different editing environment in which to write HTML.

New Office 97 Features for Web-Authoring

Word 97 includes a capable HTML version 3.0 authoring environment. This environment, which we'll call *HTML Mode*, is entered when you either:

- tell Word you want to create a new HTML document or
- open a file with the suffix .htm or.html.

Word has most of the bells and whistles of the standard Word environment, including all of the Word formatting options that are also supported in HTML. Using HTML Mode, you can quickly create a simple document in Web-friendly HTML and send it to your Web site.

In HTML Mode, you can't apply any formatting to your document that Word can't save in HTML. Tabs have no effect, and there's no hard page break. Your document onscreen looks essentially as it will look in most Web browsers (although Word will be glad to show you exactly how it looks in your favorite browser with the press of a button). Keep this in mind as you construct your Web pages in Word—if it can't be done in HTML, Word won't let you do it while editing.

FYI: File Extensions

Kevin: By convention, most PC-developed Web pages end in the suffix .htm. UNIX-developed Web pages end in .html. As we'll see in the chapter on Access, Office sometimes uses .htm and sometimes .html just to keep things interesting.

Mac-developed Web pages end in .html, but if you point out that the convention began on UNIX, they'll insist they only do it because it's the best way anyway.

Microsoft has also added the following Web-friendly features to Word 97:

- **e-mail links**—If you type something that looks like an e-mail address (a string of text in the format <something>@<somewhere>.<xxx>), Word assumes it's an e-mail address and automatically creates a live connection (a hyperlink) between the words you typed and the Web. If the document you typed the e-mail address into is saved to the Web (or to a corporate intranet or even a plain old document file), anybody clicking on that e-mail address will be able to send a message to the person answering to that address. The same holds for Uniform Resource Locators (URLs), which identify the unique address of any page on the World Wide Web (like http://www.megacorp.com). Type one into your document, and anybody clicking on it finds themselves viewing that page in their favorite Web browser.

- **a wizard**—The Web Page Wizard works in much the same way as other Office wizards, ushering you along a path toward a final product (a Web page, in this case) that is about 90 percent useful and needs some painstaking adjustments to be really ready for prime time.

- **lots of kEwL stuff**—(that's Web-speak for "really interesting") Multimedia enhancements that are ready to use in your pages: graphical bullets and lines, background sounds and textures, scrolling text ("MICROSOFT—THIS PAGE BROUGHT TO YOU BY MICROSOFT—THIS PAGE"), embedded video clips, and much, much more! Of course, the content-to-bandwidth ratio of these features is really small, but they look very nice.

Entering HTML Mode

There are two ways to enter HTML Mode. The first is to open a document that is saved with the suffix .htm or .html. This tells Word that the document is probably written in HTML, and it responds appropriately. The second way is to start a new document based on the HTML document template. To do this, select File | New from the menu bar. One of the tabs in the resulting dialog box is labeled Web Pages; click on it. You should have three templates to choose from: a Blank Web Page, More Cool Stuff, and the Web Page Wizard. All will take Word into HTML Mode.

HTML Mode looks about the same as standard Word editing mode, except that there are changes to the menus and a new toolbar is available. These menu changes are summarized in Table 3-1 (commands or menus not listed are common to both modes):

Menu	Command	Standard Mode	HTML Mode
File	Save as Word Document		✔
	Save As HTML	✔	
	Web Page Preview		✔
	Versions	✔	
Edit	Object	✔	
View	Form Design Mode		✔
	Master Document	✔	
	Header and Footer	✔	
	Footnotes	✔	
	Comments	✔	
	HTML Source		✔
Insert	Break	✔	
	Page Numbers	✔	
	Field	✔	
	Comment	✔	
	Footnote	✔	
	Caption	✔	
	Cross-reference	✔	
	Index and Tables	✔	
	Horizontal Line		✔
	Text Box	✔	
	Video		✔
	Background Sound		✔
	Forms		✔
	Scrolling Text		✔
Format	Paragraph	✔	
	Text Colors		✔
	Borders and Shading	✔	
	Columns	✔	
	Tabs	✔	
	Drop Cap	✔	
	Text Direction	✔	
	AutoFormat	✔	
	Style Gallery	✔	
	Object	✔	

Menu	Command	Standard Mode	HTML Mode
Tools	AutoUpdate		✔
	Track Changes	✔	
	Merge Documents	✔	
	Protect Document	✔	
	Mail Merge	✔	
	Envelopes and Labels	✔	
	Letter Wizard	✔	
Table	Table Properties		✔
	Cell Properties		✔
	Borders		✔
	Table AutoFormat	✔	
	Cell Height and Width	✔	
	Headings	✔	
	Formula	✔	

Table 5-1: Word menubar options compared in Standard and HTML Mode.

For the most part, the Word menu is a superset of the HTML one. The HTML menus lack some of the formatting available in Word mode, such as text direction, revision tracking, and markups pertaining to printing or paragraph formatting, since these attributes are irrelevant online. In only a few cases does HTML Mode provide features not found otherwise in Word, such as background sound and embedded video; most of these features are actually available in submenus in Word mode.

So you can safely assume that, if you have a decent grasp of Word's standard menu selections, you should be able to find what you're looking for in the HTML mode menus. If you can't find it, it's probably not there.

Designing the Basic Web Page

To demonstrate the use of Word's HTML editing features, we're going to create a few sample Web pages. They'll be included in the grand example at the end of the book, and you're welcome to follow along in your copy of Word or to use and modify them as you please. Keep in mind that while Word can create competent Web pages, these pages aren't going to win any awards for graphic design. However, they'll get your point across, and nobody will laugh at them.

If you're new to page design and layout, refer frequently to those screen prints you took of pages you like. If you like them, somebody else will, too. Look at the things that make them interesting—the layout of objects on the page, the color scheme, the relationship between text and white space. Don't get too wrapped up in appearances at this point—we'll get to that later. Remember, content is key. But, just the same, have a picture in your mind of what you eventually hope to create.

The Site Sketch

Because you can't read my mind, I'll include here a rough sketch of the page we're going to create using the simple tools provided in Word. As the chapter progresses, we'll augment and modify this page slightly, but we'll keep coming back to this sketch (Figure 5-5), generated on the back of a cocktail napkin after work.

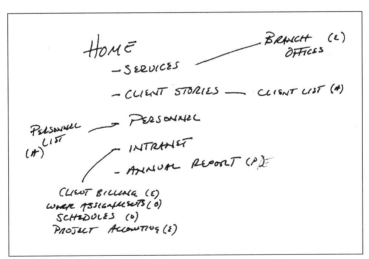

Figure 5-5: The MGL site sketch.

Laying Out the Web Page in Word

The pages we create need to have a consistent look. Sure, we can mix different type styles and make things flash and blink, but we're worried about our corporate image here. We need a page that projects the strength of our company, provides some level of functionality, and gets done in five days. After some brainstorming, Figure 5-6 is the "home page" for the site that we're envisioning.

Figure 5-6: The MGL home page sketch.

Looks like we're ready to go. First, we'll create the page in Word. Most of what we want to do is available in Word's native document format and this book assumes that you're comfortable working in Word already. Figure 5-7 is what our first cut at the MGL home page might look like as a Word document.

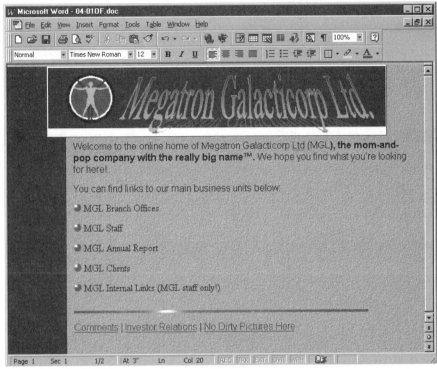

Figure 5-7: The MGL home page layout in Word.

You'll notice that it includes faces from two type families (Arial and Times Roman), some boldfacing and bulleted text, a graphic logo (created in Word), a graphic margin, and a page background. It took about five minutes to create.

That snappy logo is pretty easy to draw, using the Drawing toolbar in Word. In actuality, your company probably already has a logo, and it might even be in electronic format for you to use, so it doesn't seem like we should go into the details of playing with the graphic tools here. The next chapter shows how to use PowerPoint's native tools (which are very similar to Word's) to create a similar logo. That's appropriate, because PowerPoint is about glitz and flash, and we're just trying to get content on the page in Word.

Not a bad start, but it lacks flash, and it's pretty non-functional. After all, each of the references to the other pages in our Web site don't actually *do* anything yet, and the page is sitting here on our PC, where nobody can see it but us. Now for the fun part—converting the Word document we just created into HTML for the world to see.

Converting Word Layouts to HTML

To convert the page to HTML, simply select File | Save As HTML from the menu. Word will convert the page and reopen it in HTML mode. Once you've converted it, we'll go over the conversions Word made and make some changes and additions of our own.

Caution

If you created your logo (or any other graphics on the page) in Word (using WordArt or the drawing tools), you might want to save a backup copy of your page in .doc format. While the Word HTML Help file (wordhtm8.hlp) says that drawing objects converted from .doc to .htm *should* be automatically saved as graphic files, we have not been able to reproduce that functionality consistently and have to conclude that it is not a perfect implementation. *Save your work before converting it to HTML.*

Word converts your page to HTML, and the result is Figure 5-8.

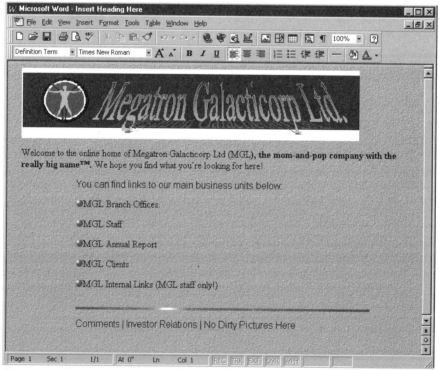

Figure 5-8: The MGL Word layout converted to HTML (browser view).

What you're seeing isn't really HTML, any more than what you see when editing in native Word mode is what is saved on the disk. Word is acting like a Web browser here, interpreting the ugly HTML code it just created and showing you what it might look like online.

Word should convert your graphics to GIF images (you'll see them on your disk in the current directory as Image1.gif, Image2.gif, and so on) and place them in about the right place on the Web page.

Hey! Where did the graphics go? The page looks about the same as it did before, with the noticeable absence of the drawn rectangle in the left margin. It's gone because sometimes Word doesn't save drawing objects that aren't saved elsewhere in a file. Sometimes it works; sometimes it doesn't. Thus the warning above to save a backup copy. We'll put them back in a minute. There's a demonstration of this bug on the enclosed CD as *disappearing graphics.avi.*

We created the MGL logo used here entirely in Word, using WordArt. Unfortunately, unlike a dedicated graphics program, there's no way to manually save a graphic (except for a Chart; see below) as a standalone graphic file in Word. This makes working around the disappearing graphics problem quite painful. For example, to save the MGL logo as a graphic, we had to take a picture of the page and put it on the Windows clipboard (using the Print Screen button), open Windows Paint and paste it into a blank page, crop it, and save it as a bitmap. Whew!

In Word's default document template, called NORMAL.DOT, some default styles for document text are made available to you. They include Normal, Default Paragraph Font, and a few more. Where Word changes to HTML Mode, a new global document template, HTML.DOT, is loaded. This template includes formatting tags for most of the standard features of HTML, freeing you from the drudgery of entering all of these tags manually. By selecting a region of text in the MGL home page, you can see in the Formatting toolbar (Figure 5-9) what kind of HTML formatting Word has applied to your document.

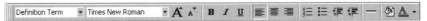

Figure 5-9: The HTML Mode Formatting toolbar.

Note that the styles available to you in HTML.DOT, while extensive, don't even come close to exploiting all of the features of HTML. They're just the features that Word is prepared to support and display for you.

FYI: If Word Can't Do the HTML Conversion...

For HTML tags that Word doesn't include in the default template, you can use the "HTML Markup" style to insert raw HTML tags directly into your document. Word won't show you how they'll look online, but at least you can use them if you know what you're doing. For more information about inserting HTML code into Word, see "Tweaking," below.

Text Formatting

HTML provides some standard ways of selecting text style and size. Text with no formatting tags is called Normal. As you can see from the toolbar, there are a few things we can do with Normal text with little effort:

- **Boldfacing**
- *Italicizing*
- <u>Underlining</u>
- or any combination of these three.

HTML supports six different type sizes and any number of text colors. These can all be adjusted from the Word toolbar. There are several additional type styles that HTML supports. See Appendix B for a comprehensive listing of HTML tags.

Serif & Sans-serif Text

You'll notice that Word has made all of the text in our document Normal, but has used different fonts for the serif and sans-serif text. In addition to adding to the clutter of the page, there's no good reason for us to use two different typefaces, and some Web browsers won't recognize the difference between the two anyway. So let's make all of the text in our document Normal for now.

What Is....

serif: Literally, *hat.* A serif typeface is one with horizontal lines at the top and bottom of most characters, like Times Roman or Courier.

sans-serif: Literally, *without hat.* Sans-serif typefaces include Arial and Helvetica.

attributes: Characteristics of individual letters (font, bold, italic) as opposed to the shape of blocks of text (paragraph formatting).

To change the style of the text in the document to Normal:

1. Select all of the text on the page with the mouse or keyboard.

2. Click on the Styles pulldown menu and select the Normal style from the drop-down list.

Almost there. Now select just the line that used to be three hyperlinks (at the bottom of the page) and apply the Normal style to them again. Now everything is the same typeface, but we've lost some formatting as well, as you can see in Figure 5-10.

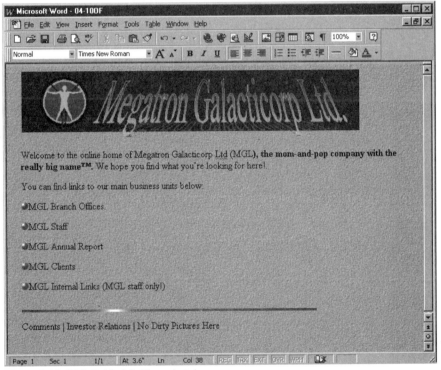

Figure 5-10: HTML Mode's Normal style.

FYI: Undoing Each Attribute

You had to apply the Normal style twice because the hyperlinked text contained two formats: one was the hyperlink, and the other was the font. Each time you applied the Normal style, you removed one layer of fancy formatting.

Text Alignment & Headings

Word incorporates text alignment and headings into its default toolbar and the HTML style. Typically, HTML pages use heading styles to emphasize text that begins a section or paragraph; it would be just as effective to specify a font and size for the heading text, but these styles predate browsers that could directly modify text characteristics. Likewise, text might have a Center style applied to it to center it horizontally on the page.

In general, the largest text on a page is of style "Heading 1," denoted as <H1> in arcane HTML and displayed as a large, bold line of text in the browser's default typeface. The HTML specification defines six levels of headings, more than you should ever need. Using headings is preferable to using detailed font commands because they produce more consistent results on different browsers and they require fewer bytes to transmit.

For our example, use the Center button on the Word toolbar after selecting the related links at the bottom of the page to center them horizontally. We don't have any headings in this example, but you can apply a heading style to any text in the same way that you'd normally apply a style.

Lists

HTML includes support for six types of lists. Of these, Word includes direct support for four:

- Bulleted lists
- Numbered lists
- Definition lists
- Unordered lists

The first three of these are available from the toolbar as styles. The fourth, unordered lists, are implemented as indentations in Word. Since the unordered list element in HTML has the effect of indenting the text included in it with no indication (a bullet, number, and so on) that each line of text is a list element, it can be used to provide paragraph indenting that is not otherwise available in HTML.

This use of indented lists is not well known, but it gives you quite a bit of flexibility in the placement of text. This is one case where Word makes it easy to take advantage of an otherwise obscure feature of HTML.

The uses of bulleted and numbered lists should be obvious. Word provides some control over the format of the bullets and numbers through the Format menu selection; once you have applied the bulleted list or numbered list format to a block of text, you can change the bullet or number style with the Bullets and Numbering submenu. HTML supports the six numbering styles that Word provides and three bullet styles: disc, circle, and square.

FYI: Bullets

Word chooses to implement only the default disc type of bullet. All the other types are implemented as graphical bullets (see below). You could always use the HTML Markup style, or edit in raw HTML, to change the bullet style if you didn't want a disc and didn't want to include images.

Let's change the style of the bullets we've used in our text. Select the lines that we want to change; then use the Bullets selection on the toolbar, or select Format | Bullets and Numbering from the menu. Figure 5-11 shows the result.

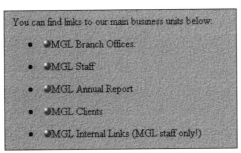

Figure 5-11: Applying the Bulleted List style to the text.

Whoa! Why did the application of the Bullet style add more bullets, rather than change the existing bullets? It's because Word converted the bullets in our original Word document to images when we converted the document to HTML. This is unfortunate. We can delete the spherical bullets manually and keep going. If you don't want to do this yourself, you can see it from the safety of your own desktop by viewing *bullets.avi* on the enclosed CD.

However, we might consider using another graphical bullet rather than the boring disc Word uses by default. Word makes this easy by including support for graphical bullets. To browse the selection of bullets that comes with Word, select the bulleted list you just created and right-click somewhere in the selection. Choose the Bullets and Numbering menu option and click on the Bullets tab. The selection in Figure 5-12 will appear, and it's just the beginning.

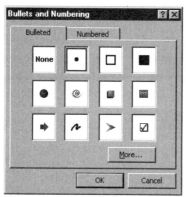

Figure 5-12: The Bullets tab of the Bullets and Numbering dialog.

But wait—there's more. Clicking on the More button at the bottom brings up a standard file selection dialog, loaded with several image files that can be applied as bullets to your list. You can select one and it will replace the boring disc bullets on your page with snazzy graphical bullets. You can even add your own graphics to this list; they're just image files stored in C:\Program Files\Microsoft Office\Clipart\Bullets (if you've installed Office in the typical fashion). You can even replace different lines of text in your list with different bullets by selecting them and replacing the standard bullets one at a time. Note that selecting a bullet graphic other than the standard will make it your default bullet for the rest of this Word session.

Our Take: Will the Real Bullets Please Stand Up?

Kevin: All's not well in Oz, however. Astute Word users will note that, after the bullet replacement is made, you can now select the *bullets themselves* as well as the text. Furthermore, if you re-select the list and try to change the bullets, Word just adds more bullets! There's more: notice that the Bullets button on the toolbar is no longer depressed, and see what happens if you select Undo after applying graphical bullets. (They're deleted one line at a time, and your bulleted list is just a bunch of lines with no bullets at all.)

What's going on here? In its desire to help you make graphically interesting HTML pages, Microsoft has implemented the graphical bullets feature as if it's native HTML, which it's not. When you apply any bullet style to your list except the boring, default one, Word removes the bullet formatting and inserts a reference to the file containing the bullet you select into your document. We'll talk more about embedded images in the next section, but this has the effect of removing the list character of your list and making it plain text with images at the beginning of each line. This isn't necessarily a bad thing, but you might want to be aware of it.

Jeff: When is this kind of thing just the implementation of a good idea, and when is it an attempt to corral you into using Microsoft's browser? The answer is: It depends on how paranoid you are. Sometimes programmers just like to do neat things because they think it's a good idea.

This doesn't look bad. Let's add some more and see if we can approach overkill.

Images

A Web page without eye-catching graphics is like *USA Today* without color. The information's probably all there, but it's no fun to look at. Indeed, if the early versions of the Mosaic browser had not supported embedded images, the Web would probably not be what it is today.

In fact, the ease with which images can be copied from pages and inserted into other pages has resulted in a copyright quandary of epic proportions. If you put a copyrighted image on your page, and I copy it into mine without attributing the source or getting permission, am I violating your copyright?

Probably, but let's say I do it anyway. It's a pretty neat graphic, so somebody else copies it to their page, and so on. Eventually, it makes it to a CD-ROM of clip art that somebody makes money from. Clearly, there's a violation at this point, but the poor soul putting together the CD might or might not have known where the image originally came from.

The point is that you shouldn't use any images that you can't trace the source of. Sure, you might not be breaking the law for whatever reason, but why help propagate the problem? If you buy clip art from a reputable vendor, that's probably fine. If someone represents to you that the images on their page are free for the copying and that they don't know of any copyright problems with them, you're probably OK. But artists need to make a living, too.

I'll step off of my soapbox. You can find several clip art archives (with copyright information included) on the Web, or you can find collections for a few dollars at most computer stores. For this example, we can design the graphics ourselves. We want to replace that vertical rectangle that we made in Word that disappeared when we converted the document to HTML. Unfortunately, placing it as we did in the original, along the left margin, is not easy in HTML. You see, HTML doesn't provide any facility for precise placement of objects, at least not in HTML version 3.0 and earlier. So we're going to use a little sleight-of-hand to place a graphic all along the left side of the page.

FYI: Precise Placement of Graphics

HTML version 3.2, just adopted, does permit the precise placement of graphics, but it's not yet supported by most browsers, and Word doesn't give you any direct facilities to use its new features.

Inserting Images

Before we start playing with our page, you should know that inserting graphics into your Web pages in Word's HTML mode is just like inserting graphics into Word's normal mode. Select Insert | Picture from the menu. Word gives you several choices of where the Picture will come from:

Clip Art Office 97 comes with hundreds of royalty-free (that means you can use them with impunity) images for you to include on your pages. Selecting this option brings up a selection dialog that gives you previews of available images, from which you can select one. You can even search the collection by keyword.

Only a few of all of the images available are copied to your hard disk when you install Office. For the biggest selection of clip art, have your Office 97 CD in your CD-ROM drive when you select this menu option and Word will include it in its search for clipart.

In an excellent implementation of Web-enabling, the clip-art browsing screen includes an icon that looks like the logo for Microsoft Internet Explorer. Click it and you'll connect to a Microsoft Web site (http://www.microsoft.com/clipgallerylive/) with even more clip art for your use, which will be added to your local clip art directory if you so desire.

Some of the clip art included in the Microsoft Clip Gallery is not really "clip art." It includes sound and video files that you can embed into your pages. Note that not all browsers support the playback of embedded audio and video, and these files tend to be large and increase the transmission time of your page significantly.

If you have another CD (or diskette) that contains clip art you use frequently and wish to copy to your copy of the Clip Gallery, you can select the Import Clips button to select the art you use from another directory or disk. You will then be prompted to specify keywords describing the clip (for searching) and what category(ies) it belongs in.

From File   This selection starts a standard Office file selection dialog, from which you can retrieve a graphic from anywhere on your LAN, including your own disk drives or CDs.

Browse Web Art Page   This option starts your default Web browser and takes you directly to the Microsoft Clip Gallery Live (described above), where you can select more images.

Chart   Selecting this starts Microsoft Chart, which is included with Office and allows you to make pretty sophisticated graphs and organizational charts. The chart you design is saved as a GIF image when you exit Chart, which is embedded into your document.

Our Take: Save As .GIF?

Kevin: This feature is especially bothersome, because if you create a chart in any other mode, there's no way to save it as a graphic. It's as if there's a hidden Save As GIF function in Microsoft Chart that's not available to users. The positive spin on this is that you can use Word to create snapshots of graphs for use in other applications. Start a new HTML document in Word, create your chart, save the HTML document, and delete the HTML document from your disk. The chart will remain as a GIF file in the same directory as the HTML page, called Image*X*.gif (where *X* is a number).

Jeff: What a fun way to create a GIF. I hope Word works better with the Web when Office 2000 comes out.

That's all there is to inserting simple images into your documents. They will display on the page exactly where you insert them; if your cursor is in the middle of a sentence, that's where the picture will appear. Be careful about cursor position when inserting graphics. Where they appear might not be where you want them, but you can get close if you know where you are when you click on Insert.

FYI: Disappearing Graphics

Kevin: If you're one of the unlucky souls whose images were lost upon saving your document to HTML, this section is for you. Because we were prescient and saved our logo in a .doc file before we converted our page to HTML, we haven't lost anything yet. You might be tempted to copy your Word-created graphic out of its original .doc file and just paste it into the Web page you're working on. If you do, it will seem to work, and then your graphic will disappear without a trace when you try to save the page. You have to change your Word-drawn graphic into an image file in order for it to be saved with your Web page.

You can use any number of utilities to save your graphic, but the easiest way to do it is this:

1. Display the graphic, enlarged to a size that will fit comfortably on a Web page, in Word.

2. Press Print Screen to copy your entire desktop to the Windows Clipboard.

3. Open a graphics editor, like Windows Paint or Paint Shop Pro (on the Companion CD-ROM).

4. Paste the screen shot into the editor by selecting Edit, then Paste from the menubar.

5. Crop the graphic using the editor's tools until only the logo remains. You might have to cut and paste it again within the drawing application.

6. Save the graphic as a GIF or JPG image.

To insert an image from a file into a Web page, select Insert | Picture | From File and select the file to paste it into your Web page.

What Is...

bitmap: A graphic image that is saved as individual points of color and brightness (pixels). Bitmaps tend to take up a lot of disk space and don't scale very well. Photographs are examples of bitmaps. Web browsers typically only read bitmapped graphic files.

vector: The opposite of bitmapped is vector, where a picture is drawn using colors and lines. Vector graphic files tend to be smaller because only the endpoints of the lines need to be stored on disk. Theoretically, any image can be either a vector or a bitmap, but can you imagine a photograph stored as lines? Some applications, like most clip art, are better suited to vectors and are typically distributed that way.

Image Width

We have the graphic logo at the top of the page, where we had it in the first place. If it's not there and you're following along at home, insert it from a file, move the text down by adding carriage returns before the first line, and move the graphic to the top of the page. You might wish to resize it if necessary once it's in place. Don't try to extend it to the full width of the page, because Word is pretending it's a Web browser and there is no right margin to a Web page.

FYI: Web Page Width

One technique that works well, if you're really concerned about the way your pages will look as people resize their browsers, is to include a graphic image that's the same width as you want people to set their browsers. Something like a double-headed arrow with the text "resize your browser to this width" will get people to view the page the way you intended for it to be viewed.

Inserting the vertical bar along the left margin is harder, since HTML doesn't have any concept of wrapping text around an object. If Word saved it for you upon conversion, it probably doesn't look like you want it to; if not, nothing is lost, since we don't like the way it usually converts anyway. If the dark vertical bar has been inserted in your page as a graphic, delete it by selecting it and pressing the Delete key on your keyboard.

We'll fix the dark vertical bar on the left margin in a few pages. However, consider the way the left-justified black text is going to end up on top of the dark margin bar—that's unacceptable. To fix the text-on-bar problem, select the text and indent it until it's clear of the bar. Alternately, you could make the bar narrower, but it's wide for graphic effect.

Transparency

The logo looks pretty good, but you might see a small, white horizontal line under it where it overlaps the background. That logo was created on a white background, and Word assumes the white background is part of the image. So where it overlaps the background, Word includes the white area. Ideally, that white area should be transparent, so we can see the background beneath it. Figure 5-13 shows the difference between a transparent background and an opaque one.

Figure 5-13: A transparent image allows the background to show.

If Word saved your graphics for you as GIF images, you might not see the white bar. That's OK; you should still know how to fix the transparency problem should it arise.

Largely in response to the demands of the Web, the GIF image format has evolved a couple of new features. One is animation, which is a topic for a different book. Another is transparency, which is the solution to our problem. If you're having a transparency problem because you inserted a graphic from a file on disk, open the image in a good image editor like Paint Shop Pro and re-save it as a GIF with a transparent background (that option is usually specified during the save process).

That's all you need to know to get going in the world of image placement in Web pages. There are a lot more things you can do, and we'll talk about a couple of them below. But first, let's mention some of the more common HTML elements you might wish to use in your pages.

Horizontal Lines

Horizontal lines are a mainstay of most Web pages; they break up long passages of text and add emphasis to regions that need to be set off from the rest of the document.

The only options available in HTML to affect the formatting of a horizontal line set are width and thickness. Word, however, provides a slew of graphical lines that you can choose from; these are inserted as graphics, not true lines, but there's no visible difference to your viewers.

In our example, a horizontal line above the related links at the bottom of the page would set them apart from the main text for emphasis.

Adding Backgrounds

Web page backgrounds come in three flavors: nonexistent, solid colored, and bitmapped. To make the background of your page the default color defined by the viewer's browser, do nothing. The default color on most browsers out of the box is a light gray. You shouldn't depend on that, since users can and do change their default background color. But if it doesn't matter, sticking with the default background color minimizes the amount of time it takes for a page to load and minimizes the impact on the memory resources of the viewing machine.

Solid Color

If the background color matters to you (for graphic effect, or because you use some images that depend on a certain background color), go ahead and set it. Making the background a solid color doesn't increase downloading time significantly, and it can lend your page a certain cachet. Then again, it might just make the page unreadable without a lot of tinkering.

To use a solid color background, simply select Format | Background, and select a color from the palette shown. Depending on how your local Windows machine is configured, you might see from 16 to about 40 colors on the first dialog available. If those aren't enough, click on the More Colors tab and select a color from the entire palette of colors available to you. If this still isn't enough, select the Custom tab on the More Colors dialog, and you can design your own personal color from all of the colors Windows can put together. Unless you need a very specific background color, this is not a great idea; most users will have their computers configured to view 16 or 256 colors, and their machine will make its best guess as to what color to use if you get too fancy. One of the colors on the first screen (16 or 40 colors) is your best bet.

Our Take: Web Activism

Kevin: For a while after the passage of the "Telecommunications Decency Act" by the U.S. Congress in 1996, many sites changed their background color to black. The law placed restrictions on what could and could not be placed on Web sites and made ISPs responsible for the legality of the content placed on their sites; the backlash among the Web community was swift, albeit ineffective. It was pretty striking at the time to surf the Web and see black page after black page.

Jeff: I was annoyed at this display of solidarity because I thought it was just children rebelling against Mom and Dad. Then I realized I was looking at Web pages from all over the planet and the creators had a common purpose, had adopted a common way of expressing it, and had implemented the method, all in just a few days. No government on Earth could match that feat.

Background Images

You can create some really spectacular effects by using background images. Background images can change the whole feel of a site and make the design memorable in its own right, regardless of the content. Some sites use a background of floating clouds to suggest peacefulness or removal from the cares of the everyday world; others use vivid colors and images to evoke excitement or a sense of urgency. Some backgrounds are more practical, such as muted company logos or ruled pages that look like a notebook.

Whatever background image you choose, if you choose one, remember to keep it small so as not to bog down the remote machine's data connection, and to keep your page legible. A photo of the most beautiful Irish glen might look nice on your Windows desktop, where the icons are opaque and applications hide it when they run, but it's pretty busy for a Web page with text superimposed.

We used a background in the MGL home page example above to get the "marbled" effect that implies corporate strength. It's one of the several background images that come with Office 97 and are available for your use.

To insert a background image from the selections that come with Word, follow the same steps as for a solid color, above. Instead of selecting a color from the palette, select the Fill Effects button. You'll be given a small selection of backgrounds to choose from. Not enough choices? Click on Other Textures and you'll be presented with a file selection dialog. If you have your Office CD in your CD drive, you'll find several more textures than you can shake a stick at under \Clipart\Backgrnd, and the other Clipart subdirectories contain photos that might or might not be useful, depending on your requirements.

Remember the background we placed on the page when we were still in Word mode? That's just a graphic image, stored on your local disk as a GIF file. Take a look at it in Figure 5-14.

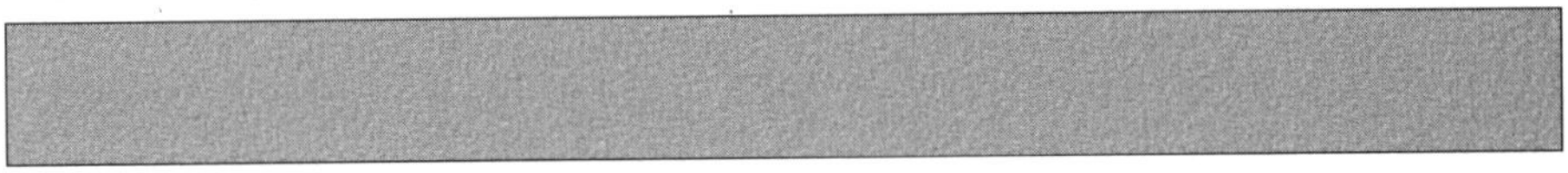

Figure 5-14: A background image.

What Is...

JPG: A graphics file format, like BMP, GIF, and TIF. All of these are just abbreviations for the name of the method that's used to store the image on the disk. Some make smaller files, some make more accurate reproductions. Web browsers generally recognize images of formats GIF and JPG. JPGs are often smaller (and they transmit faster by extension), but they might lose resolution depending on how they were saved. **GIF**: A graphics file format, like BMP, JPG, and TIF. GIFs are exact copies of the original, and they can be very large.

This image looked a lot bigger when it filled the entire background of our page! In fact, if you look closely, you'll see that the image is *tiled*—that is, it's copied over and over next to itself—so it fills the entire page. Skilled artists can create these backgrounds with patterns that connect perfectly to themselves on all four sides, and the Web browser tiles the image by default.

To add our vertical bar to the left side of the page, we're going to modify the image slightly. Note that this isn't really inserting an image into the page, as discussed above; rather, we're going to modify the background property of the page by changing the background image.

In a nutshell, here's what we're going to do:

1. Open the image in your favorite image editor (Paint Shop Pro from the Companion CD-ROM is a good choice).

2. Put our blue bar on the left side of the resulting image.

3. The changed image will look something like Figure 5-15.

Figure 5-15: A modified background image.

4. Now save it, using the same name as before. Reload your Web page and you should see something like Figure 5-16.

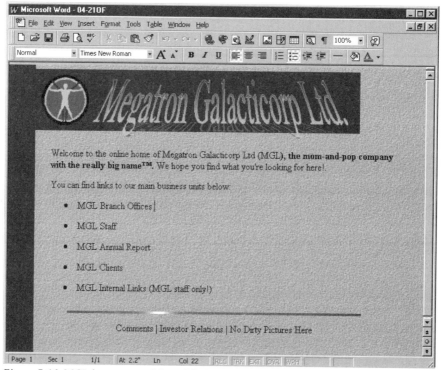

Figure 5-16: MGL home page with modified background.

Voila! It's back! Notice that the browser doesn't try to plaster the new, wide image all over the screen; if you enlarged your browser to an area wider than the image, you would see it start to tile horizontally. When creating this kind of image, try to make it wider than most people will ever make their browsers. About 800 pixels is a good bet.

Our Take: Paint Shop Pro Rules

Kevin: Paint Shop Pro (PSP) excels at making useless images into great backgrounds. PSP (http://www.jasc.com) includes a number of "filters" that, when applied to your images, change them into something still recognizable but indelibly altered. Company logo too loud? Try applying the Emboss filter and it becomes a gray shadow of itself that looks as if it's been pressed into paper. Or reduce it to 16 colors, and then change those colors to pastel reminders of their original selves by editing the palette. It's a good idea to reduce your image's colormap to as few colors as possible before saving it to make it smaller; PSP makes this a snap.

Jeff: Kevin introduced me to PSP, and I now have a good reason for using a PC. Other than playing games, of course.

A good background can add distinction and tone to your page. A bad one can make the page annoying and unreadable. A too conservative background is generally a better choice than a too loud one.

Creating Templates

Once you settle on a background image that you like, why not be consistent and apply it to every page on your site? For that matter, why not apply the overall design (in the case of the MGL home page, the vertical bar and logo at the top) to your other pages? HTML templates in Word work just like other Word templates. When starting a new page, you can select a template file to use as the basis for your new page and thus ensure consistency.

To create an HTML template, you create the template page as you want it to appear. Then do the following:

1. Select File | Save As.

2. In the Save As Type window, select Document Template (*.dot).

3. In the Save In window, navigate through your disk until you reach the location of your HTML templates—usually C:\Program Files\ Microsoft Office\Templates\Web Pages.

4. Choose a name for your template that describes it to you. Remember, a preview of your template will not be available when you're trying to start a new page.

5. Click on the Options button.

6. Two-thirds of the way down, in the Save Word Files As window, select HTML files. Click on OK.

7. Now click on Save to save your template.

   The next time you start a new document (by clicking on the New button on the toolbar or selecting File | New from the menubar), you'll be able to select your template from the Web Pages template group. But you're not done yet.

8. Bring up the Save As dialog again by selecting File | Save As from the menubar.

9. Click on Options.

10. Change the Save Word Files As window to Word Documents (*.doc). Click on OK.

11. Now click on the Cancel button to exit this dialog.

> **Caution**
>
> Saving HTML templates severely restricts your ability to edit the files later. Whenever you save an HTML file in .dot format, be sure also to save a copy as standard HTML.

That seemingly futile procedure just saved you from saving all of your documents from now on as HTML files. You're welcome.

Templates help enforce good page design and can be used to promote continuity and consistency across a site. You could even establish a central site on your LAN for document templates and include a standard template for your company's Web pages.

Creating Hyperlinks

The one feature that makes the Web a web is the ubiquitous hyperlink, which transports the viewer from one page to another. Without hyperlinks, a Web page would be static and paper-like. With hyperlinks, any element of a Web page is potentially a link to another page, possibly on another server, any-where in the world. Hyperlinks can be used to link to related pages outside of your home site, to provide a structured means of navigation through a Web site (through Forward and Backward references, for example), or to provide a means of giving more detail on a given topic without breaking up the flow of the main page.

Bookmarks

A hyperlink can refer to a specific place in a document, or it can just connect to the top of the referenced page. The places in documents to which hyperlinks may attach are called *bookmarks*, and they are inserted in documents by their authors. So while you can create a hyperlink to a page on someone else's site, there is no way to jump directly to the middle of that page unless the original author has provided a bookmark for you to connect to. You will have to settle for the top of the page.

FYI: Anchors & Bookmarks

Most people refer to HTML bookmarks as anchors. Word is in the minority using the bookmark terminology, but we'll use it here for consistency. Note that bookmarks are different from hyperlinks, discussed later. A hyperlink is the stepping-off place that takes you to a bookmark, or anchor.

To create a bookmark in Word, you select the text you wish to anchor to and select Insert | Bookmark from the menu. The Bookmark dialog appears and asks you what to name the bookmark, as shown in Figure 5-17.

Figure 5-17: The Bookmark dialog for creating an anchor.

Choose your bookmark names consistently and carefully. Most documents will have only a few, making later reference to them relatively easy, but a large document can have hundreds. Consider using easily remembered codes for figures and tables (like F- and T-) and not being too skimpy as to the length of the bookmark name.

Once you name a bookmark, you will not see any evidence that you have inserted it. If you wish to see a reminder of where your bookmarks are, select Tools | Options from the menubar and turn the View Bookmarks option on. They will appear as square brackets around the text you marked. Bookmarks can enclose any amount of text, but the point where they begin is all that really matters.

When inserting a hyperlink later, you will be given a list of available bookmarks to link to, if you desire. Word gives you the option of using *hidden* bookmarks. These do not normally appear in the bookmarks list and are used for internal document management, as opposed to external linkages.

Path Names

Whether or not you create any bookmarks in your document, you will almost certainly want to create hyperlinks. A hyperlink refers to a document (whether it's the current document, another on the same site, or somebody else's entirely) in one of three ways:

- by referring to the full path of the file on the local file system (e.g., "c:\documents\deflist.htm")

- by using the relative path to the file from the current document (e.g., "../htdocs/tables/t1-6.htm")

- by using a Uniform Resource Locator (URL) (e.g., http://www.mgl.com/deflist.htm.)

Our Take: Relative & Fully Qualified URLs

A loyal reader writes: "I do not understand the differences between full path and relative path and a complete URL. I have read many explanations of them, including Laura LeMay's, and I still don't see the point."

Kevin: Far be it from us to tread where Laura has already been, but here goes. A fully qualified URL specifies the path to a page from anywhere on the Web. The fully qualified URL to my home page will work in any browser, anywhere in the world. A relative URL requires knowledge of the "base URL" for the document. For example, if I have a dirty picture at " http://www.mysite.com/home/pictures /scandalous.gif" (a fully qualified URL), I could use that URL (as in <IMG SRC="http://www.mysite.com/home/pictures/scandalous.gif" >) anywhere in any page on any server and it would work. But it's a lot of typing, and it makes my index pages difficult to maintain. If I move the whole site to a different server, I have to change all of my references.

➡

On the other hand, if I just use <IMG SRC="scandalous.gif"> (a relative URL) in a page that's already in the /home/pictures directory, the Web server can find the page faster and the page is less cluttered and more portable.

Jeff: If you create your Web pages with fully qualified URLs and then move a document, your pages break. If you use a relative URL, some pages might break and others might not. If you use relative URLs and move an entire directory structure to another machine, you'll have less to fix than if you use absolute URLs. On the other hand, if someone saves one of your Web pages locally for later use, they will not be able to find any of your pages. This can be a good or bad thing, depending on how protective you are of your Web pages.

The first method, a fully qualified path, is almost never used. It allows remote users to know the organization of your disk (which might not be a good idea), and it might specify pages to which external users do not have access due to Web server permission settings. If you used this method and made a mistake, you might not realize you had a problem until you published your pages.

The second method, a relative path, is very commonly used to refer to pages residing on the local server. Since most Web pages are built within a structured directory hierarchy, a page is not likely to move relative to the other pages in the hierarchy even if the whole structure is picked up and moved to another server. This minimizes maintenance, since hard-coding of variables (like the name of the server or hard drive) has been avoided. The main disadvantage of this method is that you can still refer to pages that remote users cannot access, due to server permissions.

The last method is the best for referring to pages that are publicly accessible, or to pages on remote hosts. Specifying a URL for a linked page forces the user of the Web server to retrieve the page, minimizing potential security risks. It doesn't prevent linking to local pages; either the local pages will be located in the Web server's document directories, or the local URL designator "file://" can be used instead of "http://".

The Hyperlink Dialog

Live hyperlinks are generally noted in HTML documents by text in a different color from other text on the page, usually light blue. Hyperlinks that you have visited previously appear in a different color, often dark blue. Any object on an HTML page can be a hyperlink, including images. This facilitates the creation of *buttons*, small graphic images that load a new page when clicked on.

To create a hyperlink in Word, first select the object or area of text that your users will click on to be transported away. In general, you should mark as little text as is reasonable as a hyperlink so your entire document does not appear in screaming light blue. Next, select the Hyperlink button from the toolbar, or select Insert I Hyperlink from the menu. The Insert Hyperlink dialog will appear (Figure 5-18).

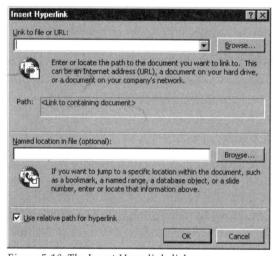

Figure 5-18: The Insert Hyperlink dialog.

If the document is on your local disk, you can use the Browse button to search for it; selecting the Use Relative Path for Hyperlink button at lower left avoids the fully qualified path name problems detailed above. If you know the URL for the page you wish to link to, enter it in the Link to File window. If the link is to an anchor on the current page, you need not enter anything in this window. Whether or not a bookmark is in the current page, you should enter the bookmark name in the Named Location window at the bottom of the dialog. A list of bookmarks in the current page is available.

Tables

One of the seminal advances in the state of HTML authoring was brought to us by the folks at Netscape. Realizing that the inability to accurately line up objects on a page was a real liability from a graphical design point of view, Navigator began to support standard row/column tables embedded in HTML documents. In an early Web example of the tail wagging the dog, the <TABLE> tag was adopted as a standard in HTML version 2.0 soon thereafter.

An HTML table is usually used just as a table is used in a run-of-the-mill document: to line up related data in columns and rows. You can create a standard Word table in Word mode; upon conversion to HTML, it will still look pretty much the same. To create a table while in HTML mode, use the Table menu selection just as you would in Word mode. For all practical purposes, you can do everything you can do with a Word table with an HTML table, either converted or created in native HTML.

But wait—there's more. Advanced HTML authors sometimes use tables as a way to enforce precise placement of objects on the screen. Think of it this way: What if there were a huge, invisible table on your Web page, and you could control what was in every cell? If you assume that HTML tables allow cells to overflow when their content exceeds their capacity (which would be correct), you can see how this table would act as a large grid for placement of images, text, and similar items.

Furthermore, the ability of HTML tables to change width as the browser window is resized gives you the ability to place things where you want them on the screen, and know that their relative proportions will be preserved as your viewers change their browser width. This feature isn't supported in Word by default, but it's easy enough to turn on. This is relatively advanced stuff, however, and it's not at all necessary unless you really want this feature.

Tweaking HTML

The features included in Word 97 for Web support aren't perfect, as you've probably figured out by now if you've been reading. Sometimes they're fine, but sometimes they don't take full advantage of all of the features that HTML provides, or sometimes they take too much advantage (as in the "Scrolling Text" section later). In any case, you're not stuck with what Microsoft gives you right out of the box, because HTML is a friendly language that you can easily modify. It's just a matter of getting the hang of all of those triangle brackets and slashes, kind of like the sounds that you have to make deep in your throat to speak German.

When editing HTML, you always want to have easy access to a comprehensive list of available tags. There's one in the back of this book as Appendix B; copy it and put it in your wallet. The format and length of that guide are a matter of choice, and there are several good style guides available on the Web. If you want to keep up to date with the latest happenings in HTML, one very good, very concise reference is Kevin Werbach's "Bare Bones Guide to HTML," available online at http://werbach.com/barebones/. It lists all tags in current use, including proposed and browser-specific tags of general interest.

When writing or reading HTML, remember the following general rules:

- All tags are enclosed in triangle brackets, like this: <PRE>

- All tags begin with a tag in the form above and end with the same tag preceded by a forward slash, like this:

```
<BLINK>This is annoying, blinking text!</BLINK>
```

- Tags can be nested to any level, and the end of an embedded style should precede the end of the style it's embedded in. Example:

```
<B><I>This text is both bold and italicized!</I></B>
```

There are exceptions to every one of the above rules, but they are generally true. So when trying to understand a block of HTML code, remember to look for the beginning and ending tags for each format, and you will be able to see it on the Web browser in your mind.

Werbach's guide lists almost 200 tags; Word directly supports about 100 of them in various ways. What about the other 100? Some don't have a lot of practical use, such as the rare <CITE> tag (usually italicizes and indents reference work citations), and some are downright arcane (such as the Relationship tag, <A REL="***">, which has no function in most browsers). In some cases, Word inserts the tags for you with no prompting (such as the required <HTML> and <BODY> tags). And some tags are useful, but are simply beyond the reach of the software, such as the incredibly able image map tag (<IMG SRC="URL" ISMAP>) that turns different areas of embedded images into hyperlinks.

What if you have a good handle on HTML and want to insert an unsupported HTML tag into your document? There are two ways to do this without leaving Word:

- Change to the View as HTML mode and edit the tags directly; or

- Insert the new tags using the HTML Markup style.

The first is probably the simplest, but it requires a little comfort with HTML. After you've saved your work, select View | HTML Source. Word reopens your document in all of its ugly HTML glory. You can replace, insert, or edit the tags directly in this mode, and Word will preserve (although it won't necessarily display) your changes. Additionally, most of the standard text editing features of Word, including search and replace, are available in HTML mode.

Caution

You can't view a document template (.dot) file as HTML, nor can you convert one to HTML. If you decide to use HTML document templates, you should also save a normal HTML version of your template in case you need to edit it later.

Using the HTML Markup style isn't a lot harder. Position the cursor at the point in the text where you wish the new tag to appear, and type the tag. Then apply the HTML Markup style (from the style list on the toolbar) to your new entry.

Tweaking Tables

Word doesn't take advantage of the ability of HTML tables to resize themselves to fit the width of the browser. Tables created in Word will run off the right side of the screen if left to their druthers, and that's not very attractive. But a minor change to the <TABLE> tag that defines the table structure can make a table resize itself relative to the width of the current browser window. We'll use method 1, below, to change the properties of the existing table to something Word can't do (but interprets correctly—figure that out). We'll also use method 2 to make some text blink on and off—a standard HTML tag that's not available from within Word.

HTML Markup Example, Method 1

1. Save your work.
2. Change to HTML Source mode by selecting View I HTML Source.
3. Don't panic as the screen fills with HTML code. Look through the document (you can use Word's Search tool) for the word TABLE. It will be in uppercase.
4. The TABLE tag starts with a less-than mark (<) and ends with a greater-than mark (>). Look for the greater-than mark associated with the TABLE tag. It will probably say something like <TABLE CELLSPACING=0 BORDER=0 CELLPADDING=7 WIDTH=638>.

    See the WIDTH property in that tag? That's the absolute width of the table, in pixels. To make it a relative measurement, rather than an absolute one, change it to read WIDTH="90%" (quotes required).
5. Click on the Exit HTML Source button on the toolbar. This will return you to your document, which—surprise—recognizes the change.

HTML Markup Example, Method 2

1. Save your work.

2. Move the cursor to a point in the table where you want to insert blinking text. Maybe it can be a title, in the top leftmost cell.

3. Type a blink specification in HTML. How about: <BLINK>Hey! I'm Talking To You!</BLINK>.

4. Change the style of the text you just typed to HTML Markup by selecting it and then selecting HTML Markup from the Styles pulldown on the toolbar.

5. Don't panic. Word doesn't know what to do with a BLINK tag, so it hides it and it seems to disappear from the page. To make it visible again, turn on hidden text from the Tools menu (Tools | Options | Hidden Text). Your HTML Markup text will appear in day-glo red.

That's all there is to it. Note that you can choose any relative width you like; you can even have tables side by side if you like, all adjusting nicely to the width of the browser window. A group of well-adjusted tables makes a mom's heart happy.

After you make changes, you should view your tags in a real Web browser to verify that they work. Word makes this pretty easy by providing a button on the HTML toolbar that launches your default browser with the current page. It's always a good idea to check your changes often, before you get too far along. Don't forget to reload the browser page after you make and save each change in Word.

Embedding Objects

If you've used Word to create a Web site, and if you use Office products to manage your business, you might feel a little, well, limited by Word's abilities. There's a lot more to business information than simple text, or even the snazzy, formatted text that some of the Web formatting options in Word give you. You've got financials in a spreadsheet, dying to be posted on the company intranet. The presentation that Murray gave to the Brotherhood of Widget Salesmen last month has some good stuff in it and should be where it can be seen. What about the contact information that's in the database?

All of the Office 97 products include some kind of hook to the Internet (and most to the Web). In general, you can use the tools that come with the applications to publish stand-alone pages that contain data extracted from the parent application. In some cases, the data can even be dynamic (updating itself based on query or form actions). We'll discuss the specific Internet-enabling features of each Office application in a separate chapter, but we should give some details on how to include static data from your other Office applications in your Word-generated Web pages while we're talking about Word.

Spreadsheets

Let's say that you have a spreadsheet containing sales figures for a given business unit, and you want to put that on the Web. One way to go about it is to embed the spreadsheet into an already written Word Web page.

There are two ways you can get your Excel data online via Word: as a graphic image or as a mail merge. Let's look first at the image idea.

Spreadsheet Data as Graphics

When you insert a spreadsheet into a Word document by cutting and pasting it you actually use a part of both Word and Excel called the Object Linking & Embedding (OLE) service. The application where the data originates is called the OLE Server, and the destination application is the OLE Client. The actual data that is transferred between the two applications is called an OLE Object. An accomplished Windows programmer can write programs that use the OLE service in both applications to actually update OLE objects while they sit in place in the Client applications; that's how the Link option works when you paste an OLE object into an OLE Client. When you choose Link as you paste the object in, you actually tell the Client application to query the Server application when appropriate and get the new data for the inserted object.

The Client application in Word, which handles any data pasted into Word from other OLE-compliant applications (including, but not limited to, other Office applications), makes the pasted data look just like it looked in the originating program. Thus a spreadsheet pasted into a Word document still looks pretty much like a spreadsheet; see Figure 5-19 for an example.

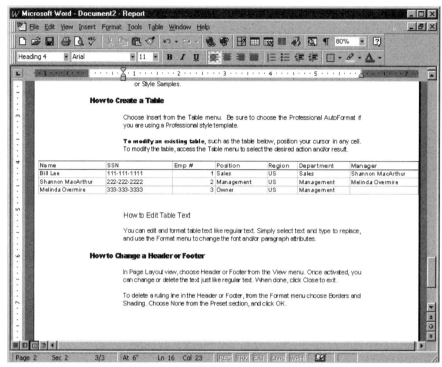

Figure 5-19: A spreadsheet pasted into Word.

If you double-click on the table, an instance of Excel will start, and you can edit the table. If this appearance is exactly what you're looking for, you can make your life easy by taking advantage of it. You can save a representation of the inserted spreadsheet as a static image and paste that image into your Web page. It's not sexy, it doesn't update, but it's really fast. Word will even do it for you; if you insert a spreadsheet into a Word document and save that document as HTML, Word will save the spreadsheet as a graphic (called something like Image12.gif) for you.

You can drag and drop into an HTML page opened in Word just as you can into a blank standard Word document. The resulting graphical table looks just as it did in Word mode.

That's the easy way, and it's useful in 90 percent of all cases, when you can get your data formatted in Excel just right. If you need Word to format your data, or if you want to change it after it enters Word and get Excel out of the picture, you can use the mail merge method.

Spreadsheet Data from Mail Merge

This section is not for the faint of heart. For some reason, the innocent-sounding mail merge feature of every word processor on Earth strikes fear into the hearts of secretaries and Web gods alike. Part of the reason for the confusion probably has to do with the similarity that the mail merge feature has with database design.

As with the design of tables in a database, you have to think of your information in terms of *fields*, or groups of data. For example, if you're working with a spreadsheet (a highly topical example for this section), you might think of the columns of your spreadsheet as collections of fields. If you can envision titles for your columns, then you've grasped the idea of *field names*. A group of columns containing exactly one instance each of all of the fields you've defined is a *record*—you can think of it as a row in your spreadsheet. The spreadsheet that holds your data is called a *data source*, or *primary merge file*. Finally, the Word document you'll create is the *secondary merge file*. Still with me?

The data you create in Excel for use in Word must be in the format of what's called a *list*. In a nutshell, that means that it should be separated from the rest of the data in a workbook by at least one blank row or column, and it should have titles at the top of every column. It's a good idea to boldface or otherwise distinguish these title cells from the data in the rest of the list. Finally, avoid cells with no data in them, like blank rows and rows full of dashes or underlines. In the best-case scenario, there's nothing in the spreadsheet but your data and titles on the columns. A typical list containing employee information might look like Figure 5-20.

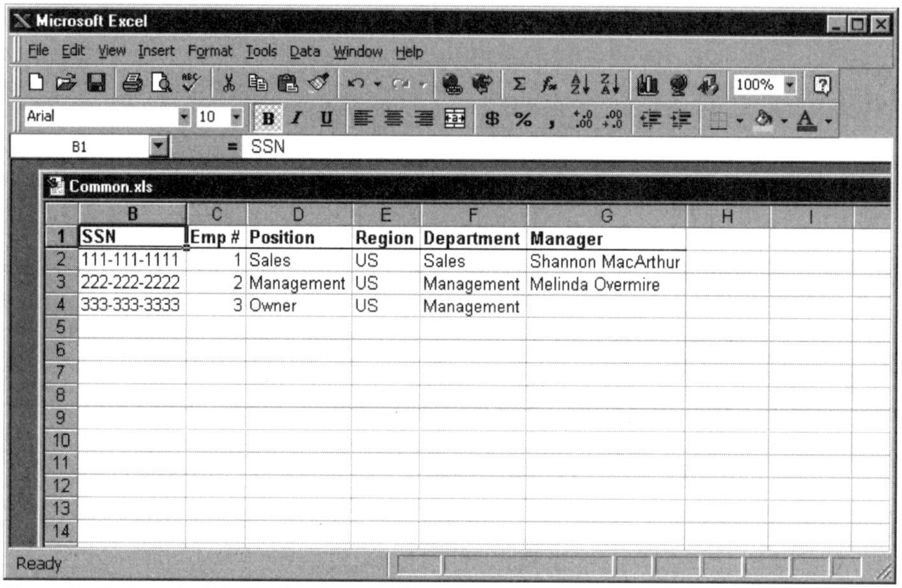

Figure 5-20: A typical list in Excel, ready for merging.

Once your list is in place, save it in a normal Excel file (.xls) and exit Excel. Up to here, the preparation hasn't been much different from the method above for inserting spreadsheets as graphics. Now you're ready to rock.

Imagine that the list above is a spreadsheet that your Personnel Department uses for listing employees, and you want to put some employee information on your Web site. But there's too much information in the spreadsheet to put online—SSNs, for example, and the employee numbers aren't necessary. Personnel won't let you modify the spreadsheet. Okay, I know you could copy it and delete the columns you don't want, but for the sake of this example, let's say that you can't—maybe you don't even have a copy of Excel.

Here's what we're going to do in Word. We'll start a new document and tell Word that the data for our mail merge is coming from the Excel file on the network. Then we'll tell it where to get the data inside the spreadsheet (this is much easier if there are blank lines and columns around the data cells). We'll tell Word which fields we want to use from the Excel file and where to put them on the page. Then we'll tell Word to finish up and get the data. Finally, we'll convert the whole shebang to HTML. A nuisance? Maybe. But as the amount of data increases, the usefulness of this method increases as well. And since HTML pages have no breaks, there's no reason why you can't merge a file that's hundreds of records long into one document.

Word holds your hand pretty well through the mail merge process. Still, it's easy to forget where you were if you think too hard. Open a blank document, or you can even position your cursor at the point where you want the data placed in an existing document. Click on Tools | Mail Merge.

Next, click Create. You'll have several options to choose from, but for Web page authoring, you'll almost always want Catalog. Next, decide if the data will be merged into the current document (most likely) or you want Word to start a new page for you.

Next, select Get Data | Open Data Source. (You'll notice by now that the logical next step becomes available to you as you finish the previous step.) You'll see a normal file selection dialog, which you can traverse to select the Excel file containing the spreadsheet. You'll have an easier time of it if you change the default file type at the bottom of the window from *.doc (Word files) to *.xls (Excel files). When you find it, select Open.

Word will do a quick read of the file you've selected and will ask you where the data list is in the spreadsheet. If it comprises the whole spreadsheet, Word will detect this and offer Entire Spreadsheet as an option. For more complicated spreadsheets, you'll be able to select a range of cells. Choose the appropriate data location and continue. Remember, if you're not sure, don't do it. You can always click Cancel, open Excel again, find your data and make sure it's where you think it is, and get back into Word and finish. In fact, as long as you're still in the same document, Word will even remember which steps of the merge process you've already been through, so you can pick up where you left off.

Since you've not yet set up your Word document to accept any merged data, you're then prompted to Edit Word Document, which means "tell me where to put the stuff I pull out of the spreadsheet." When you click on the only button available to you, you're returned to your document, and all is as it was—except that there's a new toolbar at the top of the screen. (We're almost done—hang in there.) This toolbar is full of arcane and scary symbols; see Figure 5-21.

Mail-Merge Helper

Figure 5-21: The arcane and scary Mail Merge toolbar.

This part is like meeting a strange dog for the first time—if you don't let Word know you're unsure of yourself, it won't know any better. The name of the game here is to insert *merge fields* into your document. These are just placeholders for the data from your spreadsheet, which will be copied into the placeholders you enter in any fashion you like. Here is the real power of mail merge. Want one record (group of fields) per page? You can do it. Want it in a table? No problem. In a different arrangement? Sure. Here's how: Move the cursor to the place in the document where the first merge field (like the employee's name in this example) should go. Click on the toolbar button marked Insert Merge Field. See the button marked Name? That came right off the top row of your spreadsheet, and it told Word where to find all of the names. Click on it, and Word inserts a merge field into your document like **<<Name>>**. When the time comes to tell Word to get the data, it will put exactly one employee name into that placeholder, and it will create identical placeholders for the rest of the names.

Next, do the same thing for the rest of the fields in the Insert Merge Field pull-down list. You might want to leave out data that you don't want to appear in your final document, like SSNs and the like. Put them anywhere on the page. Change their font. Make them purple. Feel the creative power flowing through your fingertips on the keyboard. Whoa—too exciting!

When you've finished putting all of your merge fields on the page, it might look like Figure 5-22.

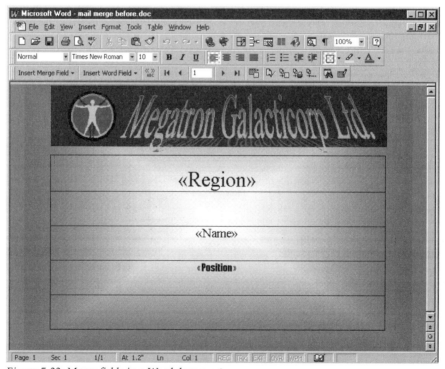

Figure 5-22: Merge fields in a Word document.

Snazzy. Now it's time for the real magic. If you're satisfied with the way the fields are laid out, click on the Mail Merge Helper button on the toolbar (see Figure 5-23). Click on Merge and then Merge again. Voila!

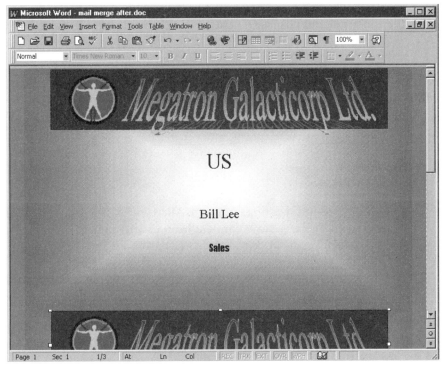

Figure 5-23: Completed merge.

Word either inserts sequential instances of your data, record by record, in the current document or it creates a new one, depending on your choice very early in the process. Once that's done, if you like what you see, you can simply Save as HTML, following all of the caveats earlier in this chapter about doing that, and you'll have your spreadsheet data in a custom Web page.

Presentations

Your options for embedding PowerPoint presentations in your Word pages are pretty few. If you were going to keep your document in Word format, you could embed any PowerPoint presentation directly into any document and view it without ever leaving Word. In much the same way that double-clicking on a spreadsheet embedded in Word starts an instance of Excel to edit it, double-clicking on an embedded slide show starts the show. All of the controls of PowerPoint are available, since you're really running PowerPoint.

Unfortunately, there's not a lot you can do once your Word page becomes HTML. PowerPoint can natively produce some very nice Web pages and entire presentations (see Chapter 6), but embedding a presentation in Word and saving it as HTML saves only the first slide, and it becomes a static picture. You'd have better control over the organization of your pages if you worked from PowerPoint and saved each slide as a GIF file before inserting them into your Word-authored Web pages.

If, for whatever reason, you don't want to work from within PowerPoint, you can use Word to put the title slide of a presentation on a Web page. But that's about it.

Databases

Your options for inserting data from Microsoft Access into a Word document are essentially the same as for data from Excel, but both more and less. Huh? It's like this: You can't drag and drop from Access into Word, as you can in Excel, but the mail merge capabilities are infinitely better.

In Excel, you can grab a spreadsheet by the title bar and drag it, kicking and screaming, into the current Word document. Access isn't as compliant; dragging a table only moves the table to the edge of the visible screen. The other method of OLE object insertion, choosing Edit | Insert Object from the menubar and selecting an Access database, creates a clickable icon in your Word document that can be used to open an instance of Access. You can't see your data in Word this way. You could open an Access table or form and take a screen shot of it; you could then paste the image into your Word document. Really kludgy.

The right way to do this is through mail merge. Unlike Excel spreadsheets, database tables automatically have fields, or column headings. This makes it insanely easy for Word to figure out where the data is in an Access database, unlike a spreadsheet, where the data set could be anywhere on the page. It's nearly impossible to format the data in a database so mail merge won't work. Follow the instructions above for mail merge with an Excel data source, but substitute your Access database everywhere the previous example calls for a spreadsheet file.

If you're a real organization nut, consider pulling your Excel spreadsheet into Access before mail merging it. This sounds like a lot of work, but it ensures that the mail merge will go smoothly. Frankly, if you have spreadsheet data that needs to be mail merged, you're probably using the spreadsheet as a database, and you'll be better off using a real database anyway. Spreadsheets are for performing calculations on groups of data, and they aren't very good at storing data efficiently. Databases are for storing and retrieving data, and you can do some calculations if you need to.

OLE Objects

When you install a "well-behaved" Windows application, the application should inform Windows that it has been installed, where it lives, and what options Windows needs to know to handle it correctly (usually display and printing data, as well as information on how to work with other programs). The place where that information is stored is called the Windows Registry, and this poorly documented and rightfully maligned feature of Windows comprises the long-term memory of your PC's operating system. It's stored in several files, which will remain nameless here, and is not meant to be tinkered with. That said, you can see what's in your Registry by using the Windows REGEDIT program. To run REGEDIT, click on the Start button, then select Run, and finally type **regedit** in the window. Then press OK. What you'll see looks like Figure 5-24.

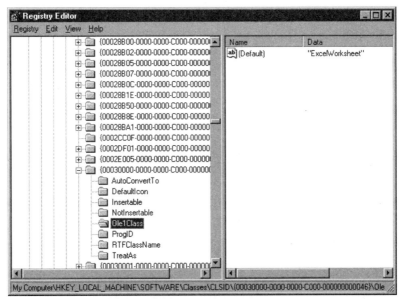

Figure 5-24: The Windows Registry in REGEDIT.

> **Caution**
>
> The entries in your Registry are critical to the performance of your system. Changing them can make your system unusable and maybe impossible to recover. Nothing in this section requires you to change any settings in the Registry, and you won't miss much if you don't try this at home.
>
> That said, if you do start REGEDIT, consider making a backup of your Registry files before you explore further. To make a backup, select Registry, then Export Registry File and save it on a floppy disk in case the worst happens.

REGEDIT works very much like Windows Explorer; categories are listed in the left pane as folders, and the details are shown on the right for viewing and editing. Applications you install usually save information about themselves in the folder called HKEY_LOCAL_MACHINE, in a subfolder called SOFT-WARE. Information about the types of files that each application considers itself competent to handle are in a subdirectory of SOFTWARE called Classes. The figure above shows the OLE entry for Microsoft Excel; this tells Windows that any file with the extension .xls is an Excel file, and Excel files are included in the OLE category called Microsoft Excel Worksheet.

Now, back to reality. If you exit REGEDIT (hope you didn't change anything) and return to Word, you can select Insert | Object from the menubar. The list of file types you'll see in the Object Type window (Figure 5-25) is extracted from the Registry. Whenever you install a new application that is OLE capable, Windows notes this in the Registry, and Word detects this when you start it. This permits you to exchange objects between the two applications more or less at will.

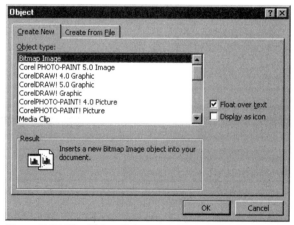

Figure 5-25: The Object dialog.

In the figure above, you'll note several objects that are native to CorelDraw and Corel PhotoPaint, which are installed on the machine from which the picture was taken. Selecting one of these objects will start the appropriate application, which will allow you to create the object; when you exit the other application, you'll return to Word and your object will appear on the page as a little gift box. This box is really a link to the application that created the object, and double-clicking on it will start the necessary program to edit or view the object.

Similarly, if the object already exists, you don't need to specify the application. Just choose the From File tab and select the file in the file selection dialog you are presented. Windows knows what type of object it is from the file extension and inserts the gift box in your document.

Now, if you're really lucky, the object inserted in your Word document will look just like it does in the associated application. This is often true of image files, no matter the format; the associated application translates them for Word. This is a real bonus for Web page development.

Consider this: you are creating a Web page in Word, and an associate hands you a disk full of clip art. Unfortunately, it's in a format Word doesn't understand, like CorelDraw's native .cdr. If CorelDraw isn't installed on your machine, there's nothing you can do. If it is, however, you don't even need to convert those files to an HTML image format (*.gif or *.jpg) before using them. Just insert them into your document; when you save it as HTML (or if you're already in HTML mode), Word will use CorelDraw to convert them to the appropriate image type and they'll look great in your Web page. Doesn't get a lot easier than that.

Forms

Next to mail merge, the "forms" feature in Word is probably the most useful and least-used goodie in the Office suite of applications. People who use Word only for simple text documents won't use it, but just about every high-power word processing Ninja has created a form in Word at one time or another. Most people use simple underlines and tabs to line up form elements and print a document that permits simple data entry, which is later collated by hand.

Woe are they, for they have not seen the light. Word includes an extensive set of tools for creating online forms that can greatly simplify the collection of any kind of data in an organization. If your office is full of PCs running Word, you have very little excuse for not creating online forms and letting users print them out after they've completed them. If you don't want to do online data collection, you can still make terrific-looking forms with Word's form tools. And the included tools also make decent Web forms!

That's the good news. Now for the bad. Where Word is really lacking is in the collection of the data that is entered into the forms. If you're creating online forms in Word, you can write Word macros (beyond the scope of this text) to collect the data, maybe as comma-delimited text, and later bring it into Access or Excel for analysis. However, if you create the forms for eventual publishing on the Web, they'll look great—but they won't do anything. A Word-created Web form that's put on the Web without some serious Webmaster work will sit there, and when a user presses the Submit button, it will continue to sit there.

That's because there's no programming behind the form, and Word doesn't provide any facilities for adding the necessary code. It's hard to imagine the discussions at Microsoft that resulted in the decision not to include even some rudimentary forms-processing code as part of the package of controls that come with Office. The disclaimer they've included, that you'll need to talk to your Web support staff before implementing any forms you create, seems like a cop-out.

Nevertheless, if you're handy with CGI programming under Windows, you can go ahead and whip out some really slick forms in Word. The included Web Wizards create some good, basic forms that you can customize for your own use.

Web Wizard

When you start a new HTML page, you'll notice three templates to select from: Blank Web Page (pretty self-explanatory), More Cool Stuff (discussed below), and the Web Wizard. True to the form of Wizards in previous editions of Microsoft products, the Web Wizard takes you through a few questions (exactly two) and builds a page for you based on your answers.

The selections for pre-built pages are actually pretty comprehensive. It's conceivable that you could build an entire simple site using just these. In fact, you'll notice that the MGL home page looks a lot like one of these. There's a reason for that.

The pre-built page styles included with Word 97 are:

- **Blank.** Exactly what it says.
- **2-Column.** A simple layout with two columns of graphics or test defined.
- **3-Column.** Similar to above, but with three columns.
- **Calendar.** A simple grid into which you can add dates.
- **Centered Layout.** A simple, mostly centered text page, suitable for a title page.

- **Form-Feedback.** A very nice customizable feedback form.
- **Form-Registration.** A form to collect demographic information about people.
- **Form-Survey.** A form to ask users questions.
- **Personal Home Page.** A page to describe yourself and your reason for being, for the whole world to see.
- **Simple Layout.** A page with a little text and a list.
- **Table of Contents.** A page with a grid set up for listing page references or hyperlinks.

This sounds great, but it's not as nice as it looks. The pages still need content added—that's a given. But there are some surprising lapses on the part of the Wizards' designers that will lull some unsuspecting aspiring Web designer into a false sense of security. The Calendar page isn't really a calendar; it's an empty grid into which you can insert numbers for dates. You'll need to manually create a new page for every month. The forms look nice, but they don't do anything, despite the fact that all include a Submit button. There's no program code behind the form, code which must be there for the form to work. In fact, the online help for "form elements" includes the following basic truth: "Because forms require additional support files and, therefore, additional server support, it is recommended that you consult your network or Web administrator when planning the form." This could have been implemented better. If you're an experienced Web programmer, you'll have no trouble with these forms. If not, they're not of much use.

Each form can be rendered in one of eight styles, including Contemporary and Outdoors. Applying these styles changes the page background (they're all bitmapped images of one kind or another) and inserts matching bullets and horizontal lines where appropriate. You could choose one of these for your entire site and do well, but don't go overboard with these.

In short, you can throw together a simple site in half an hour with the Web Wizard, but it won't garner any bookmarks.

Microsoft Enhancements

One of the recurring problems in Web design is the selfish attempts of the large, multinational corporations to make more money, heaven forbid. One of the ways they do that is by trying to gain market share, thus elbowing everybody else out of the market; one way to gain market share in the Web browser market is to make your browser freely available and add features to it that nobody else supports.

This practice is kind of like inventing a kind of street sign that's only visible through the windshield of a certain brand of car. It's great if you want to read those signs and happen to drive the right kind of car, but it's annoying to everyone else. With that image in mind, imagine if every auto manufacturer developed its own sign standards. Pretty soon, the median would be so crowded that you would have trouble reading even the signs that were supposed to be readable through everybody's window.

Sound extreme? It's exactly what's happening in the world of Web browsers. There actually *is* an international standards body for HTML, the Internet Engineering Task Force (IETF), but it's been relegated to the role of peacemaker and apologist by Netscape and Microsoft, with help from several other companies. Both companies have added their own "extensions" to HTML that only their browsers can read. If you want to see or use those features, you have to use the appropriate browser. If enough people switch browsers, the company in control of the browser of choice controls the prospective standard, further freezing out everybody else. The problem has become so pervasive that Ziff-Davis, the computer magazine publisher, has started a (probably futile) petition drive (http://www3.zdnet.com/) to get the big boys to play nice and slow down.

As a Web designer, what can you do? You could confuse everybody by using both Netscape and Microsoft features in your pages (bad idea). You could choose one or the other, making your pages unreadable, ugly, or boring when viewed in the other guy's browser (bad idea). Or you can stick to standard, generally accepted HTML that everybody can read, since the name of the game is "content," not flash (good idea). All of the features described below are only visible in Microsoft's browser. *Caveat emptor.*

Portable Network Graphic Format

A new file format, Portable Network Graphic (PNG), is supported directly by Word 97. PNG is a *lossy* format, which means that it loses resolution as the image is compressed. This is fine for small images, since the loss of detail is generally not noticeable in a small picture, but it is more problematic for large images or when small images are blown up. PNG images are designed to be used on Web pages, although no Web browser currently available supports them directly; they are generally limited to 256 colors and include image transparency features. By combining the transparency features of GIF images with the compression (and therefore network-friendliness) of JPG images, Microsoft hopes PNG will become a standard in Web graphics.

Video

Microsoft believes that the inclusion of support for streaming data, such as video and audio, on the Web is forward-thinking, so they've installed support for a few audio and video formats in Internet Explorer. When you embed a video clip in a Web page, you guarantee a couple of things:

- That it will take a long time to load, because video files tend to be large and downloading them over a busy network takes time, and

- Only people running Internet Explorer (or specially modified versions of Netscape Navigator) will be able to view them.

With those limitations in mind, Word makes the embedding of video clips into your Web page as easy as embedding a still graphic. Assuming the video clip is in a file on a disk, it can be inserted at the current point in your HTML file by selecting Insert | Video. Word opens the dialog box shown in Figure 5-26.

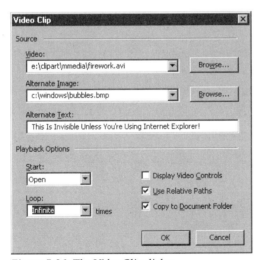

Figure 5-26: The Video Clip dialog.

In the top window, enter the source for the video clip. This can be a filename, a path, or a URL. In the second window, space is provided for the name of an alternate still image to use in the event that the remote browser doesn't recognize video, which is quite possible. Below that you have an opportunity to enter a text string describing the video for those who are running their browsers in a text mode.

A few options are configurable for video clips. You can specify that the clip starts running when the page is first opened, when the mouse passes over it, or both. You can make the clip restart from one to five times, or keep replaying forever like The Rocky Horror Picture Show.

Scrolling Text

Another "gee whiz" feature brought to you by the Boys in Redmond. We have no need for it on our MGL home page, and most browsers (including Netscape's) will not be able to see it. But it's fun anyway. To insert a scrolling line of text into your page, move the cursor to its intended location and select Insert | Scrolling Text from the menubar. You should see the dialog in Figure 5-27.

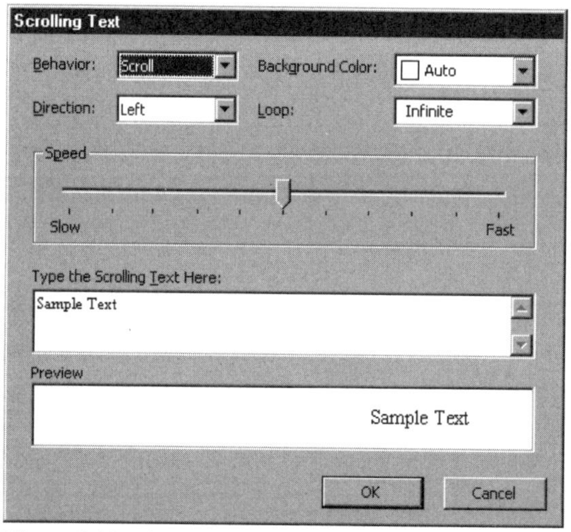

Figure 5-27: The Scrolling Text dialog.

The options here are pretty self explanatory, but we can save you a little time by describing them:

- **Behavior (Scroll, Slide, or Alternate).** Scrolling text exits off of one side of the screen and reappears at the opposite side. Sliding text slides and stops at the window edge. Selecting Alternate makes the text bounce back and forth between the edges of the window.

- **Background Color.** The color of the background behind the text. The text will always be black, and you have no control over the font.

- **Direction (Left or Right).** The direction the text should move.

- **Loop (Infinite, 1-5).** Only available with the Scroll or Alternate behaviors. How many times should this effect annoy viewers of your page? You get to decide.

- **Speed.** This slider sets the speed that the text moves across the page, from Slow (really glacial) to Fast (still pretty slow).

- **Type the Scrolling Text Here.** Guess what you do in this window?

- **Preview.** What your effect would look like on a fast machine with no network traffic. Is this effect useful? Not if it can't be seen on most browsers.

AutoUpdate

HTML changes often. Since each browser manufacturer is constantly trying to one-up the others, and the many varied uses of the Web continue to exceed even the dreams of its most fervent apostles, the standard for the language keeps expanding.

It would be unreasonable to expect that Word could properly interpret every HTML tag, but Microsoft has left itself an escape route to implement old and new tags alike without delaying the release of their product. It's called AutoUpdate, and it is supposed to automatically apply changes (sometimes called "patches") to your copy of Word as they become available.

AutoUpdate, found on the Tools menu in HTML mode, works through an existing Internet connection to contact Microsoft and determine if an update is available. At this writing, there are none, so the actual behavior of AutoUpdate is as yet untried. But, if Microsoft announces an update, you might want to give AutoUpdate a click.

More Cool Stuff?

The last choice you have when starting a new Web page in Word is the enigmatically marked More Cool Stuff icon. Selecting it opens a static page that includes a link to Microsoft's Web site (http://www.microsoft.com/OfficeFreeStuff/Word/), where you can download additional controls and add-ins for your pages. These add-ins are typically ActiveX controls (currently only readable by Microsoft's browser). If you look around, you can find some new background styles that update your Web Wizard, but that's about it so far. The "coolest" thing about More Cool Stuff is the page background, a 3D stylized puzzle motif in medium gray. Now *that's* useful.

Moving On

We've explored just about everything you can do to create a Web page using Word. For simple pages and sites, Word is a capable authoring tool. Word also simplifies converting existing documents to HTML files for Web use and the AutoUpdate feature has real promise if Microsoft uses it to add functionality as HTML evolves; it would be nice to see an application keep itself up to date without asking for a credit card number for a change.

Word does have its limitations as an HTML authoring tool, though. As your site becomes more complex and increases its functionality, you will probably find you need a dedicated authoring tool.

For Web sites with a little more pizazz, you might consider using Microsoft PowerPoint as your authoring environment. It includes most of the features of Word, but it places more emphasis on style than on content. Sometimes, this is a good thing.

chapter 6

PowerPoint 97

You're feeling good about how well the new Web site is going. You figured out how to do some neat things with Word 97, you created some Web pages, the corporate logo looks good, and things are starting to take shape.

As you work on a particularly tricky Web page, your boss's boss happens by and looks over your shoulder. You continue to work, wondering what he will say. After watching you load the new Web page in your browser, he compliments you on how well you are doing, but you can tell he's less than overwhelmed.

"Can you make the logo look a little better," he asks, "and give the whole page some more color? I want more oomph, more pizzazz, more sparkle. What you've got here is fine, but I wanted something more."

"Sure," you say, wondering how you're going to do it. He pats you on the shoulder, smiling at you, confident he has picked the right person for the job.

As you are ruminating on the best way to handle changes to the Web site, your phone rings. It's the vice-president, and he commends you on the company annual report you presented at the meeting yesterday. He wants you to make the slides available to everyone in the company. You agree, wondering how to preserve the impact of the color slides without the expense of color printing.

As you hang up the phone, panic begins to creep up on you. How can you create a whiz-bang Web site when all you've ever done on the Web is browse? And how can you give everyone a copy of your full-color slides without incurring the wrath of your boss, the department supervisor, for wasting money on color printouts?

Despair sets in. You wonder what the job situation is like in Canada. You never really liked working here anyway, and you've heard Canada is lovely this time of year. Ottawa is highly recommended.

But wait, don't panic! You'll have time to set up the Web site, throw in a few bells and whistles, and still have a power lunch with the vice president tomorrow. At lunch, you can tell the VP how you made the slides available on the company Web site.

All you have to do is use PowerPoint 97. PowerPoint makes it easy to create images of all kinds and save them in GIF or JPEG format for the Web. As for the slides, just use the Save as HTML feature of PowerPoint 97 to save the slides you created in PowerPoint as HTML pages.

Anyone interested can see the slides in full color, and the vice president will applaud your ingenuity. Your boss will take credit for your idea to use the Web site for displaying presentation slides, and everyone will be happy.

Our Take: What PowerPoint Feature Is Most Useful for Creating Web Presentations?

Jeff: The HTML Wizard in PowerPoint is cool. It takes all of your slides, turns them into GIFs, creates a table of contents page for the presentations, and can also add a link for users to download the original PowerPoint file. That automates a whole bunch of stuff that could take a long time.

Kevin: I agree. This is most useful when applied to an existing PowerPoint file. Seems like everybody wants to convert their existing presentations to HTML, and the way the Save As does it is really slick and really easy. Problem is, once it becomes known that you know how to do this, everybody will want you to do their slides for them.

Planning Your Web Site Additions

It's back-to-the-napkin time as you plan your Web site additions. You did save the original napkin you used to create your first few Web pages, didn't you? It's always best to try and lay out new additions in a visual manner so you can keep the new Web pages straight as you create them instead of trying to make it up as you go along.

Before you dive in and start splashing colors and images around, it's a good idea to have a plan for what you want to do. Not only do you need to know ahead of time where everything should go so you can create hyperlinks as you need them, but you should also consider the impact your changes will have on Web users.

PowerPoint is graphically oriented where Word is text oriented. You can use Word to create graphics by using the Drawing Toolbar or WordArt, and you can use PowerPoint to create text, so there is some overlap. However, the underlying purpose of the two applications is completely different.

The boss wants color and oomph and pizzazz. For a full-blown, image-laden Web site, you need PowerPoint and the tools it gives you for creating images, presentations, animations, charts, graphs, and other colorful Web content. Even someone who knows as little about the Web as your boss's boss will be impressed when he sees what you can do with PowerPoint.

Making Wise Use of Bandwidth

One point to keep in mind as you add graphical content to your Web site is how much bandwidth your Web pages will require. Remember, everything on a Web page must be downloaded from your Web server to the user's machine before it can be displayed by the user's Web browser.

Web servers excel at transporting text over the network. When a Web page is all or mostly text, it downloads quickly even over slow connections. When a Web page contains images, however, things slow down a little or a lot, depending on the number of images.

Why the slowdown? Because image files are binary data (mostly numerical data, much like program code), and cannot be compressed as much as text files. This makes it harder to transmit them over a network.

Compression programs such as WinZip or gzip are able to take a huge 2-megabyte text file and squeeze it down to 25 percent of its original size without losing any data by looking for repeated strings (such as *Office 97* or *In my opinion*) and replacing them with a *token*. The token is a much smaller text string that represents the original. A dictionary of tokens is created as a file is compressed and each instance of the string is replaced with a corresponding token. If a text file is mostly blank spaces or contains a lot of repeated text, it can be compressed more than a file that rarely repeats strings. Obviously, the smaller the file, the quicker it transmits across the network.

Binary data, on the other hand, is mostly numerical, and floating-point numbers are not often exactly repeated, so the compression scheme doesn't work as well. Many types of binary files can be compressed only a little or not at all.

What Is...

binary files: Binary files are used to store anything other than ordinary text that runs on your computer, such as program code or numerical information, as in computer image files.

text files: Normal computer files you can read with any text editor, such as Word.

data compression: Converting a file into a different format so it takes up less disk space.

color map: A list of colors contained in a computer image.

What does this mean to you? It depends on how you access the Web site. If you are on the company network at your desk and you download a Web page, it's quick to load. On the other hand, if you are trying to download a Web page over a modem from home, it can take much longer.

Be sure to evaluate the needs of your users before you create huge images for your Web pages that will give your Web server a hernia trying to transmit them. In some cases it might be a good idea to create a low-bandwidth version of the Web pages that are most visited on your site. Give the user a choice of plain-but-fast pages or snazzy-but-slow pages, as shown in Figure 6-1.

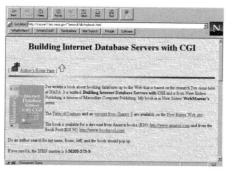 

(a) Plain but fast   (b) Snazzy but slow

Figure 6-1: Low-bandwidth pages consist mostly of text (a); high bandwidth pages contain a lot of graphics (b).

Make images as small as possible and with as few colors as possible. Images with a large color map are larger, because the more colors, the more information stored in the image file itself.

An image has a set of colors that are present in the image itself. Each pixel in the image has to have a color, even if the color is marked as transparent. Each pixel is mapped to a color in the image's color map. As the number of colors increases, the size of the color map increases. An image with 16 colors might not look as good as one with 64,000 colors, but it might be one-tenth the size.

Controlling Web Page Presentation

Another thing to consider when jazzing up your Web site is how to present the graphics so everyone sees them in the same way. HTML does not handle horizontal spacing very well, and every Web browser seems to go out of its way to interpret HTML tags in a way never envisioned by a Web page author.

Since you are on the company intranet, you have more control on the browser used to view Web pages. In fact, the IS department has mandated the use of a standard Web browser for everyone, so you don't have to worry about supporting other Web browsers. Anyone using a nonstandard browser gets what they deserve.

Our Take: What Is PowerPoint's Biggest Weakness When Creating Web Presentations?

Jeff: One thing is the Save as HTML Wizard will create a billion files even if you just want a single GIF of one slide. That's annoying. Another is that everything you do in PowerPoint gets the same shape, like an 8 ½" x 11" sheet of paper on its side. If you create a GIF with a different shape, you have to pull it into another graphics program and crop it to the size you want it. That is tedious and unnecessary.

Kevin: Generally, the images produced by PowerPoint when saving as HTML are too small. If the slides contain anything more than a few bullets (and most people tend to put way too much on their slides anyway), the detail is almost invisible in a Web browser. Most people end up downloading the whole presentation so they can read the detail.

What about employees who dial into the network from home? The IS department has no control over what browser they use on their computers at home. In an effort to be as user-friendly as possible, you should lay out your Web pages as carefully as possible to minimize browser differences.

Another browser-dependent item you cannot control is the size and type of font users select in their Web browsers. HTML is not meant to be rigidly controlled, so the best idea is to let the browser handle the text formatting as much as possible and just take over when absolutely necessary.

Allowing for Monitor Resolution & Colors

One of the things that makes MS Windows so useful is its ability to display using different resolutions and color depths to match the capabilities of a user's monitor and video card. One of the worst things about creating Web pages is having to accommodate all of those resolutions and colors.

It's worse than that. Have you ever visited a Web page that seemed to be long and skinny and didn't use the entire browser window? Or one that was short and fat and was wider than your default browser?

Browsers for different platforms have different default shapes. UNIX browsers like to be tall and skinny. Windows browsers tend to be short and fat. Macintosh browsers tend to be almost square. This is because of the shape of the monitors most commonly used on the various platforms.

What does this mean for you? If every machine on the intranet uses the same monitor, uses the same resolution, and has the same number of colors available, you have no problem. But what about users dialing up from the road on their laptops? If your Web pages are on the Internet, the variety of browsers can make you throw up your hands.

Evaluate the video capabilities and preferences of the computers your users will be using to view your Web pages. Pick a standard to design to, such as 640 by 480 resolution at 256 colors, or 1024 by 768 at 64,000 colors. If you have a wide variety of resolutions and color depths to support, keep that in mind and create your Web pages to be as flexible and user-friendly as possible.

Webifying PowerPoint Presentations

Creating presentations to use in a controlled environment such as a conference room is one thing. Putting presentations on the Web is something completely different.

In the conference room, you can control the timing of when slides appear on the screen, make things happen as a result of your actions or on a timer, and even hide slides so you don't have to talk about them unless a particular question comes up. You are in complete control of what happens when.

Not so on the Web. You will probably never know who sees your presentations or which slides they look at, how long they spent on each slide, or if they got enough information out of them to do them any good. Users are in complete control of what they see in their Web browser.

As a result of this difference between actual presentations and copies of slides for a presentation on the Web, if possible you should make your Web presentations self-sufficient. Give users controls to help them navigate through your slides in a logical manner. Also help them go directly to the slides they want to see if they already know what they are looking for. Don't just put a pile of Web pages in a directory and expect the user to figure them out.

To help you out, PowerPoint 97 gives you tools for putting your presentations on the Web and lets you add controls for Web visitors to control their own path through your Web site. Just be sure you add more than the default controls added by PowerPoint if your Web presentation needs them. If you want to link Web pages created in PowerPoint to pages not contained in the current presentation, you can add text hyperlinks or use button images that link to other pages.

Once you've considered these topics, jotted down a few ideas, drawn a rough site map on a notepad, and gotten a few ideas by playing with PowerPoint's tools, we'll take a look at how to create a Web site using PowerPoint 97.

Creating the Logo

As a first step, let's dress up the company logo. The boss didn't tell you exactly what he wanted, but you know what he meant. The first thing a user sees when visiting the company home page is the company logo at the top of the page. The logo should be sleek, sophisticated, colorful, tasteful, and vivid.

FYI: Learning to Use PowerPoint

Before you try and produce a PowerPoint Web page, plan to spend some time just playing. Create a few shapes with the drawing tools, add some text, toss in a line or two, and then study how the special effects change them.

Look over the WordArt choices and experiment with changing fonts and font sizes. Try dark text on a light background, light-colored 3D shapes on a dark background, and so on. Once you feel comfortable with the tools and you have an idea what they do, you can start creating your real Web pages.

If you try to jump right in and try to create Web pages right away, you will either mess things up so badly you'll have to start over anyway, or your images will be plain and unsatisfactory. Play first, then use what you learn to do the real stuff.

Okay, it's impossible to do all of that with one image. But you can do your best. Let's take a look at what PowerPoint 97 has to offer that can improve the logo you created in Word. The original logo is shown in Figure 6-2. How was the logo created? With just a few simple steps, using the Drawing Toolbar. Let's recreate it now.

The Drawing Toolbar does the same thing in Word, PowerPoint, or Excel. We recommend you create images in PowerPoint, however, because image creation is PowerPoint's strong suit and, as you saw in the Word chapter, Word sometimes has trouble saving images.

Figure 6-2: The Megatron Galacticorp company logo.

Creating an Image in PowerPoint

For those readers who prefer to *see* how things are done, there is a movie file on the CD that accompanies this book that shows how to create the Megatron Galacticorp company logo. Use Windows Explorer to look in the resource\demos directory on the CD for the *makelogo.avi* file. Double-click on the file, and the Windows Media Player will run the movie for you.

First off, choose the Rectangle object from the Drawing Toolbar. It's the one next to the arrow that points down and to the right. Draw a rectangle on your canvas and choose a fill color. That's the picture of the bucket. I made mine blue. What color did you choose? See, this isn't so hard! A nice rectangle. Take a break, you're sweating.

Next, choose the Insert WordArt button on the toolbar. It's the one that looks like the letter A that's had too much coffee. The WordArt Gallery pops up, as shown in Figure 6-3. Look the styles over carefully, perhaps trying out a few.

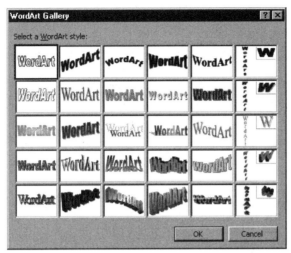

Figure 6-3 : The WordArt Gallery.

We chose the style in the second row up from the bottom and the third column over from the left. When you select a style, you'll get a box to edit text in. For our company, we typed in Megatron Galacticorp Ltd. Unless your company just happens to be named the same, you might want to enter some different text. Our company sounds like a Transformer that flies a spaceship, but yours can be whatever you like.

We picked a different font from the font box, Book Antiqua, and then pressed the OK button. The text is generated onto the PowerPoint page and we moved it directly on top of the blue rectangle, and the result is shown in Figure 6-4. Once again, this isn't so hard, is it? PowerPoint does most of the work for you.

Figure 6-4: Adding text to the blue rectangle to create the company logo.

Only one piece remains. Where did the little picture come from that looks like a Leonardo Da Vinci drawing? It's an image from the clip art collection included with Office 97. To get to the clip art, choose Insert from the menu at the top of the screen, then pick Picture. From the list of possibilities, choose Clip Art and you will see the Microsoft Clip Art Gallery, shown in Figure 6-5. Prepare to lose a lot of time here.

Figure 6-5: The Microsoft Clip Art Gallery.

FYI: More Clip Art

You'll see a lot more clip art in the Gallery if your Office97 CD is in your computer when you start it. PowerPoint automatically looks for the CD and includes the clip art on it in the Gallery if it's present.

The Da Vinci image is in the Healthcare and Medicine category, the category shown in Figure 6-5. Select it (lower right hand corner) and press the Insert button. The image will be added to your canvas. Placement of the image will depend on the size and resolution of your monitor, so if you don't see it immediately, try scrolling around the canvas until you see it.

Surely you noticed it's in black and white, where our logo is in color. (The figures in the book are black and white, of course, but you can see them in color on the CD that comes with the book. All of the Web site examples in the book are on the CD.) Colorizing the image is just a matter of choosing a fill color for each piece of the image. Watch the *makelogo.avi* video to see how it's done.

FYI: Ungrouping Images

The images in the Clip Gallery can often be broken into component images so you can apply different colors or effects to each piece individually. Just select the image on your canvas and choose Draw|Ungroup from the menu. If the image can be divided, it will be. Now you can move each piece around and work with it as you see fit.

So, just add the colored image to the logo and, voila! Instant logo. You'll probably want to group all of the pieces together so you can move them as a unit when you want to place the logo on your Web page. To do so, use the mouse to draw a box around the entire logo, and choose Draw | Group from the Drawing Toolbar. All of the disparate pieces are combined in a single image. If you want to break them up, just reverse the process. Each piece retains its integrity.

Dressing Up the Logo

Now it's time to dress up the logo a bit, as the Big Guy requested. The original logo looks pretty good, but there are a few things you can do to it to add sparkle using PowerPoint 97. PowerPoint is designed to create impressive images, and many of its features translate to the Web.

Inevitably, if you start playing with the appearance of an image, you will cross the line from wow to gaudy. Where is this line? It's in a different place for different people. In this case, the line is what your boss's boss will like. You think you have a good feel for his tastes, so you look at your company logo with a goal in mind.

PowerPoint is fun to simply play with, if you have a few minutes (hours?) to spend. You'll find yourself adding just one more effect to your images until you've added about 20 "just one more" effects. Don't be afraid to experiment, because you can always press the Undo button to wipe out as many changes as you want. Just remember at some point you have to declare an image *done* and stop playing with it, um, improving it.

The more time you spend playing with PowerPoint's drawing tools (which are the same tools available in Word), the more experience you'll have creating and editing images. In a short time, you will be producing professional-quality images that everyone will swipe off of your Web pages without so much as a thank you.

So, let's go to work on the company logo. First off, you know your boss's boss likes things to have a 3D look. Using the Drawing Toolbar, which is shown in Figure 6-6, you can give images a 3D look, create shadow effects, change image colors, and just generally make the company logo so gaudy everyone who sees it will wish they had sunglasses.

Again, for those who like to see things being done, dressing up the company logo is shown in the *sparkle.avi* video clip in the resource\demos directory on the accompanying CD.

Figure 6-6: The Drawing Toolbar.

This should look familiar to you if you read the previous chapter, because it's the same drawing toolbar Word uses. Unfortunately, or perhaps fortunately if you have no taste, the visual effects can't be used together, so that prevents you from creating a logo that looks like a flying saucer zipping through the sky, plus embossing the letters in the company name, plus putting a big shadow under the saucer. You have to choose the one effect you like best. Of course you can change the look of the text separately, so you can create interesting effects that way as well.

Oops, we've been playing for quite some time, so we need to get something accomplished. Let's break the logo back into its separate parts for now, to make things easier to work with, as shown in Figure 6-7.

Figure 6-7: The ungrouped parts of the company logo.

The text is the most noticeable part of the logo, so let's add a 3D effect to that part. Select the text on your canvas, then choose the 3D button from the Drawing Toolbar. It's the button on the extreme right end. From the menu of items displayed we picked Style 12, which is three rows up, all the way on the right end. It makes the text look like Figure 6-8.

Figure 6-8: Logo text in 3D format.

If you want to tweak the 3D effects even more, choose the 3D Settings option at the bottom of the 3D menu page. You'll get the toolbar shown in Figure 6-9. With this toolbar, you can tweak the color, surface texture, lighting effects, and rotation of the image.

Figure 6-9: The 3-D Settings toolbar.

Like many of the PowerPoint tools, this is a magic toolbar. It can make 30 minutes disappear in a puff of smoke as you use it. Be careful, because the puff of smoke might be coming out of your boss's ears if he sees you having so much fun on company time.

Next, let's put a shadow behind the background rectangle. Select the rectangle on your canvas and pick the Shadow button from the Drawing Toolbar. It's the button second to the right, next to the 3D button. Pick your shadow type. We picked the one on the top row, second from the left.

For more fine tuning of shadows, choose the Shadow Settings button at the bottom of the Shadow menu. You will see the toolbar shown in Figure 6-10. With this toolbar, you can change the shadow color or nudge the shadow to the left, right, top, or bottom.

Figure 6-10: The Shadow Settings toolbar.

Select the Da Vinci image on your canvas and choose the Shadow button once again. Pick the shadow in the bottom-left-hand corner. This will give the image a subtle, embossed look.

Now only one more step remains. The Big Guy wanted "sparkle." Choose Autoshapes from the Drawing Toolbar and pick Stars and Banners. From the resulting menu, choose the four-point star. Place the star on the descending *g* in Megatron and choose a fill color of white. That adds the Big Guy's sparkle.

Now, let's put all the pieces together. Group them using the Draw | Group item on the Drawing Toolbar, and the result is shown in Figure 6-11. Do you think the boss will like it? Save a copy of it now, because we'll be working on it more in just a bit.

Figure 6-11: A 3D company logo complete with sparkle.

Turning Images Into Links

Wouldn't it be neat to create "hot spots" on a company logo so that when a user clicks on a hot spot, it acts as a hyperlink and transports them to another Web page? This is the traditional definition of an image map, where the Web page creator specifies different areas of a graphic image that correspond to different URLs.

What Is...

image map: An image with pieces mapped to different URLs. When a user clicks on a part of the image, the image acts like a hyperlink and takes the user to another Web page.

While the Microsoft marketing literature *says* PowerPoint 97 will let you create image maps, if you read the fine print PowerPoint can only fulfill this promise if you allow Microsoft to redefine *image map*.

PowerPoint has several built-in images that are used as controls on a PowerPoint slide. The images are control buttons and are located on the Slide

Show | Action Buttons menu. These 12 buttons, shown in Figure 6-12, can be mapped to perform a variety of actions depending on interaction with the user.

Figure 6-12: PowerPoint action buttons.

Where a traditional image map is a complete image that has pieces mapped to URLs, Microsoft says you can cluster several mapped Action Buttons together on a Web page in an image map. The functionality is the same, but the flexibility and esthetic appeal are completely lost when you can only use the limited number of images PowerPoint 97 gives you and you cannot create custom images to map actions to.

Having said that, there are many occasions where PowerPoint's Aaction buttons can come in handy, and it is simple to add one to a Web page. Just choose the Slide Show | Action Buttons menu and pick an action button.

Press and hold the left mouse button on your canvas and create a box outline that is the size you want your button to be. Don't worry, you can always resize the button later if you change your mind about the size. Release the mouse button, and the dialog box shown in Figure 6-13 will appear to let you choose the action associated with the action button.

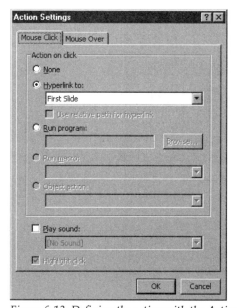

Figure 6-13: Defining the action with the Action Settings dialog.

You can choose the action to occur when the user presses the action button or when the user's mouse moves over the action button. You can also pick a sound to play when the action is activated. We'll cover playing sounds later on in the chapter when we discuss animation.

Importing Graphics Into PowerPoint 97

Have you ever heard the saying "A picture is worth a thousand words"? That can be especially true when creating documents for the Web. PowerPoint 97 gives you more than one way to add charts to your Web presentations.

Remember the vice president and the annual report? You created the fancy graphs using PowerPoint's embedding features to include charts and spreadsheets. Luckily for you, those will also export in HTML format so you can include them on the company Web site as is. Whew! But don't tell anyone. Let them think you worked long and hard at it. And start counting your bonus money now.

Adding Charts

You can use Microsoft Chart to insert a variety of chart formats. Select the Insert | Chart menu item and a new chart will appear in your PowerPoint slide. If you put the mouse arrow anywhere on the bars in the bar graph and click the right mouse button, one of the options that appears is Chart Type. Select that menu item and the Chart Type form appears, as shown in Figure 6-14.

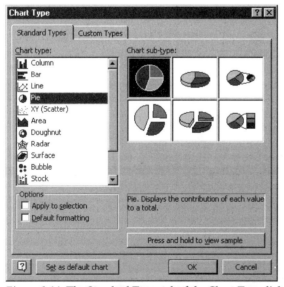

Figure 6-14: The Standard Types tab of the Chart Type dialog.

The Standard Types section shown in Figure 6-14 gives you a large variety of chart types to choose from. If you prefer one type over all the others, you can set that one as the default chart type and all new charts will default to that type. If you choose the Custom Types tab, shown in Figure 6-15, you can pick a chart type from an even larger selection, or if none of the built-in types suit you, you can create your own.

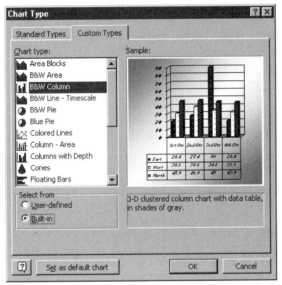

Figure 6-15: The Custom Types tab of the Chart Type dialog.

Once you decide on a graph type you like, you can edit the X- and Y-axes, change the legend, change the data, and add or delete graph elements. If you need to present data in a simple, graphical format, Microsoft Chart will do anything you need.

Embedding Excel Spreadsheets

If you have data already in Excel spreadsheet format, you can embed it directly into your PowerPoint presentation. If you are creating a spreadsheet and just prefer to use the Excel environment to construct the spreadsheet, you can do that too. You can embed the spreadsheet data itself or use an Excel Chart.

Creating the Excel Spreadsheet in PowerPoint

The simplest way to start a new Excel spreadsheet in a PowerPoint slide is to just look for the Insert Microsoft Excel Worksheet button on the PowerPoint toolbar and press it. You get to choose the size of spreadsheet to insert, and then PowerPoint drops a spreadsheet window into your presentation.

Our Take: Strange Behavior of Office 97 Applications

Jeff: Here's a fun party game for you and your friends. Start up a new PowerPoint slide. Press the Insert Microsoft Excel Worksheet button and select any size spreadsheet. Wait a few seconds while your computer puts the spreadsheet on the screen. Now, use your mouse to grab a corner of the new spreadsheet window and try to change the size of the window. Under Windows 95, I get an error message that says "This program has performed an illegal instruction" and the spreadsheet disappears. This does not happen under Windows NT.

Now, here comes the fun part. Try to exit PowerPoint. The Office Assistant tells you that you have embedded objects in your PowerPoint presentation and you must shut them before you can close PowerPoint. Only the embedded object isn't there any more and can't be deleted.

If this happens to you, just use the Ctrl+Alt+Del key combination to bring up a list of running processes, select PowerPoint from the list, and wait a few seconds while Windows tries to shut it down. No stupid computer tells *me* how to turn off a program!
Kevin: Works fine on my machine. Go figure.

Type your information or formulas directly into the cells and then click outside of the spreadsheet area to go back to PowerPoint. You can always double-click the spreadsheet to edit it if you need to add or change anything. You might have a problem trying to resize the worksheet to be more readable.

FYI: Moving Excel Spreadsheets to the Web

If you just want to put a simple Excel spreadsheet on the Web, there is no need to go to the trouble of using PowerPoint. You can save the spreadsheet directly from Excel using the Save as HTML Table feature.

Inserting an Excel Chart into PowerPoint

The Excel Chart tool is similar to the Microsoft Chart tool that is in Word and PowerPoint 97, but it is more powerful. With Excel Chart, you can perform true spreadsheet operations such as the summation of a row or column of data, create formulas to average the values of selected cells, and so on.

To insert an Excel Chart into a PowerPoint slide, choose the Insert|Object menu item on the Standard Toolbar and the Insert Object form will appear, as shown in Figure 6-16. Select Microsoft Excel Chart from the Object Type list box.

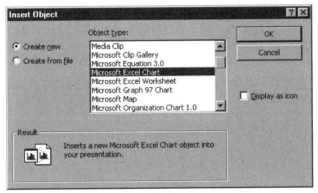

Figure 6-16: The Insert Object dialog.

If you are creating a new chart, select the Create New option. If you have an existing Excel chart to insert, choose the Create From File option. Once you make your selection, press the OK button. Your chart will be inserted into the PowerPoint slide, and the PowerPoint toolbars will change to give you the Excel toolbars for working with your data, as shown in Figure 6-17.

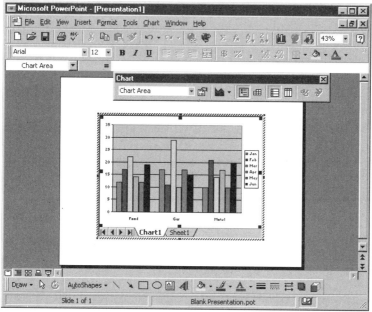

Figure 6-17: Embedding an Excel chart in a PowerPoint slide.

While you are working with the Excel Chart, you will feel as if you have switched to Microsoft Excel. Once you finish with the Chart data, clicking outside of the chart area will return you to PowerPoint.

Our Take: More Strange Behavior

Jeff: Well, the fun continues. If I try to resize the Excel Chart, the same error occurs that happened when I tried to resize the Excel Worksheet. I tried completely reinstalling Office 97 to fix it and it did no good. Again, it does not happen under NT.

Kevin: Just goes to show you that weird stuff happens even to gurus sometimes.

Adding Other Object Types

You are not limited to embedding just Microsoft Excel objects in your PowerPoint slides. As you saw in Figure 6-16, there are a whole bunch of objects you can add to slides.

Keep your audience in mind before you go crazy adding every kind of multimedia application available to your slides. If your presentation will be shown on one computer with you in control, knock yourself out. If the presentation will be put on the Web, limit what goes onto the slides.

Some objects, such as audio and video clips, might not export to the Web at all, or they might require browser plug-ins that require licensing on a per-user basis. Multimedia makes things interesting, but don't make promises your presentations can't keep.

The ability to create your own images that can be converted for use on the Web is a wonderful feature of PowerPoint 97. If, instead of creating your own images from scratch, you have existing graphics that you want to add to a PowerPoint slide show or Web page, PowerPoint 97 can import a variety of image file types, as shown in the following table:

Image File Type	File Extension
AutoCAD Format 2D	.dxf
Computer Graphics Metafile	.cgm
CorelDRAW	.cdr
Encapsulated PostScript	.eps
Enhanced Metafile	.emf
Graphics Interchange Format	.gif
JPEG File Interchange Format	.jpg
Kodak Photo CD	.pcd
Macintosh PICT	.pct
Micrografx Designer/Draw	.drw
PC Paintbrush	.pcx
Portable Network Graphics	.png
Tagged Image File Format	.tif
Targa	.tga
Windows Bitmap	.bmp, .rle, .dib
Windows Metafile	.wmf
WordPerfect Graphics	.wpg

Table 6-1: Image file types that can be imported into PowerPoint.

As you look over the list, however, keep in mind that not all image formats are natively supported by PowerPoint. In many cases, PowerPoint requires a filter to handle a particular image type. If you don't install the graphics filters you need when you install PowerPoint, you can always go back and add the filters you need by using the Add/Remove Programs program in the Windows Control Panel.

Another thing to be mindful of is that some aspects of a particular image type might not be supported even with the correct filter installed. For instance, while PowerPoint can import GIFs, if you want to use a multi-image GIF, only the first image in the set will be imported. PowerPoint 97 does not support animated GIF images. Support for other image formats can have similar shortcomings.

Making Things Move on Your Web Page

While PowerPoint 97 does not support animated GIFs, it does have several built-in animation formats that you can add to your Web page presentations.

Some people really like images moving around on a Web page. Some people find them distracting. Others find them downright annoying. As with anything else, animations on a Web page have their place. The trick is to use them sparingly and not inundate the user with too much motion and color all at once.

This method of animation is intended to facilitate drawing attention to one item at a time as a presenter talks to an audience. If animations never stopped, there would be some mighty confused people trying to figure out what a presentation was all about.

Animations in PowerPoint do not endlessly loop. They are designed with presentations and slide shows in mind. One item in a PowerPoint slide can do one thing, then another item can do something else, and so on. The animation can start at a user action or automatically as a slide is displayed.

What Is...

loop: When an animation plays through to the end, then starts over and plays again.

This type of animation can translate to the Web, but anyone viewing the animation must either have the PowerPoint Animation Player add-in already added to their Web browser, or it gives the user a link to go get it. The PowerPoint online help says the Animation Player supports Microsoft Internet Explorer 2.0 or 3.0 or Netscape Navigator 1.22 or 2.0. One would assume it supports later browser versions as well.

Installing the PowerPoint Animation Player

The Animation Player is included on the Office 97 CD in the ValuePack/
Pptanim directory. If you use the Windows Explorer, shown in Figure 6-18,
and double-click on the Axplayer.exe file in the above directory, the Animation
Player will install itself. When installed for this book, the installation program
correctly identified the existence of both Internet Explorer and Netscape
browsers, but the installation only worked for Internet Explorer.

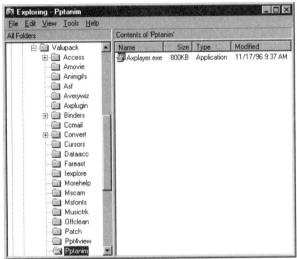

Figure 6-18: Using the Windows Explorer to install the PowerPoint Animation Player.

So what do you do if you want to use Netscape to view your animated
PowerPoint Web pages? Well, you can try Plan B. If you save your PowerPoint
presentation as HTML (which will be detailed later in "Creating a Web Slide
Show"), PowerPoint 97 adds a hyperlink to the Animation Player download
site. Any presentation that requires the Animation Player includes this
hyperlink on the Table of Contents page. If Netscape users click on the link,
they can download and install the player—but it will still not work.

Maybe the problem occurs because the installation program finds two
different browsers? Maybe you should uninstall Internet Explorer and try
again? I wouldn't. According to Microsoft's Knowledge Base, "Microsoft
Office 97 for Windows requires that Microsoft Internet Explorer 3.01 be installed for proper Internet and HyperText Markup Language (HTML) functionality." That's Article ID number Q159707, if you're interested.

Our Take: No Choice of Browsers

Jeff: So what is the bottom line on using the Animation Player with Netscape? Microsoft wants you to use their Internet Explorer Web browser. Microsoft has seen to it that you will use IE to view animated PowerPoint Web pages. If Microsoft really wanted to give you a choice of Web browsers, the installation would really work for both Netscape and IE.

Kevin: Remember the scrolling text so prominently featured in Word? Same problem.

Caution

The PowerPoint Animation Player is a Microsoft ActiveX control. What does this mean? It means only users viewing your Web pages under Windows 95 and Windows NT can use the Animation Player plug-in with their browsers. Do *not* create Web pages that require the Animation Player if you expect UNIX or Macintosh users to visit your Web pages. They will not be able to see any of your Web pages that include PowerPoint animations.

Now that you have the Animation Player plug-in installed (if you use the Internet Explorer Web browser), let's add a couple of animations to our company logo. If you still want to use the Netscape Web browser, you can try calling Microsoft's technical support line.

Adding Animations to Web Pages

If you want to see a video clip of how pieces of the company logo are animated, watch the *animate.avi* video in the resource\demos directory on the accompanying CD.

Reload the PowerPoint slide that contains the company logo. We will be animating the Da Vinci image and the four-pointed star, so in order to make sure those images are individually accessible you will need to ungroup the images.

Use your mouse to draw a box around the logo and then select Draw | Ungroup from the Drawing Toolbar. It is possible to group different images together in subgroups within an overall group, so make sure the Da Vinci image and four-pointed star can be selected individually.

If you created the background of the logo, added the text, and then grouped those two items using the Draw | Group command from the Drawing Toolbar, that would create one subgroup.

If you colorized the Da Vinci image, you had to ungroup its elements first, add the colors, then regroup the elements. That becomes another subgroup.

You can add the Da Vinci image to the rest of the logo and group them together, which becomes yet another subgroup.

When you add the four-pointed star and grouped that with the existing logo, that becomes the topmost level grouping. In order to work with individual pieces of the logo, you will have to continue ungrouping items until you get to the individual images you want to animate.

The simplest solution is to put all of the elements together as you like them and create just one group, but you can group items together as you like to make your images easy to work with. If you want to add items to the logo in the future, it would be easier to just add the item and group everything together, but it might make more sense to ungroup everything, add the new item, and regroup everything. Keep this in mind as you continue to work with your PowerPoint images.

So, make sure you have the Da Vinci image and the star as individual items and set off on the canvas, as shown in Figure 6-19. Our plan is to animate the Da Vinci item so it spins in a circle, and when the spinning stops, the star will appear as a flash. Remember, PowerPoint animations only occur once and stop. If a Web visitor wants to see the animations again, they have to reload the Web page.

Figure 6-19: Ungrouping the company logo for animation.

There are two ways to animate an object in your presentation. Under the Slide Show menu item, both the Preset Animation and Custom Animation selections let you add an animation to an object.

The Preset Animation selection gives you a pre-selected list of animations to apply to an object. If your needs are simple, just pick an animation from the list and keep going.

The Custom Animation selection gives you much more control over your animation effects. If you want to reorder animations or set conditions on how they are used, you will need to use the Custom Animation form.

If you use a lot of animations or you just want to have the animation effects at your fingertips all of the time, look for the Animation Effects icon on your Formatting toolbar. When you press it, the Animation Effects toolbar pops up, as shown in Figure 6-20. This toolbar puts the Preset Animation and Custom Animation menu items on your screen at all times.

Figure 6-20: The Animation Effects toolbar.

For the first animation, we want to make the Da Vinci image spin. Select it on your canvas and choose Slide Show | Custom Animation from the main PowerPoint menu, or just select the Custom Animation icon on the Animation Effects toolbar.

Choosing Your Animation Effects

The Effects section, shown in Figure 6-21, allows you to select which animation to apply to an item and the sound effect the user will hear. Once the animation is complete, you can select what the item does and whether it changes color, disappears, or sits and looks at the user.

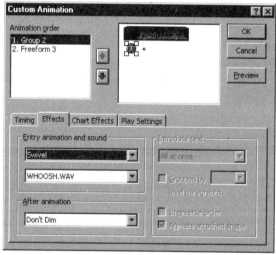

Figure 6-21: The Effects tab of the Custom Animation dialog.

If the item being animated is text, you can choose how to animate the text. If you have more than one or two sentences, you can group the text together and only show parts of it at a time to make it easier for the user to follow.

Because Windows controls any sound driver installed under the operating system, a Web browser can play sound files just like any other Windows program, assuming the user's computer has a sound driver installed. Web visitors who view your Web pages from platforms other than Windows must have their own form of sound drivers installed or they will not hear your sound effects.

If you don't like any of the built-in sound files offered by PowerPoint, just choose Other Sound from the list of sound effects and an Open File dialog box will appear for you to find the sound file you want.

Besides the Effects tab of the Custom Animation dialog, there are three other sections for customizing PowerPoint animations:

- Timing
- Chart Effects
- Play Settings

The top-level dialog box shows you a small image of your PowerPoint slide, allows you to set the order that animations occur, and lets you preview the animations to help you decide which ones to use.

Timing Your Animations

The Timing section, shown in Figure 6-22, lets you decide which items to animate, how to initiate the animation for each animated item, and when the animation should occur. The user can start an animation sequence by clicking on something with their mouse, or the sequence can start automatically when a Web page is loaded. Individual animations can proceed one after another, or you can place delays between them for effect.

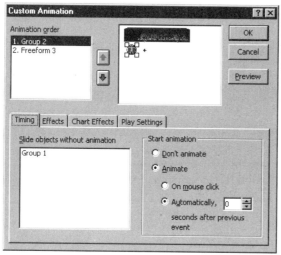

Figure 6-22: The Timing tab of the Custom Animation dialog.

Animating Charts

The Chart Effects tab, shown in Figure 6-23, lets you animate chart items in the same way the Effects section allows you to animate other items. The animation effects and sound files available are the same. We will use the Chart Effects later, in the section "Using Charts & Graphs."

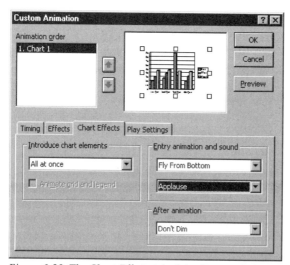

Figure 6-23: The Chart Effects tab of the Custom Animation dialog.

Play Settings

If you want a sound or movie clip to play during a whole presentation or just for the duration of a single slide, you can insert a sound or movie object using the Insert | Movies and Sounds menu item. Choose which type of object to embed and then select the sound or video clip that will play. When you do, the Play Settings tab of the Custom Animation dialog will appear, as shown in Figure 6-24, for you to customize how the clip plays during your presentation.

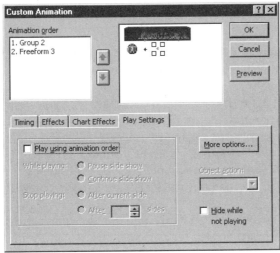

Figure 6-24: The Play Settings tab of the Custom Animation dialog.

The Play Settings will not work with the sound or video action buttons on the Slide Show menu. Action buttons are controls placed on a Web page for the user to interact with. The Play Settings only work with a sound or video object embedded in the slide.

Applying Animation to the Megatron Galacticorp Web Page

Select the Da Vinci image with the mouse and bring up the Custom Animation form by choosing the Slide Show | Custom Animation menu item. Choose the Effects tab (Figure 6-25) and, in the Entry Animation and Sound box, press the down arrow to display the available effects.

Look for *spin*. Scroll the box up and down and look some more. The effects are in alphabetical order, so you can't miss it. What's that you say? There is no spin effect? That's correct, and you have learned another important lesson about PowerPoint 97's animation effects. *Do not assume it has the one you want.*

For round images especially, it would be an obvious choice to have an effect to spin the image in a circle. Even if it sounds like a good idea, it isn't an option. So what do you do? Start selecting effects one at a time and use the Preview button to see what they do. It can be tedious, but when your first choice isn't available, you do what you can.

For this case, the *swivel* effect will probably do. It rotates an image around a vertical axis, instead of spinning an image in a circle, but it's the closest effect available. Select the swivel effect and a sound effect if you want. Make sure the After Animation box (in Figure 6-25) says "Don't dim" so the image remains on the screen after the animation is over.

Now select the Timing tab. For a Web page, it's a good idea to have the animation start automatically, instead of reacting to a mouse click. Some users whiz by Web pages so fast they would never even see the animation. You aren't doing all of this work for nothing, so make sure every Web visitor is treated to your animations by selecting the Animate Automatically option. It might be a good idea to put a second or two delay to allow a Web page to load completely before the animation starts.

To make sure the Da Vinci image spins as it should, press the Preview button and watch it. Smile to yourself, pat yourself on the back, and watch it a few more times. Then stop congratulating yourself and get on with it. We aren't finished yet.

There is no need to close the Custom Animation box just yet. Select the Timing tab and look in the box that says: Slide Objects With Animation. Select the 4-pointed star from the list.

If PowerPoint has decided the star is no longer a star but is a Freeform object, the star will appear in the list labeled as *Freeform* instead of *4-pointed star*, as shown in Figure 6-25. If you don't know which item is the star, just keep selecting items from the list until the star is selected in the preview window. Once you select the star, Animate It Automatically 0 seconds after the previous event. If you prefer the star to appear with a second or two delay, feel free to set it up that way.

Now select the Effects tab. In the Entry Animation and Sound box, choose the *Appear* animation and the *Laser* sound effect. This will make the star appear with a bang once the Da Vinci image stops spinning. Figure 6-25 shows the Custom Animation form with the two items selected for animation.

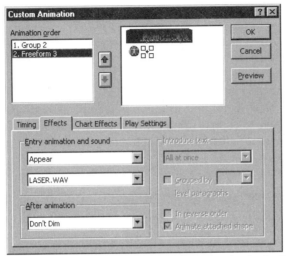

Figure 6-25: Selecting logo elements for animation in the Custom Animation dialog.

Be sure to preview the animation effects, complete with sound effects, several times, preferably at high volume. This will attract your nearby co-workers, who will ooh and ahh in delight at your cleverness. The noise they make will attract management, who is always looking for an excuse to tell employees to get back to work.

Once the managers arrive, they will attract your boss and his boss until everyone is standing around offering suggestions on what *they* would do to make the logo better. If your boss's boss has any suggestions, listen carefully, even writing them down so you can meticulously detail why you didn't follow his suggestions later if you need to.

Creating a Web Slide Show

Now it's time to put the company annual report on the Web. This year's report was longer than necessary, as usual, but we will create three simple slides out of the report. It's a small company, in spite of the name Megatron Galacticorp Ltd. (MGL).

We will recreate all three slides and then save them as HTML pages to put on the Web using the Save to HTML option on the PowerPoint File menu.

Creating a Title Page

Every good presentation has a title page. Ours is no exception. The title slide will include our fancy new company logo at the top, with the company mission statement underneath. The title and date of the annual report will complete the contents of slide number one.

Choose the File | New menu item and you will be presented with a lot of presentation templates to choose from, as shown in Figure 6-26. We will be using the Whirlpool template because it's blue to match our company logo and, besides, it looks cool.

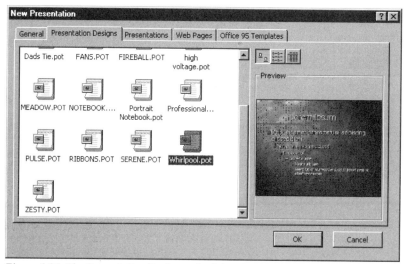

Figure 6-26: The Presentation Designs tab of the New Presentation dialog.

Once you choose a template format, you will see the New Slide dialog, where you get to choose a slide format that kind of fits what you plan to do with the slide. The one we will choose for the title page is highlighted in Figure 6-27.

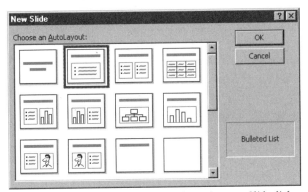

Figure 6-27: Choosing a slide layout from the New Slide dialog.

Delete the text box at the top of the page and replace it with our company logo (you do remember the file you saved it in, right?), add the company mission statement as text, include the title and report date as text, and add a Next button to the bottom of the page using the Slide Show | Action Buttons menu option. The final product is shown in Figure 6-28.

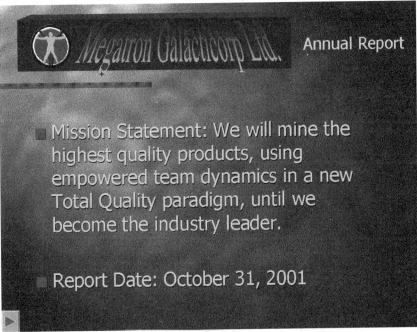

Figure 6-28: Annual report title page after modification to the slide template.

Creating an Organization Chart

Now it's time to create the company organization chart. Use the Insert | New Slide menu item to add another slide to the presentation. This time, choose the organization chart layout, which is shown highlighted in Figure 6-29.

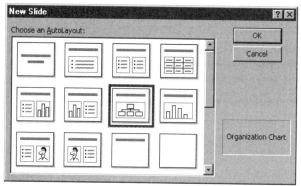

Figure 6-29: Selecting the Organization Chart template from the New Slide dialog.

Copy and paste the slide elements from the title page to the top of this slide. Double-clicking on the organization chart icon brings up the Microsoft Organization Chart tool, as shown in Figure 6-30.

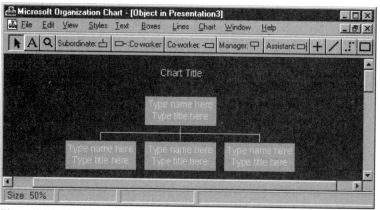

Figure 6-30: The Microsoft Organization Chart tool.

Enter your organizational information using Organization Chart. You can spend a lot of time here moving boxes around, changing colors, adding new boxes, and so on. After a while you'll remember you had a purpose and you'll get back to work.

The MGL organization chart is shown in Figure 6-31. Sometimes it can take a while to move boxes around so they show up big enough to read on a slide. This is especially true for slides to be viewed from the Web. Don't forget to add a Previous and Next button to the slide.

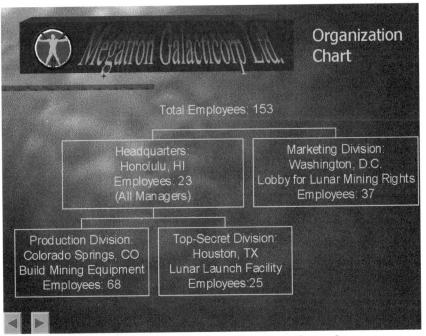

Figure 6-31: The MGL organization slide after modification to the template.

Creating an Income & Expense Chart

This financial slide presents income and expenses for each division of the company. This is an excellent opportunity to use a chart to graphically display numerical data in a more readable form.

For this slide, we will use the chart layout, which is shown highlighted in Figure 6-32. The chart layout includes an embedded chart object that we can double-click to start creating our graph.

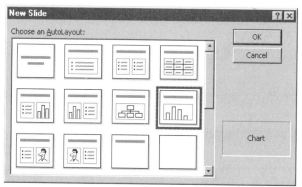

Figure 6-32: Selecting the chart layout from the New Slide dialog.

Once you put the company logo and slide title at the top of the slide, double-click the chart icon and bring up Microsoft Chart to change the legend and axis labels, and enter the financial data. Add a Previous and Next button and the finished slide is shown in Figure 6-33.

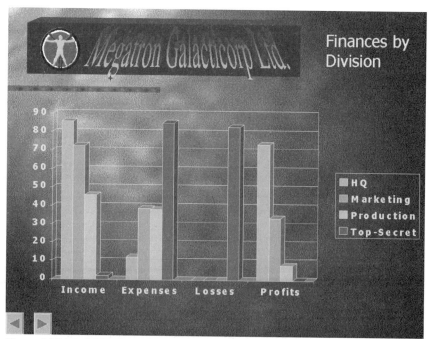

Figure 6-33: The MGL Finances by Division slide after modification to the template.

Creating Hyperlinks

A neat thing to do for this, or any other slide, is to include hyperlinks to other Web pages. In this instance, if each of the company divisions has its own Web pages, it might be useful to hyperlink the name of each company in the chart legend to its corresponding home page. This can be done in a few easy steps.

The first thing to do is ungroup all of the chart information so you can connect hyperlinks to individual chart objects. Select the chart object and chose Draw | Ungroup.

Caution

When you ungroup an embedded object you lose the associated functionality of the attached program. For example, if you ungroup the chart, you lose the ability to use Microsoft Chart to edit the chart itself. Ungrouping an object breaks it into individual pieces that are no longer associated with an underlying program. Make sure you have performed all necessary edits before you ungroup an embedded object.

Select an object you want to add a hyperlink to and either press the Insert Hyperlink icon on the PowerPoint toolbar or choose Insert | Hyperlink from the menu. When you do, the Insert Hyperlink form will appear, as shown in Figure 6-34.

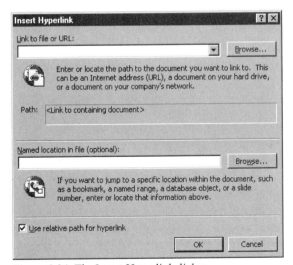

Figure 6-34: The Insert Hyperlink dialog.

The hyperlink can refer to a file on your computer, a file on the company's file server, or a Web page somewhere on the Internet. In this way, you can include information from anywhere in the world in your PowerPoint presentation.

Converting PowerPoint Slides With the HTML Wizard

We have completed our slide presentation on the company's annual report. Now we are ready to create the Web version of the presentation. Choose the File I Save as HTML menu option and the Save as HTML Wizard will appear, as shown in Figure 6-35.

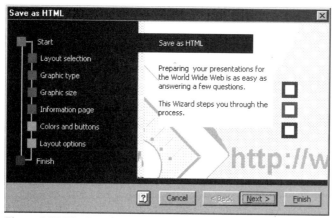

Figure 6-35: The Save as HTML Wizard.

The HTML Wizard is a program that will guide you through a series of steps to turn your PowerPoint slide show into Web pages. At the bottom of each Wizard page are the four buttons: Cancel, Previous, Next, and Finish. You can cancel the Wizard at any time without creating anything. You can go back to a previous step if you change your mind about something. All of the information you enter is kept, no matter what page you go back to. Once you finish a step, you use the Next button to proceed to the next step. And if you want to create Web pages using only the information you have entered up until now, press the Finish button. If you create Web pages before you go all the way through the Wizard, you might have a lot of file editing to do to be sure the Web pages work correctly.

On the first page, press the Next button to start entering information about your Web presentation. The first step of the Wizard is shown in Figure 6-36 and lets you choose an existing layout you have used before or create a new one. If you want your Web site to have a consistent look and feel throughout, it is easy to create a layout the first time you use the Wizard and then use it for each presentation from then on. The layout contains information about how to display your images, where to put control buttons, and so on.

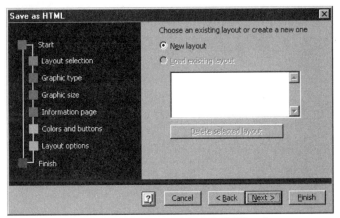

Figure 6-36: Selecting page layout with HTML Wizard.

Next you can choose the frames or no-frames option, shown in Figure 6-37. Here you can choose the standard Web page layout or one with frames. The frames layout makes it easier for a user to navigate your Web site, but the standard layout allows for a larger section of each Web page to appear on screen.

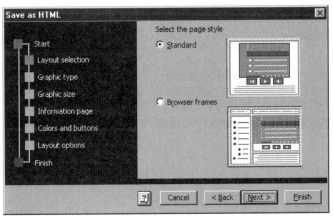

Figure 6-37: Selecting frames or no-frames with the HTML Wizard.

If your images need to be bigger so they can be read more easily, choose the standard layout. If you have a large number of slides, maybe the frames layout would be the better choice. Our images need as much space as possible, so we will choose the standard layout.

Once you choose a Web page layout, press the Next button to go to step two of the Save as HTML Wizard, which is shown in Figure 6-38. Here you can choose the graphics format your images should be saved in. If you have decided to use the Animation Player, as we have here, select that option. Otherwise, select either GIF or JPEG.

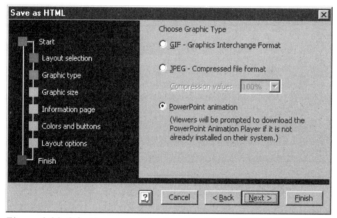

Figure 6-38: Selecting a graphics format with the HTML Wizard.

After selecting your graphics format, select the Next button to customize your Web presentation to fit the monitors of the people who will see it (Figure 6-39). The higher the resolution you choose (indicated by the larger numbers), the bigger your images will be.

If you choose 1024 by 768 and most of the monitors at your company are in 800 by 600 mode, your Web pages will probably be too big to see without scrolling the Web browser window. It is usually important to be able to see all of a slide at once, so choose the resolution carefully.

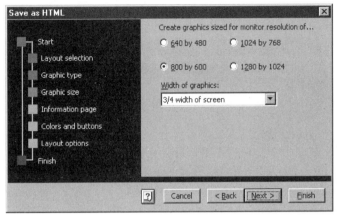

Figure 6-39: Selecting monitor resolution with HTML Wizard.

We will be conservative and choose 800 by 600 and make the graphics occupy three-fourths of the width of the screen. This will let the graphics be displayed on all but the smallest of monitors.

Press the Next button to go to the screen that allows you to include the e-mail address and home page of the company Web site (Figure 6-40). Any other information you add here will be displayed on the title page of the Web presentation. You can also give the user the option of downloading the presentation in PowerPoint format. If you want to include a button for downloading the newest version of Internet Explorer, you can do that as well.

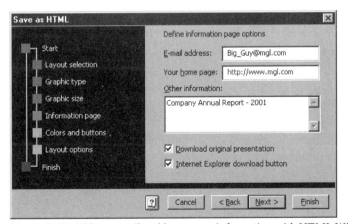

Figure 6-40: Adding e-mail and home page information with HTML Wizard.

Pressing the Next button will take you to the choice of making your presentation use the user's default browser colors or choosing your own (Figure 6-41).

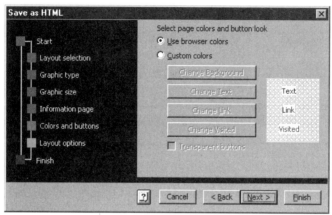

Figure 6-41: Choosing browser colors with HTML Wizard.

Be user-friendly here. Users choose their own color schemes for a reason. If you override their choice of colors for no good reason, you can irritate them unduly. If, however, you have images with transparent backgrounds and the text cannot be read unless it is on the proper color background, or if you have a background color that would hide normal text, you can change the colors so everything is easy to read. We will be using the default browser colors.

On the next page of the HTML Wizard, you get a choice of button styles to place on each page. As you can see in Figure 6-42, the choices are limited; but they will get the job done. These buttons give the user controls to go to the Table of Contents page, to the home page you specified earlier, and to a text version of the presentation.

FYI: Graphics & No Graphics

Every Web presentation created with the Save as HTML Wizard that uses the PowerPoint Animation Player is saved in graphical and text formats. This lets anyone view your Web pages, but they will make sense only if you include informative text on each slide.

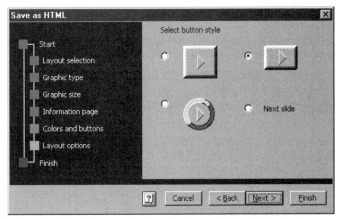

Figure 6-42: Selecting navigation buttons with HTML Wizard.

The final step of creating your Web presentation lets you choose where to place the control buttons, as shown in Figure 6-43. PowerPoint presentations tend to be wider than tall, so placing the buttons on the top or bottom of Web pages leaves more room for the slides themselves. If you have notes with your slides, you can choose to put them on the Web as well by checking the Include Slide Notes In Pages box.

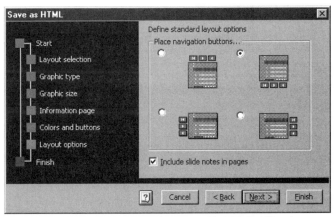

Figure 6-43: Placing navigation buttons with HTML Wizard.

Once you have made all the decisions on how your Web presentation should look, you must put the files somewhere. Specify a destination directory in the form shown in Figure 6-44.

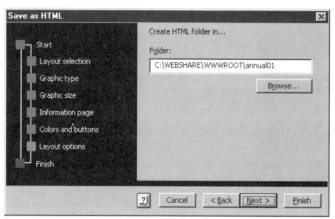

Figure 6-44: Saving the Web page files to a directory.

If you want to save your PowerPoint presentation to its own directory, there is no need to create a new one. The HTML Wizard creates a subdirectory under the directory you specify.

And you're done! Press the Finish button and wait for a while as PowerPoint chugs along, converting everything into HTML documents. Depending on the number and complexity of the slides in your presentation, the conversion process can take a while.

Viewing the New Web Pages

Once your presentation is saved, fire up your Web browser and take a look! Every PowerPoint presentation saved as HTML will get a Table of Contents page, which is shown in Figure 6-45.

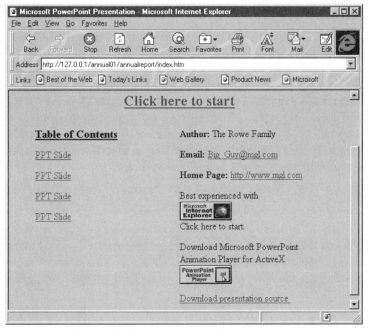

Figure 6-45: The HTML Wizard creates a Table of Contents page.

FYI: Editing the Table of Contents

Unless you consulted the Psycho Friends Hotline before you installed Office 97, you had no idea the organization you entered in a form during the installation would show up on your Web pages. (See where it says "The Rowe Family"?) You can use any text editor, such as Word 97, to edit the Table of Contents and remove it, if you entered something inappropriate.

To assure yourself the slides look okay, click on the Click Here to Start hyperlink to look at the first slide. But wait, what happened to the animated Da Vinci image? Instead of swiveling, as we told it to, it does some lame fade-in. What happened? Did we do something wrong?

Not all PowerPoint Animations can be transferred to the Web. When you save a presentation as HTML, the animations that can't be viewed on the Web are changed for you to an animation the Animation Player can view.

CAUTION

Unfortunately, PowerPoint doesn't tell you which of your animations can't be used on the Web when you save a presentation as HTML. The problem is that Microsoft neglected to build support for all of PowerPoint's animations into Animation Player.

What does this mean for you? It means you have to check every PowerPoint animation you convert to HTML to make sure it works properly before you put it up where the world can see it. If your animation isn't supported, you have two options: you can live with the substitute animation, or go back and choose a new animation that you know (hope) will be supported.

Now it's time to call the vice president and schedule that golf game tomorrow. As he's putting on the 18th hole and he needs a birdie to beat you, casually mention that you put the annual report slides on the Web yesterday and they look pretty good. Maybe he'll miss the putt, you'll beat him, and he'll be so excited about the new Web pages he won't mind. But don't count on it.

Finding More Help

Microsoft wants to make sure you have plenty of help and new ideas for creating Web pages with PowerPoint 97. In addition to the online help and the Value Pack on the Office 97 CD, Microsoft has lots of goodies online for you to use via the Web.

Using the Value Pack

The Value Pack on the Office 97 CD contains lots of goodies for you to discover. Discover is the key word here, because there is very little documentation that tells you exactly what is on the CD. You are practically reduced to just looking over the CD contents using the Windows Explorer.

There is some help to be found, however. You can use the Windows Explorer or PowerPoint to open the file: Valupack\Overview.pps, which is a PowerPoint presentation about some of the Value Pack contents. By clicking on the provided links, you can get a little better idea of what is on the CD.

Also, when you attempt to insert a clip-art image for the first time in any Office application, the Clipart Gallery will incorporate the clip-art collection that comes on the Office CD into the clip-art viewer so you can access all of the images. Just about every illustration in this book was created using

PowerPoint and the clip-art collection.

Using PowerPoint Central

If you look under the Tools menu, you will see an item called PowerPoint Central. If you click on that link, the Office Assistant will tell you how long it's been since you last visited the Microsoft Web site for the latest product updates on PowerPoint 97. You have the option of connecting to the Web site if you want.

Whether you do visit the Microsoft site or not, the PowerPoint Central slide show will appear. PowerPoint Central is chock-full of good advice and even a quick-start demo to show you how to use many of the features of PowerPoint 97. Running the demo is highly recommended even if you're a PowerPoint guru. There's some good information there.

Visiting the Microsoft Web Site

For a company that barely acknowledged the Web existed until recently, Microsoft has jumped on the Web in a big way. One of the ways they have adopted the Web to the user's advantage is by setting up an extensive set of Web pages dedicated to Microsoft products.

Under the Help menu is an item entitled Microsoft on the Web. Choosing this item brings up a list of several Web sites dedicated to help you get the most out of PowerPoint 97. You can find free software, get the latest information on bug fixes or plug-in enhancements, or query the Microsoft Knowledge Base to find the answer to your questions about PowerPoint. With PowerPoint 97 and the Microsoft Web site, help is just a mouse click away.

Moving On

By using PowerPoint 97, you can create some visually gorgeous Web pages that will entertain just about any Web visitor. Existing PowerPoint presentations can be put onto the Web, and your own custom graphics can grace your very own Web pages. PowerPoint 97 is perhaps the most Web-friendly of the Office 97 applications.

In the next chapter, "Access 97," you will discover how Microsoft Access 97 has been enhanced to use the Web and the Internet to share your database information with anyone who has a Web browser.

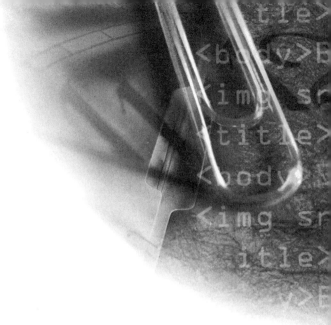

chapter 7

Access 97

The "beep" you just heard means there's incoming e-mail. You bring up your mail client and know immediately that it's not exactly a pat on the back.

You quickly scan the message . . . they want an online catalog. Just when you thought this Web site was done and wrapped up, they want an online catalog. Okay, so Internet commerce is the latest thing, and your Megatron Galacticorp Ltd. (MGL) bosses figure they might as well try to cash in on some of it. But a catalog isn't static—new items are added and deleted from one all the time, and prices change. This isn't going to be easy.

There are a couple of ways you could write Web pages for the items in the catalog. One would be to create a separate page for every item in the catalog and stay on top of it as the catalog changes. But it would be pretty cumbersome for people to have to go through the entire list every time they wanted, say, an MGL ballcap. Another might be to have one big page with everything in the catalog listed on it. Still cumbersome. What you need is a database—an indexed collection of information that can be organized in many different ways. With a database, people could search for specific items in the catalog, and the online version of the catalog could be kept up-to-date with the version you're using in-house. But how do you put a database online, and how do you create Web pages that change as the database changes?

What Is...

database: An online collection of related data, organized for easy changes and additions. Microsoft Access is a program that creates and manages databases.
datasheets: A tabular view of the data in the database, much like a spreadsheet.
dynamic pages: Web pages containing collections of data retrieved from a database in response to a specific, spontaneous request from a user.
static pages: Web pages containing collections of data retrieved from a database in response to a predefined request from a database programmer, triggered by a user.
reports: Paper collections of data retrieved from a database.
forms: Online screens designed to facilitate the entry of data into a database.
queries: Formal requests to a database to return data.

When confronted with a problem like this, most people either (1) find a workaround that doesn't require the use of a database program or (2) find a database programmer. The first solution invariably leads to an unmaintainable site, and the second can be expensive. Since we know your budget on this project, and you're eager to make this as easy to maintain as possible, let's consider option (3): create a catalog in Access and put it on the Web.

The number of options you have when considering how to put a database on the Web is staggering, and it could be the subject of its own book.

Our Take: Web Databases

Jeff: It certainly could be its own book. I wrote it. Um, sorry for the blatant plug, but Web/database connectivity is not easy and it's what I do for a living. Using Microsoft Access is about as easy as it gets under Windows, but only if you use a third-party product.
Kevin: I think that will change. If Microsoft is to position Access as a business-capable database management system, it's going to need to integrate it directly into IIS better than it has with Active Server Pages. Maybe in the next version?

Even if you limit yourself to the environment we're primarily concerned with in this book, Microsoft Access running on a Windows NT operating system, talking to the Web with Internet Information Server (or Peer Web Services, or Personal Web Server—they're all the same thing), there are several decisions you have to make early in the design process to create the right kinds of Web pages. You need to create the database, for starters. Then you need to decide:

1. Will users be allowed to ask questions of the database (*queries* in *dynamic pages*), or will you tell them what you think they want to know (*static pages*)?

2. Will you present the data in simple tabular form (*datasheets*), as a formatted page (*reports*), or in an attractive page that users can use to add data to the database (*forms*)?

3. Finally, do you want your database pages to work correctly in all Web browsers, or just in Microsoft Internet Explorer?

There's good news and bad news here. The bad news is that some of the decisions above are mutually exclusive, like good-looking forms and non-Microsoft browser compatibility. The good news is that you can still achieve most of this enormous functionality without sacrificing too much style. One way or the other, it's possible to get your data to the masses effectively and still have your Web pages look good.

Unfortunately, there's more bad news: using Office to put a database on the Web is a little like teaching a child to use the potty. It can be done, but it takes a long time to get it right and you're always wondering if you'll ever be done with the process. Some of the screen shots in this chapter took days to complete, and some never did work out, as you'll see.

What Is...

Active Server Pages: Microsoft's technology for making its Web server (IIS) talk to ODBC data sources (like databases). The term is also used to refer to the actual Web pages this technology creates. These pages can only be viewed with a Microsoft Web browser.
dbWeb: Another Microsoft product to handle communication between databases and a Web server. This product was actually purchased by Microsoft from another company and is not database- or server-specific.
Cold Fusion: Yet another product that makes databases talk to Web servers. This one has no association with Microsoft at all.

Microsoft's Web-page generator using its proprietary Active Server Pages format is still in its infancy, and you might be much better off using a database connector application such as Microsoft's dbWeb or Allaire's Cold Fusion. Both of these products, and a host of others, were built from the ground up to support database connectivity to the Web, and they sport large user bases and thousands of success stories. When you do get set to take the plunge, be ready to spend plenty of time browsing newsgroups and Microsoft's Web site for clues. It can be done, but it's not easy, and it's not as automatic as it should be.

Databases 201

Hey! What happened to "Databases 101"? It's not here. It's beyond the scope of this book to teach basic database theory and design, so we're going to assume a certain amount of knowledge. To successfully put a database on the Web using the techniques in this chapter, you need to know how to:

1. Create tables in Access and use standard terms in referring to table elements (records, fields).

2. Define relationships between tables.

3. Create simple forms in Access, including combo boxes and text boxes.

The level of sophistication of your Web site is directly related to your ability to create a cohesive, content-appropriate database structure. If you're not creating the database, you can probably get away with just understanding how it's put together.

Creating a Sample Database

We're going to create an Access database called *catalog* to hold the data we wish to put on the Web. It's on the enclosed CD, but you can create it yourself if you prefer. Start Access 97, create a new, empty database (call it catalog, natch). A database needs at least one table to be useful (unless it's a library database, but that's a different book), so click on the Tables tab in the database window and then select New to create a new table. Start in design view, and create a table structure as shown in Figure 7-1.

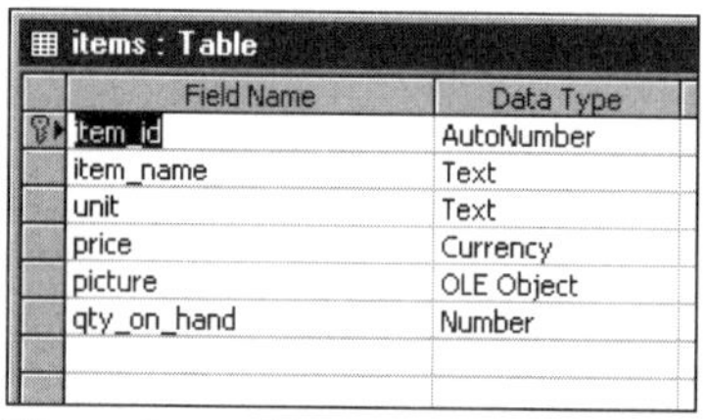

Figure 7-1: Table design created for the catalog.

Make sure you set the field Item_id to be a primary key, as shown. This will prevent the accidental entry of items with duplicate Item_id's into the database.

Next, you might wish to enter some sample data into the table. A table with data already entered is on the enclosed CD, but you can add data either in the Datasheet View of the table or by creating a simple form. Note that the field Picture is of type OLE Object. It will contain an image of the each item in the database. To store data in an OLE Object field, select the picture cell on the form or datasheet and right-click. Select Insert Object from the menu that appears and select an image file on disk to be imported into or linked to the field.

After you have data in the table, save it. When you're prompted for a name, choose Items and exit Access.

The examples later in this chapter will use some forms, queries, and reports in the catalog database to show how each of these items become Web pages. They're all on the enclosed CD, but you can create your own and follow along if you like.

For comparison with the HTML pages you'll create later, you need to know how each of the Access objects (forms, tables, reports, queries) we're going to turn into Web pages look in native Access. To follow along, click on the tabs at the top of the database window in Access. The table Items is a standard Access table with the structure shown in Figure 7-1. The query "Low Stocks" is a simple SQL statement:

```
SELECT items.item_name, items.price, items.picture, items.qty_on_hand FROM
items WHERE (((items.qty_on_hand)<100));
```

The form catalog is intended for use in viewing records in the table Items. If used in Access on a PC, it could be used to add or remove records from the table. It looks like Figure 7-2.

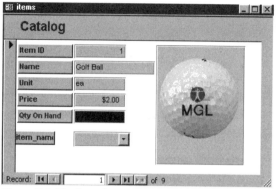

Figure 7-2: The form for editing or adding catalog items.

Lastly, the report Printed Catalog shows all of the available merchandise in the Items table in a form suitable for printing. It's intended only to display data, not to accept input. It looks like Figure 7-3.

items

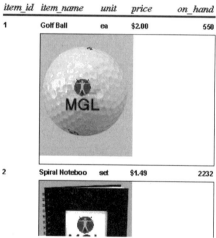

Figure 7-3: The printed catalog page.

ODBC: The Lingua Franca of Databases

Just because you have an Access database ready to go doesn't mean that the world will be able to get to it with their Web browsers. You could put the file containing the database where people could download it, but that's not really "putting a database on the Web." What you need is to find a way to make your Web server get the data people need out of your database.

If you go back to Chapter 5 and reread the discussion of using mail merge in Microsoft Word, you'll happen upon a discussion of data sources. In Word, a data source is a table in another application (a *server*) that provides data to the requesting application (a *client*) when needed. The server application must be present on the machine when the data is requested, and it must know where to find the data (in most cases, the client tells it where to look). So if you define a Word mail merge data source as an Excel spreadsheet, and Excel is no longer on the machine, there will be nobody available to serve the data and an error will result. The facility that allows this kind of data sharing is called Dynamic Data Exchange, or DDE. For the most part, there's no need for you to worry about the mechanics of DDE—it's automatic.

The standard for making databases accessible to applications other than the one that created them is called Open Database Connectivity, abbreviated ODBC. You're going to need to make your Access database into an ODBC Data Source by registering it with the Windows operating system, thus telling the Web server where to find it. Then you'll be able to create Web pages that talk directly to the database, using Windows as a middleman.

For example, let's say that you have an Access database that another application on the same machine (a client) wants access to (no pun intended). There are probably two ways you can do this, depending on the client:

- You can have the client query Access directly for the data.
- You can have the client query the operating system for the data.

The first option has two innate disadvantages:

- It requires Access to be installed and working on the PC being queried.
- Access has to start before it can provide the data, which creates a delay.

If you use the second option instead, with a little set-up ahead of time, Windows can get the data right out of the database without starting Access.

Before we get into the mechanics of setting up ODBC, you should realize that ODBC can be used to provide a means to query any data source, providing an appropriate ODBC driver is installed. These drivers are often provided with the application that manages the data. Access's ODBC drivers are installed when you install Access using the Typical installation. Secondly, you might note that Internet Information Server (IIS) uses ODBC to query local data sources, thus forcing our hand. We can't set up IIS to do a Word-style mail merge (although Word can use ODBC data sources).

What Is...

OLE (Object Linking and Embedding): Manages parts of documents ("objects") that are cut and pasted from one application to another. An Excel spreadsheet embedded in a Word document is using OLE. A small, limited version of Excel is actually running whenever you edit that embedded spreadsheet.

DDE (Dynamic Data Exchange): Permits the operating system to manage data that is shared between two applications, like an Outlook address list that is used as the basis for mailing labels in a Word mail merge. When Word needs the data, it starts Outlook; Outlook provides the requested data and then dies.

ODBC (Open Database Connectivity): Permits the operating system to manage data created in applications. Any application that can create tabular data can be an ODBC data source, given the appropriate drivers. When the data is needed, the operating system retrieves it without opening the application that created the data.

DSN (Data Source Name): The name of a table or procedure that retrieves data from a database of any type. ODBC makes referencing data sources on a given system easier by giving each data source a unique name, or DSN.

ODBC driver: A piece of software that tells Windows's ODBC system how to read and write data to a specific application. For example, the Access ODBC driver is typically installed when Access is installed. Most applications that can take advantage of ODBC install their own drivers when they are installed.

User DSN: A DSN that is only available to the user who configured it and only on the machine on which it was originally installed.

System DSN: A DSN that is available to certain users on certain machines in the local network. Typically, a system DSN is made available to all members of a user group or to all users of a given machine. Most data sources for use with third-party software, like Web servers, are configured as System DSNs.

File DSN: A DSN that is available to all users on the local network who have an appropriate driver for that data source installed locally. Rarely used.

IIS: Microsoft Internet Information Server, the Web server provided with Windows NT.

client: A machine or software application that requests data or services from another (the "server").

server: A machine or software application that provides data or services to another (the "client").

Installing and Configuring ODBC

To install and configure ODBC, there is a little work to be done on your Web server. In the examples in this section, the ultimate goal is to configure the Access database called Catalog as a system data source.

From the Windows desktop, select the Start I Settings I Control Panel. In Control Panel, double-click on the icon marked 32-Bit ODBC (in Windows 95) or ODBC (in Windows NT). The ODBC Data Source Administrator should start and look like Figure 7-4.

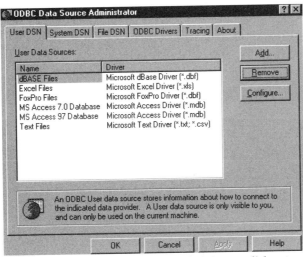

Figure 7-4: The ODBC Data Source Administrator dialog.

What Is...

configure: Set the options of a piece of software to perform a specific set of tasks most efficiently.

DSN (Data Source Name): The name of a table or procedure that retrieves data from a database of any type. ODBC makes referencing data sources on a given system easier by giving each data source a unique name, or DSN.

system data source: A DSN that is available to certain users on certain machines in the local network. Typically, a system DSN is made available to all members of a user group or to all users of a given machine. Most data sources for use with third-party software, like Web servers, are configured as system DSNs.

You might have only some of the entries shown in Figure 7-4, depending on what ODBC-compliant applications are installed on your system. The entries shown are samples to tell you what kind of data sources you can immediately use; none of the entries in the list are initially configured.

We're going to configure the Access database called Catalog as a system data source. This makes it open and available to anyone connecting to your system, including your Web server. The default data source type is User, which limits its use to the user who creates it; since we want the Web server to use the source we're creating, we should create a system data source. Select the System DSN tab at the top of Figure 7-4 and then click on the Add button.

The ensuing dialog, titled Create New Data Source, gives you a list of drivers to choose from for the data source you're about to create. Select the appropriate one (in this case, the Microsoft Access Driver) and click on Finish.

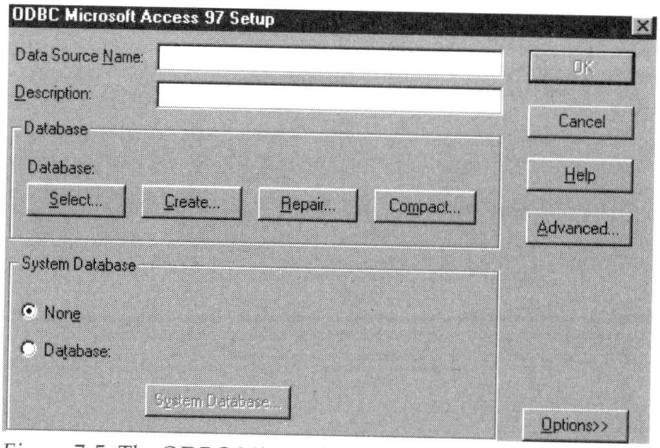

Figure 7-5: The ODBC Microsoft Access 97 Setup dialog.

Let's go through the configuration options listed here one at a time:

■ **Data Source Name**—Each data source of any type must have a name by which it is referenced by other applications. You can be pretty creative with the name, but it's best to pick something simple and descriptive so you don't have to struggle later to figure out what you named your data source. For this example, enter **Catalog**. Simple and easy to remember.

■ **Description**—Here's where you can get verbose. This description is typically only useful to someone coming in behind you and examining the ODBC settings.

- **Database**—Four options appear. They are:
  - **Select**—Press this button to start a file selection dialog, and select the file containing your Access database, Catalog. When you select it, the path to it will appear above the Select button.
  - **Create**—If you hadn't created the Access database yet, pressing this button would start Access and allow you to create one. Upon saving the new database and exiting Access, you'd be returned here and the database would be selected for you.
  - **Repair**—Occasionally, databases become corrupted due to hardware problems or software errors, usually in the operating system or database program. If you were trying to select an existing database and could not because it was corrupted, you could select the Repair button and fix it before continuing.
  - **Compact**—As databases are used, they can become somewhat disorganized and accessing data in them can become somewhat slower. To reorganize a well-used database into optimal shape, select the Compact button and select the database.

- **System Database**—Access can be configured to require passwords from users and to restrict and control access to specific parts of specific databases. The database in which such security information is stored is called System Database and is usually saved as system.mdb or system.mda. These special databases can also be data sources for ODBC, but they're not particularly useful as data sources for the Web. The None option should be checked in this box.

- **Advanced**—The only potentially useful option in the Advanced dialog is the default username and password to be used when accessing the data source. If you're intending to publish a database that has security enabled (see System Database, above), you can enter a default username and password in the Advanced dialog for the Web server to use when retrieving data. Typically, you would configure the database with a user called www_server or the like and assign it appropriate rights. Then you could use the special username and password here. Most databases will not require these settings to be used or modified.

When you've made all of the appropriate selections, press OK to return to the ODBC Data Source Administrator dialog. Finally, click on OK to close the ODBC Data Source Administrator.

Creating the Web Pages to Retrieve the Catalog

Now you're ready to write a Web page that retrieves data from the catalog database under Windows 95.

What Is. . .

tables: These basic descriptions of data are the linchpin of an Access database. All table information is available and accessible via the Web.

queries: Queries provide the means by which your Web server will retrieve or store data in your Access table(s). You can create queries in Access's convenient Query Builder, then obtain the SQL equivalent (by switching to SQL View) and use that in your Web page if you like, or you can use Access's Publish to the Web tool to save your queries in a Web-compatible format if you prefer.

forms: Getting data into and out of tables while in Access is usually performed with forms. Spending a lot of time designing nice-looking Access forms for use on the Web is probably a waste of time, however, since only one of the three methods Access provides for publishing your data makes any use of your forms at all. Even if you use the one method that preserves your form layout, any Visual Basic for Applications code you embed in your form will be ignored.

reports: One way to get data out of your tables is with Access reports, which are static, paper-destined representations of stored data. They work the same way on the Web.

macros and modules: These are of no use on the Web. Stored procedures in Access are not accessible from external applications, like Web servers.

If you've built any Access applications of any complexity at all, you should be realizing now that putting your project on the Web isn't going to be as simple as pushing a button. The simplest conversion method, which we'll describe below, provides only a simple, flat, dead view of your data. As the complexity of the conversion increases, so does the number of restrictions on your browser software. As you'll see in a minute, getting data out of the database is pretty easy, but getting it in (or getting it current) isn't.

Publishing Your Database

There comes a time in every project for some hard choices, and it's time for one of them now. Access supports three ways of putting your data on the Web (without using any third-party tools, of which there are many):

- **Static HTML**—Convert existing Access forms and tables into unchanging HTML pages.

- **Dynamic HTX/IDC**—Queries are passed to the Web server, which gets current data from the database and returns it to the requester in standard HTML.

- **Dynamic ASP**—Queries are passed to the Web server, which gets current data from the database and returns it to the requester using proprietary ActiveX controls.

Static HTML

Access's built-in Save As HTML option will save any table, form, report, or the results of any query (any Access object except macros and modules) in a simple, tabular grid and arrange it as an HTML table. These simple pages can be modified later or created with a template to improve their appearance. They can be viewed by any modern browser.

The data in these pages cannot be changed (except by directly editing the page, which has nothing to do with the database) once they are created. This kind of representation is appropriate in cases where the data really is static, or where speed of production is more important than appearance.

Our Take: Automatic Updating

Kevin: I can envision an Access application that could run on a Web server, updating its data sources through local use or by automatic update, and spitting out these static pages on a timed or demand basis. Say, for example, that you have an instrument that is attached to your PC and saves its data in just about any format. You could create an Access database, attach the table the instrument is updating (as a linked table), and write an Access module that writes HTML pages to the documents directory of a Web server whenever the data changes. Anybody with access to the Web could then see the state of the instrument, but they could not modify the database remotely. Cool.

Dynamic HTX/IDC

In order to use Dynamic HTX/IDC pages, you have to have your pages on a machine that is running a Microsoft Web server, like Internet Information Server (IIS) on Windows NT or Personal Web Server on Windows 95. HTX/IDC gives you a way to permit real-time, live requests for information against your database without sacrificing browser compatibility.

Using the data source we created earlier, Access creates HTML pages that include nonstandard HTML. These files have the extension .HTX. When a remote user opens one of these HTX files, the Microsoft Web server looks for an associated file with the same name and an extension .IDC. These IDC (Internet Data Connector) files contain the name of the data source and an SQL command that retrieves the data from the specified data source. The Web server then plugs the retrieved data into the HTX file and passes it on to the remote requester as standard HTML. This process is shown in Figure 7-6.

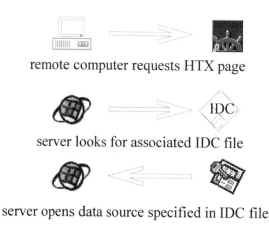

remote computer requests HTX page

server looks for associated IDC file

server opens data source specified in IDC file

server fills in data fields in HTX file

server returns filled-in HTML to remote computer

Figure 7-6: The data retrieval process with HTX/IDC files.

Since a live query is performed every time a remote user accesses a page, this kind of data access is called *dynamic*. Access will set up tables, forms, and queries for you in this format, but only as tabular datasheets. No fancy formatting here. However, if you want to modify the HTX file Access creates to make it look a little snazzier, you can do so and still take advantage of the dynamic nature of the medium.

Your fields are still limited to simple text boxes, however; even though HTML provides some additional useful controls (such as scrolling selection boxes and option groups), they're not supported by the current version of the Publish to the Web Wizard. Let's hope they are in a future release.

FYI: A Wizard by Any Other Name

From a loyal reader: *Why is this called "Publish to the Web Wizard" when it's just HTML Wizard in the other applications? Or is this Wizard somehow different?*

The HTML Wizards just save to the local disk. The Publish Wizard actually talks to a live WWW server and uploads your pages to it.

Dynamic ASP

If you want to get really fancy, this mode of publishing will allow you to do almost anything you want. Got a nice-looking form? No problem. Custom controls, like calendars and tabs? Can do. Embedded video? Sure. Of course, you've got to have the pages on a machine that's running a Microsoft Web server. That's no big deal; we had to do that for the HTX/IDC files above, too. There's only one more catch—you have to sell your soul to Bill Gates. ASP (Active Server Pages) work by embedding ActiveX controls in the pages. These ActiveX controls communicate directly with the Web server, bypassing HTML altogether. The problem is that ActiveX controls are only visible in Microsoft's Web browser, Internet Explorer (IE). So if you are comfortable limiting your audience to PC users running IE (less than 40 percent of all Web users at this writing), you can bake this concoction.

Most Access objects look about the same in ASP pages as they do in HTX pages, except for forms. Your carefully designed form is supposed to have its controls converted to their ActiveX equivalents and saved in the HTML page for you, preserving most of the functionality (and appearance) of the original Access form. If you're designing for an Innernet (Jeff's name for Intranets), you might be able to get away with this if everybody's on a PC and is running IE. If your pages are intended for the world at large, this isn't a good choice. Finally, it doesn't always work right, as explained below.

Choosing Your Publishing Approach

How can you decide what kind of page you're going to create? First of all, you're not stuck with one kind of page for your entire site. If some of your data tables are well suited to static representation, you can use static pages for those. If some require the latest data from the database, choose HTX for those. And if some are only going to be used by internal users with access to Internet Explorer, you can go to town with ActiveX controls in ASP pages.

The decision process you'll follow for each database object (tables, forms, queries, reports) looks something like Figure 7-7. In fact, you can use that decision tree to help you make your decision.

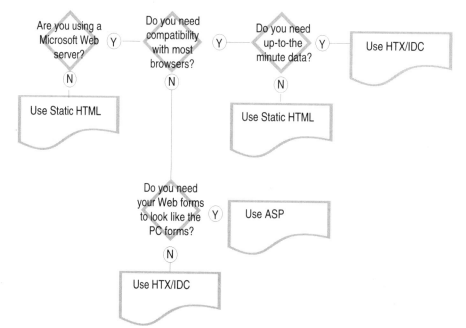

Figure 7-7: Decision process for selecting the publishing approach for each page.

Once you've decided what kinds of pages you're going to make, it's time to get cracking on them. This is the easy part. Really.

Access HTML Templates

If you're at all serious about putting a site together using Access, you'll need to take some positive control of the appearance of your pages. Access doesn't do a very good job of it for you, although Microsoft does provide some decent sample templates to start with. If you're not comfortable working in HTML, you'd better stick with the templates provided with Access and available on Microsoft's Web site.

Access HTML templates are different from the Access internal form and report templates you might have used, and they're unlike templates in any other Office application.

Understanding how templates work requires some knowledge of the way HTML is interpreted by browsers. When writing HTML, you insert tags in a text file that the browser on the remote computer interprets and displays. For example, if you insert an <EM> tag (emphasis) in your document, the remote machine is free to decide how to display that (although most browsers will italicize the text the tag encloses). In Access HTML templates, you insert special non-HTML tags that Access interprets and changes to standard HTML when you use the Publish to the Web Wizard. There aren't many of these special tags, and you'll only use a few of them for most pages. You can insert these special template tags in any HTML file; you might do well to create your template in Word or PowerPoint and then insert the appropriate Access tags in the raw HTML that they generate.

Access Template Tags

For reference, the following special tags are recognized as placeholders by Access in Access HTML template files. HTML templates are typically enclosed in triangle brackets, and these are used in the same way:

- **<!--AccessTemplate_Body-->** This is where the data extracted from the Access database is placed. Without this tag, your template isn't of much use. This tag should be placed somewhere in the <BODY> region of the template file. Note that the tag shown in the online Access help topic About HTML Template Files for this function, AcessTemplate_Body, is misspelled.

- **<!--AccessTemplate_Title-->** A placeholder for the title of the document, which is specified during the Publish to the Web process. The HTML document title is usually displayed in the title bar of the Web browser. This tag is usually inserted in the HTML <TITLE> tag:

```
<TITLE><!--AccessTemplate_Title--></TITLE>
```

- **<!--AccessTemplate_FirstPage-->** This tag creates a hyperlink to the first page of a series of Web pages created in one batch by the Publish to the Web Wizard. If desired, this should appear somewhere in the <BODY> of the template file and would normally be used as part of a hyperlink tag:

  ```
  <a href="<!--AccessTemplate_FirstPage-->">Beginning</a>
  ```

- **<!--AccessTemplate_PreviousPage-->** Hyperlink to the previous page.

- **<!--AccessTemplate_NextPage-->** Hyperlink to the next page

- **<!--AccessTemplate_LastPage-->** Hyperlink to the last page in a series.

- **<!--AccessTemplate_PageNumber-->** Inserts the current page number. Note that HTML pages don't have any concept of length or of page breaks, so this tag really represents the order of a given page in a series or hierarchy of pages. It might appear several screens down on the remote browser. You'd probably use it at the end of the <BODY> region in your template.

FYI: Access Tags Embedded in HTML Comment Tags

HTML-savvy readers will notice that the Access template tags are surrounded by the standard HTML comment tags, <!-- -->. This prevents errors when the Wizard can't fill in the tags and they get sent to the remote browser, or if there's a typo in the tag itself. The worst that can happen is that nothing will appear where the inserted object is supposed to be.

Access expects templates to be located in the directory C:\Program Files\Microsoft Office\Templates\Access. If you desire your templates to be located elsewhere, change the HTML Template option in Access Options. Finally, make sure that any images included in your HTML file are located in the folder to which you will be saving your HTML output. If you're working on one project, you might do well to keep your templates, images, and output all in the same directory. Just make sure your options are set appropriately and make sure you use unique filenames for your template files to tell them apart.

Our Take: Tags Within Tags Within Tags?!

Kevin: Since HTML is a standard language, companies have to find a way to differentiate their products from each other. One way to do this, as we alluded to earlier, is to add extensions that enhance the standard by adding functionality or style. In HTML, it's a tenet that any browser should be able to ignore any tags it doesn't understand. So you see a few custom tags being created, like the Microsoft <MARQUEE> monstrosity ("MMM"?), but it's much more common to add the really extensive additions in the form of tags inserted into standard HTML comments, which look like this: <!--comments here-->. It's a particularly nasty kludge, because you're never sure if a comment is really a comment anymore.

Jeff: Microsoft isn't the only company to do this. As an example, the Cold Fusion Web/database gateway product has a complete set of extension tags (which all start with <DB> or <CF>) that are added to HTML pages. The Cold Fusion program intercepts the page before it is returned by the server and replaces the tags with the data they request. Programming languages such as JavaScript add parameters to existing HTML tags to enhance the functionality of a Web page.

Web pages are created by using HTML tags, so it's natural to create new tags and attributes since users are already familiar with how tags work. The problem with this is not all products work as well as others, a tag for one product can clash with an identical tag from another product, and some browsers might not recognize the new attributes at all. The simple world of ubiquitous HTML is just a memory as users demand more functionality from the Web and companies respond to these demands with new products.

Creating an Access Template

Let's put some of this knowledge of Access template tags to work in creating a template for our catalog page. We've already created several pages, so we can work from one of those. The home page we created in Word is a good starting point, so if we open it in Word we can switch to View/HTML Source to do the editing. We see something like Figure 7-8.

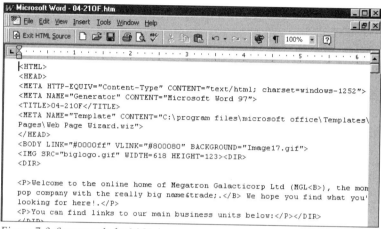

Figure 7-8: Source code for MGL home page.

Most of this gibberish is entirely unnecessary, so we'll delete it. First, save the file to a folder where you're comfortable working with it, since we're going to make some drastic changes. This might be a good time to create that working area we discussed above.

FYI: Creating a Save As Folder

You can create a new folder in the "Save As" dialog that all Office applications use to save files. Just move to the parent of the soon-to-be created folder, and click on the Create New Folder button (the third button from the left; it looks like a folder with a star peeking out from the upper right-hand corner). Type the name of the new folder, and then double-click on it to go into it and save your file.

A good place to put that working area might be C:\Program Files\ Microsoft Office\Templates\Access*project_name*, where *project_name* is whatever name you find easy to work with. For this example, we'll use MGL and call the file t_home.htm. The *t_* prefix makes it clear that this is a template. You can use any convention you like.

Now we need to do some editing. In a template file, we don't need all of the <META> tags; they're there for Office's convenience, not yours. And most of the stuff between the <BODY> and </BODY> tags can go away, too. Be careful not to delete the <BODY> tags themselves, though; they contain important information about the page background and other elements of the page design. When you're done cutting, your file should be similar to Figure 7-9.

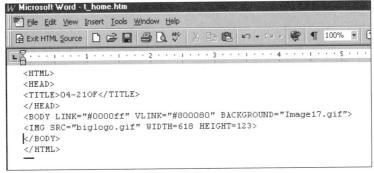

Figure 7-9: Edited source code of the MGL home page.

Notice that we left the <IMG SRC> tag at the beginning of the <BODY> region intact. That's the MGL logo, and we want it to appear on all of our pages.

Now it's time to insert some of the Access-specific template tags defined above. We should replace the document title, include the data tag in the <BODY> region, and maybe add some navigation links at the bottom. The navigation links will be useless unless we create a lot of pages at one time, but they're easier to remove later than they are to insert. After making the replacements we want, the template document looks like Figure 7-10.

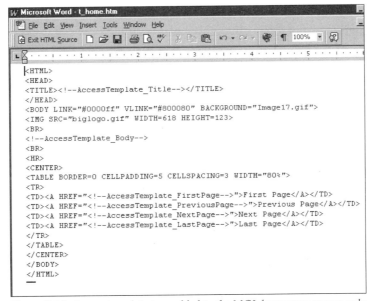

Figure 7-10: Access template tags added to the MGL home page source code.

We've inserted the Access title in the <TITLE> tag and the data object in the <BODY>. There's a little fanciness at the end; the navigation hyperlinks are arranged in an HTML table, side-by-side on one line. Finally, a few <BR> tags insert line breaks at strategic points to space things out a little. If we look at the template we just created in a browser (or Word's HTML mode), it looks like Figure 7-11.

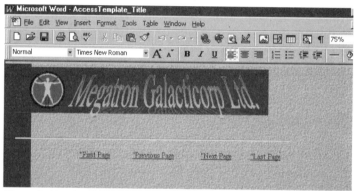

Figure 7-11: Edited MGL home page viewed from browser.

Not bad. A couple of things to notice: the title of the page is "AccessTemplate_Title," which will be replaced when we run the Wizard, and the hyperlinks at the bottom each have a double-quote (") before them. This is due to the unusual convention of having a comment within quotation marks, which HTML doesn't like. It will go away after we add data to the page.

Using Access's HTML Wizard

Creating any kind of Web page in Access starts with the Publish to the Web Wizard, which is started by selecting File | Save As HTML in Access. About halfway through its progression of windows, you're asked to decide on the format (HTML, HTX/IDC, or ASP) of your pages. Depending on your selection, there are several additional options, but you always end up with a page or series of pages in the directory you specified at the start.

Access's Publish to the Web Wizard includes an indexing function that will create a table of contents for your site (assuming the whole site is created from Access data objects at one time, which is unlikely). It can also transfer your files to a Web server locally or remotely after they're created if you choose.

The Publish to the Web Wizard is more helpful than most Office wizards, guiding your effort to publish a database all the way through pushing the newly created pages onto your Web server. Unlike most wizards, however, this one works best with some preparatory work, including writing templates and establishing your server.

The catalog database we're using for our examples includes at least one table, form, query, and report. The data in our product catalog rarely changes, so by following the decision tree in Figure 7-7 we can quickly see that Static HTML is a reasonable output format for this database. But we'll try all three methods on it for completeness.

No matter what format you're going to create, you'll start by selecting File | Save As HTML from the menubar. The Publish to the Web Wizard starts and looks like Figure 7-12.

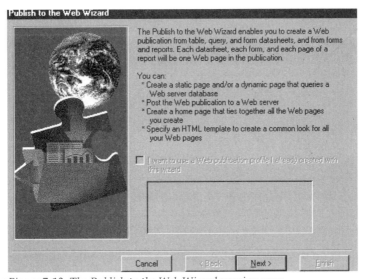

Figure 7-12: The Publish to the Web Wizard opening page.

The set of options you specify in the process of creating a Web site, including template files and file directories, can be saved as a *Web Publication Profile*. These profiles can be reused with other databases or can be reapplied to the same database later to regenerate the pages with new data or data objects. If you had saved any profiles, they would appear on the dialog in Figure 7-12 and could be selected.

What Is...

profile: A collection of settings that you wish to reuse.
template: A file that acts as a basis for new Web pages, sometimes including graphics, backgrounds, and navigation links.

For now, pressing the Next button takes you to a dialog where you can choose the elements of your database to be Webified, as shown in Figure 7-13.

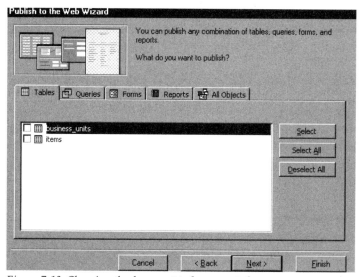

Figure 7-13: Choosing the document to be converted.

Clicking on the selection boxes to the left of the names of the tables, queries, forms, and reports shown in each of the tabbed property sheets of this dialog selects them for publishing as HTML. For a bird's-eye view of the whole database, select the All Objects tab.

We'll select the Items table, the Low Stocks query (which reports items whose stock quantity is low), the Catalog form (used to enter or edit objects in the Items table), and the Printed Catalog report. Pressing Next takes us to the next dialog, shown in Figure 7-14.

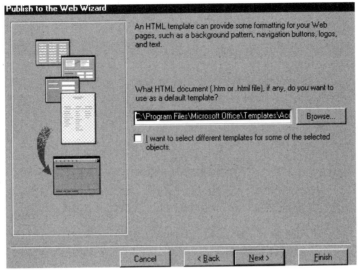

Figure 7-14: Choosing an Access template for your HTML conversion.

Time to put the template we created earlier to good use. Click on the Browse button and select the template you wish to use as a basis for your pages, if any. Several Access templates come with Office, but you can't preview them here. You can, however, start your Web browser at this point and look at the templates provided before choosing one.

An option at the bottom of the screen allows you to choose different templates for different database objects. Clicking on this box and then pressing Next brings up a spreadsheet-like dialog listing each selected database object and allowing you to independently assign templates to each object. For this example, we'll use the basic MGL template for all of the pages.

Selecting Next brings us to the dialog (Figure 7-15) where we have to decide on the format for the pages to be generated: Static HTML, HTX/IDC, or ASP.

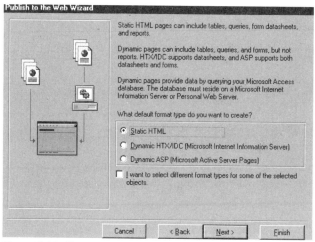

Figure 7-15: Choosing the type of page.

As above, we can specify different formats for each object page, if desired. We'll go through all three formats with all four objects, but let's go on to the next dialog for now because it's the same for all the page formats.

Once you've selected your page format, press Next to specify where the pages should go. The resulting dialog is shown in Figure 7-16.

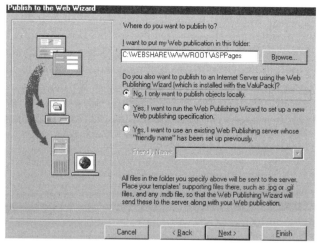

Figure 7-16: Selecting the destination of converted pages.

The Access Wizard gives you three choices of where to put your converted pages:

- Put the pages in a local folder, like the folder containing the template file, or in a folder on a locally connected Web server;
- Define a remote Web server to Windows using the Web Publishing Wizard and publish to it;
- Use a remote Web server already defined and save the pages on it.

The details of the Web Publishing process are explained in Chapter 4, so we'll publish the pages locally for these examples.

Selecting Next brings you to a dialog asking if you want to create a home page. This home page is really an index of the pages you're about to create and you can link to it from another page in your site if you're publishing several similar tables, forms, or reports. There's nothing lost (except a few seconds) by creating it, so click on the Yes, I Want to Create a Home Page box and accept the default page name, imaginatively titled Default.

FYI: The Web Index Page

Most Web servers recognize pages called default.htm or index.htm as starting points for remote users. So if a remote user specifies the directory containing your pages but doesn't specify a file, the Web server will show them one of these two files if they exist. If your server has Allow Browsing enabled, it might be a good idea to always create an index file to prevent snooping eyes from viewing your entire file structure.

We're almost home free. Access finally asks if you want to save your selections to a Web publication profile, discussed above. Save the profile if you wish and press Finish to create your Web pages in the format you chose.

FYI: Reinventing the Wheel

From a curious reader: *If you don't save the profile, what happens?*

If you save a profile, you can go through this whole set of dialogs again and Access will show you the options you chose when you saved the profile. You can change them then if you wish. If you don't save a profile, you have to start from scratch every time you publish (or re-publish) your pages. Once you get it right, there's little to lose by saving one basic profile and reusing it.

Creating Static HTML Pages

For our first example, let's assume you chose Static HTML in the page format dialog in Figure 7-15. Once you finish the rest of the Wizard option dialogs, you should see several new files in your template directory. They represent the HTML versions of the database objects we exported and are more or less ready to put on the Web site. Let's look at the pages one by one.

The Default.html Index Page

Access created the default index page we requested (Figure 7-17).

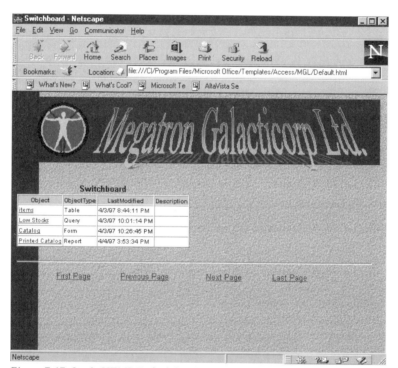

Figure 7-17: Static HTML Default.html index page.

It's been titled Switchboard for us, and it contains a list of all of the database objects we saved as HTML. Furthermore, they're already connected as hyperlinks from this page, which will make navigating among them pretty easy. Notice also that our template layout has been preserved, and the funny extra quotation marks before the navigation links at the bottom of the page are now gone. We might or might not want to use this page on our site, but it will make debugging a lot easier.

FYI: One Ringy-Dingy

From an inquisitive reader: *What's with the switchboard?*

Microsoft likes to suggest that Access applications be built with a central form called a *switchboard*, from which navigation is provided to all other forms. The example Northwind database included with Access works like this. The default home page Access creates is also in this switchboard format, which you may or may not like. At least they're consistent.

FYI: Adjusting Pages

The Switchboard table Access created for us doesn't look too good pressed up against the left margin like that; a little editing of the HTML source code could center the table on the page or indent it one notch to the right and make it look a lot better. It's going to be this way in all of the exported pages. In the examples on the CD, the template has been modified to correct this alignment problem.

The Publish to the Web Wizard created all of our pages with the UNIX suffix .html instead of the Windows .htm. This shouldn't cause any problems, but it's worth noting as you work with your pages. If you manually create links to these pages, remembering that they have an unusual suffix will save you grief later.

Moving right along: let's see how the Items table fared. Click on the hyperlink marked Items.

Tables Exported as Static HTML

Figure 7-18 shows how a table saved as static HTML appears in Netscape.

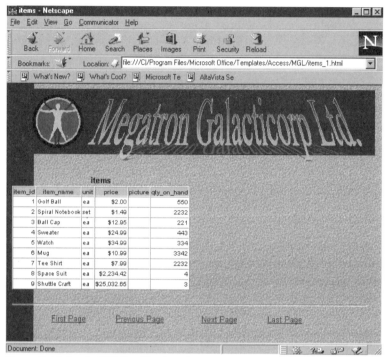

Figure 7-18: Static HTML table viewed in Netscape.

This datasheet-like display of the Items table is obviously limited; most of the data is there, but it's far from exciting. Still, it would be pretty easy to spruce it up by directly modifying the HTML table the data is in. Using Word's HTML mode, you could easily delete the column qty_on_hand showing quantity available (probably doesn't belong on a public Web site).

What about the picture field? Access can't export embedded OLE objects directly; to do so would require saving each of them as individual files and inserting a link to the files in the page. Of course, *you* can do that pretty easily. Since the images we've embedded are already saved on disk, they just need to be moved to the Web server's public documents area (or wherever this document ends up) and linked in manually. For example, we can add the picture of the golf ball by finding the table row containing the golf ball information, and changing the line of HTML that reads

```
<TD BORDERCOLOR=#c0c0c0 ALIGN=RIGHT><FONT SIZE=2 FACE="Arial"
COLOR=#000000><BR></FONT></TD>
```

to

```
<TD BORDERCOLOR=#c0c0c0 ALIGN=RIGHT><FONT SIZE=2 FACE="Arial"
COLOR=#000000><IMG SRC="1931.gif"></FONT></TD>
```

(bold added for emphasis). This makes the table look like Figure 7-19.

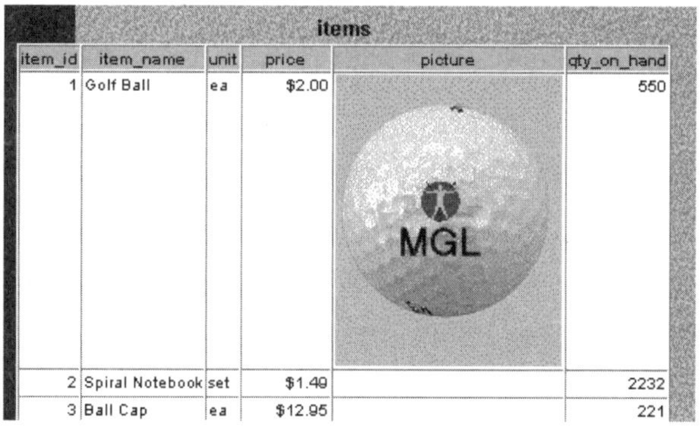

items					
item_id	item_name	unit	price	picture	qty_on_hand
1	Golf Ball	ea	$2.00		550
2	Spiral Notebook	set	$1.49		2232
3	Ball Cap	ea	$12.95		221

Figure 7-19: Static HTML table with image embedded.

It's not beautiful, but you get the idea of how you can directly modify the source HTML to drastically improve the presentation of your pages.

The navigation links at the bottom of the page still don't do anything. That's because a single table fits on a single HTML page. That's not the case with a form, where a separate instance of the form can be created for every element in the source table. Let's see how the Catalog form fared. Click on Back in your browser, and then select the hyperlink marked Catalog to continue.

Forms Exported as Static HTML

Figure 7-20 shows how the Catalog form fared.

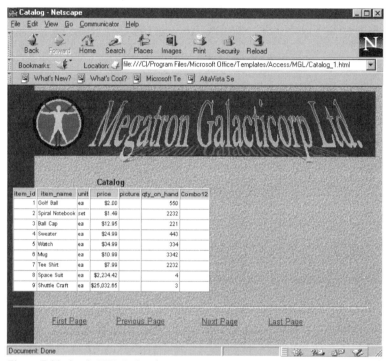

Figure 7-20: Static HTML Catalog page.

This looks amazingly like the output for the table on which it's based, Items. That's because Access makes no attempt to save the format of an Access form unless it's saved in ASP format. All of the form elements are here, including the blank space where the pictures ought to be, but there's really no difference between this and the index page (Figure 7-18) except one table is titled Switchboard and this table is called Catalog.

Next up is the query Low Stocks. Go back a page in your browser and click on Low Stocks to see what's next.

Queries Exported as Static HTML

Not a lot of excitement in Figure 7-21.

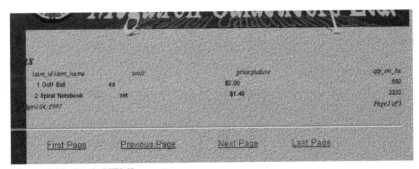

Figure 7-21: Static HTML query page.

Again, we have a table representation of the results of the query—those items with quantities less than 10.

Reports Exported as Static HTML

Since reports are, by their nature, static, you'd expect pretty good results from exporting a report as a static page. What you get is Figure 7-22.

Figure 7-22: Static HTML report page.

As you can see, you're likely to be a bit disappointed. But wait! All is not lost here. Let's examine what we've got and why it happened.

First of all, you'll notice that the title of the report, Items, is left justified and invisible on top of the blue sidebar. That's because the default title color that Access uses in creating a simple report from a table is dark blue; on any other color background, it would probably look fine. Additionally, we've still got the problem of the output data appearing too close to the left margin, which will have to be moved by manually going into the source code.

At last, the navigation buttons at the bottom of the screen actually do something: they take you from page to page in the report. Why are there only two records per report page? Because there are only two records per report page in the Access version. In Access, however, a picture of each item takes up a lot of the page; here, the pictures don't come across, so it looks like the page is skimpy.

A little work can improve this page noticeably. First, the Access report should be reformatted so it looks better on a dark background. Since we know the pictures won't come across, we should either plan on including them manually or remove the field in which they're displayed altogether. You might consider not using the template for reports, because you can do much more careful formatting of them directly in Access. There's no reason why an Access report can't look just fine coming through the converter, if it's set up right. In this case, however, the raw table output looks better than the carefully formatted report. *C'est la vie.*

In short, static HTML pages are best used only in situations where the appearance of the page doesn't matter; say, pages intended for internal use or pages that will be manually manipulated later.

Creating Dynamic HTX/IDC Files

Picking up where we left off earlier, in the progression of the dialogs of the Publish to the Web Wizard, if you select Dynamic HTX/IDC (Microsoft Internet Information Server) as your default page format (Figure 7-15), the data source selection dialog in Figure 7-23 appears.

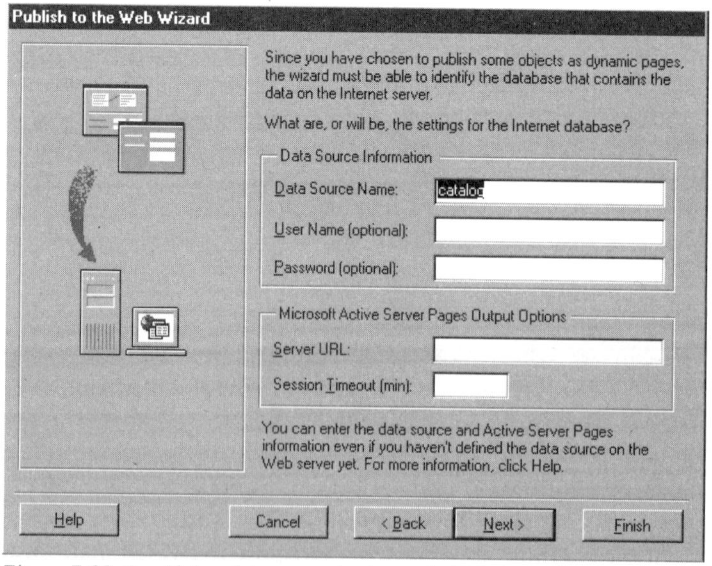

Figure 7-23: Specifying data source in dynamic HTX/IDC format.

CAUTION

Remember, to use any kind of dynamic page format without additional program-
ming, you have to be serving the pages from a machine running IIS or Personal
Web Services, where the background programming is built in for you.

We created our data source ahead of time anticipating this dialog. The Web
server will need to know where to get the data requested by the HTX templates it's about to create, and this dialog is where you tell it. A username and
password are only required if the ODBC data source requires them. Our data
source is called Catalog, and it's filled in for us since Access assumes we were
bright and named the data source the same thing as the database. It's right. We
are indeed bright. Select a destination for your pages, choose to create a home
page, save your selections if you like, and press Finish to create your HTX/
IDC document pairs in the directory you chose.

Tables Exported as Dynamic HTX/IDC

Starting from the newly regenerated default home page (which looks exactly
like it did in the previous example, Figure 7-17), select the Items page in your
browser. If you're viewing these pages as local files, you'll see Figure 7-24.

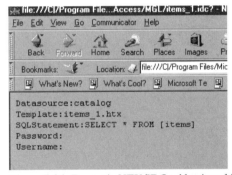

Figure 7-24: Dynamic HTX/IDC table viewed locally.

What happened? Remember, HTX (and IDC) files are interpreted by the
Microsoft Web server (whichever one you're using) and are returned to the
remote requester after formatting by the server. If you're viewing the files
directly, there's no server involved and you get to see the raw innards of your
files. Fire up your server, store the pages in a directory your server can get to,
and try again. The Items page should look like Figure 7-25.

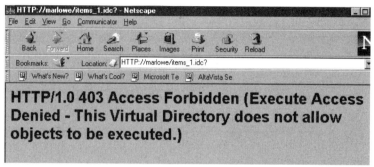

Figure 7-25: Dynamic HTX/IDC table viewed remotely without correct permissions.

Huh? If you see this, fire up the administration routine for your Web server and see if you've allowed Execute permissions on the directory you put the documents in. Since the default permission is read only, it's unlikely that execution of scripts (which is what an IDC file really is) will be allowed by default. Add execute permission for the affected directory and try again. Third time's a charm. Figure 7-26 shows what you should see.

item_id	item_name	unit	price	picture	qty_on_hand
1	Golf Ball	ea	2.0000		550
2	Spiral Notebook	set	1.4900		2232
3	Ball Cap	ea	12.9500		221
4	Sweater	ea	24.9900		443
5	Watch	ea	34.9900		334
6	Mug	ea	10.9900		3342
7	Tee Shirt	ea	7.9900		2232
8	Space Suit	ea	2234.4200		4
9	Shuttle Craft	ea	25032.6500		3

First Page   Previous Page

Figure 7-26: Dynamic HTX/IDC table viewed remotely with correct permissions.

Very nice. This looks a lot like the page we got with much less work in Static HTML (Figure 7-18), but with one critical difference: *the data is up-to-the-second.* Anybody viewing this page, on just about any browser, will see the absolute most current data. In the Static HTML example, the data is current only at the moment the page is generated. If your data isn't static, HTX/IDC provides a browser-independent way of performing live queries against your database.

As before, there are some minor formatting quirks here (note the decimal place problem in the prices—you can fix this by specifying the number of decimal places in the table design), and the pictures didn't come through. But we know what to do about that now.

Buoyed by our success, let's continue on to queries. Go back a page and select the Catalog form page.

Forms Exported as Dynamic HTX/IDC

Figure 7-27 shows what comes up in our browser.

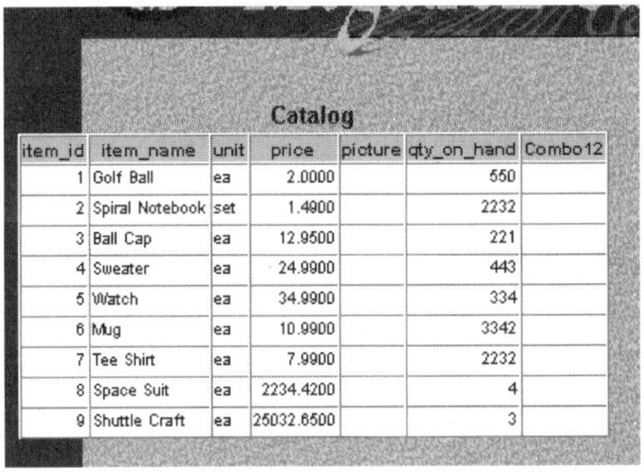

item_id	item_name	unit	price	picture	qty_on_hand	Combo12
1	Golf Ball	ea	2.0000		550	
2	Spiral Notebook	set	1.4900		2232	
3	Ball Cap	ea	12.9500		221	
4	Sweater	ea	24.9900		443	
5	Watch	ea	34.9900		334	
6	Mug	ea	10.9900		3342	
7	Tee Shirt	ea	7.9900		2232	
8	Space Suit	ea	2234.4200		4	
9	Shuttle Craft	ea	25032.6500		3	

Figure 7-27: Dynamic HTX/IDC Catalog page viewed remotely.

Looks just like the static form in Figure 7-20, except that we're guaranteed of current data. Yawn.

Queries Exported as Dynamic HTX/IDC

Go back a notch in your browser and select the Low Stocks page. Figure 7-28 shows the results of the simple Low Stocks query in HTX/IDC.

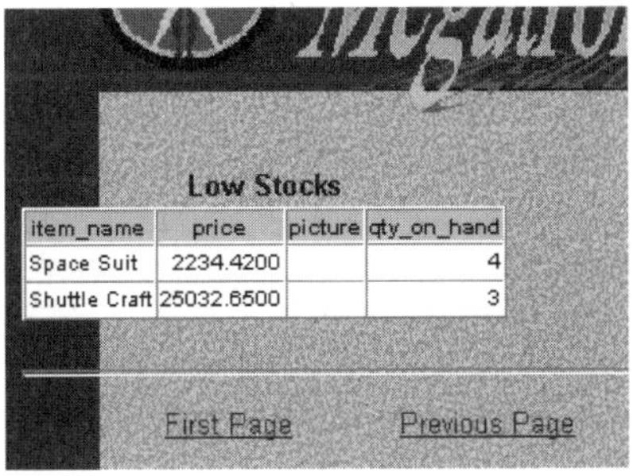

item_name	price	picture	qty_on_hand
Space Suit	2234.4200		4
Shuttle Craft	25032.6500		3

First Page   Previous Page

Figure 7-28: Low Stocks_1.idc.

More boredom, except that the data is current. Last try—how about that report?

Reports Exported as Dynamic HTX/IDC

If you're following along and you took a look in the directory into which you're storing your HTX/IDC files, you'll notice that the files created for the report Printed Catalog all have the suffix .html instead of .htx and .idc. If you check some of these files out, you'll see that they're exactly identical to the reports we ran earlier, using the static HTML format. The data is current in these reports, at least as of the time you created them, but they won't be updated as people access your pages. They're static.

Why didn't we get dynamic reports? It's hidden in the fine print, but there's no reason for a dynamic report. A report, by definition, is a snapshot of the database at the time it's created. If you want the absolute latest information in the database, you'll have to create a form to show it. If you try to publish a dynamic report, you'll notice that it remains eerily static.

Having run both static HTML pages and dynamic HTX/IDC pages, we can now see that they look amazingly similar. The only real difference is that you must run HTX/IDC pages on a Microsoft Web server, and the data is current as of when the user requests the page. Since any browser can view HTX/IDC documents in all their glory, there's no reason not to use them if you need up-to-date data.

The same is not true of Active Server Pages (ASP), explained below.

Creating Dynamic ASP Files

Harkening again back to Figure 7-15, we go for broke and select Dynamic ASP (Microsoft Active Server Pages). This time, we've modified the template slightly; for clarity, the gray background has been changed to a stippled white, and the <!--AccessTemplate_Body--> tag has been put in a couple of unnumbered list (<UL>) elements to indent it slightly. Following through the dialogs, we come again to the data source selection dialog, with some settable options for the ASP format (Figure 7-23, above).

There are two options specific to ASP here that we haven't used before: Server URL and Session Timeout (min). The information you enter here is stored as part of the ASP files Access will create. You have to enter the base URL of the server that will be providing your pages and the name of the directory from which these pages will be served here. For example, if you're using Internet Information Server (a good idea, because we've had pretty rotten luck doing this with Personal Web Server), you might keep your Web pages in \InetPub\wwwroot\catalog on the server www.megacorp.com. The entry for this block, then, would be http://www.megacorp.com/catalog. Additionally, if the remote server is heavily used, you might want to force external users to relinquish their control of an external data source after several minutes of inactivity; you can choose a time limit here. There is darned little documentation on how these options are supposed to work, but at least the first one is absolutely required. You read it here first.

There's one more caveat. Just because you're using a Microsoft Web server doesn't mean that it can read an Access data source, even through ODBC. If you try to use your ASPs, even in a Microsoft browser on a Microsoft server, you'll still have problems unless you install the Microsoft Access Desktop driver. This is usually installed when you install Access, but not necessarily.

You might be in luck: if you performed a full installation (not a typical installation) of Office 97, you probably installed the Access driver. (You can check to see if you have it—start the ODBC Administrator from Control Panel, click on the Drivers tab, and see if the Access driver is installed.) If so, you'll know soon enough as you follow the steps below. If not, this will do it for you. This driver is installed by starting the server configuration dialog and selecting the ODBC Drivers and Administration option, and then selecting the Microsoft Access Desktop driver. If you're using Personal Web Server, however, you have to install this driver from the ODBC Administrator under Windows. If you're running Internet Information Server on Windows NT Server, you can also use the installation procedure in "Installing Active Server Pages" below if you like.

The destination of our ASP files is a little more critical than it was in the cases of the static and HTX/IDC pages. It would be a good idea to publish these pages directly to your Web server's public directory, since you'll have to use the server to access these pages anyway. After following through the dialog until we get to the familiar Finish button, our ASP pages are created and we're back to where we started.

Tables Exported as Dynamic ASP
Okay, let's start at default.html and open the Items page in Netscape. Figure 7-29 results.

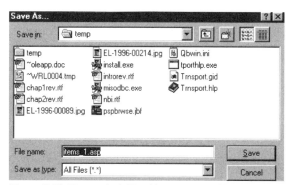

Figure 7-29: Dynamic ASP table page opened in Netscape.

Whoops. We have to use Internet Explorer to open these pages. Remember, anybody not using a Microsoft browser is going to be out of luck if you use ASPs. Trying again using IE, we get Figure 7-30.

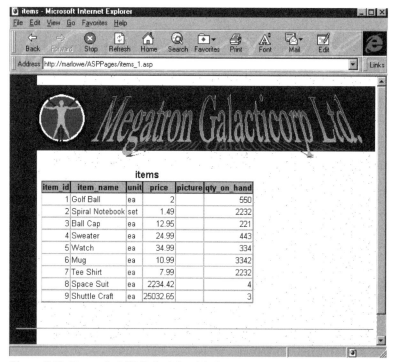

Figure 7-30: Dynamic ASP Default.html index page.

Notice how the table is easier to read on the stippled (instead of gray) background and how it's indented to get out of the dark margin? It still looks pretty boring, but how much can one ask from a simple table? The query that provides this live data takes less than five seconds on a Pentium-166 PC.

Forms Exported as Dynamic ASP

Now we'll go back to the home page and call up the Catalog form, the object in which the ASP format should really excel.

There are a couple of things that can go wrong while you're trying to do this, and the generation of an ASP file containing ActiveX controls (like the Catalog form) is a good way to test your system. First of all, you need to ensure that your Web server is aware of the existence of the directory that your pages are living in and that the permissions on that directory include both Execute and Read. If external users can't execute the ASP files, they will get blank pages when they try to access them. Using the Administration facility of your Web browser, set up a virtual directory for the folder in which you've put your pages and set the permissions.

FYI: Separate Executable Files From Static Web Pages

It's not a good idea to have executables in the root directory of your Web site because it's not generally a good idea to have executable files in directories that also have read permissions. Consider creating subdirectories for executable files. Note that the Publish to the Web Wizard will only save your files (and all the referential hyperlinks) in one directory, so if you want the ASP files in one directory and HTM files in another, you'll have to do some manual editing.

Secondly, ensure that you have installed the Active Server Pages extensions in your Web server. If you're running IIS (or Peer Web Services under Windows NT), it's an option at installation time and it's installed by default. If you're using Personal Web Server under Windows 95, it's not automatically installed, and you're likely to see the VBScript contents of your Active Server Pages in your Web browser.

Installing Active Server Pages

Here's the tricky part: The ASP extensions aren't included with the distribution files for Personal Web Services, so you have to get them manually from http://www.microsoft.com/iis. You'll need to fill out the registration and go to the download page, but you can then unselect everything except the Active Server Pages files to save some time. The file you want is called asp.exe and it's about 9MB, which will take awhile to download at 28.8 kbps. A good alternate site for this file is http://msie.www.conxion.com/msdownload/iis/activeserver/i386/en/asp.exe. If you're lucky enough to have a copy of Windows NT 4.0 around, you can just run asp.exe off of the NT CD and it will install nicely on your Windows 95 system.

If you're really unlucky, you will see only the template and the navigation links at the bottom of the page. This is a symptom of an incorrectly installed Internet Explorer, and it's apparently a very common problem. There is a file called isctris.ocx that is supposed to be installed when you first install Internet Explorer, but sometimes it doesn't get copied. If your page seems to load, but you see no data in it, you should launch Internet Explorer (even if it's not correctly installed) and go to http://www.microsoft.com/ie/download/layout.htm. The control will automatically download from Microsoft's Web site and install itself on your PC. This should solve the problem.

If you go to this site using a different browser, you'll need to download the file to your C:\Windows\System directory and then register it by typing **C:\Windows\System\Regsvr32.exe c:\Windows\System\isctris.ocx** (one line) in an MS-DOS window. Try again after that's installed, and all should be well. Since this is a client problem, there's only so much you can do from the authoring end, but at least you tried.

FYI: HTML Layout Control

Why not put a disclaimer at the bottom of your page: "If this page appears blank, and you're running Internet Explorer, click here to install the HTML Layout Control, which is required to view this page." Make the word "here" a hyperlink to the URL above and you've saved your viewer a lot of trouble.

Figure 7-31 shows how the Catalog form appears when you get it right.

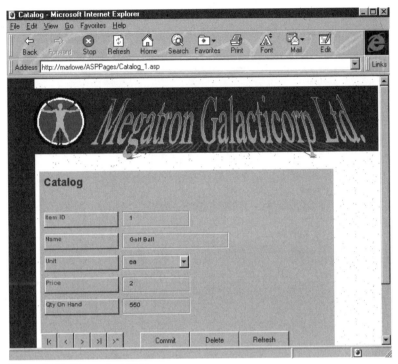

Figure 7-31: Dynamic ASP form page.

Looks good, except for the missing picture. As you create your own forms, you might find that they do not look exactly like the forms they are based on. Besides trivial issues of spacing and font (which are supported in a limited way online, since HTML is not yet capable of perfectly placing page objects), there are several objects that you can use in Access forms that will not appear on Web pages, even ASP-formatted ones. They include:

- Page breaks
- Lines and rectangles
- Tab controls (as opposed to tabs, which do export)
- Images (sigh)
- Background pictures

Apparently, problems loading and writing forms in ASP format are common, so common that Microsoft has set up an online troubleshooting guide. Unlike most online troubleshooters, this one really does get to the heart of the problem for most issues. You can try it at http://www.microsoft.com/support/tshoot/accessasp.htm.

Moving right along. Let's see how our simple query comes out.

Queries Exported as Dynamic ASP

Loading our list of items with low quantities, we get Figure 7-32.

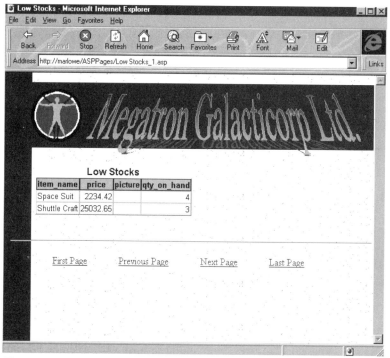

Figure 7-32: Dynamic ASP query page.

Nothing surprising here, as the query returns data in a datasheet format by default, and we've already seen that datasheets export relatively well.

There's no sense in checking out the report we generated in ASP, because reports are static and Access just creates a standard HTML page (with current data) for any reports specified during the Publish to the Web Wizard process.

Moving On

Access is an excellent, inexpensive, full-featured database application. Its handling of standard SQL commands is complete, and its extensions are logical and more or less useful; the application development environment Access provides, especially in the Access 97 version, makes Access programming feasible even for large, complex applications.

Unfortunately, the Web development tools Access provides are difficult to understand and poorly documented. While they are adequate to the task of simply *putting* an Access database on the Web, you will quickly find that you need to move up to third-party tools to effectively integrate your Access database with your Web site.

In the next chapter, we'll continue the tour of Office 97 by discussing publishing Excel 97 spreadsheets on the Web .

chapter 8

Excel 97

Y ou've gotten kudos from all your co-workers for the speed with which you constructed the company Web site. The company Annual Report is on the Web as a PowerPoint presentation, and the vice president is happy. You're basking in the afterglow of a job well done, when your phone rings. You know what is about to happen, but you answer the phone anyway.

It's Ted from the Accounting Department. "We heard about your nifty new Web site," he tells you. "We heard you created the company site to help disseminate information to everyone. Is that true?"

What can you say? "Yes," you say, "that's true."

"Great!" Ted says heartily. "The Head of Accounting just got chewed out by the Big Guy because we're spending too much on office supplies. We whipped up an Excel spreadsheet that shows how much we've spent over the past few months and we were about to print it out and hand it to everyone in the company, but we decided that would be wasteful of office supplies. Heh, heh."

Ted has a typical accountant's sense of humor.

"So," Ted continues, "we heard about the company Web site and figured it would be perfect if you could put our spreadsheet on the Web for everyone to look at. Can you do that for us?"

This time you're prepared. You know PowerPoint 97 can embed Excel spreadsheets and publish them to the Web, and you vaguely remember reading something about Excel's being Internet-enabled as well.

"Sure," you tell Ted. "Attach your spreadsheet to an e-mail message and send it to me. I'll see what I can do." You hope figuring out how to send e-mail will keep Ted busy for awhile, but Ted has been studying too.

"Will do. I'll fire up Outlook and send the spreadsheet to you. Thanks, bud. You're a pal!"

You hang up the phone and grab your mouse. You've got some work to do! Luckily, Microsoft Excel 97 will make your work easy for you. The Excel HTML Wizard can convert your Excel spreadsheets into Web pages in no time.

Creating Spreadsheets for the Web

The first thing you have to do when publishing Excel spreadsheets to the Web is to create a spreadsheet. True to his word, Ted sends his e-mail 10 minutes later with the spreadsheet attached. You save it to a file and open it in Excel 97. Ted's boring spreadsheet is shown in Figure 8-1. Watch it! You're yawning.

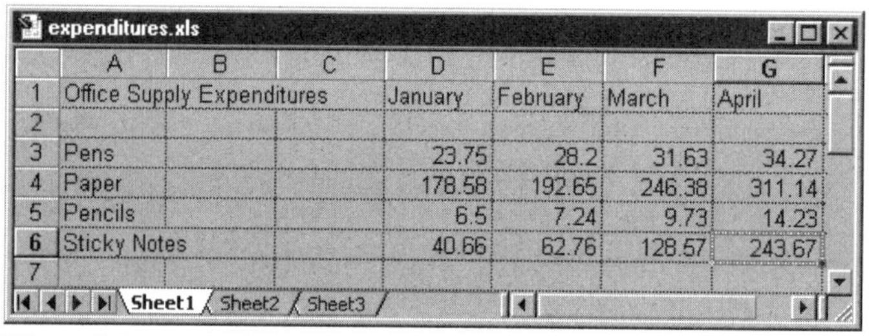
expenditures.xls

	A	B	C	D	E	F	G
1	Office Supply Expenditures			January	February	March	April
2							
3	Pens			23.75	28.2	31.63	34.27
4	Paper			178.58	192.65	246.38	311.14
5	Pencils			6.5	7.24	9.73	14.23
6	Sticky Notes			40.66	62.76	128.57	243.67
7							

Sheet1 Sheet2 Sheet3

Figure 8-1: An unadorned Excel spreadsheet.

The information you need to create a nice Web page is all there, but it would look better as an Excel Chart. Accountants can comprehend numbers directly, but normal humans need some sort of numerical translator to give raw numbers meaning. We're talking bar graph here.

However, Ted and his accountant friends would probably take offense that their nice, neat spreadsheet wasn't good enough for you to convert directly to the Web. To make Ted and his friends happy, as well as giving the regular company employees something visual, you can do both.

Converting a Spreadsheet to a Chart

First, let's create an Excel Chart that is based on Ted's data. Excel's tools make this a cinch. Just press the Chart Wizard button (it's the one that looks like a bar graph) on the main toolbar or choose the Insert | Chart menu item. This will bring up the Chart Wizard.

If you want to see Ted's spreadsheet converted into a chart, there is a video clip on the CD that will show you how it's done. Look in the demos directory for the *chartwiz.avi* file. If you double-click on the file in Windows Explorer, the Windows Media Player will appear and you can run the video.

The first step of the Chart Wizard, Chart Type, shown in Figure 8-2, gives you a large selection of chart types to choose from. For Ted's spreadsheet, we'll choose the Custom Types tab and pick the Columns With Depth chart type just because we like it. You can choose any style you like. Once you choose the visual representation you want to use, press the Next button. This takes you to the second step of the Chart Wizard to customize the source data.

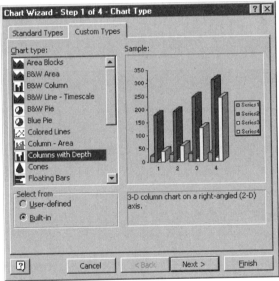

Figure 8-2: The Custom Types tab of the Chart Wizard dialog, Step 1.

FYI: Changing Chart Wizard Choices

All of the choices you make in the Chart Wizard can be changed on the final chart that is produced by the Chart Wizard. Just right-click on the chart and choose an option from the menu displayed. Each step of the Chart Wizard is available as a menu item, so you don't need to fret about making all of your choices correctly the first time. If you mess something up, it can be fixed.

On the Data Range tab of Step 2, Chart Source Data, which is shown in Figure 8-3, you can select the range of data cells that should appear in the chart and tell the Chart Wizard whether to chart the data in row or column format. Using row format groups data in horizontal cells on the chart. Using column format groups vertical cells on the chart.

You can create your spreadsheet in your favorite way and then adapt the chart to fit your preferences, or graph your data in a new way that shows different relationships among the data points.

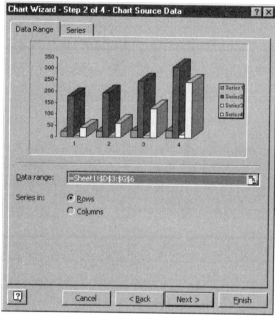

Figure 8-3: The Data Range tab of the Chart Wizard dialog, Step 2.

The Series tab of Step 2, Chart Source Data, shown in Figure 8-4, is used to customize legend and axis labels and bind cell values to a chart series. A series is represented by a particular color on the chart, so you can give a label to each bar color in the chart. The labels we will use for Ted's data are shown in Figure 8-4. Once you have labeled your chart, press the Next button to go to the next page.

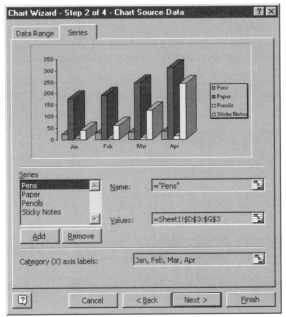

Figure 8-4: The Series tab of the Chart Wizard dialog, Step 2.

Step 3 of the Chart Wizard contains seven different tabs: Titles, Axes, Gridlines, Legend, Data, Labels, and Data Table.

The Titles tab of Chart Options, as you can see in Figure 8-5, is used to enter the title of the chart and the labels for each of the chart axes. Try not to put too much textual information on your chart so that people who see it can grasp the intent of the chart without having to spend much time deciphering tiny text.

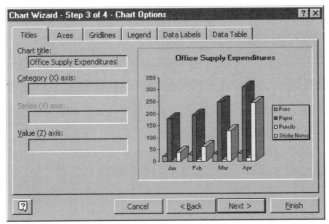

Figure 8-5: The Titles tab of the Chart Wizard dialog, Step 3.

When you advance to the Axes tab, which is shown in Figure 8-6, you can choose which of the available axes should appear on the chart. You can turn one or more axes off to alter the appearance of the chart data and see the results in the right-hand box. In some cases, only one axis might be significant when presenting your data in a chart. Some chart formats present data differently as well, so be sure to pick a chart that shows your data to best advantage.

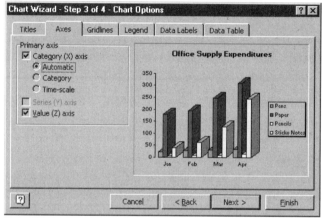

Figure 8-6: The Axes tab of the Chart Wizard dialog, Step 3.

We will use the Gridlines tab to give the chart a three-dimensional feel, as shown in Figure 8-7. You can choose the density of the gridlines with check boxes. You can also choose a two-dimensional or three-dimensional representation for the gridlines with the 2D Walls and Gridlines check box. Use these options to make your chart easier to read. Using a few gridlines can be easier to read than using them all. The 2D effects work better on some chart formats than others. The Excel Chart Wizard lets you play with the chart as you create it to present your data in the most informative way possible.

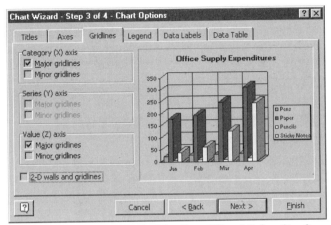

Figure 8-7: The Gridlines tab of the Chart Wizard dialog, Step 3.

The Legend tab, shown in Figure 8-8, lets you choose where to put the legend box, if you want to use one at all. To turn the legend off, uncheck the Show Legend box. If you choose to show a legend, use the placement selections to preview how it will look on the Web page. Using a legend makes the chart itself smaller, because the legend takes up valuable screen real estate. On the other hand, if you use no legend at all, the meaning of your chart might not be very clear. Use a legend to add meaning to your chart. Don't use it if it just gets in the way.

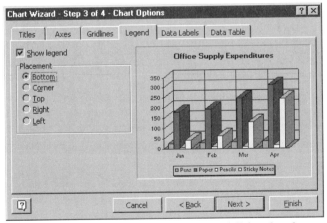

Figure 8-8: The Legend tab of the Chart Wizard dialog, Step 3.

Moving to the Data Labels tab, you can include labels on each element of the graph, and you can include a legend key as well, as you can see in Figure 8-9. If you have a lot of words on your chart, it can distract users from being able to quickly grasp the meaning of a chart. Use labels and other chart elements sparingly to prevent confusion.

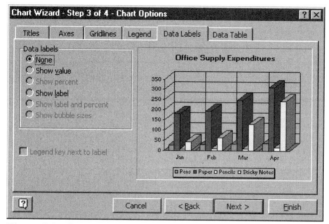

Figure 8-9: The Data Labels tab of the Chart Wizard dialog, Step 3.

The final tab on Step 3 of the Chart Wizard dialog is the Data Table tab. From here, you can include the spreadsheet cells as well as the graphical chart representation of the data on your page by checking the Data Table box, as shown in Figure 8-10. If you include a data table, you can include a legend alongside the data labels as well. Keep in mind that using both representations on the same Web page can make all of the information impossible to read if your chart has a lot of elements. Once you finish customizing your chart on the Step 3 dialog, press the Next button.

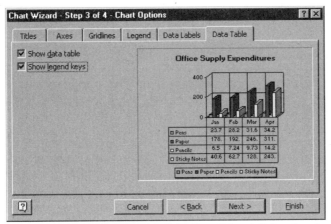

Figure 8-10: The Data Table tab of the Chart Wizard dialog, Step 3.

Step 4, shown in Figure 8-11, is the final page of the Chart Wizard. This dialog lets you embed the chart as an object in the spreadsheet itself or create a separate chart page that is a full-sized chart. What's the difference? In the next section, when we convert the spreadsheet to an HTML document for the Web, you will see how each type is displayed. For now, we'll embed the chart in the spreadsheet.

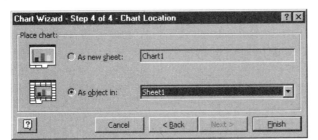

Figure 8-11: The Chart Location dialog of the Chart Wizard, Step 4.

Now you've completed the choices necessary for creating an Excel chart. Press the Finish button, and the Chart Wizard will create the chart and add it to your spreadsheet, as shown in Figure 8-12.

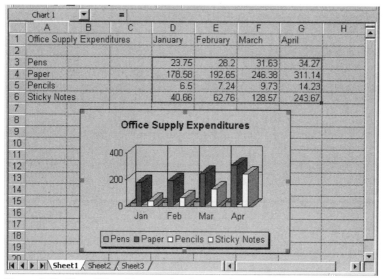

Figure 8-12: Chart Wizard inserts the chart in the Excel spreadsheet.

Moving Excel Spreadsheets to Web Pages

Once you've finished the creation of your spreadsheet, complete with chart graphics, you are ready to save the spreadsheet as an HTML document for viewing on the Web.

Fire up the Excel Internet Assistant Wizard by choosing the File | Save as HTML. If you don't see that choice on the File menu, it's because the Internet Assistant was not installed when you installed Office 97.

Installing the Internet Assistant Wizard

If you chose to install everything when you were installing Office 97, or you knew to choose the Internet Assistant Wizard during a Custom installation, you have the Internet Assistant. If you chose the Typical installation, the Internet Assistant was copied to a subdirectory under the Excel directory, but it needs to be made available to Excel before you can save spreadsheets as HTML.

To install the Internet Assistant, choose the Tools | Add-Ins menu item and the Excel Add-Ins form will appear. Select the check box next to Internet Assistant Wizard, as shown in Figure 8-13. Press the OK button and the add-in will quickly be installed.

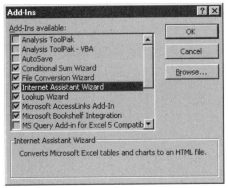

Figure 8-13: Installing the Internet Assistant Wizard from the Add-ins dialog.

Converting Excel Data to HTML With the Internet Assistant Wizard

The Internet Assistant Wizard collects information on how you want to display the Excel spreadsheet information on your Web page.

The first page of the Internet Assistant Wizard (Step 1) lets you choose which elements of your spreadsheet to convert to HTML, as shown in Figure 8-14. We will convert both the data and the chart into an HTML page.

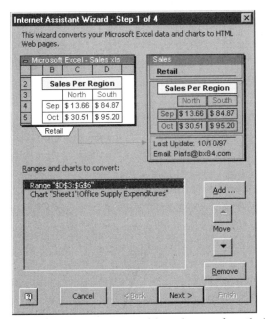

Figure 8-14: Selecting spreadsheet elements from the Internet Assistant Wizard dialog, Step 1.

Press Next to move to page two (Step 2) of the Internet Assistant Wizard. This dialog lets you choose to create a brand new HTML document or add the spreadsheet elements to an existing Web page, as shown in Figure 8-15.

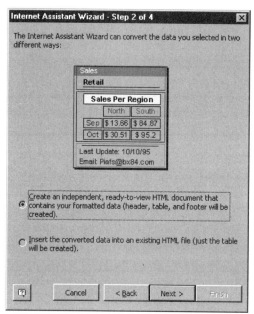

Figure 8-15: Choosing the Web page for your Excel spreadsheet with Internet Assistant Wizard, Step 2.

Editing Web Page Source Code to Incorporate Excel Data

If you choose to add your spreadsheet to an existing Web page, you will need to edit the target Web page source code before proceeding. Call up your favorite HTML editor (Word 97 works just fine, as well as any ordinary text editor) and open the target Web page. Locate the point in the file where you want the spreadsheet to appear, and insert the following tag on a new line:

```
<!--##Table##-->
```

The new spreadsheet data will be added at the point you selected with the above tag, and the tag itself will be replaced with the spreadsheet data.

Once you have decided to create a new HTML document or use an existing one, press the Next button to proceed to Step 3 of the Internet Assistant Wizard.

Step 3 allows you to enter the text that will surround the spreadsheet itself. As you can see in Figure 8-16, you can add a Title, Header, or Description, HTML horizontal line breaks before and after the spreadsheet, and information about who created the document and when, and whom to contact if you have questions. Once you fill in the appropriate data, press the Next button to proceed.

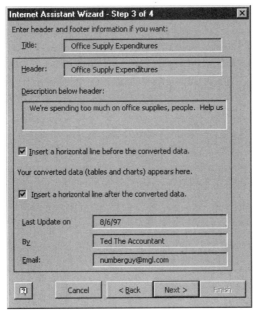

Figure 8-16: Adding descriptive information to the target Web page to accompany the Excel data using Internet Assistant Wizard, Step 3.

Step 4 of the Internet Assistant Wizard is shown in Figure 8-17. In Step 4, you have a choice of code pages for your HTML document and a choice of where to save the Web page on your hard drive.

Some languages have accented characters not available in the standard American alphabet, and some languages use a completely different alphabet. Changing the code page changes the way your Web page is displayed.

Keep in mind this will only work if those who read your Web pages have the same code page available in their Web browser. You can't just switch code pages to translate a Web page to Japanese.

What Is...

code page: Character set used on your Web page.

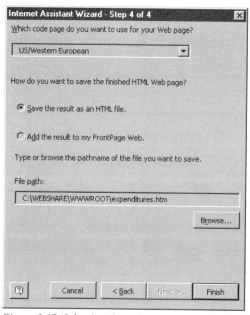

Figure 8-17: Selecting the code page and where to save your Web page with Internet Assistant Wizard, Step 4.

If you use Microsoft's Front Page publishing software and your ISP supports Front Page extensions, you can use the Internet Assistant Wizard to save your new Web page directly to your Web site. You don't have to save the file and then upload it to your Web site. Front Page does that for you.

If you don't use Front Page or you want to save the Web page somewhere else, enter the file path to tell the Wizard where to save your file. Press the Finish button, and the Wizard will create your new Web page or add to an existing one. The finished Web page is shown in Figure 8-18.

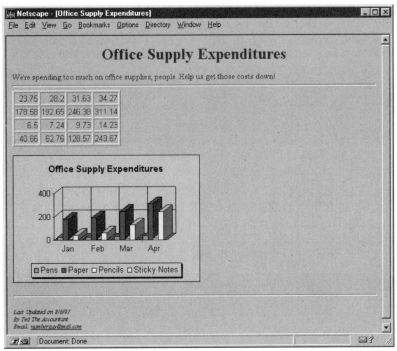

Figure 8-18: Completed Web page with Excel chart embedded in the spreadsheet.

Internet Assistant Wizard saves the Excel information as a graphic and inserts it in the Web page along with the description provided in Step 3 (Figure 8-16). Now you get to see the difference your choice makes. If the chart was saved as a separate page in the spreadsheet, it will be converted into HTML, so that it looks like what is shown in Figure 8-19.

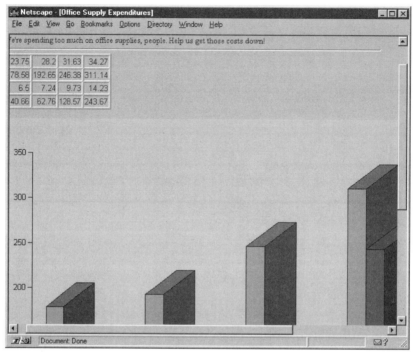

Figure 8-19: Completed Web page with Excel data saved as a chart.

The Internet Assistant for Excel 97 does not give you the choice of what size to make your images, as does the Internet Assistant for PowerPoint 97. The chart is saved as a separate GIF image no matter which way you create the chart image, so embedding the chart gives you a small image, and creating a separate sheet gives you a huge one. Keep this in mind when you create charts that will be converted into HTML.

If you want to change the size of the GIF created by the Internet Assistant Wizard, you can use a graphics editing program to do so. There are several on the CD that accompanies this book. We recommend Paint Shop Pro, but you can pick the one you like best.

Configuring Excel to Collect Data From the Web

What you've done so far is all that Ted from Accounting has asked for. However, you've got a feeling that others will see your handiwork and show up at your cubicle asking you to make Web pages for them as well. Some of the other features of Excel 97 might come in handy when you're creating more advanced Web pages.

Instead of just presenting information to the user, you might need to allow users to enter information into a Web form, then collect the information into a file or directly into a database. Excel 97 allows you to do this, but it requires some work on your part, as well as a few extra utility programs Microsoft makes available on their Web site.

If you are using Microsoft's Personal Web Server or Internet Information Server (IIS), you can use Excel 97 to collect user input into an Access database or other ODBC data source. If you are using a different Web server that supports CGI, you can collect user input into a tab-delimited file for later import into an Excel spreadsheet.

Setting up your system to use Excel from the Web is not a no-brainer, but with a little patience and perseverance (and the instructions in this chapter) you can succeed. If you would like to see how to create a simple Web form in Excel, look in the resource\demos directory on the CD and double-click the *webform.avi* file in Windows Explorer. The Windows Media Player will appear, and you can watch the video.

Before we step through the process of creating a Web form in Excel, here is an overview of how it works.

The process to collect data from the Web using Excel 97 involves:

1. Creating a Web form in Excel.

2. Starting up the Web Form Wizard.

3. Using the Web Form Wizard to map the elements on the form to database or spreadsheet fields so the data entered by the user is put into the correct place.

4. Choosing either the IIS or CGI method of data collection.

5. Choosing a location to put the Web form and associated files.

6. Creating a confirmation message that tells the user their data was accepted.

7. Recording the URL to the database file in which the data will be collected.

8. Adding an ODBC data source to your system and editing a configuration file to point to the data source if you chose the IIS method.

First, you will use Excel's Web Form Wizard to create a Web form that contains the fields you need to collect information from users. The Web Form Wizard creates the form a user sees, plus it creates the scripts necessary for the Web server to process the information.

Users can click a hyperlink that points to the Web form, or they can open the Web form directly with Excel. You can even send the Web form as an e-mail attachment for the user to activate.

The Web form is downloaded to the user's computer. In reality, the Web form is an Excel workbook, so Excel 97 is started to process the workbook. Obviously, using this method of gathering user input requires everyone who wants to use your Web form to have Excel installed on their computer.

FYI: The User Must Have Excel

Consider carefully before electing to use Excel's Web Form Wizard. If you are on a company intranet and can ensure everyone who accesses your Web site has Excel 97, this method will work for you just fine. On the other hand, if you are deploying a Web site on the Internet and you want to get user information, do NOT use this method. The vast majority of Web users will not have Excel 97 and will not be able to enter information.

And no, you cannot substitute the Excel Viewer for Excel 97. The Excel Viewer does not support user input, so it will not work.

Once the user enters the requested information, Excel 97 sends the information to the Web server via the HTTP protocol. Excel then closes the Web form and shuts down.

The information is received by the Web server, and the scripts created by the Web Form Wizard process the information and put it into a database or an ordinary text file, depending on the capabilities of your Web server.

FYI: The CGI Method Requires Perl

If you choose the CGI method, the Web Form Wizard will create a Perl script that will process the user information. If you do not have Perl installed on your system, the script will not work. You can download the Perl program from http://www.activeware.com.

Creating a Form in Excel

For this example, we will create a Web form that could be used by Ted and his band of accountants. They want to collect information on office supplies, so let's create a Web form that allows users to record office supplies as they remove them from the supply cabinet.

Choose the View | Toolbars menu and select the Forms toolbar, which is shown in Figure 8-20. When creating your Web form, use only the controls on this toolbar, because these are the only form controls supported by the Web Form Wizard.

Figure 8-20: The Excel Forms toolbar.

Creating forms in Excel is an art in itself and is beyond the scope of this book. For an in-depth look at all that Excel 97 has to offer, including forms, try the *Excel 97 Power Toolkit* (Ventana, 1997). However, as you must create a form before you can use the Web Form Wizard, I will show you some simple steps to create a usable form in Excel.

The Web form we need to accept user information about office supplies only needs four fields for the user to enter the quantity of pens, pencils, paper, and sticky notes that they remove from the supply cabinet. That sounds simple enough, right?

Start off with a blank spreadsheet. We will make the background black, and the area where the entry fields reside will be white. Use the mouse to highlight all of the visible cells in the spreadsheet. Choose the Fill Color icon on the Formatting toolbar (it's the one that looks like a bucket pouring paint) and pick the color black.

As our work area, use the mouse to select a 5 x 10 cell area and choose the fill color as white. Click the Borders icon and put a border around the white area. Add labels by double-clicking in the appropriate worksheet cells and entering text. Lastly, color the four fields where the form will accept data in bright yellow so not even Ted could miss them, and sprinkle lightly with your choice of border accents. The final form is shown in Figure 8-21.

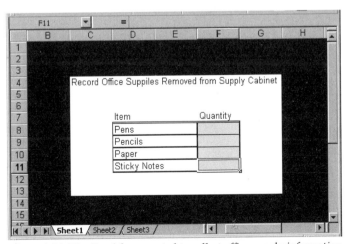

Figure 8-21: The Excel form created to collect office supply information.

Setting Up Data Collection Files With Web Form Wizard

Now that we have a form, the next step is to use the Web Form Wizard to create a version that can be used on the corporate intranet. Choose the Tools | Wizard menu item and select Web Form to start up the Web Form Wizard. The first page (Step 1) is just an introduction, so press the Next button to continue.

In Step 2, we need to select the cells that will be used to collect user information. The information entered into the selected fields will be put into our specified database or flat file. For this form, use the Add a Cell button to add a selected spreadsheet cell to the list of controls and cells. When you click the Add a Cell button, you are allowed to select a cell from the spreadsheet and add it to the list. Figure 8-22 shows the four spreadsheet cells selected.

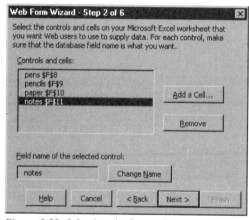

Figure 8-22: Selecting the form cells to accept user input with Web Form Wizard, Step 2.

Use the Change Name box and button to give each cell a recognizable name so the information collected will make sense without your having to go back and look at the Web form. If you choose to store records in a database, the names you give the Web controls will be used to name the database fields when the Web Form Wizard creates the database for you. When you are finished with Step 2, press the Next button to continue.

Step 3 of the Wizard gives you a choice of how your data will be collected, as shown in Figure 8-23. Your decision here will generate one of two completely different Web collection techniques.

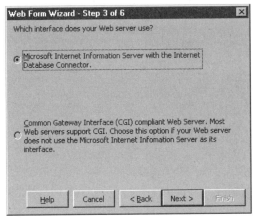

Figure 8-23: Selecting the data collection method with Web Form Wizard, Step 3.

The first technique uses Microsoft's Internet Information Server with the Internet Database Connector (IDC). If you are using IIS and want your data collected into a Microsoft Access database, choose the first option. The Web Form Wizard will generate an Access .mdb database file to hold your data, and an .idc file, which you will edit to tell the IIS where to find your Access database file.

The second option uses the Common Gateway Interface, which almost all Web servers support. If you are not using IIS or you prefer your data to end up in a tab-delimited file format instead of an Access database file, choose this second option and the Web Form Wizard will generate a .pl file (a Perl script) for the Web server to use for processing your data and a .txt file (plain text) to store the information in. Once you have made your decision, press the Next button to continue.

In Step 4, you choose where to save your database files. You can save the files to your local machine, or you can use Microsoft FrontPage to save the files to a remote Web site. To use FrontPage, you must have FrontPage open and running or the Web Form Wizard will not allow you to choose that option.

You will also need to enter a complete path that tells the wizard where to save your files, as shown in Figure 8-24. Once you enter the pathname and tell the wizard how to save your files, press the Next button to continue.

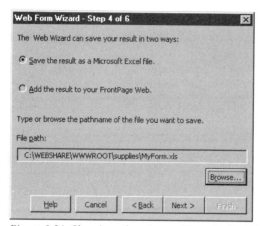

Figure 8-24: Choosing where to save files with Web Form Wizard, Step 4.

Step 5 of the wizard lets you customize the results page the user sees after they submit their data. Choose a title that will appear in the title bar of the Web browser, a header to headline the page, and an informative message assuring the user their information was received correctly.

If you decided to use the IIS and Access database to store your data, Step 5 will have a box for you to enter the URL of the .idc file created by the Web Form Wizard, as shown in Figure 8-25. The URL tells Excel where to send the information entered by the user.

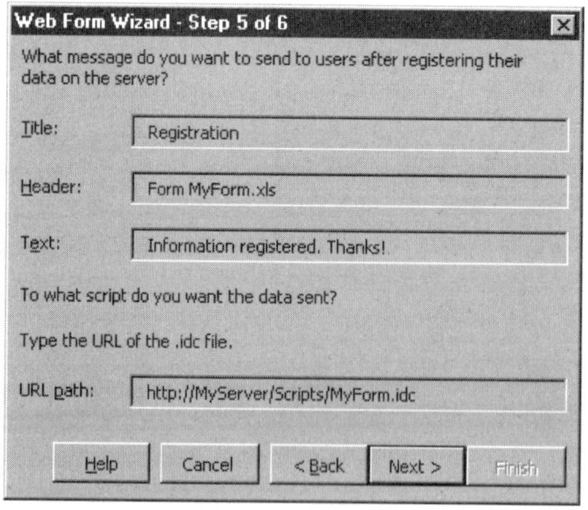

Figure 8-25: Customizing your Web form and designating where to store Access database data with Web Form Wizard, Step 5.

If you decided to use CGI and Perl to store your data, Step 5 will have a box for you to enter the URL of the Perl script the Web Form Wizard is about to create, as shown in Figure 8-26. The URL is the location to which the information entered by the user will be sent.

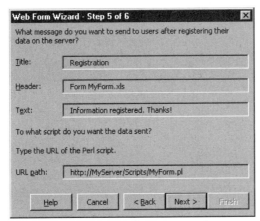

Figure 8-26: Providing information on where to store CGI and Perl script data with Web Form Wizard, Step 5.

Once you have finished Step 5, press the Next button and the Web Form Wizard will process the information you have entered, and it will generate the appropriate files. You still have a couple of things to do, depending on the data collection method you decided to use. The next two sections will show you how to finish setting up your Web form to use IIS or CGI.

The files created by the Web Form Wizard are prefixed with the name MyForm by default. We will use that name for the examples presented here. Naturally, if you named your files something else, use your name in place of MyForm.

Setting Up Data Collection Methods

There are two ways to collect user input from an Excel Web form. One is to use a Microsoft Access database file and Microsoft's IIS Web server. The other is to use a Perl program to put information in a plain text file; this will work with any Web server. The following sections will show you how to use both methods.

With IIS

Once you've set up your data collection files with IIS and Access, you must register the Access database file created by the Web Form Wizard with your system so any program can find it and add data to it. To do this, you will need to go to the Windows Control Panel and start up the ODBC Data Source Administrator. For a more detailed discussion of how ODBC and data sources work, see Chapter 7, "Access 97."

FYI: Setting Execute Permissions

When using the IIS to collect your data, the Web Form Wizard creates four files. If you are concerned about making your Web site as secure as possible, Microsoft suggests moving the .idc, .htx, and .mdb files into a folder with execute permissions but without read permissions. This will let people use your programs without letting them read the files. This keeps them from learning about possible loopholes to exploit on your Web server. You can set folder permissions with the IIS Directory Properties, as detailed in Chapter 4. If you decide to do this, do it BEFORE you register your ODBC data source. Once you set the path of the database file, you can't move the database file, or the Web server won't be able to find it.

Press the Start | Settings | Control Panel. In the Control Panel folder, locate the 32-bit ODBC icon. Double-click the icon, and the Data Source Administrator will open. Press the System DSN tab, as shown in Figure 8-27.

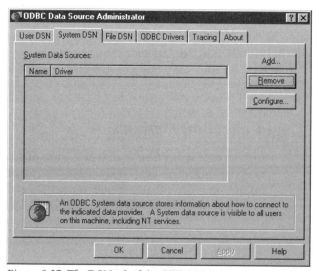

Figure 8-27: The DSN tab of the ODBC Data Source Administrator dialog.

On the System DSN form, press the Add button. This will present you with a list of the available ODBC drivers on your system. Choose the Microsoft Access Driver, as shown in Figure 8-28, and press the Finish button.

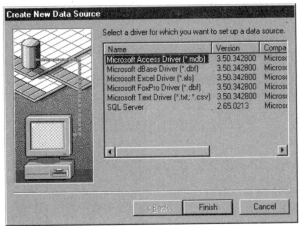

Figure 8-28: Selecting the Microsoft Access ODBC Driver from the Create New Data Source dialog.

You will now see the ODBC Microsoft Access 97 Setup form. As shown in Figure 8-29, you should give your data source a descriptive name and add a brief description. Here we've chosen the name Office Supplies. Remember the name you choose for the data source, because you will use it again later. Now, under the Database label, press the Select button.

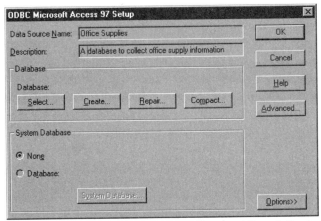

Figure 8-29: Providing the Data Source Name and Description in ODBC Microsoft Access Setup dialog.

Press the Select button in the Database section. This will bring up a File Open dialog box for you to locate the .mdb file the Web Form Wizard just created for you. In this case, the file is MyForm.mdb. Click on the filename and press the OK button. The database file you just selected will appear on the ODBC Microsoft Access 97 Setup form if everything worked correctly. Press the OK button to finish the process. The new data source will appear in the System DNS form, as shown in Figure 8-30.

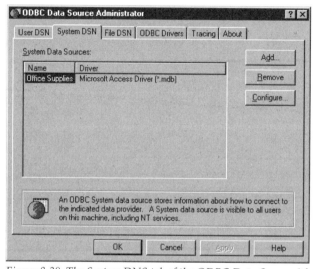

Figure 8-30: The System DNS tab of the ODBC Data Source Administrator dialog.

You will need to modify the text in MyForm.idc with a text editor (Word 97 will work just fine). You should find the file in the same directory as the MyForm.mdb. Open the file in the text editor; it should contain text similar to that shown below:

```
Datasource: Your datasource
Username: Your username
Password: Your password
Template: MyForm.htx
SQLStatement:
+ INSERT INTO Sheet2
+ (c7, c6, c5, c4)
+ VALUES('%c7%', '%c6%', '%c5%', '%c4%');
```

Change the words "Your datasource" to the name of the data source you just added to your system. In this example, the name is Office Supplies. The edited file should be similar to the one shown below:

```
Datasource: Office Supplies
Username: Your username
Password: Your password
Template: MyForm.htx
SQLStatement:
+ INSERT INTO Sheet2
+ (c7, c6, c5, c4)
+ VALUES('%c7%', '%c6%', '%c5%', '%c4%');
```

Save the file with the new information, and the IIS will now be able to find your database.

FYI: Data Source Permissions

You can require a username and password before users get access to a data source. When accessing a database file from the Web, this precaution is rather pointless. The username and password must be written into the .idc file in place of the words "Your username" and "Your password." The Web user doesn't have to know the password to get access to your database, so what's the point?

With CGI

As mentioned before, the CGI method requires that you have Perl for Windows installed on your system. While you're downloading Perl, you might as well get PerlScript and Perl for ISAPI, which are available from http://www.activeware.com.

What Is...

CGI: Common Gateway Interface. This is a method used for Web servers to execute programs and send the results to a user's Web browser.
Perl: A programming language.
PerlScript: A program that enables you to put Perl variables and programming code in your Web pages.
ISAPI: Internet Information Application Programming Interface. A method of writing programs for Microsoft's IIS Web server that is an alternative to CGI.

PerlScript is a program that allows you to put Perl variables and programming constructs into your Web pages. Perl for ISAPI is a program that lets your Perl programs execute in the IIS and bypass CGI. PerlScript is an easy way to add Perl programming capabilities to your Web pages. Perl for ISAPI is a way to speed up your Perl-based Web programs.

All three programs come in self-extracting files. Just use the Windows Explorer to double-click on the files, or enter the name of one of the files from a DOS window. The Perl programs will ask you for the name of a directory to install Perl into and will install all the necessary files for you.

Before your Perl programs will work, you must associate the .pl file extension with the Perl program. To do this, choose the View | Options menu item in the Windows Explorer. This will bring up the Options window. Press the File Types tab and scroll down the list of file types until you find PL File, as shown in Figure 8-31.

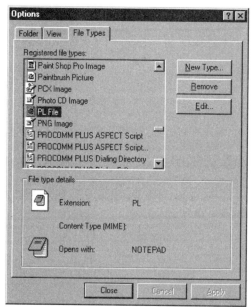

Figure 8-31: Selecting the Perl extension from the File Types tab of the Options dialog.

If the program associated with the .pl extension is not Perl, you will need to edit the file type. Press the Edit button of the File Types tab to open the Edit File Type dialog. In the Actions: list, highlight the Open action, as shown in Figure 8-32, and press the Edit button of the dialog to open the Editing Action form.

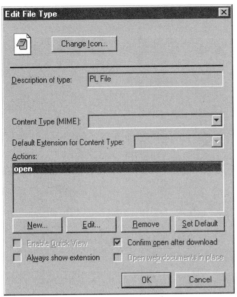

Figure 8-32: Associating programs with the correct extension with the Edit File Type dialog.

On the Editing Action For Type dialog, change the name of the application used to perform the open action by entering the path to the Perl program, or press the Browse button to search for the Perl executable. Once you find it, as shown in Figure 8-33, press the OK button, and you return to the File Types dialog. Be sure to enter the path to Perl on your system if it is different from what is shown here.

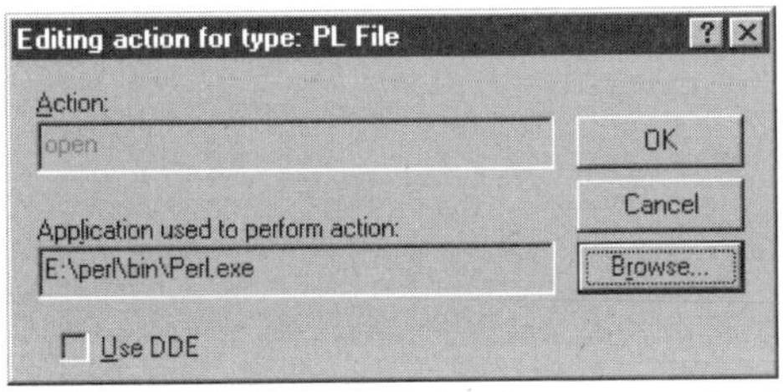

Figure 8-33: Changing the application associated with an action with the Editing Action for Type dialog.

Press the Close button on the Edit File Type dialog, and Perl should appear on the File Types form as the program that is now associated with the .pl file extension, as shown in Figure 8-34. Now Windows will automatically use Perl to execute any Perl script named with a .pl extension.

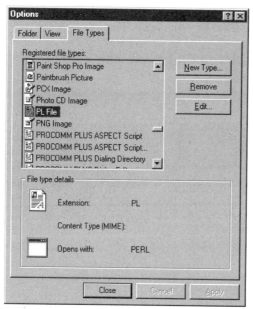

Figure 8-34: The File Types tab of the Options dialog indicating files with the .pl extension will execute in Perl.

Editing the Excel Web Form

Now that you've set up the data collection files and a means of collecting the data, you're ready to look at your handiwork with a Web browser. Open your Web browser and enter the path to the MyForm.xls file created by the Web Form Wizard, or the filename you created instead. Windows will launch Excel 97 and open the Web form you created, as shown in Figure 8-35.

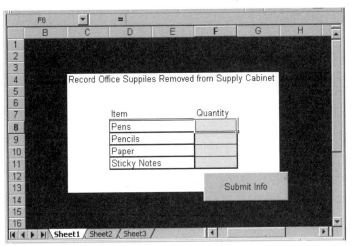

Figure 8-35: The Web form viewed in Excel.

As you can see, the Web Form Wizard added a really ugly looking Submit Info button to the Web form. You will probably want to change the size and location of the button. Just right-click on the Submit button and use your mouse to move and resize the button.

Wait a minute. You will notice you just used Excel to edit the form users will access on your system! Hold on, because actually Excel opens a local copy on the user's machine, and the original on your Web server remains intact. Whew! However, if you want to prevent users from entering input anywhere other than the four cells designated to accept user input and make sure users can't move and edit the Submit button, you'll need to edit the copy of MyForm.xls.

Use Excel 97 to open the copy of MyForm.xls that resides on your Web server. Right-click on the Submit Info button and choose the Assign Macro menu item to open the Assign Macro form. Highlight the SubmitInfo macro, which is shown in Figure 8-36, and press the Edit button.

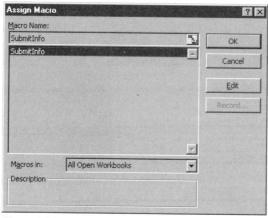

Figure 8-36: Providing the editing action with the Assign Macro dialog.

Don't panic! While it might seem like everything on your computer screen was just replaced with something overwhelming and unfamiliar, this is just the programming environment used with Visual Basic for Applications. All Office 97 programs can use Visual Basic for Applications to write programs. We will use the Visual Basic editor, shown in Figure 8-37, to lock the Excel Web form so users can't do anything undignified with your Web form.

Take a deep breath. You're going to change code!

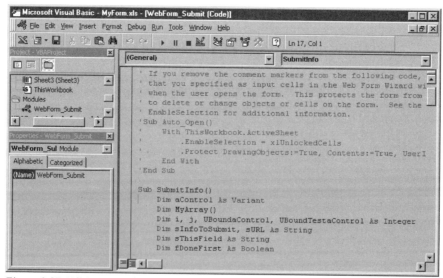

Figure 8-37: Editing macros in Visual Basic for Applications.

If you read the comments at the top of the program (all comments in Visual Basic start with the ' character and appear as green text in the editor), they will tell you what to do. Just uncomment the Auto_Open function by removing the ' character from the beginning of each line, and your Web form will only allow input in the cells you have selected. Once you complete your edits, the program will appear as shown in Figure 8-38.

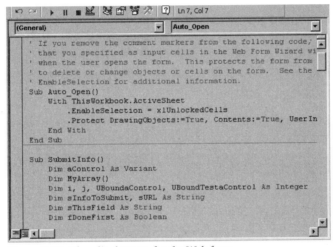

Figure 8-38: The edited macro for the Web form.

Choose the File | Save MyForm.xls menu item to save your changes, then choose the File | Close and Return to Microsoft Excel menu item and you will be returned to the familiar Excel environment. Move and resize the Submit Info button to suit yourself. Save the MyForm.xls file, and it is now protected so users cannot edit the copy their Web browser downloads to their local machine.

If you close the file, then reopen it, you'll notice you can't click on any cells outside the four cells that you designated to accept user input, nor can you move the Submit Info button. That wasn't so hard, was it? You'll be a programmer in no time!

Now you can collect information from Web users in a database or flat file and analyze it at your leisure. This is much easier than keeping records on paper and enduring the inevitable errors that occur when transcribing information from paper into a database. At least this way you only have the original data entry errors, and not another set on top of that. (Accountants have to take pleasure in the small joys of life.)

But your data-collection process is not quite complete. You have the data collected neatly in a file, but how do you open the file, extract the data, and do something useful with the information? The following section tells you.

Collecting Data Directly From a Database With Excel

Excel is one of the most popular Office 97 programs because it enables users to store and manipulate simple data. Another Office 97 program, Access 97, is better at storing more complex data, but Access lacks the capabilities of Excel when it comes to analyzing the data. Wouldn't it be nice if you could store information in Access 97, and then use Excel 97 to write formulas and analyze the information?

With a little work, you can do exactly that. In fact, you are not limited to using Access 97. You can use virtually any data source that is recognized by Windows. You can even import data from database files on the Internet, such as the database file you created with the Web Form Wizard to collect information on office supplies.

Querying the Web Page With Excel

To collect Excel data from another computer, you will need to construct a query to tell Excel where the file is, and you will also need to write a program to find the data and return it to your Excel spreadsheet.

Obtaining the Office 97 Resource Kit

To import data from an external database on the company intranet or the Internet, you will need to add a module to Excel 97 to allow Excel on your computer to gather dynamic data from an Excel form on a remote computer. The module is available as part of Microsoft's Office Resource Kit (ORK) on the Web. Point your Web browser to the URL: http://www.microsoft.com/office/ork/ and you will see the ORK Home Page.

The ORK has a lot of useful information not available anywhere else, including software add-ins and utilities to make Office 97 more useful. We are interested in the Excel 97 Web Connectivity Kit, which is available from a hyperlink in Appendix A of the ORK. Use your Web browser to open http://www.microsoft.com/office/ork/AppA/AppA.htm.

Click on the World Wide Web and Intranet Tools hyperlink at the top of the page. It will take you to the Microsoft Excel 97 Web Connectivity Kit section of Appendix A. There is a hyperlink that says Click Here and Follow Instructions, as shown in Figure 8-39. Click on this hyperlink.

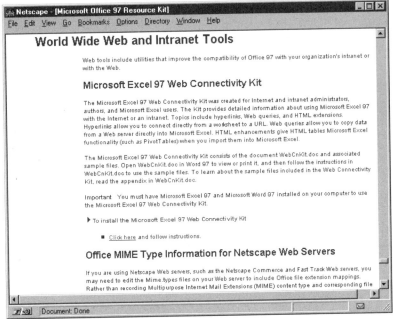

Figure 8-39: The Web Connectivity Kit for Excel 97.

You will see a list of available resources. The one we want is the Web Connectivity Kit. Bookmark this site so you can come back later, and then click the Web Connectivity Kit hyperlink. You will see the Microsoft Office 97 Free Stuff Registration Wizard.

The Registration Wizard requires you to register with Microsoft using your Product ID for Office 97. You will enter a password for future access. Once you register, you do not need to register again to access this site in the future. When you complete your registration, your Web browser will be taken back to the Web page where the whole thing started. Click on the Web Connectivity Kit hyperlink once again, and you will be able to download the kit to your local machine.

You'll notice the hyperlink that told you to "click here and follow instructions" actually never gave you any instructions. What do you do with the file you just downloaded?

Use the Windows Explorer to locate the file you just downloaded, which is named Webcnkit.exe. (You do remember where you put it, don't you? If not, try to download it again and notice the directory where your Web browser intends to save it.) Double-click on the name of the file in the Windows Explorer and follow the instructions that appear on your screen. Honest, this time you will be instructed on how to continue.

You can also point your Web browser to the URL: http://www.microsoft.com/excel/webquery/to get more information about downloading and installing the Web Connectivity Kit for Excel 97.

Once you have installed the kit, use Word to open the WEBCNKIT.DOC file that comes with the kit. This document contains a lot of useful information about using Excel 97 on the Internet, an intranet, or the Web. Spend a few minutes reading the information contained in WEBCNKIT.DOC and you will be amazed at some of the things Excel 97 can do for you in reference to the Web and Internet.

Constructing a Web Query

A Web query file is deceptively simple to create and consists of a maximum of four lines. You can create a Web Query with any text editor, and simply save the file with a .iqy file extension to tell Excel what type of file it is.

If you want to create a Web query to access the text file created by the Web Form Wizard using the CGI method, it looks something like this:

```
WEB
1
http://your.host.name/your_directory/get_supply_data.pl
```

The first two lines of the file are optional, but if they are included, they must look just like the first two lines shown above. The first line is also case-sensitive. The words "web," "Web," and so on will cause an error when you try to run the query from Excel.

The third line is the important one. It is the URL to the program on the remote Web server that will return the information you are looking for. Naturally, you will replace your.host.name with the name of the desired Web server and replace your_directory with the path to the program. Save the file into your msoffice/queries directory or another directory of your choice. Don't forget to use the .iqy file extension. Our file will be called get_supply_data.iqy.

Now comes the important part. Nowhere in all of Microsoft's documentation do they bother to tell you that you have to write the program called by the Excel Web Query. All Excel does is read the Web query file and send an HTTP request to the remote Web server for a program. Excel expects the results to be in HTML format. Microsoft neglects to give you any examples of how to write the necessary program.

Instructing Excel to Expect HTML Response

The topic of Perl programming is far beyond the scope of this book, but you can adapt the simple program below for your own needs without needing to know much about Perl. As an example, I will show you how to write a simple

Perl program to access the MyForm.txt file where users enter data using the MyForm.pl file created by the Web Form Wizard.

Our Take: What Do You Think About Microsoft Using Perl in Their Flagship Office Product?

Jeff: I think it's hilarious. I'm glad they seem to have admitted they don't have to write proprietary tools to do everything when there are tools out there that work just fine. I just wish they had been more up-front with it and documented how to use Perl with their CGI interface. It would have eliminated a lot of confusion for many users and made Microsoft look less grudging about using Perl.

Kevin: I'm just waiting for them to add proprietary extensions to it and make it MS-Perl. Actually, I wouldn't be surprised to see this feature either (1) find its way into the other Office products as patches and the next version are released, or (2) go away altogether, as useful as it is.

The program must be named the same as the program you entered in the get_supply_data.iqy file. In this case, the program will be named get_supply_data.pl, and it looks like this:

```
print "Content-type: text/html\n\n";
open(IN_DATA, "<MyForm.txt") or die "Cannot open data file\n";
while (<IN_DATA>) {
 print $_;
}
close(IN_DATA);
```

Simple, eh? The first line returns the necessary document header for Excel to understand it is receiving an HTML document as it expects. The next line opens the MyForm.txt file for reading and prints an error message if it fails. You can change the name of the file to open as you need to. Then the program just reads each line of the file and sends it to the Web server for relay back to your Excel spreadsheet. The last line closes the text file, and the program exits.

Returning Remote Dynamic Data as a Spreadsheet

Because the data contained in MyForm.txt is in tab-delimited format, Excel receives the data and creates a spreadsheet for it. To run a Web Query, choose the Data | Get External Data menu item and select Run Web Query to open the Run Query form. Choose the get_supply_data.iqy file, as shown in Figure 8-40, and press the Get Data button.

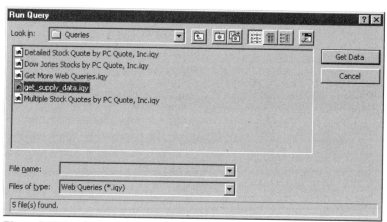

Figure 8-40: Retrieving Web page data with the Run Query dialog.

Before Excel executes the Web query, after you click on the Get Data button, you are asked to choose a form for the retrieved data with the Returning External Data to Microsoft Excel form shown in Figure 8-41. With this form you can choose where to insert the returned data and whether to put the data in the current worksheet or create a new one. If you want to get fancy, you can press the Properties button and customize how the results are displayed.

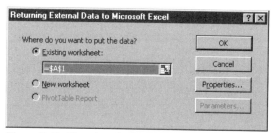

Figure 8-41: Choosing the form of the retrieved data with the Returning External Data to Microsoft Excel dialog.

When finished with the form, press the OK button, and Excel will execute the Web query. The results are returned by the remote Web server and put into an Excel spreadsheet, as shown in Figure 8-42.

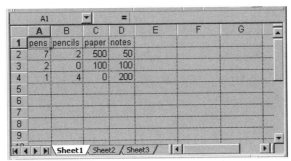

Figure 8-42: Query results displayed as an Excel spreadsheet.

FYI: Error 403

If you have problems getting information back, be sure the get_supply_data.pl file is in a directory on the remote Web server that has execute permissions. If the error code returned is 403, that's probably the problem. Use the Web Administrator to set the correct directory permissions, and you should have no more problems, as long as Perl is installed on the remote system.

That takes care of the data collected using the Perl program, but what about the information collected in the Access database? It is much harder to construct a program that extracts data from an Access database and return it via the Web. That is better done with Access 97 itself, as detailed in Chapter 7, or with a third-party product. However, Excel can import data from an Access database file without using a Web server. That method is detailed in the next section.

Querying Other Databases With Excel

As long as you have the correct ODBC driver installed for your data source, Excel can extract data from other databases equally well. For this example, we will get data from an Access database.

Our Take: Why Import Data From a Database Into Excel? Why Not Use the Database Tools Instead?

Jeff: There are a lot of people who are more comfortable using Excel than mucking about with a database. The concept of rows and columns is more familiar to them than records and fields, even though the concept behind the two is similar. Excel just gives users another way to use a database without having to learn yet another programming environment. Whatever makes the user feel more comfortable and still gets the job done is the best thing for everybody.

Kevin: I get a little concerned, though, when I see mission-critical databases written as spreadsheets, and it happens all of the time because people are so afraid of databases. Teach a person to fish and they can eat forever.

Choose the Data | Get External Data menu item and select Create New Query. This will bring up the Choose Data Source form. Highlight <New Data Source> in the list of databases and press the OK button.

The Create New Data Source form will appear. Name the data source, select the Microsoft Access driver, and use the Connect button to locate the MyForm.mdb database file. When you are finished, the form should look similar to Figure 8-43.

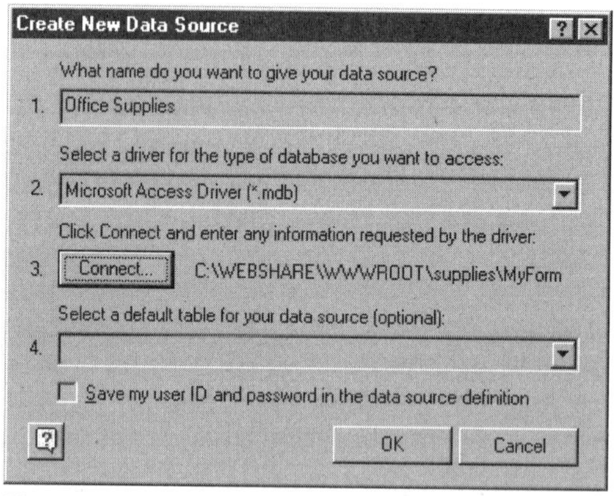

Figure 8-43: Identifying a data source with the Create New Data Source dialog.

Press the OK button, and the new data source will appear in the Choose Data Source form, as shown in Figure 8-44. Now the Web database will be accessible for Excel to query information from.

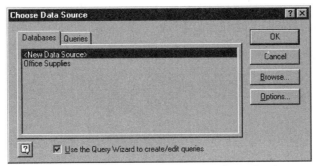

Figure 8-44: Identifying the new data source for an Excel query.

Double-click on the Office Supplies data source that we just created, and the first page of the Query Wizard will appear. You will work your way through four forms using the Query Wizard.

On the first form, select all four columns for the query, as shown in Figure 8-45, and press the Next button.

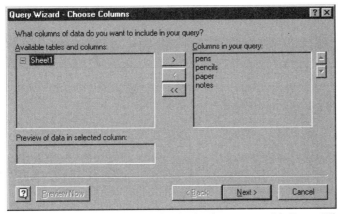

Figure 8-45: Selecting columns for the database query with Query Wizard's Choose Columns dialog.

The second screen of the Query Wizard lets you set up data filters to fine tune the results imported into Excel, as shown in Figure 8-46. In this case, we want all of the data regardless of what it is, but by using filters on a large database, you can decrease the amount of data imported into Excel and make your data analysis more meaningful by eliminating unwanted data. We don't need a filter for our example, so press the Next button.

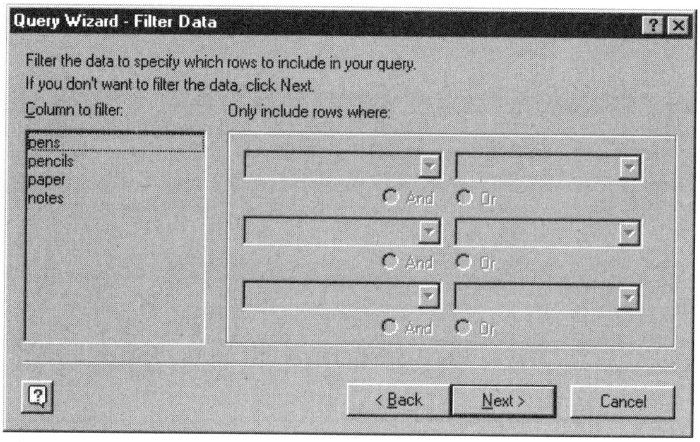

Figure 8-46: Limiting the data retrieved with Query Wizard's Filter Data dialog.

The third screen of the Query Wizard lets you sort the data, as shown in Figure 8-47. In our case, we are using numerical data that doesn't lend itself well to sorting, but if you want to import character data you can sort it in a variety of ways to present the data in a more organized manner.

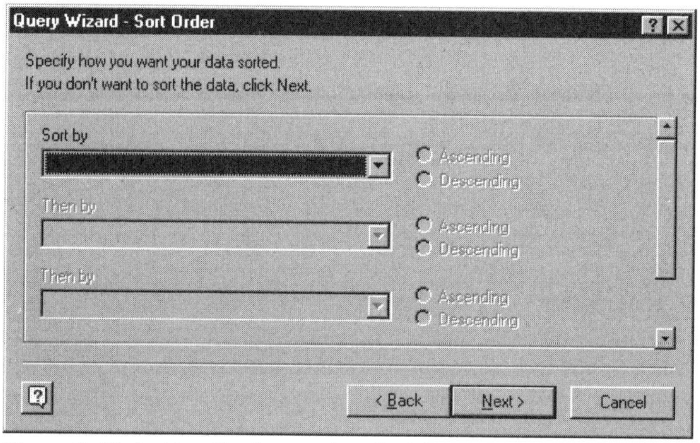

Figure 8-47: Sorting the data retrieved with Query Wizard's Sort Order dialog.

The fourth screen of the Query Wizard lets you import the data directly into an Excel spreadsheet, or you can call up the Microsoft Query program to construct a more complex database query, as shown in Figure 8-48. Microsoft Query enables you to detail your database query to a very fine-grained level not available in the simple approach of the Query Wizard.

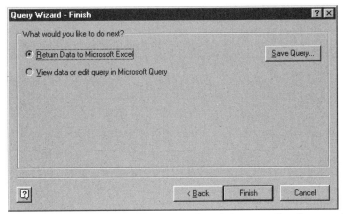

Figure 8-48: *Choosing to create an Excel worksheet or refine the query in Query Wizard's Finish dialog.*

If you have a lot of data or you need to perform a complicated query, use Microsoft Query to further edit your database query. Once you have finished editing your query, don't forget to save it with the Save Query button so you can use it again in the future. Press the Finish button to exit the Query Wizard.

Once you have defined the data source for the query and have constructed the query itself, the Returning External Data to Microsoft Excel form appears, as it did when you executed the Web query (Figure 8-41). Choose where to insert the new data, and press the OK button. The resulting spreadsheet is shown in Figure 8-49.

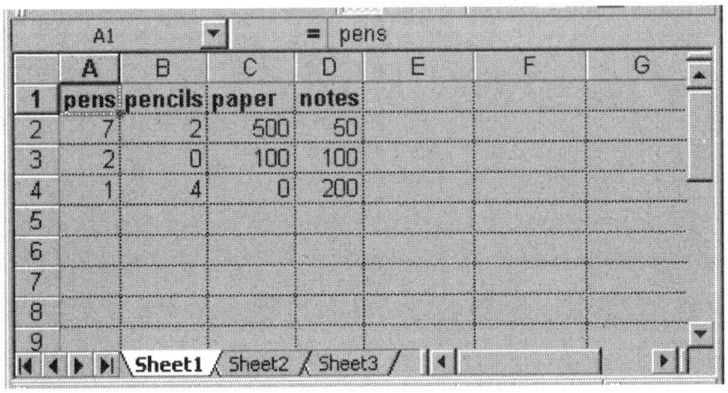

Figure 8-49: *Data imported from an Access database into an Excel spreadsheet.*

It looks familiar, doesn't it? This is the same information collected by the Perl CGI program, MyForm.pl, and imported via a Web query using the get_supply_data.pl program. This version was collected using the Internet Database Connector and the Internet Information Server.

No matter which way you choose to collect your data from the Web, you can import it into an Excel spreadsheet and analyze the data, generate reports, and save the results as HTML for others to see. Excel 97 gives you the tools you need to make the Web and the Internet work for you.

Moving On

In this chapter, you learned how to save Excel spreadsheets and charts as HTML documents for Web users to see. You also learned how to use Excel Web forms to collect information from Web users and store the data using IIS or CGI. You also learned how to import the collected data into an Excel spreadsheet, either via the Web or by accessing the database files directly. Of all the Office 97 products, Excel 97 gives you the most complete set of tools to manage Web data.

There's one more Office application to look at: Outlook. It's new and it's big. Read on.

chapter 9

Outlook

For the last several hours (or days, or weeks), you've been setting up a Web site for your company using the Office 97 suite of products. By now, you've chosen an ISP, set up a Web server, and used Word, PowerPoint, Access, and Excel to create Web pages. There's good and bad news at this point. The good news is that you're done writing Web pages. The bad news is that there's still more work to do. Nobody's even going to think to ask you to take on this chore, so the boss won't be calling you for this one. It's strictly extra credit. And it has absolutely nothing to do with the Web. Interested? Read on.

If you've never used an office-coordinating application or Personal Information Manager (PIM) before, then Microsoft Outlook 97 is going to look like a three-headed lizard to you. Centered on an exceptionally rich address book and calendar, Outlook is filled with so many features that it will take you weeks just to explore all of them, much less integrate them into your office environment. If you are already using a scheduler or online address book, then Outlook is worth a good, hard look. With tightly integrated e-mail, auto dialing, and group scheduling features, it can and should make your secretary fear for his or her job. When combined with the considerable features of Microsoft Exchange Server, it's a killer.

That said, Outlook is not Web-enabled in the traditional sense. Devotees of previous versions of Office (and even of Outlook's predecessor in Office 95, Schedule+) will immediately look for the Save As HTML selection on the menubar. It's not there. Microsoft's claim that "you can save files in HTML pages from any Office 97 program" (http://www.microsoft.com/office/97tour/answers/EU006.htm) is slightly specious. You can, indeed, save your Outlook data in HTML pages, but it's not easy and they're not particularly useful.

Furthermore, Outlook is rapidly being eclipsed by other products. There are a myriad of other information managers on the market, and more appear every week. It is fair to say that few are as broad as Outlook; you've got to ask yourself, though, "Do I really need all of this?"

Outlook has come a long way from its roots. From an ignominious birth as Schedule+, an unannounced and well-hidden scheduler originally bundled with Windows for Workgroups, Outlook seemed destined to become Microsoft's flagship front-end product. It can be used to replace the Windows Explorer and manage the myriad of files on your hard drive. It can replace your e-mail program, and it even permits the use of more or less English rule-based mail filtering. It can figure out when the office curmudgeon, the one who never reads his e-mail and who never returns phone calls, can make it to a branch meeting. It can even literally beam your phone book into your watch, Dick Tracy style. With some time and effort, Outlook can organize your life. It can probably help organize your workplace. But it's not a Web publishing system.

What Is. . .

Windows For Workgroups (WfWG): The version of Windows that fell between the phenomenally successful Windows 3.1 and Windows 95. WfWG combined the familiar Windows user interface with basic networking, allowing users to share files and applications on a local area network.

Windows Explorer: The application you use to view the directory of folders and files on a disk.

Microsoft Exchange: The protocol used by Microsoft programs to communicate for the purposes of sending mail and faxes.

Microsoft Exchange Server: A central computer that controls the passing of Microsoft Exchange data around a local area network. The term sometimes refers to the software program that runs on a computer to permit it to perform this task.

As feature-rich as Outlook is, it appears that it will not be the cornerstone of the next incarnation of Office or Windows, as it once appeared it might be. The Web is so important that Windows is going to have to become a browser and the browser is going to have to become part of the operating system. So much for information becoming the core of the suite; it's going to be connectivity.

There's not a lot of "development" to be done in Outlook; it's a group of utilities (programs that assist in the management of information) more than a development tool (a program that assists in the creation of other programs). So rather than try to show you how to develop Web sites or an Internet presence using Outlook, we'll concentrate on enabling the components of Outlook for your office Intranet, which is difficult enough.

Outlook & Microsoft Exchange

Outlook's primary connection to the Internet is via Microsoft Exchange, the network messaging protocol that first appeared in Windows for Workgroups. If your office is using a Microsoft Exchange Server for its mail service, you're home free and you've got a lot of work ahead of you to make Outlook do everything it's capable of. If not and your office LAN is heavily populated with Windows PCs, you might consider it, if only so you can take advantage of Outlook's features. If your LAN is already well established with UNIX or Macintosh mail servers, the additional benefit of an Exchange Server is something you'll have to evaluate.

What Is...

network messaging protocol: A language computers on a local area network use to handle e-mail and faxes.

mapped network drive: A folder on a remote computer, connected to via a local area network in such a way that the remote folder appears to be local. For example, if a directory on computer B is called "Public" and the permissions are set appropriately, it can be mapped to appear as a drive (say, the Q: drive) on computer A on the same network.

client (as opposed to user): A computer or program that requests data from another computer or program (a server).

That is not to say that you can't use Outlook if you're not using Microsoft Exchange Server. As a stand-alone application, Outlook provides very good scheduling and some very nice e-mail features. And if your office is well populated with others using Office 97, you can share a significant amount of information with them in a peer-to-peer style environment, in much the same way you might share files using mapped network drives and Windows Explorer. But Outlook's real power is contained in its application to a homogeneous intranet, where a central Exchange Server controls communication among dozens of clients.

One could write an entire book about implementing Exchange in a typical office. It isn't difficult, and the benefits of doing so, especially in a mostly Windows environment, are plenty. Unfortunately, top-of-the line communications servers aren't cheap. A typical Exchange 4.0 implementation costs almost $400 per user, which isn't likely to make any friends in the front office. There's no questioning that Exchange is a wonderful piece of software and is well worth considering for a new installation. But migrating an existing installation, especially one already running some kind of communications system (almost any generic UNIX, Lotus Notes, Netscape Enterprise Server, and so on), is likely to be costly.

Features

If there is a tool that you might need someday to manage your working life (or even your personal life, if you're particularly particular), it's in Outlook. Considering that few people are likely to purchase Office 97 for the fact that it includes Outlook ("Oh, look, Marge! The latest version of Office includes an e-mail application! Let's buy it!"), there's a lot of value in this little package. You could control your Windows desktop entirely from within Outlook.

Its features are too many to list comprehensively here. The more mundane include:

- an e-mail program
- a calendar
- a phone book (the "Contacts" module)
- a to-do list ("Tasks")
- a free-form journal
- "sticky" notes
- a "deleted" module, like the Recycle bin

Ho-hum. The real value of Outlook lies in its more esoteric features, only a few of which are listed here:

- **Automatic formatting of typed hyperlinks**. For example, if you type "http://www.microsoft.com", Outlook (in fact, any Office 97 application) changes it into a clickable hyperlink in my document. This has real potential; for example, you could keep links to company home pages in your phone book next to the entry for your sales representative. As you've already discovered, the other Office applications also do this, even when you don't want them to. This feature is less obtrusive and more useful in Outlook than in the others, because turning text into a hyperlink adds value to the text. In a printed document, a hyperlink isn't worth much.

- **A chronological record of your day**. Outlook keeps track of everything you do with any Office 97 application during your day and stores a log containing all of your actions in its Journal module. It even remembers exactly when you performed each action and tracks how long it took. Later, you could use this data to prepare client bills, track document status, and so forth.

- **Not just a calendar.** The Outlook Calendar module includes a standard calendar (in one-day, seven-day, monthly, and annual views) and to-do list, but it also includes an appointment schedule and reminders, an editable list of holidays and recurring events, and a means for sorting your calendar by any means you desire (for example, a list of office projects grouped by person responsible, and so on).

- **Clutter management**. Any of the components of Outlook can be viewed in their own, separate window. Right-click on the title bar of any Outlook module and select Open In New Window. This allows the Inbox and Calendar, for example, to be managed as separate applications from the Taskbar—a real boon if you have limited screen space or if you like to keep one of them visible all of the time. Similarly, you can use Outlook as a window manager, starting most of your applications from within Outlook, the same way you'd use the Windows desktop.

There's more. Outlook can spell-check your e-mail messages and verify the validity of your addresses. It can automatically check for and retrieve new mail, like a good Irish setter. It can poll your co-workers to find out who wants to go to Bogen's for lunch. It dices. It slices. But that's not the point. To make full use of Outlook, you need to decide first and foremost how you want to use it, and to what level of headache you're willing to commit.

Our Take: How Much Is Too Much?

Kevin: Well, this is too much. There's an industry term for programs that have so many features that no one person can possibly use them all—they're called *bloatware*. Outlook's got so many gadgets that I keep finding new ones, and I've been using it intensively for several months. Now, I sort of like the "Swiss army knife" approach to applications—it's never boring. But wouldn't it be better (for me) if I could buy only the modules I need? Microsoft knows this, of course, which is why they sell these things in a suite. It's like a fast-food lunch combo. I don't really need the large fries, but as long as they're part of the combo. . .

Jeff: And pretty soon as you eat all those fries, *you* become pretty bloated yourself, or in this case your hard drive does. PCs get faster, hard drives get bigger, memory gets cheaper, and bigger software uses them all up so you never seem to make any headway. If you go back and run a DOS version of Word, you'll be amazed at how fast it runs. Assuming you can find anything to do with it. One reason software is so big is the unfortunate intrusion of the C++ programming language. C++ is a very bloated language, and Office is written using it. Hopefully Java will mature over the next year or so and replace C++, but that doesn't help your poor hard drive today. Just try to stay away from that buffet.

There's not a lot of sense in covering the nuts-and-bolts operation of each feature of Outlook here. They're pretty straightforward, and the online help is competent. Most importantly, though, they have nothing to do with the Internet or Internet development.

Using Outlook to Manage Your Working Life

When configuring your Outlook installation, you can keep it simple, you can go for the gold, or you can choose something in between. Regardless of the option you choose, most of the features of Outlook will be available to you. Your choices are:

Installation Option	Pros	Cons
Microsoft Exchange Client. Use your existing Internet mail server and the Outlook mail client, a local version of Microsoft Exchange.	If you already use some form of Internet mail, this option will look the most familiar to you. Except for the hassles of configuring Microsoft Exchange, this option requires the least work.	No "public folders" means no sharing of schedules, calendars, or documents.
Shared Private Folders. Your existing mail server keeps doing its job, but you set up a location where you (and others running Office applications) can share data, including calendars, and so on.	Cheap. Many of the features of Outlook are available without additional expense.	Static—data only updates when the folders are imported. Outlook's tight integration with Exchange Server and the benefits that integration brings are unavailable.
Microsoft Exchange Server. Installing Exchange Server on a centrally located PC brings some incredible functionality at some considerable cost. Outlook becomes the client for a nicely featured suite of groupware tools, not unlike Lotus Notes.	Exchange does a great job of reliably delivering mail and news. If your office includes mostly PCs, this is a great way to make them work together.	Exchange Server costs money and requires hardware and administration.

Table 9-1: Outlook configuration/installation options.

We'll discuss how to set up and use the first two options in this chapter. The third, taking advantage of an Exchange Server, doesn't fall within the scope of this book. If you're running Exchange Server, you probably have a full-time support staff to run it and manage its workgroup features, making this book unnecessary. If you're considering it but haven't bought it, you can probably afford a book dedicated to Exchange Server, and you'll need it. One you might consider is *Microsoft BackOffice 2.5: The Complete Solution,* (Ventana).

Installing Microsoft Exchange Client

A client-only version of Microsoft Exchange comes included with 32-bit Windows operating systems (Windows 95 and NT). You might have noticed it while installing Windows—it's that potentially annoying Inbox icon that you can't easily remove from your desktop. If you did remove the Inbox, or if you never installed it, you'll need to get it to use Outlook's mail features.

You can still use Outlook if you don't go through this. The Calendar will still manage your own appointments, the Contact Manager will remember your phone numbers, and the Log will track what you do and when. But you won't be able to receive or send mail or coordinate appointment information with anybody else. And this setup isn't too hard. And it's free. So what do you have to lose?

FYI: Shortcut to Control Panel

When working with Windows settings, or anytime you expect that your Windows environment is going to require some tweaking, make your life a little easier by adding a shortcut to the Control Panel to your Windows desktop. There are several ways to do this, but the easiest is to right-click on a blank spot on the desktop, select New, then select Shortcut from the menu that appears. In the Command Line: box that appears, type **c:\windows\control.exe** and press Next. Then enter Control Panel in the Enter a Name box and click on Finish. An icon will appear on your desktop for Control Panel (you might want to change the icon by right-clicking on it and selecting Properties|Shortcut|Change Icon), and you won't have to hunt for it from the taskbar again.

To install the Microsoft Exchange mail client:

1. Click on the Start button | Settings | Control Panel.

2. Select Add/Remove Programs.

3. Select the tab labeled Windows Setup.

4. Click the check box to the left of the line marked Microsoft Exchange. Make sure that the line at the bottom of the Description box reads 2 of 2 components selected. If not, click on Details and check any unchecked boxes. Figure 9-1 shows what the screen should look like before proceeding.

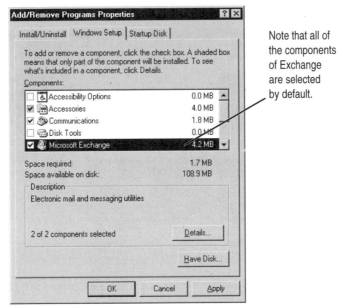

Figure 9-1: Installing Microsoft Exchange with the Add/Remove dialog.

5. Make sure your Windows CD or disks are in their appropriate drives and select OK to install Microsoft Exchange.

You can remove and reinstall Exchange in much the same way as you installed it, if you so desire. From Control Panel, go to the Add/Remove Programs dialog, select the Windows Setup property sheet, and uncheck the boxes for any components you want to remove.

Configuring the Exchange Client

Installing Exchange automatically starts the Inbox Setup Wizard, which is probably better than no help at all, but not by much. You've still got a lot of work to do, and doing it wrong is worse than not doing it at all. Since several files are created and referenced during Exchange configuration, making mistakes here can result in the wrong files being referenced, and the best fix to a botched Exchange installation might be to uninstall it and try again.

That said, to configure Exchange once the Wizard starts:

1. When prompted: Have You Used Microsoft Exchange Before?, select No, then Next.

2. When asked to automatically configure services, check the Manually Configure box at the bottom of the window and select Next. Ignore the entries automatically inserted, as shown in Figure 9-2. You might have more or less entries in your installation.

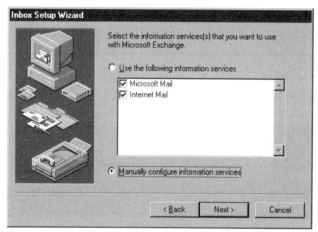

Figure 9-2: Choosing to manually configure Microsoft Exchange with the Inbox Setup Wizard, Step 2.

3. Enter your name as the Profile Name. You can use any name you like, but you might as well make it descriptive. This will identify the set of settings for an individual to use on this computer. You can set up different profiles for different people or different mail servers later, if you desire.

4. Add some services. You'll want to click on the button marked Add, then select the following services: Personal Address Book, Personal Folders, and Internet Mail. As you select each service, you'll be given some configuration options. There are no options to change for Personal Address Book. For Personal Folders, enter a filename for your personal folder. Your initials are a good choice. Configuring Internet Mail is where the work starts.

There are a myriad of settings to consider when configuring Internet Mail. This discussion assumes you have an active mail account with a provider that permits remote access to mailboxes using the standard POP3 protocol. (If you don't know what protocol your mail service uses and you have read your mail remotely before, it's probably POP3. Contact your system administrator for details if this setup procedure doesn't work.) First, deal with the Internet Mail dialog.

What Is...

POP3: A protocol often used by mail servers to allow the remote reading and sending of mail.

5. In the General tab of the Internet Mail dialog box (Figure 9-3), enter the information requested: full name, e-mail address, Internet Mail server, account name, and password. Your password will not appear in a readable form.

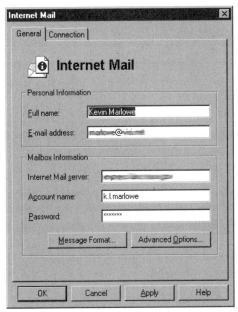

Figure 9-3: The General tab of the Internet Mail dialog.

6. Select the Connection tab (Figure 9-4) at the top of the dialog and enter the necessary information about how you receive your Internet mail: using a locally attached network (e.g., Ethernet) or using a modem. If using a modem, make sure you select the Login As button and enter your account name and password for your PPP account. These might be different from your mail account name and password.

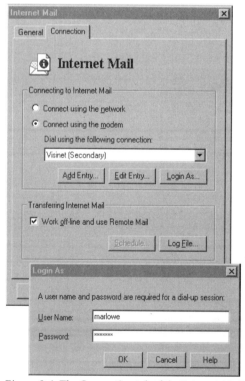

Figure 9-4: The Connection tab of the Internet Mail dialog.

7. Finally, click on OK until you're back to the Inbox Setup Wizard and select Finish to make it go away.

Congratulations on surviving Exchange client setup. You should now be able to use Outlook's e-mail client with your existing mail server, and Outlook's fax accessory should work. Now things get a little more complicated.

Sharing Private Folders

Let's say that you want to do a little more than send e-mail with your fellow cubicle-mates. In this perfect world, you're all using Outlook to manage your calendars, and you want to be able to use Outlook to set up a meeting everybody can attend. You still can't use Outlook's built-in group scheduling features, because they require the use of Exchange Server. You can, however, see everybody else's calendar if they allow it. This isn't really an Internet feature, since it depends on all of the workgroup being present on the same local network, but it's worth trying.

The technique we're about to discuss uses the concept of *folders*, an idea that recurs frequently in the world of mail and groupware clients. Each individual user of Outlook can have any number of folders in his or her profile. Each folder represents a different object in Outlook. For example, a folder might contain your personal calendar. A different folder might contain your incoming mail, and yet another your to-do list. Your folders normally contain information about only you, as everybody maintains their own folders.

You can share your folders with others by using the built-in sharing features of Windows. Typically, to share a directory in Windows, you right-click on its icon in Windows Explorer, select Sharing from the menu, and click on Share As in the dialog that follows. By default, that directory and all files in it become readable by anyone on your local network.

FYI: There Are Folders & Then There Are Folders

Windows sometimes uses the term folder to mean directories on the hard disk, while Outlook uses folder to mean a group of related data, like a calendar or task list. For clarity, we'll use *directory* in this chapter when referring to groups of files on the hard disk and *folder* to mean applications in Outlook.

To read someone else's calendar, you need to know where it is, and have access to it through the sharing mechanism described above.

There are a couple of ways to do this: users can each set up a shared directory on their own hard drives to contain their folders, or you can choose a directory on a central machine that everyone can use to save their folders to. Either way will work.

For this example, let's assume that your office has put into place the following:

■ A shared directory (C:\SHARED) on each machine will contain sharable files.

■ Everyone will update their shared calendars every Monday morning.

■ Shared folders will be named so they identify the person who created them; for example, Jane M. Eyre's calendar folder file will be called jme-cal.pst.

The steps you will take to update your shared calendar are not, unfortunately, automatic. Your calendar is actually saved deep in the directory hierarchy on your local hard drive. To make a copy of your calendar for everybody else to read, you need to do the following:

1. In Outlook, select the Calendar icon to open the Calendar folder.

2. Click on File | Import and Export.

3. In the dialog that pops up (Figure 9-5), choose Export to a Personal Folder File (.pst) and click on the Next button.

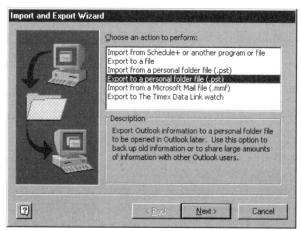

Figure 9-5: The Import and Export Wizard dialog.

4. Select your calendar on the tree that appears (Figure 9-6) and click on Next.

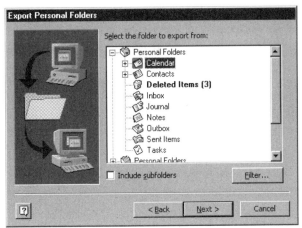

Figure 9-6: Selecting Calendar for sharing by using the Export Personal Folders dialog.

5. When you're asked where to save the exported file (Figure 9-7), choose the shared directory your office agreed upon earlier and the appropriate name for the file. Click on the Finish button to make it happen.

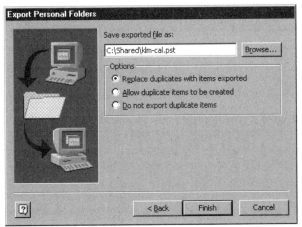

Figure 9-7: Selecting where to save the exported calendar file using the Export Personal Folders dialog.

Your calendar is now available for anyone else to read. Now, how can you read someone else's calendar? It's pretty intuitive—click on File | Open Special Folder | Personal Folder. You'll see a file selection dialog, and you can find the shared directory we talked about above and select the calendar folder for the person you're interested in. This will, in turn, open a new copy of Outlook containing that person's calendar. Read it and weep.

This technique will work for any of the folders in Outlook. You could set up an office-wide directory the same way, by sharing the head secretary's Contacts folder. You could disseminate information about a project by sharing the Tasks folder describing it. You get the idea. The problem with this approach is that the information is static—it's only as current as the last time it was edited and saved to the common area.

Using Outlook With Microsoft Exchange Server

If you decide to use Exchange Server to facilitate the sharing of information in your office, you'll find that it uses much the same kind of facility as described above to manage multiple folders for multiple people. If there's information you normally share with other people, it will be stored on the server rather than on your local machine. That way, when anyone requests a current copy of your schedule, the one they'll get is absolutely current. Furthermore, various group-enabled features of Office become available, such as seeing various people's calendars in different colors in one calendar table.

Again, if you're working in a mostly Microsoft environment and you're interested in real-time information sharing among the office, you should consider using Exchange Server.

Moving On

There's not much to move on to. You've now gotten a taste of each of the Office applications and have acquired some experience using them to create Web pages and share your data across the Internet. The only thing left to do is to put it all together—to take the pieces we've created and show that they can all work together in a Web site. This won't come as a surprise to you, but it works.

chapter 10

The Big Picture

If you've gotten this far, congratulations. You've probably put together a professional, serviceable site by now. You've seen enough of the Web to know that this isn't going to win a "Cool Site of the Hour" prize from some self-aggrandizing rater of Web worthiness, but it gets the information across and does so competently.

Where do you go from here? Well, now that the groundwork has been laid, you might consider upgrading your Web toolkit a little, since you are probably running up against Office 97's Web authoring limitations. A good place to go next is Microsoft Front Page, a sub-$100 product that organizes and indexes your site. If you've had to move a page from one directory on your server to another, you know how annoying it can be to update all of the references to and from it; FrontPage does all of that for you. There are similar shareware tools on the enclosed CD.

You might also consider a dedicated HTML editor. If you're not yet ready to go cold turkey and write native HTML in Windows Notepad, try any of the HTML editors on the CD. Even if they don't do exactly what you want, you will learn more about HTML than you ever wanted to know just by getting used to them. And the beauty of shareware is that they don't cost anything to try. Of course, if you end up liking one and using it for your production-quality pages, you really should stroke a check to the starving author(s) who gave us permission to let you take it for a spin.

Lastly, you could specialize. The art of writing Web pages is akin to a marriage of document design (the presentation of content on the written page) and graphic art, and there's always room to improve. You could concentrate on the appearance of your pages, or on the usefulness of the content. Interested in Web databases in general? You're not alone. Online multimedia presentations? It's a burgeoning field, with several competing standards waiting for you to evaluate them and show your stuff. There really isn't any limit to what you can do on the Web if you want to continue from here. Maybe cyberspace is the real final frontier, and you've got a seat on the bridge.

About the CD

On the enclosed CD, we've taken all of the examples from the previous chapters and have welded them together into one coherent Web site. In some cases, they've been slightly modified from the examples in the chapters for continuity or to match the directory structure we've settled upon, but they were all generated using only Office 97 tools. In theory, you should be able to pop this CD into your Web server (which you've set up following the step-by-step instructions in Chapter 4 and Appendices C or D, of course), copy the entire MGL_Web directory hierarchy to your Web root folder, set up permissions on your Web server and ODBC data sources if necessary, and you should be up and running. Here's a hint: modify them using your favorite text editor before you pass them off as your own, or people will think you've lost it.

The hierarchy we've set up for you is intended for readability and reference more than for organizational bliss. For example, you'll notice that the index document in each subdirectory is called index.htm. Is this a good idea in general? It doesn't hurt, but it makes the site pretty hard to administer when you have three index.htm files open in your editor and need to figure out which is which. It's set up that way on this CD so you can quickly jump from section to section without remembering a lot of filenames. For example, the online catalog is at http://yourserver/MGL_Web/ordering/. The annual report is at http://yourserver/MGL_Web/report/. There's no reason why you have to follow that convention, but it's convenient for what we're doing here.

The structure of the site is shown in Figure 10-1.

Figure 10-1: The MGL_Web Folder hierarchy on the enclosed CD.

The root of this structure could be the root of your Web site, or you could copy it as a subdirectory off the root. There are folders for each major topic covered in the book, using every application (except for Outlook) in Office 97.

You'll notice that the \internal directory contains subdirectories for each of the Excel HTML types (via Access and with Perl); likewise, the \ordering directory contains examples of static HTML, HTX/IDC files, and Active Server Pages from Access. There's even a bonus: the \personnel directory contains another set of Access ASP, HTX/IDC, and Static examples for good measure (note the difference between the hyperlinks in the HTX/IDC and Static versions). Finally, we like to keep most of the graphics we use in our pages in one directory (\images in this example). This technique minimizes duplication and makes it easier to remember where you put that #%$^ logo when you're editing pages by hand.

If you do decide to copy this site to your server and work with it, remember that you must regenerate all of the ASP files. ASP files include information about the server they were created on, and since MGL is a fictional company, you'll have some trouble running the examples without recompiling them. All of the included databases include a Publish to the Web template to make this as easy as possible. Don't forget to set up system data sources and make the directories they live in executable on your server (see Chapter 7 for details).

Troubleshooting

As you put together your master site, you'll undoubtedly stumble. Get up, dust yourself off, and try again. Sooner or later, you'll get it. Some thoughts to carry you along the journey:

- **Pages look OK but your images are missing?** You've probably not used the right relative paths in your HTML. Take a look at the source. If you see your images listed as IMG SRC="/images/logo.gif", the leading slash tells you that you're counting down from the root directory (an *absolute* path). If you see IMG SRC="images/logo.gif" (no leading slash), then the images directory is expected to be a subdirectory of your current location (a *relative* path). Confused? You can save yourself some grief by always using absolute paths.

- **Pages look OK but hyperlinks don't work?** Make sure you're going through your Web server; the URL for your pages should start with http://, not file://.

- **Access ASP pages fill the browser window with garbage?** You didn't install the Active Server Pages extensions, which work with all three versions of the Web servers but are only shipped with IIS 3.0. You can download it from www.microsoft.com/iis.

- **Can't find the home page created by the Save As HTML Wizard in Access?** Remember, it gets saved with an .html extension by default, not the .htm that everything else uses. You would do well to create it, then rename it for consistency.

- **Graphics you created in Word disappear when you Save As HTML?** It's a bug. Make sure you save them in a separate .doc file before saving as HTML, so you can find another way to save them in graphics format (like by using the screen capture in Paint Shop Pro, on the enclosed CD) before they vanish into the ether.

- **PowerPoint graphics too big on your Web pages?** Use the Save As HTML Wizard in PowerPoint to resize your images. While you might think $3/4$ of the screen at 800x600 resolution will work fine, remember you have other things on the screen as well, such as navigation buttons, titles, and so on. Some users don't like to run their Web browsers full-screen, so try to accommodate as many people as possible.

- **PowerPoint graphics too small on your Web pages?** Go back to the Save as HTML Wizard and make them bigger. Creating Web documents is not yet a science, so making mistakes and correcting them is pretty normal. What looks good on your monitor when you create a Web page might not work on many other monitors. If at all possible, view your Web pages using a variety of resolutions and monitor sizes to find a compromise that works well for a majority of users.

- **Users editing your Excel Web forms?** You need to protect all of the data cells except those intended to accept user input. Go back to Chapter 8 and read the section that tells you how to use Visual Basic for Applications to "lock out" user input for all unused spreadsheet cells.

- **Is your Perl program generated by the Excel Web Form Wizard not working correctly?** Be sure you have Perl installed on your Web server machine, and be sure your Perl program has a file extension that is associated with the Perl executable. If you need help with any of these topics, see Chapter 8.

- **Can't make your Web queries work?** Be sure your Web query files are in a directory on your Web server that allows users to execute programs. If the directory does not, your Web programs won't work. Use the Web Administrator for your Web server to add execute permissions to the directory that contains your Web query program.

- **Can't figure out what's going wrong?** Check the server error log, which can be in several different places depending on which server you're using (it's specified in the server administration pages).

CAUTION

When you download patches and features to install with your Web server, save them somewhere so you don't have to download them again should you need to reinstall or recover from a crash. Active Server Pages, for example, is about 10MB and takes almost two hours to download on a 33.6 kbps modem.

Getting Ahead of the Pack

Here's the last word: the times, they are a changin'. Anything written about the Web is practically obsolete as soon as it's printed. There's no question that the next version of Office will have better Web authoring tools. Maybe Outlook will even come along for the ride. But waiting for the technology to "stabilize" is like waiting for PC prices to drop, or for the next great buying opportunity in the stock market. You gotta play to win. And it's a lot easier to update or improve a site than it is to start from scratch, so you might as well put together the best site you can and tweak it until it's perfect. And when you write the perfect Web site, we'd like to see it, so let us know.

About the Companion CD-ROM

The CD-ROM included with your copy of the Microsoft Office 97 Internet Developer's Guide contains valuable software, including animation tools, text editors, image viewers, link checkers, and more. Plus, AVI and Web site files are included to demonstrate Internet development techniques discussed in the book.

To Navigate the CD-ROM:

The CD-ROM contains two folders, Software and Resource. The Software folder contains full- and limited-version applications, shareware, and more from a number of developers. The Resource folder contains AVI files and Web site files to be used in conjunction with the book.

Software on the CD-ROM

A complete listing of the Software Folder contents follows in Table A-1.

Program	Description
ACDSee32	Previously known as ACDSee for Windows 95, this 32-bit enhanced version of ACDSee is the fastest image viewer for Windows 95 and NT 4.0. For more information, visit ACD Systems's site at http://www.acdsystems.com.
A Smaller GIF	A Smaller GIF compresses animated GIFs, saving memory and making downloading easier without affecting image quality. A Smaller GIF provides full viewer functions—play, forward, backward, fast view F/B, pause, random access, and more. Visit http://www.peda.com for more information.
Cel Assembler	Cel Assembler 1.2 for Windows 95 is a graphical tool for building and animating GIFs. The interface allows the user to view all of the image frames at once and to move/copy/paste them intuitively. The user can also easily set delays/palettes/erasure methods as well as optimize the animation to reduce file size. A full-featured preview shows the animation in real time or a frame at a time, and can be viewed while the animation is being edited for immediate feedback. Cel Assembler makes animation building easy. To find out more, visit http://www.gamani.com.
CSE 3310 HTML Validator	CSE 3310 HTML Validator is a highly user-configurable, easy-to-use HTML syntax checking program for Microsoft Windows 95 and Windows NT. For more information, visit http://www.htmlvalidator.com.
CuteFTP	CuteFTP is a Windows-based Internet application that allows novice users to utilize the capabilities of FTP without having to know all of the details of the protocol itself. It simplifies FTP by offering a user-friendly, graphical interface instead of cumbersome command-line utility. Visit http://www.cuteftp.com.
Eudora Light	With nearly 3 million users, Eudora is the most popular and proven electronic mail software on the Internet. Eudora's easy-to-use features save you time in composing, organizing, and replying to your electronic mail. To find out more about this mail client and other products from Qualcomm, Inc., visit http://www.eudora.com.
Free Agent	This online/offline newsreader for Windows will help you to discover the world of news and information on the Internet. Free Agent makes Usenet navigation simple, and it can save you money by allowing you to read all your messages offline. For more information about this product, visit http://www.forteinc.com.

Program	Description
Gif·glf·giF	Gif·glf·giF is a simple program for producing GIF animations. Use Gif·glf·giF to produce animated software demonstrations that can be placed on the Web. The animations are viewable with a Web browser without add-ons, plug-ins, or helper applications. Visit http://www.peda.com for more information about Gif·glf·giF.
HTML Imager	HTML Imager produces Web pages, showing all GIF and/or JPEG pictures from the chosen directory. Users can select different background colors or patterns to test the appearance of each image under chosen conditions. This program makes it easy both to catalog large collections of Web design pictures and to produce online photo albums. HTML Imager can also be used to display pictures stored in the cache produced by browsers such as Netscape Navigator or Microsoft Internet Explorer. For more information, visit http://www.unige.ch/sciences/terre/geologie/fookes.
Hypercam AVI Screen Capture Software	Hypercam 1.13 captures action from a Windows 95 or Windows NT screen in any graphics mode, including cursor movements and sound. The program saves the captured movement in standard AVI movie files. Perfect for demonstrations, presentations, and tutorials. Visit http://www.hyperionics.com to find out more about this product.
IceView '95	IceView '95 is a very fast and powerful shareware image viewer for Windows 95 and Windows NT. Visit http://www.algonet.se/~mithril/iceview.html for more information.
Itsagif	Itsagif makes colorful GIFs that are not limited to 256 colors. Visit http://www.peda.com for more information.
Jasc ImageCommander	This program is a fast and powerful image viewing and file conversion program for Windows-based computers. Jasc ImageCommander offers complete control over file format associations, making it the ideal choice for your default Windows image viewer. With support for over 30 file formats including GIF, JPG, BMP, PNG, TIF, WMF, CDR, and more. This is the only image viewing and conversion program you will ever need! Visit http://www.jasc.com for more information about this and other Jasc products.

Program	Description
Jasc Image Robot	Jasc Image Robot is a fast, powerful, and easy program for image conversion and processing. Multiple tasks can be run on large batches of images to help you focus on your work and not your image manipulation. This powerful new tool can assist with even the most complex image conversions or processes, yet is very easy to use. All of your routines can be saved for future use and edited to allow for changes to the routines. Visit http://www.jasc.com for more information about this and other Jasc products.
Jasc Media Center	Jasc Media Center offers complete multimedia file management! Just a few mouse clicks will catalog the sounds, animations, and images on your hard disk, removable storage media, network, or CDs. Works with video, photo, image, sound, and music files. Includes slide show presentation features, image format conversion, and batch image manipulation. Visit http://www.jasc.com for more information about this and other Jasc products.
Kids PowWow	Kids PowWow is a PowWow version strictly for children (up to age 13). It links with Tribal Voice's PowWow for Kids home page and provides features that help provide a protective environment for children who want to use PowWow. It alerts children when an adult pages them, or when they page an adult. The adult version of PowWow (versions 3.0+) will also display a warning to the user indicating that he/she is connected to a child. The Kids home page provides a White Pages for children and children's conferences. The children's conferences have profanity filters to disallow the transmission of profanity in conference mode. To register as a PowWow kid, a valid e-mail address must exist for the child. A registration password is given out through e-mail and the password must be entered prior to using the program. For more information, visit http://www.tribal.com.
Linkbot	Linkbot is an award-winning site management tool that helps Webmasters organize, test, and repair their Web sites. Linkbot can quickly scan through a site and identify critical problem areas, such as broken links, stale content, and over-sized files. The results can be viewed in an Explorer-style interface or in an HTML report. To learn more, visit http://www.tetranetsoftware.com.

Program	Description
LiveImage	The heir to Map This!, LiveImage is a client-side, user-friendly image mapping program for Windows 95 and Windows NT 4.0. With LiveImage, you can create your first client-side image map with embedded hyperlinks in under five minutes. Features include: zoom-in up to 8x magnification; cut, copy, and paste; GIF, JPG, and PNG file format support; doesn't require a TrueColor video board—can operate from 16 colors to 16 million colors; supports dragging links from Netscape into a map; the Image Wizard allows you to create common navigation bars; product menus, and item grids; the Image Map Wizard simplifies creating a new image map; full support for HTML 3.0 image maps—can edit existing map or add a new map to an existing HTML file, and much more. For more information about Mediatech's LiveImage, visit http://www.mediatec.com.
Paint Shop Pro 4.12	A 32-bit version of Paint Shop Pro, a powerful and easy-to-use image viewing, editing, and conversion program that supports over 30 image formats. With numerous drawing and painting tools, this may be the only graphics program you will ever need! Visit http://www.jasc.com for more information about this and other Jasc products.
Perl for Win32	ActiveState Tool Corp.'s Perl for Win32 Intel/x86 binary is a port of most of the functionality in Perl, with extra Win32 API calls that allow you to take advantage of native Windows functionality. Perl for Win32 runs on Windows 95 and Windows NT 3.5 and later. The Perl for Win32 package contains perl.exe, perlx00.dll, supporting documents, and extensions that allow you to call Win32 functionality. For more information, visit ActiveState's home page at http://www.activestate.com.
PicaView32	PicaView32 was previously known as PicaView for Windows 95 and Windows NT 4.0. It is a fast and effective 32-bit File Manager "add-on" for viewing images without running external programs! For more information, visit ACD Systems's site at http://www.acdsystems.com.
PowWow	PowWow is a unique Internet program for Windows that allows up to nine people to chat, transfer files, and cruise the World Wide Web together as a group. PowWow also has Conferencing and Text-to-Speech features. PowWow now has E-mail Answering Machine capabilities and lots more! To find out more about this and other products from Tribal Voice, visit http://www.tribal.com.

Program	Description
Printscreen 95	Printscreen 95 is a printscreen/screen capture program for Windows 3.1, 95, and NT. The program supports true color images and also provides DOS screen print from Windows. Go to http://com.primenet.com/sssware to learn more.
SmartDraw	SmartDraw lets users draw great looking flowcharts, organization charts, diagrams, web images, and other business graphics. For more information, visit http://www.smartdraw.com.
StreetGraphics Unregistered	StreetGraphics is a vectorial graphics editor which supports many features only available in Painting (non-vectorial) programs: transparency, air brush, color blends, transparent bitmaps, artistic lines (e.g., calligraphic), anti-aliasing, and much more. To find out more, visit http://www.odyssee.net/~hugow.
Super NoteTab	Super NoteTab is a versatile text editor, integrating several original productivity tools. The program handles large files, and is capable of opening a large number of files as well. Features include search/replace text, clipbook window with editable templates for HTML tags and other purposes, line and character filters, and much more. For more information, visit http://www.unige.ch/sciences/terre/geologie/fookes.
TextPad	TextPad is designed to provide the power and functionality to satisfy the most demanding text editing requirements. It is Windows-hosted, and comes in 16- and 32-bit editions. Huge files can be edited by either; just choose the edition that works best with your PC. The 32-bit edition can edit files up to the limits of virtual memory, and it will work with Windows 95, NT, and 3.1 with Win32s extensions. Visit http://www.textpad.com for more information.
WinZip	This ingenious tool from Nico Mak Computing, Inc., brings the convenience of Windows to the use of Zip files and other compression formats. WinZip includes an intuitive point-and-click, drag-and-drop interface for viewing, running, extracting, adding, deleting, and testing files in archives. The optional WinZip Wizard feature uses a standard and familiar wizard interface to simplify the process of unzipping and installing software distributed in Zip files. The wizard is not targeted at experienced users, but is ideal for the rapidly growing number of PC users getting started with Zip files. Included with this WinZip package is the WinZip Self-Extractor which allows you to create files that unzip themselves. The Self-Extractor allows you to send compressed files to users who may not own or know how to use file compression software. For more information about Nico Mak Computing, Inc., products, visit http://www.winzip.com.

Program	Description
WinVN	WinVN is a Microsoft Windows, Windows/95, and Windows/NT based news reader. Its name stands for Windows Visual Newsreader. Like other news readers, it can be used to select, view, write, sort, and print Usenet News articles. Articles can be saved locally, cut into the Windows Clipboard, or forwarded to other individuals via electronic mail. WinVN offers a more visual approach to Usenet News than most other news readers. The program allows the user to navigate easily between newsgroups and articles via its point-and-click interface. It allows the viewing of multiple articles simultaneously, and on multi-tasking operating systems like Microsoft Windows NT, WinVN even allows multiple simultaneous news server connections. For more information, visit http://www.ksc.nasa.gov/software/winvn/winvn.html.
zMUD	zMUD is a game client that allows you to connect to MUD game servers on the Internet. zMUD also functions as a Telnet client. For more information, visit http://www.zuggsoft.com.
Zoc	Zoc is a powerful communications/terminal program with a wealth of features and ease of use. It allows online picture viewing, automation via the REXX programming language, and is extremely easy to configure. Check out http://www.emtec.com.

Table A-1: Software on the Companion CD-ROM.

The CD-ROM contains the complete Web site created in the book. To find the Web site files, please refer to the following subdirectories within the Resource folder: Images, Internal, Ordering, Personnel, and Report.

In addition to the Web site files, the CD-ROM contains AVI files designed to demonstrate Web site development techniques discussed in the book. These AVI files reside in the Demos subdirectory of the Resource folder. A complete listing of the AVI files follows in Table A-2.

Filename	Description
access web publish.avi	This AVI file shows how the Access 97 Publish to the Web Wizard works.
animate.avi	A file that demonstrates how to animate a PowerPoint graphic for the Web.
different browsers.avi	An AVI file demonstrating the different ways that HTML source is viewed by Netscape Navigator 3.0, Microsoft Internet Explorer 3.1, and Microsoft Word.
bullets.avi	Shows how graphical and non-graphical bullets work in Word 97's HTML Mode.
chartwiz.avi	With this AVI file, you can learn how to create an Excel chart from a spreadsheet.
disappearing graphics.avi	An AVI file that illustrates how graphical objects drawn in Microsoft Word (using the drawing toolbar and/or Word Art) disappear when converting to HTML.
internic.avi	Shows how to use Windows 95's Telnet client to connect to the InterNIC and check on domain name registration.
makelogo.avi	With this AVI file, you can learn how to create a company logo in PowerPoint.
sparkle.avi	This file shows how to use PowerPoint to enhance the company logo created in makelogo.avi.
webform.avi	Shows how to create an Excel Web form.

Table A-2: AVI Files on the Companion CD-ROM.

Technical Support

Technical support is available for installation-related problems only. The technical support office is open from 8:00 A.M. to 6:00 P.M. (EST) Monday through Friday and can be reached via the following methods:

- Phone: (919) 544-9404 extension 81
- Faxback Answer System: (919) 544-9404 extension 85
- E-mail: help@vmedia.com
- FAX: (919) 544-9472
- World Wide Web: **http://www.vmedia.com/support**
- America Online: keyword *Ventana*

Limits of Liability & Disclaimer of Warranty

The authors and publisher of this book have used their best efforts in preparing the CD-ROM and the programs contained in it. These efforts include the development, research, and testing of the theories and programs to determine their effectiveness. The authors and publisher make no warranty of any kind expressed or implied, with regard to these programs or the documentation contained in this book.

The authors and publisher shall not be liable in the event of incidental or consequential damages in connection with, or arising out of, the furnishing, performance, or use of the programs, associated instructions, and/or claims of productivity gains.

Some of the software on this CD-ROM is shareware; there may be additional charges (owed to the software authors/makers) incurred for registration and continued use. See individual programs' README or VREADME.TXT files for more information.

HTML Quick Reference

We've tried to include common tags used by all. Some tags are only used by Tibetan monks when constructing prayer mantras. We don't include those esoteric tags that are rarely used (often because we don't know what some of them are supposed to do). Some tags only work with Netscape or Internet Explorer, and we've tried to note them accordingly. Due to the speed at which browser software changes, some notations might no longer be accurate by the time this book hits the shelves. We apologize for any errors, but we're only human. As our wives tell us frequently.

For a comprehensive listing and explanation of HTML tags, check out Ventana's *HTML Programmer's Reference*. If you need or want more basic instruction in HTML authoring from scratch, Ventana publishes *HTML Publishing on the Internet, Second Edition* and *Official HTML Publishing for Netscape, Second Edition*. And finally, if you are looking for more guidance in designing your Web pages for maximum readibilty and effect, *Looking Good Online* from Ventana covers those issues thoroughly.

NOTATION:

#	A number.
%	A percentage.
***	Text.
XXXXXX	Hex code.
,,,	Comma-separated.
|	Alternative items.
(***)	An optional tag parameter.
URL	The URL of a file (absolute or relative).

BROWSER NOTATIONS:

(none)	Should work with either browser.
NS	Netscape extension.
IE	Internet Explorer extension.

THE TAGS

Now, on to what you are really here for!

<!-- --> Comment

Basic Usage: `<!-- Your comment here. -->`

<!DOCTYPE> Document Type

Basic Usage: `<!DOCTYPE HTML PUBLIC "-//IETF//DTD HTML 3.0//EN">`

<A> Anchor (otherwise known as a hyperlink)

Basic Usage: `<A HREF="URL"></A>`

Options:	HREF="#***"	link to anchor in current document.
	HREF="URL#***"	link to anchor in another document.
	NAME="***"	name an anchor.
	TARGET="***"	link to browser window or frame.

\<ADDRESS\> Address

Basic Usage: `<ADDRESS></ADDRESS>`

\<APPLET\> Java applet

Basic Usage: `<APPLET></APPLET>`

Options:	ALIGN="LEFT|RIGHT|CENTER"	align the applet output.
	ALT="***"	alternative text for non-Java browsers.
	CODE="***"	applet source filename.
	CODEBASE="URL"	URL to find applet source.
	HSPACE=#	horizontal spacing.
	HEIGHT=#	height of applet output.
	NAME="***"	applet name.
	\<PARAM NAME="***"\>	applet parameter name.
	\<PARAM VALUE="***"\>	applet parameter value.
	VSPACE=#	vertical spacing.
	WIDTH=#	width of applet output.

\<B\> Bold Text

Basic Usage: `<B></B>`

\<BASE\> Base Information

Basic Usage: `<BASE HREF="URL">`
Note: Must be in \<HEAD\> section.

Options:	HREF="URL"	URL to prefix relative paths with.
	TARGET="***"	default target window name.

<BGSOUND> Background Sound (IE)

Basic Usage: `<BGSOUND SRC="URL"></BGSOUND>`

Options:

LOOP=#	number of times to loop sound file.
SRC="URL"	location of sound file.

<BIG> Big Text

Basic Usage: `<BIG></BIG>`

<BLINK> Blinking Text

Basic Usage: `<BLINK></BLINK>`

<BLOCKQUOTE> Block Quote Section

Basic Usage: `<BLOCKQUOTE></BLOCKQUOTE>`

<BODY> Body of HTML Document

Basic Usage: `<BODY></BODY>`

Options:

ALINK="#XXXXXX"	active link color.
BACKGROUND="URL"	background image.
BGCOLOR="#XXXXXX"	background color.
BGPROPERTIES="FIXED"	non-scrolling background. (IE)
LEFTMARGIN=#	set left margin. (IE)
LANG="***"	language used in document.
LINK="#XXXXXX"	unvisited hyperlink color.
TEXT="#XXXXXX"	text color.
TOPMARGIN=#	set top margin. (IE)
VLINK="#XXXXXX"	visited hyperlink color.

\<BR\> Line Break

Basic Usage: \<BR\>

Options: CLEAR="LEFT|RIGHT|ALL" moves down the next line of text.

\<CENTER\> Center Text

Basic Usage: \<CENTER\>\</CENTER\>

\<CITE\> Citation

Basic Usage: \<CITE\>\</CITE\>

\<CODE\> Computer Code

Basic Usage: \<CODE\>\</CODE\>

\<DEF\> Definition

Basic Usage: \<DFN\>\</DFN\>

\<DL\> Definition List

Basic Usage: \<DL\>\<DT\>\<DD\>\</DL\>

Options:
COMPACT   reduce white space.
\<DD\>   data definition.
\<DT\>   data term.

\<DIV\> Section Divider

Basic Usage: \<DIV ALIGN=***\>\</DIV\>

Options: ALIGN="LEFT|CENTER|RIGHT|JUSTIFY"   placement specifier.

<EM> Emphasized Text

Basic Usage: <EM></EM>

<EMBED> Embed an Object

Basic Usage: <EMBED SRC="URL">

Options:

HEIGHT=#	object height.
SRC="URL"	source of object.
WIDTH=#	object width.

<FONT> Font Characteristics

Basic Usage: <FONT SIZE=#></FONT>

Options:

BASEFONT SIZE=#	size can be 1-6.
COLOR="#XXXXXX"	font color.
FACE="***"	font type.
SIZE="+l-#	increase or decrease font size.

<FORM> Form

Basic Usage: <FORM><INPUT ...></FORM>

Options:

ACTION="URL"	target of form data.
ENCTYPE="multipart/form-data"	file upload. (NS)
<INPUT CHECKED>	checkbox or radio on.
<INPUT MAXLENGTH=#>	max length of text data.
<INPUT NAME="***">	element identifier.
<INPUT SIZE=#>	text box size.
<INPUT SRC=URL>	image src URL. (NS)
<INPUT TYPE="CHECKBOXIHIDDENI IMAGEIPASSWORDIRADIOIRESETI SUBMITITEXT"	element type.
<INPUT VALUE="***">	default value.
METHOD="GETIPOST"	method of sending data.
<OPTION>	item in select list.
<OPTION SELECTED>	preselected item.

➡

<OPTION VALUE="***">	value of option.
<SELECT></SELECT>	select list.
<SELECT NAME="***">	element name.
<SELECT MULTIPLE>	select multiple items.
<SELECT SIZE=#>	size of scroll box.
<TEXTAREA></TEXTAREA>	text area.
<TEXTAREA COLS=#>	column size of box.
<TEXTAREA NAME="***">	element name.
<TEXTAREA ROWS=#>	row size of box.
<TEXTAREA WRAP="OFFIVIRTUALI PHYSICALISOFTIHARD">	text wrap type.

<FRAMESET> Frames

Basic Usage: <FRAMESET></FRAMESET><NOFRAMES></NOFRAMES>

Options:

BORDER=#	border thickness.
BORDERCOLOR="#XXXXXX"	border color.
COLS=,,,	column width.
COLS=#	column relative width.
FRAMEBORDER="YESINO"	border on or off.
ROWS=,,,	row height.
ROWS=#	row relative height.
<FRAME>	define a frame.
<FRAME BORDERCOLOR="#XXXXXX">	frame border color.
<FRAME FRAMEBORDER="YESINO">	frame border on or off.
<FRAME MARGINHEIGHT=#>	top/bottom margin size.
<FRAME MARGINWIDTH=#>	left/right margin size.
<FRAME NAME="***I_BLANKI_SELFI _PARENTI_TOP">	unique frame name.
<FRAME NORESIZE>	can't resize frame.
<FRAME SCROLLING="YESINOIAUTO">	frame scrollbar.
<FRAME SRC="URL">	source for frame.
<NOFRAMES></NOFRAMES>	alternate display.

<H#> Header

Basic Usage: <H1></H1> (# can be 1-6)

Options: ALIGN="LEFT|CENTER|RIGHT"   header placement.

<HEAD> Document Header

Basic Usage: <HEAD></HEAD>

<HR> Horizontal Rule

Basic Usage: <HR>

Options: ALIGN="LEFT|RIGHT|CENTER"   align the rule.
NOSHADE   solid rule.
SIZE=#   thickness of the rule.
WIDTH=#   width of rule in pixels.
WIDTH="%"   width in screen percentage.

<HTML> HTML Document Type Identifier

Basic Usage: <HTML></HTML>

<I> Italic Text

Basic Usage: <I></I>

<IMG> Image

Basic Usage: <IMG SRC="URL">

Options:	ALIGN="TOP|BOTTOM|MIDDLE| LEFT| RIGHT|TEXTTOP|ABSMIDDLE| BASELINE|ABSBOTTOM"	align image.
	ALT="***"	alternate text to display when images are turned off.
	BORDER=#	border size.
	CONTROLS	display video controls. (IE)
	DYNSRC="***.AVI"	video clip. (IE)
	HEIGHT=#	image height.
	HSPACE=#	image spacing.
	ISMAP	image is an image map.
	LOOP=#	number of times to loop video clip. (IE)
	LOOPDELAY=#	delay between video loops. (IE)
	LOWSRC="URL"	low resolution copy of image. (NS)
	START=FILEOPEN|MOUSEOVER	when to start video clip. (IE)
	USEMAP="URL"	image map configuration file to use.
	VSPACE=#	image spacing.
	WIDTH=#	image width.

\<ISINDEX> Searchable Index

Basic Usage: \<ISINDEX>

Options: PROMPT="***"   text used to prompt user.

\<KBD> Keyboard Input

Basic Usage: \<KBD>\</KBD>

\<MAP> Image Map

Basic Usage: \<MAP NAME="***">\</MAP>

Options: The \<AREA> tag defines active areas within the image map.
\<AREA SHAPE="RECT" COORDS=",,," HREF="URL" (NOHREF)>

SHAPE	must be "rect" for rectangular.
COORDS	the coordinates that define the outline of the mapped area.
HREF	links a URL to the mapped area.
NOHREF	don't map this region to a URL.

\<MARQUEE> Scrolling Text (IE)

Basic Usage: \<MARQUEE>\</MARQUEE>

Options:

ALIGN="TOP|MIDDLE|BOTTOM"	text alignment.
BGCOLOR="#XXXXXX"	scrolling area background color.
BEHAVIOR="SCROLL|SLIDE|ALTERNATE"	scroll behavior.
DIRECTION="LEFT|RIGHT"	scroll direction.
HEIGHT=#	text height.
LOOP=#	number of times to loop scroll effects.
HSPACE=	horizontal spacing.
SCROLLAMOUNT=#	amount to scroll.
VSPACE=#	vertical spacing.
WIDTH=#	text width.

\<MENU> Menu List

Basic Usage: \<MENU>\</MENU>

Options:

COMPACT	reduce white space.
\<LI>	list item.

\<META\> Meta Information

Basic Usage: `<META NAME="keywords" CONTENT="Office 97 Web Dev Guide">`
Note: Must be in \<HEAD\> section.

Options:

NAME	identifies the meta information.
HTTP-EQUIV	specifies information to be parsed by the HTTP server.
CONTENT	specifies the contents of the NAME or HTTP-EQUIV parameters.

\<MULTICOL\> Multi-Column Text (NS)

Basic Usage: `<MULTICOL COLS=#></MULTICOL>`

Options:

COLS=#	number of columns to use.
GUTTER=#	amount of space between columns.
WIDTH=#	width of columns.

\<NOBR\> No Line Break

Basic Usage: `<NOBR></NOBR>`

\<OL\> Ordered List

Basic Usage: `<OL></OL>`

Options:

COMPACT	reduce white space.
\<LI\>	list item.
\<LI TYPE="AlaIIiI1"\>	specify number type for list element.
\<LI VALUE=#\>	number for list element, continue from this number.
START	number to start entire list with.
TYPE="AlaIIiI1"	specify number type for entire list.

\<P> Paragraph

Basic Usage: \<P>\</P>

Options: ALIGN="LEFT|CENTER|RIGHT"   align the paragraph text.

\<PRE> Preformatted Text

Basic Usage: \<PRE>\</PRE>

Options: WIDTH=#   width of text area.

\<S> Strikethrough Text (NS)

Basic Usage: \<S>\</S>

\<SAMP> Sample Text

Basic Usage: \<SAMP>\</SAMP>

\<SMALL> Small Text

Basic Usage: \<SMALL>\</SMALL>

\<SPACER> Document Spacing (NS)

Basic Usage: \<SPACER TYPE=HORIZONTAL SIZE=30>

Options:
ALIGN="LEFT|CENTER|RIGHT"   align the spacer.
HEIGHT=#   height of spacer.
SIZE=#   number of spaces in spacer.
TYPE="HORIZONTAL|VERTICAL| BLOCK"   type of spacer.
WIDTH=#   width of spacer.

\<STRIKE> Strikethrough Text

Basic Usage: \<STRIKE>\</STRIKE>

\<STRONG\> Strongly Emphasized Text

Basic Usage: \<STRONG\>\</STRONG\>

\<SUB\> Subscript Text

Basic Usage: \<SUB\>\</SUB\>

\<SUP\> Superscript Text

Basic Usage: \<SUP\>\</SUP\>

\<TABLE\> Table

Basic Usage: \<TABLE\>\<TR\>\<TH\>\</TH\>\<TD\>\</TD\>\</TR\>\</TABLE\>

Options:

ALIGN="LEFTIRIGHT"	align the table.
BORDER	visible border.
BORDER=#	border thickness.
BORDERCOLOR="#XXXXXX"	border color. (IE)
BORDERCOLORLIGHT="#XXXXXX"	border light color. (IE)
BORDERCOLORDARK="#XXXXXX"	border dark color. (IE)
\<CAPTION\>\</CAPTION\>	table caption.
\<CAPTION ALIGN="TOPIBOTTOMILEFTI CENTERIRIGHT"\>	align the caption.
\<CAPTION VALIGN="TOPIBOTTOM"\>	vertically align caption.
CELLSPACING=#	space between table cells.
CELLPADDING=#	space inside table cells.
\<COL SPAN=#\>	column span. (IE)
\<COL ALIGN="LEFTIRIGHTICENTER"\>	column alignment. (IE)
\<COLGROUP ALIGN="LEFTIRIGHTI CENTER"\>	column grouping. (IE)
FRAME="BOXIABOVEIBELOWIHSIDESI VSIDESILHSIRHSIVOID"	border display. (IE)
HEIGHT=#	table height in pixels.
HEIGHT=%	table height in percent.
RULES="ALLIGROUPSIROWSICOLSINONE"	internal dividing lines.
\<TBODY\>\</TBODY\>	table body. (IE)
\<TFOOT\>\</TFOOT\>	table footer. (IE)

<TD></TD>	table data cell.
<TD ALIGN="LEFT|RIGHT|CENTER">	align text in cell.
<TD BGCOLOR="#XXXXXX">	cell color.
<TD COLSPAN=#>	columns to span.
<TD NOWRAP>	don't wrap text.
<TD ROWSPAN=#>	rows to span.
<TD VALIGN="TOP|MIDDLE|BOTTOM">	vertically align text.
<TD WIDTH=#>	width in pixels.
<TD WIDTH=%>	width in percent.
<TH></TH>	table header.
<TH ALIGN="LEFT|RIGHT|CENTER">	header alignment in cell.
<TH BACKGROUND="URL">	cell background image.
<TH BGCOLOR="#XXXXXX">	cell background color.
<TH COLSPAN=#>	columns to span.
<TH NOWRAP>	don't wrap header text.
<TH ROWSPAN=#>	rows to span.
<TH WIDTH=#>	width in pixels.
<TH WIDTH="%">	width in percent.
<TH VALIGN="TOP|MIDDLE|BOTTOM">	vertical header alignment.
<THEAD></THEAD>	table header. (IE)
WIDTH=#	table width in pixels.
WIDTH=%	table width in percent.

<TITLE> HTML Document Title

Basic Usage: <TITLE></TITLE>
Note: Must be located within the <HEAD> region.

<TT> Typewriter Text

Basic Usage: <TT></TT>

<U> Underlined Text

Basic Usage: <U></U>

<UL> Unordered List

Basic Usage: <UL></UL>

Options:

COMPACT	reduce white space. (NS)
<LI>	list item.
<LI TYPE="DISC|CIRCLE|SQUARE">	specifies bullet shape for list element.
TYPE="DISC|CIRCLE|SQUARE"	specifies bullet shape for the entire list.

<VAR> A Variable Name

Basic Usage: <VAR></VAR>

<WBR> Word Break

Basic Usage: <WBR>

SPECIAL CHARACTERS :

Description	Char	Code	Entity
quotation mark	"	&#34;	&quot;
ampersand	&	&#38;	&amp;
less-than sign	<	&#60;	&lt;
greater-than sign	>	&#62;	&gt;
non-breaking space			
inverted exclamation	¡	&#161	&iexcl;
cent sign	¢	&#162	&cent;
pound sterling	£	&#163	&pound;
general currency sign	¤	&#164	&curren;
yen sign	¥	&#165	&yen;
broken vertical bar	¦	&#166	&brvbar;
section sign	§	&#167	&sect;
umlaut (dieresis)	¨	&#168	&uml;
copyright	©	&#169	&copy;

Description	Char	Code	Entity
feminine ordinal	ª	&#170	&ordf;
left angle quote, guillemot left	«	&#171	&laquo;
not sign	¬	&#172	&not;
soft hyphen	–	&#173	&shy;
registered trademark	®	&#174	&reg;
macron accent	¯	&#175	&macr;
degree sign	°	&#176	&deg;
plus or minus	±	&#177	&plusmn;
superscript two	2	&#178	&sup2;
superscript three	3	&#179	&sup3;
acute accent	´	&#180	&acute;
micro sign	μ	&#181	&micro;
paragraph sign	¶	&#182	&para;
middle dot	·	&#183	&middot;
cedilla	¸	&#184	&cedil;
superscript one	¹	&#185	&sup1;
masculine ordinal	º	&#186	&ordm;
right angle quote, guillemot right	»	&#187	&raquo;
fraction one-fourth	–	&#188	&frac14;
fraction one-half	–	&#189	&frac12;
fraction three-fourths	–	&#190	&frac34;
inverted question mark	¿	&#191	&iquest;
capital A, grave accent	À	&#192	&Agrave;
capital A, acute accent	Á	&#193	&Aacute;
capital A, circumflex accent	Â	&#194	&Acirc;
capital A, tilde	Ã	&#195	&Atilde;
capital A, dieresisor umlaut mark	Ä	&#196	&Auml;
capital A, ring	Å	&#197	&Aring;
capital AE diphthong (ligature)	Æ	&#198	&AElig;
capital C, cedilla	Ç	&#199	&Ccedil;
capital E, grave accent	È	&#200	&Egrave;
capital E, acute accent	É	&#201	&Eacute;
capital E, circumflex accent	Ê	&#202	&Ecirc;
capital E, dieresisor umlaut mark	Ë	&#203	&Euml;
capital I, grave accent	Ì	&#204	&Igrave;

Description	Char	Code	Entity
capital I, acute accent	Í	&#205	&Iacute;
capital I, circumflex accent	Î	&#206	&Icirc;
capital I, dieresisor umlaut mark	Ï	&#207	&Iuml;
capital Eth, Icelandic	Ð	&#208	&ETH;
capital N, tilde	Ñ	&#209	&Ntilde;
capital O, grave accent	Ò	&#210	&Ograve;
capital O, acute accent	Ó	&#211	&Oacute;
capital O, circumflex accent	Ô	&#212	&Ocirc;
capital O, tilde	Õ	&#213	&Otilde;
capital O, dieresisor umlaut mark	Ö	&#214	&Ouml;
multiply sign	x	&#215	&times;
capital O, slash	Ø	&#216	&Oslash;
capital U , grave accent	Ù	&#217	&Ugrave;
capital U, acute accent	Ú	&#218	&Uacute;
capital U, circumflex accent	Û	&#219	&Ucirc;
capital U , dieresisor umlaut mark	Ü	&#220	&Uuml;
capital Y, acute accent	Y	&#221	&Yacute;
capital THORN, Icelandic	Þ	&#222	&THORN;
small sharps, German (szligature)	ß	&#223	&szlig;
small a, grave accent	à	&#224	&agrave;
small a, acute accent	á	&#225	&aacute;
small a, circumflex accent	â	&#226	&acirc;
small a, tilde	ã	&#227	&atilde;
small a, dieresisor umlaut mark	ä	&#228	&auml;
small a, ring	å	&#229	&aring;
small ae diphthong (ligature)	æ	&#230	&aelig;
small c, cedilla	ç	&#231	&ccedil;
small e, grave accent	è	&#232	&egrave;
small e, acute accent	é	&#233	&eacute;
small e, circumflex accent	ê	&#234	&ecirc;
small e, dieresisor umlaut mark	ë	&#235	&euml;
small i, grave accent	ì	&#236	&igrave;
small i, acute accent	í	&#237	&iacute;
small i, circumflex accent	î	&#238	&icirc;
small i, dieresisor umlaut mark	ï	&#239	&iuml;

Description	Char	Code	Entity
small eth, Icelandic	∂	&#240	&eth;
small n, tilde	ñ	&#241	&ntilde;
small o, grave accent	ò	&#242	&ograve;
small o, acute accent	ó	&#243	&oacute;
small o, circumflex accent	ô	&#244	&ocirc;
small o, tilde	õ	&#245	&otilde;
small o, dieresisor umlaut mark	ö	&#246	&ouml;
division sign	÷	&#247	&divide;
small o, slash	ø	&#248	&oslash;
small u, grave accent	ù	&#249	&ugrave;
small u, acute accent	ú	&#250	&uacute;
small u, circumflex accent	û	&#251	&ucirc;
small u, dieresisor umlaut mark	ü	&#252	&uuml;
small y, acute accent	y	&#253	&yacute;
small thorn, Icelandic	þ	&#254	&thorn;
small y, dieresisor umlaut mark	ÿ	&#255	&yuml;

Personal Web Server Detailed Configuration Reference

In Chapter 4, instructions are provided to step you through the setup of Personal Web Server on Windows 95. However, there are a myriad of administrative options that you might wish to consider and explore for the HTTP, FTP, and Gopher services that make up Personal Web Server. They're explained in excruciating detail here for the technically minded.

You'll never need to go through all of these options step by step. You're much more likely to need to fix a particular setting and just go straight to it (assuming that you know where it is). In this Appendix, we've described all of the options as if you were indeed reading through the options dialogs, left to right, top to bottom, to make them easier to find.

The Internet Services Administrator screen (Figure C-1) contains links that permit the detailed administration of three services that your Personal Web Server provides: HTTP (called WWW Administration on this screen), FTP, and local file sharing. It also includes links to summary pages containing product information on the Microsoft Web site. To start the Internet Services Administrator, click on the Start button, then Personal Web Server, then Internet Services Administrator.

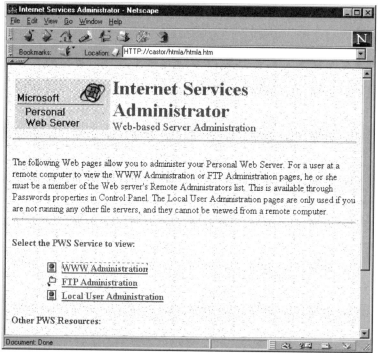

Figure C-1: The Internet Services Administrator dialog.

FYI: Where to Find Online Personal Web Server Information

Clicking on the Microsoft Personal Web Server Logo at the upper left will connect you to the Microsoft site containing information about Microsoft's Web server products. Personal Web Server's online documentation is installed in C:\Program Files\WEBSVR\docs\default.htm.

For the Web

Selecting WWW Administration in Figure C-1 brings up a dialog with three choices of tabs: Service, Directories, and Logging. In all cases, the buttons at the bottom of the screen permit any changes to be saved (OK), canceled (Cancel), or returned to their previous values without leaving the screen (Reset).

Service Tab

Click the Service tab to bring up the Internet Services Administrator dialog (Figure C-2).

Connection Timeout

This setting represents the number of seconds your server will wait for a response from a remote computer, once requested. Default: 600 seconds.

Maximum Connections

The maximum number of computers that may be connected to your Web server at any one time. The response remote users experience is directly related to how many are attached simultaneously, combined with the ability of your computer to handle their requests. Default: 300.

Password Authentication

Most Web pages do not require password by default. Personal Web Server provides some degree of security by offering several methods of controlling access to your site. You can select all, some, or none of these options:

- **Allow Anonymous (Default: On)** Permits anyone to connect to your site without a password.

- **Basic (Default: Off)** If a specific page or folder of pages is restricted to certain usernames and passwords (see Users & Groups Tabs), checking this option permits sending the usernames and passwords over the Internet in an essentially unencrypted form. Somebody watching your machine's transmissions with decoding software can easily read the usernames and passwords transmitted (and can presumably use them later).

- **Windows NT Challenge/Response (Default: On)** If the remote user is running Microsoft Internet Explorer version 3.0 or later and if your Web server machine is a member of a Windows NT Domain on your local network, Personal Web Server will encrypt usernames and passwords before sending them across the Internet.

Comment

The comment you type here will appear in the Internet Service Manager application for local users running Windows NT. It can be a description of your site or services provided. This field is for your own internal use only and is not visible outside of your local network.

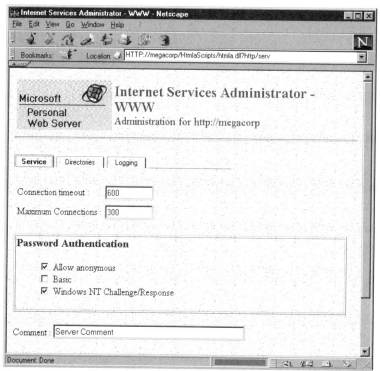

Figure C-2: The Service tab of the WWW Internet Services Administrator dialog.

Directories Tab

By default, Personal Web Server expects that your Web-destined content will be saved in the directory C:\WebShare\wwwroot. This may or may not be correct, or you might wish to add additional directories to your Web. To the external user, all of these directories will appear as subdirectories under the specified root, but they can actually exist anywhere on your file system.

You'll configure these options with the Directories tab, Figure C-3.

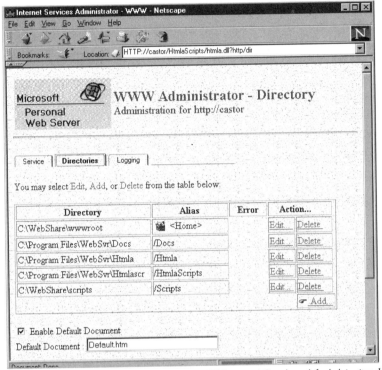

Figure C-3: The Directories tab of the WWW Internet Services Administrator dialog.

What Is...

root: The directory at the highest level of your work area or Web server.

pathname: The hierarchy of directory names, starting at the root, to where your files reside.

alias: The directory name that will appear to end users. There's no rule that says that remote clients have to know your actual directory names; you can make up any names you want.

Your options on this screen include Directory, Alias, Error, Action, and Enable Default Document/Default Document/Directory Browsing Allowed.

Directory

The fully qualified pathname to each directory you wish to make accessible from the remote user's browser. Personal Web Server sets up the following directories by default when you install it:

- C:\WebShare\wwwroot
- C:\Program Files\WebSvr\Docs
- C:\Program Files\WebSvr\Htmla
- C:\Program Files\WebSvr\Htmlascr
- C:\WebShare\scripts

Documents placed in any of these directories will be available to external users when you start Personal Web Server on your PC.

FYI: Removing Directories

Some of these directories have special functions, and you should think twice before removing them from this list. For example, all of the subdirectories of WebSvr contain documentation and the administration programs for Personal Web Server, and removing them will make it impossible to administer your server.

Alias

Directory aliases change the appearance of your file structure in the eyes of remote users. All of the directories listed above are aliased by default. Table C-1 shows the effect of aliasing these directories and a few others, for example. The aliases shown below are arbitrary; you can assign any alias you like to any directory you choose.

Directory	Alias	URL Appears to Browsers As:
C:\WebShare\wwwroot	<Home>	http://www.megacorp.com/
C:\WebShare\wwwroot\images	/Images	http://www.megacorp.com/Images/
C:\temp	/Temp	http://www.megacorp.com/Temp/

Table C-1: Aliased directories.

FYI: HTML Is Case Insensitive

HTML, like DOS (and Windows), is case insensitive; that is, you can use either upper-case or lowercase letters in your configuration or URLs and it will still work.

Error

This region will show a descriptive error message if something unexpected happens; for example, if you set up an alias and later delete the aliased directory, you will see an error message (Error! Directory not found.) here.

Action

Clicking on Delete will remove the appropriate directory from your site after the OK button is pressed. The Edit and Add functions are similar in that they both bring up a directory selection page similar to the Windows Explorer; the Edit function enters the existing information in the directory selection page, while the Add functions begins with a blank page.

FYI: Edit/Add Options

For all directories, you have several options available to you on the Edit/Add configuration pages (not shown here). You can specify any directory to be the root of your Personal Web Server site, permit external users to read files and/or execute programs in the specified directory, and specify the name remote users will use to reference each directory.

Enable Default Document/Default Document/Directory Browsing Allowed

The behavior of the Personal Web Server when a user types in your site's URL without specifying a specific page to view (e.g., "http://megacorp.com/") depends on the values of these fields as follows in Table C-2:

Enable Default Document	Default Document	Directory Browsing Allowed	Behavior
✔	Default.htm	✔	Users not specifying a particular page will see "Default.htm"; users specifying a valid subdirectory will see a file listing of that subdirectory.
✔	<blank>	✔	Users not specifying a particular page will see "Default.htm"; users specifying a valid subdirectory will see a file listing of that subdirectory.
<blank>	<anything>	✔	Users not specifying a particular page will see a directory of the root; users specifying a valid subdirectory will see a file listing of that subdirectory.
✔	<blank>	<blank>	Users not specifying a particular page will see "Default.htm"; users specifying a valid subdirectory will see an error message.
<blank>	<blank>	<blank>	Users not specifying a particular page will see an error message.

Table C-2: Effects of document options.

Logging Tab

Personal Web Server can keep reasonably extensive statistics of who connects to your site and which pages they access, as well as track server errors and warning messages, if any. You set options for logging using the Logging tab shown in Figure C-4.

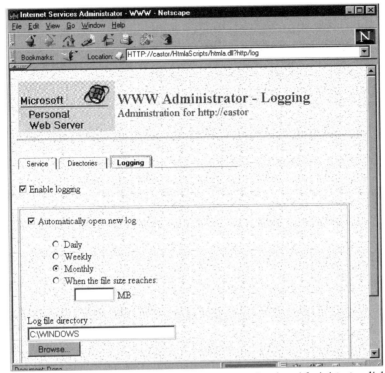

Figure C-4: The Logging tab of the WWW Internet Services Administrator dialog.

FYI: Converting Log Information to Graphics

You can easily convert your log file to statistics and graphs for display on a Web page with the help of shareware utilities like 3Dstats and AccessWatch, available at http://www.yahoo.com/Computers_and_Internet/Software/Internet/World_Wide_Web/Servers/Log_Analysis_Tools/. These utilities scan your log file(s) for events you specify, and they extract information into spreadsheet or graph form for more convenient use.

Enable Logging (Default: On)

Checking this box enables the server to log events. Clearing the check box will stop logging, but will not delete any existing log files.

Automatically Open New Log (Default: Monthly)

When a log file spans a certain number of days or reaches a certain size, the server will start a new log in the specified directory. Options for when to start a new log are:

- Daily
- Weekly
- Monthly
- When the File Size Reaches ___ MB

Log File Directory (Default: C:\Windows)

The directory in which log files are saved. Click on the Browse button to bring up a file selection dialog or type in a new directory name if desired. The log file (Figure C-5), by default, is saved in C:\Windows and is called InetServer_Event.log.

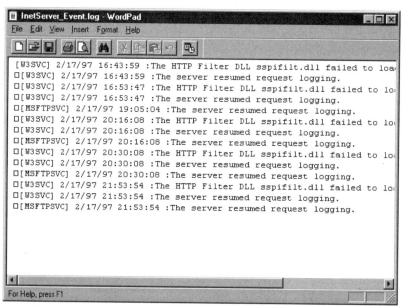

Figure C-5: A sample Personal Web Server WWW log file.

CAUTION

You can't change the default name of the log files.

To view your log files in your Web browser for remote monitoring, move them to a directory accessible to external users, as specified in the Directories dialog in Personal Web Server WWW Administrator.

For FTP

You might wish to make your Web server accessible to external users for the uploading and downloading of files. This kind of file transfer is a service typically provided by companies to allow external browsers to retrieve press releases, software, and other files; it might also be used to provide a place for clients to upload log files or descriptions of problems.

While there are a lot of configurable settings for this service, it is not difficult to set up and maintain, and its potential uses are many.

CAUTION

Permitting anonymous remote users to directly access files on your computer carries with it some degree of risk. If, by accident or design, someone places confidential information in the downloadable directory, that information becomes available to the entire Internet. There are programs (called robots) that routinely scour the Internet for files that seem to contain information that their operator (a person) considers interesting, like passwords and proprietary data.

While there is little likelihood of an external browser getting outside of your FTP directory, and no security holes of this type have been reported with this software, there are no guarantees that such an action is impossible. If you make anonymous FTP available, be aware of the potential risks, and take steps to prevent the unintended disclosure of sensitive data.

The FTP Server provides four screens for configuration: Service, Messages, Directories, and Logging. Since the Logging screen is essentially the same as the Logging screen in the WWW Administrator screen, detailed above, it won't be covered here.

Service Tab

The settings here (Figure C-6) are the same as for the Services tab in WWW Administrator (above), with the following exceptions.

Allow Anonymous Connections (Default: On)

Permits external users to connect to your server without having an account on your server or necessarily specifying their identity. By convention, users log in using the username "guest" or "anonymous" and entering their e-mail address as their password. If they do, the password used appears in your log file (if any).

Allow Only Anonymous Connections (Default: Off)

Refuses connections from any users other than *anonymous* or *guest*. Since users with valid usernames and passwords may be able to access directories outside of the FTP directories you've set up, this has the effect of limiting all users to the FTP directories you've designated.

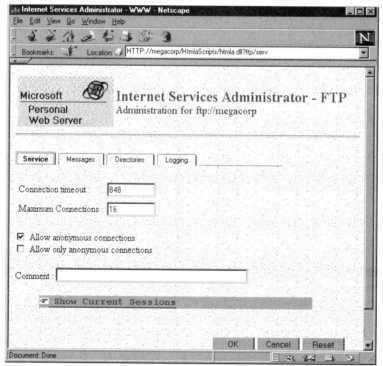

Figure C-6: The Service tab of the FTP Internet Services Administrator dialog.

Show Current Sessions

Clicking on this button brings up a screen (Figure C-7) that allows you to monitor the current status of your FTP server, including the names of people logged in. From this screen, you have three additional options:

- **Disconnect** If anybody is currently logged in to your FTP server, clicking on this button next to their name will disconnect them, terminating any file transfers they have in progress.

- **Disconnect All** Clicking here will disconnect all connected users, terminating any file transfers they have in progress.

- **Close** Clicking here will close this screen and return to the previous screen without affecting the status of any connected users.

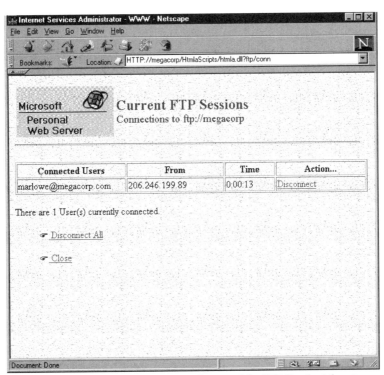

Figure C-7: The Show Current Sessions button of the FTP Service tab.

FYI: Checking Your Current IP Address

If you're using a PPP connection and want to know your current IP (Internet Protocol) address, you can log into your FTP server anonymously. The current IP address of your machine will appear as the From location of the one connected user—you. Remember that your IP address will probably be different every time you connect to your ISP.

Messages Tab

Users logging into your FTP server will see one of two messages initially and one more when they terminate the connection. All can be modified in the Messages tab, Figure C-8.

Welcome Message (Default: "Windows 95 FTP Service.")

This message appears in the remote user's FTP client when they successfully connect to your site. You may wish to enter the name of your site, an informational message, or contact information here.

Exit Message (Default: "Bye.")

This message appears when a visitor logs off your system by issuing the Quit command in their FTP client.

Maximum Connections Message (Default: "The connection limit for this server has been reached. No more connections can be accepted at this time.")

This message appears when the maximum number of users, set in the Service tab (detailed above), is connected to your FTP server.

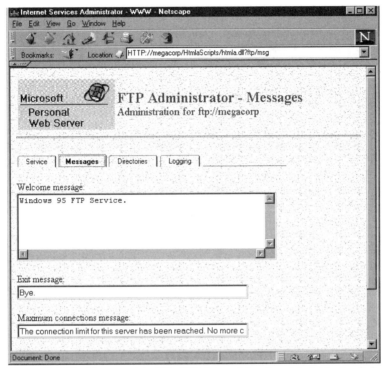

Figure C-8: The Messages tab of the FTP Internet Services Administrator dialog.

Directories Tab

The options for this tab (Figure C-9) are the same as in the Directories tab for WWW Administrator, described above, with the following exception.

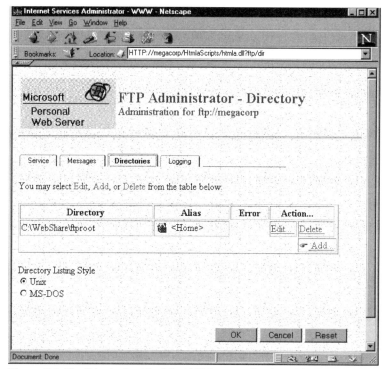

Figure C-9: The Directories tab of the FTP Internet Services Administrator dialog.

Directory Style: Unix/MS-DOS (Default: Unix)

This setting determines the way the directory tree of your FTP site will be presented to external users. Both are displayed below (Figures C-10 and C-11); the functionality is the same regardless of which style you select. You can see the difference most clearly in the file permissions, in the leftmost column in the UNIX file listing. (The FTP client shown below is Windows 95 FTP, c:\windows\ftp.exe.)

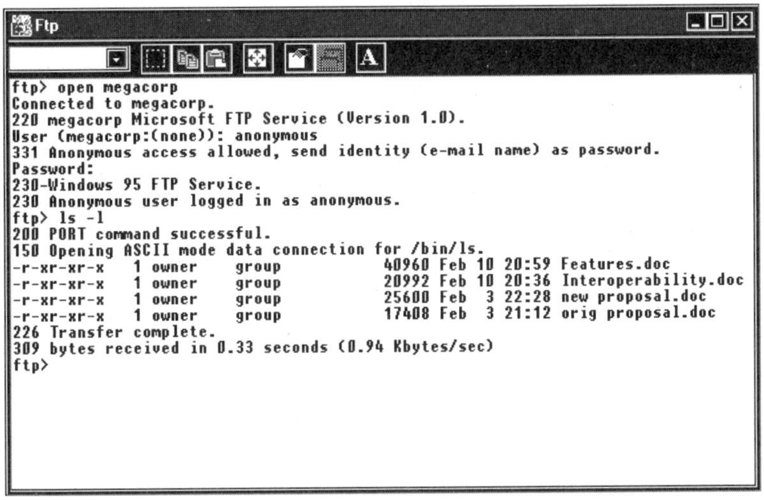

```
Ftp                                                                   _ □ ×
  ▼  ▦ ▣ ▣  ▣ ▣ ▤  A
ftp> open megacorp
Connected to megacorp.
220 megacorp Microsoft FTP Service (Version 1.0).
User (megacorp:(none)): anonymous
331 Anonymous access allowed, send identity (e-mail name) as password.
Password:
230-Windows 95 FTP Service.
230 Anonymous user logged in as anonymous.
ftp> ls -l
200 PORT command successful.
150 Opening ASCII mode data connection for /bin/ls.
-r-xr-xr-x   1 owner     group            40960 Feb 10 20:59 Features.doc
-r-xr-xr-x   1 owner     group            20992 Feb 10 20:36 Interoperability.doc
-r-xr-xr-x   1 owner     group            25600 Feb  3 22:28 new proposal.doc
-r-xr-xr-x   1 owner     group            17408 Feb  3 21:12 orig proposal.doc
226 Transfer complete.
309 bytes received in 0.33 seconds (0.94 Kbytes/sec)
ftp>
```

Figure C-10: FTP Directory, UNIX style.

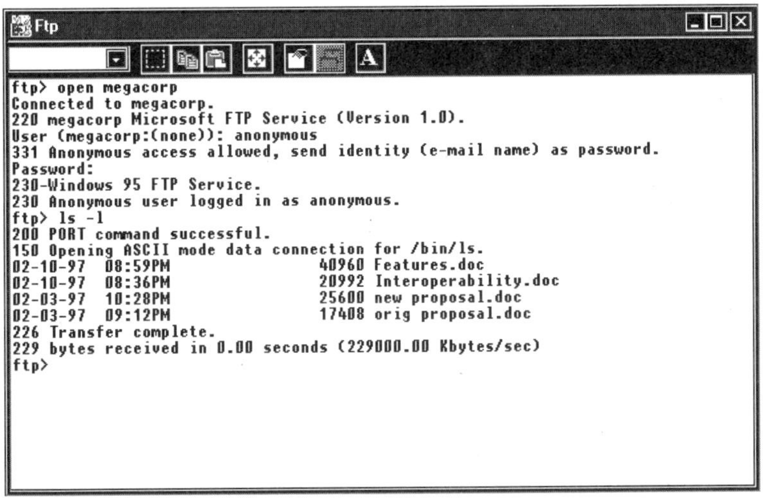

```
Ftp                                                                   _ □ ×
  ▼  ▦ ▣ ▣  ▣ ▣ ▤  A
ftp> open megacorp
Connected to megacorp.
220 megacorp Microsoft FTP Service (Version 1.0).
User (megacorp:(none)): anonymous
331 Anonymous access allowed, send identity (e-mail name) as password.
Password:
230-Windows 95 FTP Service.
230 Anonymous user logged in as anonymous.
ftp> ls -l
200 PORT command successful.
150 Opening ASCII mode data connection for /bin/ls.
02-10-97  08:59PM                40960 Features.doc
02-10-97  08:36PM                20992 Interoperability.doc
02-03-97  10:28PM                25600 new proposal.doc
02-03-97  09:12PM                17408 orig proposal.doc
226 Transfer complete.
229 bytes received in 0.00 seconds (229000.00 Kbytes/sec)
ftp>
```

Figure C-11: FTP Directory, MS-DOS style.

For Local Files

If you don't want to allow the entire world to access some (or all) of the files on your Web site, you can limit access to certain files or folders and to certain people or groups. Remote users attempting to access the protected areas of your site will be asked to enter a username and password, which you will have previously entered into your Personal Web Server, for validation.

FYI: Passwords

Users must have passwords. Personal Web Server does not accept blank passwords if you set up Local User Administrator.

You cannot use Local User Administration if you have already set up user-level access controls on your server PC. To determine whether user-level access has been enabled, do the following:

1. Click on Start | Settings | Control Panel.
2. Double-click on Network.
3. Select the Access Control tab.
4. If User-level access control is enabled, you won't be able to directly control user access to your Web pages. Instead, access will be controlled by the maintainer of the access list on the PC named in the blank at the bottom of the dialog box. If no name is listed in the Obtain List Of Users And Groups From blank, you can probably change your security to Share-level access, which is the installation default. You can then use Local User Administrator in the Web server, and also control access to specific resources on your PC (printers, files, folders, and so on) directly.

Local User Administrator provides four screens for configuration: Users, Groups, and User/Group. The Users and Groups screens are very similar.

Users & Groups Tabs

Both the Users and Groups screens (Figure C-12) contain a scrolling list of the users (or groups, as appropriate) for whom security has been activated.

Figure C-12: The Users tab of the Local User Administrator dialog.

Both screens also provide three buttons at the bottom:

- Properties
- New User (or Group)
- Remove

To add a new user to the list, select New User, and you'll see the dialog in Figure C-13.

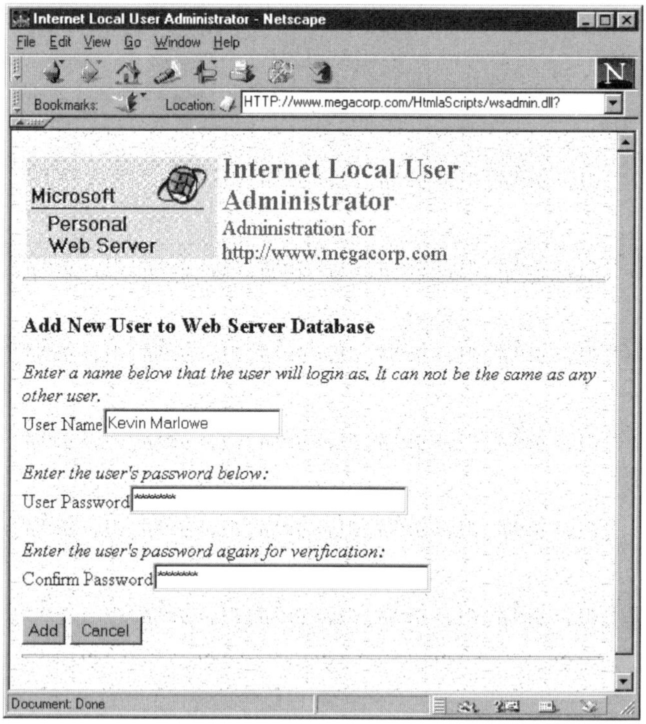

Figure C-13: The Add User dialog.

Enter the user's name (or group name) in the appropriate blank and enter the same password in both password blanks. After you click on Add, you will be returned to the Local User Administrator screen. If you enter one of the passwords incorrectly, you will be given an opportunity to correct it.

In the Groups screen, you can only enter the name of the group for which you wish to install security.

Selecting a username in the scrolling list and the Properties button brings up a configuration screen that permits changing the user's password and changing the groups the user belongs to, if any.

Clicking the Properties button in the Groups screen gives a list of users that belong to that group.

Clicking on the name of a User or Group in the appropriate screen and then selecting Remove removes the user's or group's security record.

User/Group Tab

Selecting this tab causes the following screen (Figure C-14) to be displayed.

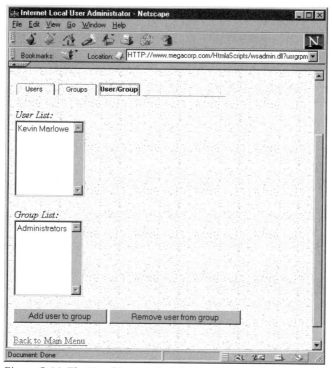

Figure C-14: The User/Group tab of the Local User Administrator dialog.

A list of users and groups is displayed, as well as buttons to add or remove users from the selected group as appropriate.

Folder-Level Security

Rather than configure security for folders or files through the Personal Web Server, you should use the Sharing mechanism in My Computer (Figure C-15). To limit access to a particular folder, first display it in the tree window in My Computer and right-click on the name of the folder (or file) you want to restrict. Select the Sharing menu item.

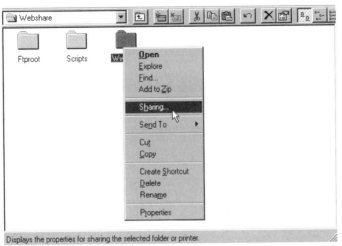

Figure C-15: The Sharing Properties window of the Personal Web Server.

Next, select the Share As radio button and click on the Web Sharing push button at the bottom of the dialog box (Figure C-16).

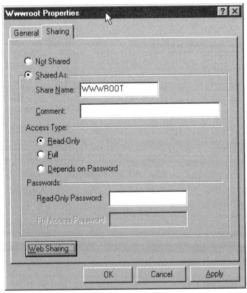

Figure C-16: The Sharing tab of the Properties dialog .

The Web Sharing Folder (or File) Properties dialog appears (Figure C-17).

Figure C-17: The Web Sharing Folder Properties check boxes.

The options are:

- **Share Folder for HTTP: Read Only (Default: On)**   Checking this box does not permit remote users to write to this directory. This is appropriate for most folders that do not contain programs, log files, counters, or other things that change content during a remote session.

- **Share Folder for HTTP: Execute Scripts (Default: Off)**   If this box is checked, remote users will be able to run any executable program in this folder.

CAUTION

This is a potentially enormous security hole. Do not enable this option unless you are aware of exactly what files are in the folder and can ensure that dangerous executable files are not placed there by others on your local network.

- **Share Folder for FTP: Read (Default: Off), Write (Default: Off)**   The Personal Web Server FTP Server does not permit restricting access to certain files or folders. You can do that here, by choosing whether FTP should be allowed at all to this folder and then choosing whether remote users can read from it, write to it, or both.

CAUTION

Another huge security hole: don't allow remote users to write to the directory and execute scripts. You have no control over the content of the scripts they might upload and execute.

Peer Web Services Detailed Configuration Reference

In Chapter 4, instructions are provided to step you through the setup of Peer Web Services on Windows NT Workstation. Having selected Windows NT Workstation as your Web server is an interesting choice politically, since you're legally (but not technically) limited to 10 concurrent users on your system. The configuration options we'll discuss here hold for Internet Information Server as well.

You'll never need to go through all of these options step by step. You're much more likely to need to fix a particular setting and just go straight to it (assuming that you know where it is). In this Appendix, we've described all of the options as if you were indeed reading through the options dialogs, left to right, top to bottom, to make them easier to find.

The Internet Service Manager provides a central control point for all detailed configuration of all of the Peer Web Services. From this point, you can configure, start, and stop all FTP, WWW, and Gopher services on all of the machines on your local network. With a glance, you can evaluate the state of your network's remote services and see problems immediately. To start the Internet Service Manager, select the Start | Programs | Peer Web Services | Internet Service Manager.

The meat of the application lies in the property settings for the FTP and WWW services. Since Gopher is so rarely used these days, we'll not discuss its configuration here. The included online documentation is excellent; see Chapter 9, "Using the FTP & Gopher Services."

For the Web

There are three dialogs available for configuring the WWW service in Internet Service Manager: Service, Directories, and Logging. After selecting a computer that is running the WWW service and clicking on the Properties button, the WWW Service Properties dialog will appear (Figure D-1).

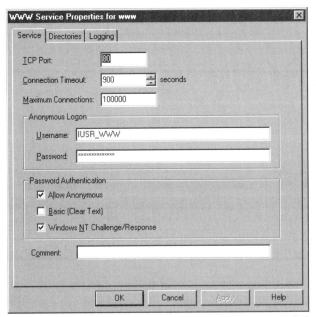

Figure D-1: The Service tab of the WWW Service Properties dialog.

Service Tab

The options here are the same as in the Personal Web Server with one addition: the TCP Port. The standard TCP port to HTTP is 80; if you change this, you will prevent remote users from seeing your Web pages unless you tell them (or they discover) the port number you choose.

FYI: Changing Port Number

Setting this port number to a number other than 80 is a great way to set up a site for development without making it readily available to the whole world. Automatic Web indexing robots will not find it, and users will probably not stumble upon it, since there are several thousand possible ports you can choose. For example, if your server is http:/ /www.megacorp.com and you configure your server to use port 1997, remote users would connect to it with the URL http://www.megacorp.com:1997.

After your site is well-tested and ready, you can just change the port to 80 and it will suddenly be available to users at the URL http:// <machine>.<company>.com.

Directories Tab

Selecting the Directories tab will display the Directories Properties for the WWW Server (Figure D-2).

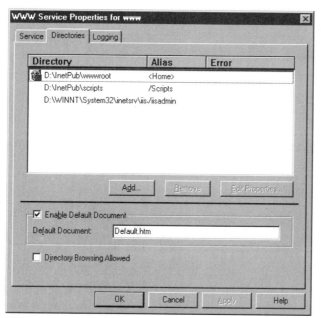

Figure D-2: The Directories tab of the WWW Service properties.

These options are the same as in Personal Web Server, discussed in the Windows 95 section.

Logging Tab

Finally, the Logging tab displays the WWW Logging Properties screen, which looks the same and has the same options as the FTP Logging Properties screen in Figure 4-35.

FYI: Different Log Filenames

Selecting different log filenames for your FTP and WWW services will reduce clutter and make searching the logs easier, should a problem arise.

For FTP

To begin configuring the FTP service, click once on the name of the computer you wish to configure on the line displaying the FTP service. Then select the Properties button on the toolbar. The dialog box for the FTP Service Properties will appear, as shown in Figure D-3, offering four tabs: Service, Messages, Directories, and Logging.

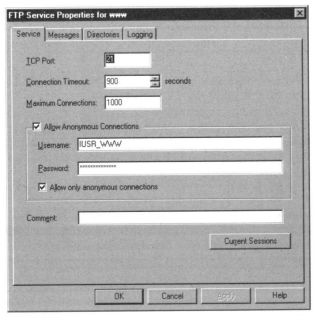

Figure D-3: The Service tab of the FTP Service Properties for the WWW dialog.

Service Tab

The options here are largely the same as for the FTP service in Personal Web Server (see Appendix C). There are a few additional options:

- **TCP Port:** the network port to which clients wishing to transfer files should attach. The standard port is 21; you can use a different port if you desire, but remote users will need to know the number of that port in order to connect.

- **Anonymous Username and Password (checkbox):** Windows NT stores different user configurations for each user of the system. By default, the installation of Peer Web Services creates a user called IUSR_<machinename> on your NT system with Guest privileges. When users connect anonymously to your server, the permissions of IUSR_<machinename> are assigned to them.

  The password is ignored for anonymous connections, but is used to log into the NT system as IUSR_<machinename>. When you install the Web server, a user ID is created on your machine with this name, and this user has only read privileges. There's no reason to change these. If you enter a different username and/or password on this screen, make sure you create a new user ID with the username and password you entered, or remote users will not be able to log in.

Messages Tab

Selecting the Messages tab starts the Messages dialog, as seen in Figure D-4.

You can use this dialog to specify friendly (or not-so-friendly) messages for remote users to see when they connect to your FTP server, when they log off, and if they connect but the maximum connections limit has been reached.

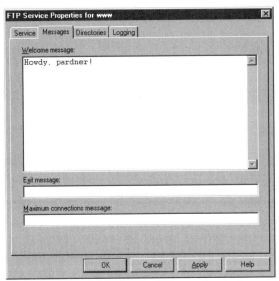

Figure D-4: The Messages tab of the FTP Service Properties for WWW dialog.

Directories Tab

The Directories tab, as in Figure D-5, allows the creation and maintenance of aliases for directories on your local system for the convenience of your remote users. Typical entries here might include aliases for the "home" directory, where remote users first log into your system; for a "pub" directory, where public files are stored; and for an "upload" directory, where you can give remote users write permissions and thus limit the locations of files they place on your system.

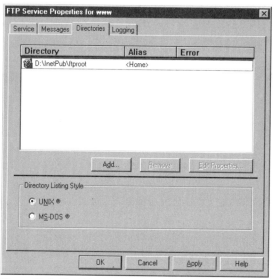

Figure D-5: The Directories tab of the Service Properties for WWW dialog.

Logging Tab

The last service to configure for FTP access controls the system logs, as in Figure D-6. As in the Personal Web Server configuration, you can disable logging, name a file to log to, and specify when new log files should be started.

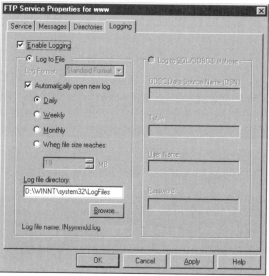

Figure D-6: The Logging Tab of the Service Properties for WWW Dialog.

Glossary

.gif   The file extension for images stored in the Graphics Interchange Format.

.gz: The file extension used for files compressed with the gzip program. Some other file extensions for other types of compression are .zip,.arj, and .lzh. The file extension identifies the type of compression used.

.html   The file extension used for HyperText Markup Language documents. Some machines use .htm instead because they can't handle more than three letters in a file extension.

.jpeg   Images stored in the Joint Photographic Experts Group format.

Active Server Pages   Microsoft's technology for making its Web server (IIS) talk to ODBC data sources (like databases). The term is also used to refer to the actual Web pages that using this technology creates. These pages can only be viewed with a Microsoft Web browser.

ActiveX   A renamed version of OLE tailored to the Web and the new version of Office.

Apache Web Server   A free Web server produced by the Apache group, hard-working, dedicated guys who want users to have a free, high-quality Web server. I get all misty eyed just thinking about it.

Applet   In the context here, an applet is a program that makes up part of the Windows Control Panel. It's also often used to refer to a certain type of program written in the Java programming language, but that's not discussed here.

Applications   Computer programs.

Architecture   The physical construction of the guts inside your computer.

Attributes   (1) Characteristics of individual letters (font, bold, italic) as opposed to the shape of blocks of text (paragraph formatting). (2) Characteristics of files (read-only, archived, and so on).

Backbone   A major piece of the Internet designed to carry enormous amounts of network traffic.

Baud rate   This is a measure of the rate at which bits flow across a communication line.

Binary Files   Binary files are used to store anything other than ordinary text that runs on your computer, such as program code or numerical information, as in computer image files.

Bit   The smallest piece of information used by a digital computer. Bits can have two values: on or off (or true or false, or 1 or 0, etc.). One bit doesn't generally tell you a whole lot.

Bitmap   A graphic image that is saved as individual points of color and brightness (pixels). Bitmaps tend to take up a lot of disk space and don't scale very well. Photographs are examples of bitmaps. Web browsers typically only read bitmapped graphic files.

Bridges   A bridge is a simplified type of router. It acts as a bridge between two networks by passing all traffic through without inspecting it for its final destination. Bridges are often used to strengthen signals over long distances.

Browser   A software program that lets you interact with the features of the Internet using a GUI.

Byte   Eight bits. A byte is typically (but not always, depending on the computer system) required to express one character.

Chat Room   One of the most useless, most maligned, and most popular features of the Internet. People who might not speak a word to anyone around them will log onto a chat room and use the computer keyboard to talk to anyone who will listen.

Child Process   A computer process spawned by another process in order to run a program while the original process accepts new requests for processing.

Client   A machine or software application that requests data or services from another (the "server").

Closed System   A system produced by one company that forces others to buy products from the company in order to use their system.

Code Page   Character set used on your Web page.

Cold Fusion   Yet another product that makes databases talk to Web servers. This one has no association with Microsoft at all.

Color Map   A list of colors contained in a computer image.

Command Line Prompt   The only way to interact with a computer before the graphical interface arrived.

Compiler   A programming language is a convenience for humans. Computers only understand 1s and 0s. Once a program is written in a programming language, it must be converted into machine language for the computer to execute. Not only that, but different types of machines require different machine languages. A compiler is a program that takes programs written by programmers and turns them into machine language. The machine language program, often called "executable code," is the version that is run by a computer.

Computer Platform   The combination of computer hardware and operating system.

Configuration   The set of options that make up the current state of a computer or piece of software.

Configure   Set the options of a piece of software to perform a specific set of tasks most efficiently.

Cookie Support   Some Web sites remember when you were there last and what you did when you came. They do this by placing an entry in a file on your local computer and checking to see if the entry is there the next time you come to their page. That entry is called a *cookie*, and checking the status of cookies requires server support.

Corel Draw   A vector-based graphics creation and manipulation program.

Corel Paint   Like Corel Draw, but specifically for working with bitmaps.

CP/M   An operating system that is the predecessor to DOS.

CPU   Central Processing Unit. The main chip in a computer.

CSU/DSU   A device that converts digital telephone signals to data computers can understand. Used in conjunction with high-speed communications lines, like T1s.

Data Compression   Converting a file into a different format so it takes up less disk space.

Database   An online collection of related data, organized for easy changes and additions. Microsoft Access is a program that creates and manages databases.

Datasheets   A tabular view of the data in the database, much like a spreadsheet.

DBI/DBD   A Perl programming interface for writing programs that communicate with a database.

DbWeb   Another Microsoft product to handle communication between databases and a Web server. This product was actually purchased by Microsoft from another company and is not database- or server-specific.

DDE (Dynamic Data Exchange)   Permits the operating system to manage data that is shared between two applications, like an Outlook address list that is used as the basis for mailing labels in a Word mail merge. When Word needs the data, it starts Outlook; Outlook provides the requested data and then dies.

Deallocate Memory   Give memory back to the operating system when a program is finished with it.

Denial of Service   If I send so many packets to your machine that other users can't get access to your system, I'm causing your computer to deny them service.

Distributed Software   Software that runs on more than one computer at a time.

DNS (Domain Name Server)   A computer program that accepts human-readable computer names and returns the computer-readable IP address. For example, a DNS server converts the computer name ftp.microsoft.com to 198.105.32.1, which uniquely identifies it.

Domain Name   A name that all of the computers in a given, arbitrary group answer to. Like surnames among humans, domain names are augmented with other names that identify specific machines. For example, "megacorp.com" is a domain name that probably doesn't belong to any one machine; "batman.megacorp.com" is probably one machine somewhere in Megacorp's network.

DR DOS   Digital Research's version of the PC operating system.

DSN (Data Source Name)   The name of a table or procedure that retrieves data from a database of any type. ODBC makes referencing data sources on a given system easier by giving each data source a unique name, or DSN.

Dynamic Link Library (DLL)   If a program needs a function that is present somewhere on a computer, there are two ways the function can be made available to the program. One is the compiler locates all necessary functions and puts them into the executable code when the program is compiled. The other way is the compiler locates the functions, but only puts the location into the compiled program, and the program only loads the functions it needs. Functions that are loaded on demand, or dynamically, are contained in computer code libraries. If a library is intended to be loaded dynamically, it is a dynamic link library (DLL).

Dynamic Pages   Web pages containing collections of data retrieved from a database in response to a specific, spontaneous request from a user.

Dynamic Routing   If a piece of the Internet goes down, computers send information via another route so packets can still get where they're going. If the broken piece comes back up, they can go back to using it. This is called dynamic routing.

Effective Throughput   No matter what the advertised transmission rate of a communications line or piece of equipment might be, that is only under ideal conditions. When you subtract the degradation of line noise from the maximum possible line quality, what is left is the *real* transmission rate, which is called the "effective throughput."

FAQ (Frequently Asked Questions) Many newsgroups see the same questions asked over and over again, so some kind soul will collect them and put them in an easily reachable spot in the hopes that dumbos will read the FAQ instead of asking the same dumb question Joe Blow asked yesterday. Sometimes it works and sometimes it doesn't.

File DSN A DSN that is available to all users on the local network who have an appropriate driver for that data source installed locally. Rarely used.

File Extension The part of a filename that comes after the ".". The extension often identifies the type of file format used to store information within the file. By identifying the extension, you know how to process the file.

Firewall This is usually a computer running special software that an external network is connected to. The firewall acts as a security guard for your network, making sure unauthorized network packets do not get access to your network.

Flame War Ouch, that hurt! If you say something dumb in a newsgroup, millions of people will read it and some of the less socially acceptable will flame you with posts that melt your eyeballs. If you respond in kind, hundreds of strangers will happily join in by posting their own flames. Pretty soon the newsgroup will melt into slag and warriors will gather in barrooms around the world to toast their cleverness.

Forms Online screens designed to facilitate the entry of data into a database.

FrontPage Microsoft's Web site creation and management software.

FTP (File Transfer Protocol) The most common language Internet-connected computers use to transfer data files (blocks of data destined for storage on a disk, not for immediate viewing). FTP, like HTTP, requires TCP/IP to work.

GIF (Graphics Interchange Format) A popular image format.

Graphical Interface Often called a GUI, which is pronounced "gooey" and stands for Graphical User Interface, a GUI is just a way of using graphics to make a computer easier to use. If you use Microsoft Windows, you use a GUI. The combination of a mouse used with windows and icons to select commands and activate programs gives the user a computer interface that doesn't require them to know much about the underlying operating system, unless they want to.

Graphical User Interface (GUI) See Graphical Interface.

Hacker The term "hacker" used to be a term of honor, used to designate a computer person who showed exceptional ability. Thanks to the media's misunderstanding the term (and much of everything else they report on), it has acquired a negative connotation.

Helper Application When a Web browser can't process a file type itself, if a helper application is defined for a particular file extension, the browser can start up the helper application and it can process the file.

High-Level Programming Language   Some languages require the programmer to do more than others. A high-level language tries to make things easier for the programmer by making the commands easier to understand and use. They don't work very well yet.

Home Page   A person or organization's main Web page.

Hop   A hop is the transmission of a packet from one machine to the next. Data moves in a series of hops until it arrives at its target machine.

HTML code   The language of the Web. HTML is not a programming language because you can't write programs in it, but it's a markup language that is intended to format text for viewing with a browser.

HTML Editor   Some kind of authoring environment for Web pages, like Microsoft Word.

HTTP   HyperText Transfer Protocol—the primary language used by computers, in conjunction with TCP/IP, to communicate on the World Wide Web.

Hub   A hub distributes network traffic from one source to several destinations. The destinations can be individual machines or entire networks. Hubs often include the ability to act as routers.

Hyperlinks   Text or an image that lets you click on it and go to another Web page.

IBM DOS   IBM's own version of a PC operating system.

ID   Each process running on a computer must be uniquely identified so the operating system can allocate resources and keep track of what a process is allowed and not allowed to do. Each process is given a number, or ID, that identifies it to the operating system.

IIS (Internet Information Server)   The Web server that is bundled with Windows NT Server.

Image Map   An image with pieces mapped to different URLs. When a user clicks on a part of the image, the image acts like a hyperlink and takes the user to another Web page.

ImageMap Support   A capability of a Web server to interpret the location of the cursor within an image on a page and return the coordinates to a program. The program then passes the location of another page to the browser. This has the effect of allowing a user to click in an image and being transported to a different URL depending on where they clicked.

Internet Assistant   Microsoft's add-on to an application that makes the application Internet-enabled.

Internet Hooks   Functionality added to Microsoft Exchange so Exchange can use the Internet and, therefore, so can its users.

Internet-Enabled   Software that can use the Internet to do things, like send and receive mail and share data.

InterNIC   The organization that maintains the master registry of domain names.

Intranet   A computer network usually used within a company. An intranet works in exactly the same way as the full-fledged Internet, but it's safer because it has no connection to the outside world. If your network is isolated from the Internet, no outside force (such as a hacker) can get to the computers on your network by using the Internet.

IP Address   The unique number that identifies a specific computer on the Internet.

IP   Stands for Internet Protocol, and defines the common language that Internet computers use to talk to one another.

ISDN (Integrated Services Digital Network)   The cheapest digital phone line you can buy. Data transfer rates over ISDN range from 64 kbps to 512 kbps (depending on configuration), as compared to today's typical modems at around 30 kbps. ISDN service requires some specialized equipment up front, and you pay by the second rather than paying a flat rate.

ISP (Internet Service Provider)   A company that provides connectivity services for individuals or other companies wishing to attach computers to the Internet.

Java   Java is a new programming language invented to run TV cable boxes. Someone decided it would be neat to use on the Web, and some of the greatest hype in history was born.

JavaScript   A programming language invented by Netscape for use in their Web browsers.

JDBC (Java Database Connector)   A standardized method of communicating with a database using the Java programming language.

JPG   A graphics file format, like BMP, GIF, and TIF. All of these are just abbreviations for the name of the method that's used to store the image on the disk. Some make smaller files, some make more accurate reproductions. Web browsers generally recognize images of formats GIF and JPG. JPGs are often smaller (and they transmit faster by extension), but they might lose resolution depending on how they were saved.

Kbps   Thousands (K) of bits per second (bps). Usually refers to the speed at which data is sent over a wire.

Key Manager   A utility to control the encryption options for your server.

LAN (Local Area Network)   A computer network that is (usually) comprised of machines located in close physical proximity.

LiveWire Pro   Netscape's product for writing Web applications that communicate with a database.

Log Files   As a program runs, it can generate a report of what it is doing. Errors are reported, program requests by users are reported, and so on, and all of these reports must go somewhere. A Web server writes all reports to a set of files, which make up a fairly complete log of what the server is doing.

Loop   When an animation plays through to the end, then starts over and plays again.

Lotus 1-2-3   VisiCalc's successor.

Macros and Modules   Programs written in Office for use only on the local network. These aren't of any use in Web-enabled applications.

Mapped Network Drive   A folder on a remote computer, connected to via a local area network in such a way that the remote folder appears to be local. For example, if a directory on computer B is called Public and the permissions are set appropriately, it can be mapped to appear as a drive (say, the Q: drive) on computer A on the same network.

MB   Millions (M) of bytes (B), pronounced as "megabyte." Typically used to express amounts of data, usually for files or disks.

Memory Leak   When a program runs, it uses computer memory. The program asks the operating system for a piece of memory, and the operating system finds an unused portion and reserves it for the program. If the program keeps asking for memory without reusing what it already had or giving it back to the operating system, these memory leaks can cause a badly behaved program to use up all computer memory and crash the system.

Microsoft Exchange Server   A central computer that controls the passing of Microsoft Exchange data around a local area network. The term sometimes refers to the software program that runs on a computer to permit it to perform this task.

Microsoft Exchange   The protocol used by Microsoft programs to communicate for the purposes of sending mail and faxes.

Microsoft Office   Microsoft's suite of programs, including a word processor, a spreadsheet, presentation software, a database (in the professional version), and whatever other application they choose for the current version of Office. In three versions of Office, the fifth application has changed three times. In Office 97, it's Outlook.

MiniSQL   A shareware database server.

Moderated   A human being reads each posting to a single moderated newsgroup before it is posted to determine its acceptability.

MS Word   Microsoft's word processing software.

MS-DOS   The most common PC operating system.

MUD (Multi-User Dungeon)   The real reason the Internet exists, MUDs are much more fun than chat rooms and give you rewards for killing things. It doesn't get any better than this.

Multihoming   The ability of the Web server to answer to more than one name, say, www.megagcorp.com and ftp.megacorp.com.

NetBEUI   Microsoft's networking protocol for sharing Windows computer resources.

Netscape Communicator   Netscape's Web browser.

Network Messaging Protocol   A language computers on a local area network use to handle e-mail and faxes.

Network   A collection of computers connected together so they can communicate.

NFS (Network File System)   A method used by UNIX computers to share file systems across a network. This is not sharing files, mind you, but actually sharing the hard drives themselves.

Noise   Communications lines carry signals. If something interferes with those signal, it introduces errors and the signals must be retransmitted until they are received correctly. The errors in a communication line are collectively called "line noise."

Notes (Lotus Notes)   A popular computer program for sharing information among a group of people.

Object-Oriented (OO) Language   This one is tough to describe to non-programmers and to some programmers. Basically, an OO language lets (forces?) you write programs as if they were a cabinet. If you want users to reach into the cabinet and pull something out or move it around, you must program a cabinet door in just the right place. This keeps users from pulling the wrong thing out of your cabinet.

ODBC (Open Database Connectivity)   Permits the operating system to manage data created in applications. Any application that can create tabular data can be an ODBC data source, given the appropriate drivers. When the data is needed, the operating system retrieves it without opening the application that created the data.

ODBC driver   A piece of software that tells Windows's ODBC system how to read and write data to a specific application. For example, the Access ODBC driver is typically installed when Access is installed. Most applications that can take advantage of ODBC install their own drivers when they are installed.

OLE (Object Linking & Embedding)   Manages parts of documents ("objects") that are cut-and-pasted from one application to another. An Excel spreadsheet embedded in a Word document is using OLE. A small, limited version of Excel is actually running whenever you edit that embedded spreadsheet.

One-step publishing   A more-or-less automated way of sending pages you've authored to the server, like Microsoft's Publish to the Web Wizard.

Open System   A system produced by one company that allows others to write their own programs to interact with the system.

Operating System   Software that runs on a computer and translates commands entered by the user into instructions a computer can understand. Linux, Solaris, MS-DOS, and OS/2 are operating systems.

OS/2   An advanced operating system produced by IBM (with some help by Microsoft, long ago) that has rabid fans but doesn't get the publicity that Windows does.

Packet   A standardized piece of information that travels over a network. Any machine receiving a packet can read the information to make sure the packet gets to its destination.

Packet Storm   If too many packets are being sent across a network due to network errors or users generating too much network traffic, this can result in a large amount of data flooding a network at one time, possibly overwhelming the network. The network will certainly slow down for a time as it tries to handle the load.

Paint Shop Pro   A shareware graphics program.

Parameter   A value given to a program to tell it what to do. Based on the value of the parameter, the program can do different things.

Path   Where to find a file on a computer's hard drive.

PC Clone   When IBM introduced the PC, other companies created their own copies of the PC, called "clones." Eventually the clones became more popular than IBM's version because they were cheaper.

PC (Personal Computer)   Popularized by IBM.

Peer   A member of the same group. In "Peer Web Services," Microsoft is implying that the NT Workstation version of their Web server is only robust enough to handle small numbers of clients.

Perl   A programming language that has its own religion.

Ping   A computer program used to see if another computer is alive and receiving packets.

POP (Point of Presence)   A major hub of one of the major telephone companies. A POP is usually placed where there is a large amount of network traffic, such as in a large city, so they can be assured of enough bandwidth to handle the load.

POP3   A protocol often used by mail servers to allow the remote reading and sending of mail.

Port   A computer uses a port to send and receive data. The more powerful the computer, the more ports it has available. Each port has a number so you can attach a program to a port, and outside computers can attach to just the right port and gain access to that program.

Post   Send a message to a newsgroup.

PostScript   A language for constructing documents that will be sent to a printer. The printer must understand PostScript for this to work.

PPP (Point-to-Point Protocol)　A common way to connect computers to the Internet using a modem and a standard phone line.

Primary Key　A field in a database table that is guaranteed to be unique. For example, lists of people often use Social Security Numbers or Employee IDs as primary keys, because no two people will have the same one.

Profile　A collection of settings that you wish to reuse.

Protocol　A standardized language computers use to communicate.

Queries　The means by which your Web server will retrieve or store data in your Access table(s).

Reports　Static, paper-destined representations of stored data.

Root Directory　A file system is constructed something like an upside-down tree, with the root being the topmost directory. By defining a root directory for your Web server, you prevent Web users from accessing anything outside of the specified directories.

Router　A device that receives streams of network traffic and segregates it so only data intended for machines attached to its other end passes through.

Routing Table　Just about every computer on the Internet has a database of computers and IP addresses. Computers consult this "routing table" so they know where to send packets.

Run Time　The moment at which a program is run, as opposed to ahead of time.

Sans-Serif　Literally, "without hat." Sans-serif typefaces include Arial and Helvetica.

Schedule+　The predecessor to Outlook.

Scripting Language　Scripting languages allow programs to be compiled "on the fly" instead of all at once. With a programming language such as C, you write the program and then compile it into an executable. If you need to make changes, you have to recompile the whole thing. This can be a time-consuming process. Scripted programs, such as Perl programs, can be easily changed because they are compiled each time they are run. Compiled programs are a bit faster because they are compiled once and can be run directly. Scripted programs are a bit slower because they must be compiled before they are run, but they are easier to modify quickly.

Secure Sockets Layer (SSL) Security　A generally accepted security standard for Web servers that makes the transfer of information between Web client and server somewhat more secure. It's typically used for financial transactions over the Web.

Serif　Literally, "hat." A serif typeface is one with horizontal lines at the top and bottom of most characters, like Times Roman or Courier.

Server　A computer that serves software to users or a software program that provides a service to users, such as a Web server or database server.

Sockets   A socket is basically another term for port.

Spam   Not only an unappetizing meat (by?)product, spam is also a name applied to unwanted junk postings or e-mail sent to large numbers of people, usually for the purpose of getting money.

Spreadsheet   A way of organizing information into columns and rows for easier analysis.

SQL (Structured Query Language)   A more-or-less standard language for making requests of databases.

SSL (Secure Sockets Layer)   The operating system support for encrypted communications between your Web server and clients.

Standard Operating System   A common operating system that doesn't change from computer to computer, even if the computers are manufactured by different companies.

Static Pages   Web pages containing collections of data retrieved from a database in response to a predefined request from a database programmer, triggered by a user.

Suite   Multiple applications packaged together and hyped as everything you ever needed.

System Data Source   A DSN that is available to certain users on certain machines in the local network. Typically, a system DSN is made available to all members of a user group or to all users of a given machine. Most data sources for use with third-party software, like Web servers, are configured as System DSNs.

T-1 line   A digital phone line, as opposed to the analog phone lines most of use in our homes. A digital T1 can generally carry up to 50 times the data a standard 28.8 kbps analog modem can pump out. Not many people need one of these.

T-3 line   A very large communications line that can transmit truly phenomenal amounts of information in an astonishingly tiny amount of time. Not many governments need one of these.

Tables   These basic descriptions of data are the linchpin of an Access database. All table information is available and accessible via the Web.

Tags   Tags are HTML identifiers that tell a Web browser how to display information.

TCP/IP (Transport Control Protocol/Internet Protocol)   The language used by computers to communicate on the Internet.

Telecommuting   One day I will sit at my computer at home and do my work on a machine many miles away, *and I will get paid for it*. This is telecommuting.

Telnet   A program that establishes a connection to another machine and lets you issue commands to execute programs on the remote machine.

Template   A file that acts as a basis for new Web pages, sometimes including graphics, backgrounds, and navigation links.

Text Files   Normal computer files you can read with any text editor, such as Word.

TIN (The Internet Newsreader)   One of a large number of useful, arcane programs used to read Usenet newsgroups.

Toolkit   A set of software tools that makes programming a computer easier.

Uniform Resource Locator (URL)   A magical incantation used in a Web browser to find a site on the Web. The URL tells the Web browser what machine to look for and what Web page to look for.

UNIX boxes   This is a term used by those who work closely with big computers that run the UNIX operating system. There are so many different types of UNIX computers that instead of trying to identify one, it's easier just to refer to one generically as a "UNIX box."

UNIX   A powerful, robust, unfriendly, hard-to-use operating system that's commonly used in high-end computing applications, especially in science and academia.

Unmoderated   Usenet newsgroups where no one reads posts before they are posted. Welcome to chaos.

URL (Uniform Resource Locator)   The unique address of a page of the World Wide Web.

Usenet   A collection of newsgroups that are published to computers all over the world. Readers can post new messages or respond to other messages. If you post something stupid, you better be wearing flame-proof underwear.

User DSN   A DSN that is only available to the user who configured it and only on the machine on which it was originally installed.

User Interface   A way to convert the requirements of a person using software to commands a computer can understand. The DOS command line is a user interface. The channel-changer on your TV is, too. See "Graphical Interface."

VBScript   A programming language invented by Microsoft for use in their Web browsers. Netscape had one, and Microsoft wasn't about to use it because that would have implied Microsoft thought Netscape had a good idea.

Vector Drawing Tool   A drawing program that works in lines and shapes (a la Picasso) rather than dots (a la Matisse).

Vector   The opposite of bitmapped is vector, where a picture is drawn using colors and lines. Vector graphic files tend to be smaller because only the endpoints of the lines need to be stored on disk. Theoretically, any image can be either a vector or a bitmap, but can you imagine a photograph stored as lines? Some applications, like most clip art, are better suited to vectors and are typically distributed that way.

Vi Editor   A common editor found on every UNIX computer.

VisiCalc   An old spreadsheet program.

Visual Basic   Microsoft's programming environment for their Basic programming language.

Visual J++   Microsoft's Java programming environment. Careful, there's proprietary code in that there Java.

WfW (Windows for Workgroups)   Windows 3.1, updated to version 3.11, and with networking features added. Windows 3.11 is not the same as Windows for Workgroups, which is sometimes erroneously called Windows 3.11.

Windows Explorer   The application you use to view the directory of folders and files on a disk.

Windows NT   Microsoft's workstation-class version of Windows, intended for use in business environments where the demands the user places on the operating system are more extensive than those imposed by a typical home user.

Windows   Microsoft's graphical interface to MS-DOS.

XView   A shareware graphics program for UNIX.

Index

http://www.vmedia.com

VENTANA

Net Security: Your Digital Doberman

$29.99, 312 pages, illustrated, part #: 1-56604-506-1

Doing business on the Internet can be safe . . . if you know the risks and take appropriate steps. This thorough overview helps you put a virtual Web watchdog on the job—to protect both your company and your customers from hackers, electronic shoplifters and disgruntled employees. Easy-to-follow explanations help you understand complex security technologies, with proven technologies for safe Net transactions. Tips, checklists and action plans cover digital dollars, pilfer-proof "storefronts," protecting privacy and handling breaches.

Intranet Firewalls

$34.99, 360 pages, illustrated, part #: 1-56604-506-1

Protect your network by controlling access—inside and outside your company—to proprietary files. This practical, hands-on guide takes you from intranet and firewall basics through creating and launching your firewall. Professional advice helps you assess your security needs and choose the best system for you. Includes tips for avoiding costly mistakes, firewall technologies, in-depth reviews and uses for popular firewall software, advanced theory of firewall design strategies and implementation, and more.

VENTANA

Java Programming for the Internet

$49.95, 816 pages, illustrated, part #: 1-56604-355-7

Master the programming language of choice for Internet applications. Expand the scope of your online development with this comprehensive, step-by-step guide to creating Java applets. The CD-ROM features Java Developers Kit, source code for all the applets, samples and programs from the book, and much more.

The Visual Basic Programmer's Guide to Java

$39.99, 450 pages, part #: 1-56604-527-4

At last—a Java book that speaks your language! Use your understanding of Visual Basic as a foundation for learning Java and object-oriented programming. This unique guide not only relates Java features to what you already know—it also highlights the areas in which Java excels over Visual Basic, to build an understanding of its appropriate use. The CD-ROM features comparative examples written in Java & Visual Basic, code for projects created in the book and more

VENTANA

Java 1.1 Programmer's Reference

Daniel I. Joshi, Pavel Vorobiev
$49.99, 1000 pages, illustrated, part #: 1-56604-687-4

The ultimate resource for Java professionals! And the perfect supplement to the JDK documentation. Whether you need a day-to-day reference for Java classes, an explanation of new APIs, a guide to common programming techniques, or all three, you've got it—all in an encyclopedic format that's convenient to refer to again and again. Covers new Java 1.1 features, including the AWT, JARs, Java Security API, the JDBC, JavaBeans, and more, with complete descriptions that include syntax, usage and code samples. **CD-ROM:** Complete, hyperlinked version of the book.

For all platforms • Intermediate to Advanced

Migrating From Java 1.0 to Java 1.1

Daniel I. Joshi, Pavel Vorobiev
$39.99, 600 pages, illustrated, part #: 1-56604-686-6

Your expertise with Java 1.0 provides the perfect springboard to rapid mastery of Java 1.1 and the new tools in the JDK 1.1. Viewing what's new from the perspective of what you already know gets you up to speed quickly. And you'll learn not only what's changed, but why—gaining deeper understanding of the evolution of Java and how to exploit its power for your projects. **CD-ROM:** All the sample Java 1.1 programs, plus extended examples.

For Windows NT/95, Macintosh, UNIX, Solaris
Intermediate to Advanced

The Comprehensive Guide to the JDBC SQL API

Daniel I. Joshi, Rodney Runolfson
$49.99, 456 pages, illustrated, part#: 1-56604-637-8

Develop high-powered database solutions for your Internet/intranet site! Covers the basics of Java and SQL, interface design with AWT and instructions for building an Internet-based search engine. **CD-ROM:** OpenLink Server-side JDBC driver, SQL databases and tables from the book, sample code, JDBC API specification and example sites.

For Windows 95/NT • Intermediate to Advanced

VENTANA

The Mac Web Server Book

$49.95, 662 pages, illustrated, part #: 1-56604-341-7

Get the most from your Internet server with this hands-on resource guide and toolset. The Mac Web Server Book will help you choose the right server software; set up your server; add graphics, sound and forms; and much more. The CD-ROM includes demo software, scripts, icons and shareware.

The Windows NT Web Server Book

$49.95, 680 pages, illustrated, part #: 1-56604-342-5

A complete toolkit for providing services on the Internet using the Windows NT operating system. This how-to guide includes adding the necessary web server software, comparison of the major Windows NT server packages for the Web, becoming a global product provider and more! The CD-ROM features Alibaba™ Lite (a fully licensed web server), support programs, scripts, forms, utilities and demos.

The UNIX Web Server Book, Second Edition

$49.99, 752 pages, illustrated, part #: 1-56604-480-4

Tools and techniques for building an Internet/intranet site. Everything you need to know to set up your UNIX web site—from basic installation to adding content, multimedia, interactivity and advanced searches. The CD-ROM features Linux, HTTP, CERN Web Server, FTP daemon, conversion software, graphics translators and utilities.

To order any Ventana title, complete this order form and mail or fax it to us, with payment, for quick shipment.

TITLE	PART #	QTY	PRICE	TOTAL

SHIPPING

For orders shipping within the United States, please add $4.95 for the first book, $1.50 for each additional book.
For "two-day air," add $7.95 for the first book, $3.00 for each additional book.
Email: vorders@kdc.com for exact shipping charges.
Note: Please include your local sales tax.

SUBTOTAL = $ _____

SHIPPING = $ _____

TAX = $ _____

TOTAL = $ _____

Mail to: International Thomson Publishing • 7625 Empire Drive • Florence, KY 41042
☎ **US orders 800/332-7450 • fax 606/283-0718**
☎ **International orders 606/282-5786 • Canadian orders 800/268-2222**

Name _____

E-mail _____ Daytime phone _____

Company _____

Address (No PO Box) _____

City_____ State_____ Zip_____

Payment enclosed ____VISA ____MC ____ Acc't # _____ Exp. date_____

Signature _____ Exact name on card _____

Check your local bookstore or software retailer for these and other bestselling titles, or call toll free:

800/332-7450

8:00 am - 6:00 pm EST